Essential Clinical Social Work Series

Series Editor

Carol Tosone, Silver School of Social Work, New York University, New York, NY, USA

The Essential Clinical Social Work Series provides state-of-the-art theoretical and clinical knowledge for clinical social workers and other mental health practitioners.

Carol Tosone • Kirk "Jae" James
Linda Lausell Bryant
Editors

Reframing Social Work with an Anti-Oppressive Lens

A Guide for Beginning Practitioners

Springer

Editors
Carol Tosone
Silver School of Social Work
New York University
New York, NY, USA

Kirk "Jae" James
Silver School of Social Work
New York University
New York, NY, USA

Linda Lausell Bryant
Silver School of Social Work
New York University
New York, NY, USA

ISSN 2520-162X ISSN 2520-1611 (electronic)
Essential Clinical Social Work Series
ISBN 978-3-031-91390-7 ISBN 978-3-031-91391-4 (eBook)
https://doi.org/10.1007/978-3-031-91391-4

This Springer imprint is published by the registered company Springer Nature Switzerland AG
The registered company address is: Gewerbestrasse 11, 6330 Cham, Switzerland

This book is dedicated to anti-oppressive practitioners (past, present, and future) committed to challenging inequities, amplifying marginalized voices, and advocating for systemic and geo-political change in the now. Forward ever, one step at a time, toward a world in which all humans can self-actualize free from oppression.

Acknowledgments

We have many people to thank for bringing this book to fruition, beginning with our outstanding DSW student contributors who inspired the project and shared their practice wisdom so generously. We are also grateful for the support of Dean Michael Lindsey and our colleagues at New York University Silver School of Social Work who embody the values of social justice and anti-racism. Our team at Springer Nature, spearheaded by Janet Kim, carefully reviewed the manuscript and offered valuable suggestion to enhance the delivery of its content. Lastly, we want to give a well-earned shout out to Usha Kaul, MSW, MPH, our Editorial Project Manager, for her skillful coordination and dedication in seeing this book through to completion.

On a personal note, Carol would like to thank her co-editors for making this such a rewarding experience. She is especially grateful to Dr. Bob Raiber for his ongoing support for all her professional endeavors. Jae would like to thank the DSW team, Usha, and everyone who made this book possible. Linda would like to acknowledge her husband, Marshall, her daughter Jasmine Yesenia and her stepchildren, Antoine, Dyami, Gabriel, Gideon, Sara, and Alice. She also acknowledges Caroline Williamson, Marc Manashil, and Mary Burns for being dear partners on adaptive leadership, Carol Tosone for her mentorship, Jae James for his friendship and the brilliant DSW cohort that worked on this book. Pa'lante!

Contents

About the Editors and Contributors

Editors

Kirk "Jae" James, DSW is Clinical Associate Professor and Director of the DSW Program in Clinical Social Work at New York University's Silver School of Social Work. Jae received his DSW from the University of Pennsylvania's School of Social Policy and Practice, and in 2018 he was inducted into their Alumni Hall of Fame. He is also the recipient of the 2020 NYU Dr. Martin Luther King, Jr. Faculty Award. As an immigrant and formerly incarcerated black man, Jae is committed to creating a world in which everyone can self-actualize. He has dedicated his life to creating liberatory spaces to heal and dismantle systems of oppression for all people. Jae has authored numerous academic articles and book chapters and speaks internationally. He has written and shared his lived experience and research with *HuffPost, the Jamaican Gleaner*, *Truth Out*, *Forbes Magazine*, and *Bloomberg news*. He is currently completing a book entitled *94A6325: Coming of Age in the Era of Mass Incarceration,* which is a reflection and amalgamation of his lived experience and research within carceral systems.

Linda Lausell Bryant, PhD, LCSW is Associate Dean for Academic Affairs and Clinical Professor at New York University Silver School of Social Work. She also directs the Adaptive Leadership in Human Services Institute at NYU Silver, while serving as the Katherine and Howard Abel Executive-in-Residence. Prior to this, she was the Director of the DSW program at Silver. In her 38-year career, she has been the Executive Director of Inwood House, associate commissioner at the NYC Administration for Children's Services, and was appointed by former New York City Mayor Michael Bloomberg to the New York City Panel for Education Policy. She is currently president of the board of Justice + Joy National Collaborative. She is the recipient of the Latino Social Work Coalition's 2021 Lifetime Achievement Award, NYU Silver's Distinguished Contribution to Student Engagement Award, and the 2022 Martin Luther King, Jr. Faculty Award. She has co-edited *Transforming*

Careers in Mental Health for BIPOC, co-authored *A Guide for Sustaining Conversations on Racism, Identity and Our Mutual Humanity* and *Social Work: A Call to Action*. She is a sponsor and contributing author to *Latinx in Social Work*, a book of narratives for healing and justice.

Carol Tosone, PhD, LCSW is Professor at New York University Silver School of Social Work and recipient of the NYU Distinguished Teaching Award. Carol is a Distinguished Scholar in Social Work in the National Academies of Practice in Washington, D.C. Currently, she serves as Co-Director of the NYU Trauma-Informed Clinical Practice Program and Co-Director of the Crisis Counseling Post-Graduate Certificate Program. Carol is Series Editor for the *Essential Clinical Social Work Series*, published by Springer Nature. She is Editor Emerita of the *Clinical Social Work Journal* (Springer), having served for 15 years as its Editor-in-Chief. She was the Founding Director of NYU's DSW Program in Clinical Social Work. She completed her psychoanalytic training at the Postgraduate Center for Mental Health in New York City where she was the recipient of the Postgraduate Memorial Award. In addition to serving as a visiting professor at universities globally, Carol received a Fulbright Senior Specialist Award at the Hanoi University of Education in Vietnam and served as the Distinguished Visiting Lydia Rappaport Professor at Smith College School for Social Work. Carol is author of numerous professional publications and executive producer and writer of training and community service media. During her career, Carol has delivered over 300 national and international presentations in various venues. Carol was the 2023 recipient of the Lifetime Achievement Award by the American Association of Psychoanalysis in Clinical Social Work (AAPCSW).

Contributors

Erin George is National Director of Policy at The Bail Project, where she leads the development and execution of the organization's systems change strategies to build a more equitable and just pretrial system. Erin has dedicated her career to ending criminalization and structural racism through legislative and grassroots advocacy. She received her BA in Psychology from the University of California at Santa Barbara and her MA in Social Work with a Minor in Public Policy from Columbia University.

Phara Gladden, DSW, LCSW-R has 20 years of experience in the mental health field. She is currently employed by the New York State Office of Mental Health (OMH) and has worked in various clinical and supervisory roles, both inpatient and outpatient. Phara has a private practice in Rockland County where she provides counseling to individuals, couples, and families.

Fengtao Huang, DSW, LCSW, CASAC is a bicultural therapist and social worker supervisor, Fengtao has been working with underserved communities, focusing on clinical practice, integrated treatment, and community education. Her practice is focused on maternal mental health, immigration and generational trauma, and parent–child relationships.

Kirk "Jae" James, DSW is Clinical Assistant Professor, Interim Director of the DSW Program in Clinical Social Work, recipient of the Dr. Martin Luther King, Jr. Faculty Award, and Chair of the Diversity, Race, Oppression, and Privilege (DROP) curricula area at New York University Silver School of Social Work.

Susan B. Koenig, DSW, LCSW is a high school social worker for 15 years, she is committed to honoring and incorporating anti-oppressive practices in clinical settings while incorporating her advanced training in contemplative psychotherapy and trauma-informed treatment in work with adolescents and young adults.

Caitlin Krenn, DSW, LCSW is a national Policy Fellow with the Network for Social Work Management (2020). Caitlin's research yielded a dynamic four-pronged model of civic empowerment in shelter spaces. Caitlin represented her cohort as the NYU Urban Doctoral Fellow (academic year 2022–2023).

Linda Lausell Bryant, PhD is Associate Dean for Academic Affairs and Clinical Associate Professor at the NYU Silver School of Social Work. She also directs the Adaptive Leadership in Human Services Institute at NYU Silver, while serving as the Katherine and Howard Abel Executive-in-Residence. Prior to this, she was the Director of the DSW Program in Clinical Social Work.

Daisy Lopez, DSW, LCSW holds an MSW from Fordham University and a DSW from NYU Silver School of Social Work. Daisy is an experienced clinician integrating a trauma-informed and client-centered approach to support those experiencing or healing from physical and sexual violence.

Juhi Malhotra, DSW, LCSW is a Clinical Assistant Professor at New York University Silver School of Social Work specializing in the evolving pedagogy of practicum education. She is the Seminar in Field Instruction (SIFI) Coordinator and teaches and advises students. Through her doctoral studies, she is committed to bridging learning gaps between the classroom and the community.

Allison McCullough, DSW, LCSW focuses her research on the intersection of gender and incarceration and seeks to find ways to bring anti-oppressive work to carceral spaces. Allison has been working as an advocate within the criminal legal system for the past five years, and as a social worker in New York City for the past 13 years. Her current work focuses on decarceration efforts with women detained on Rikers Island.

Heather Menzer, DSW, LCSW holds an MSW and Post-Master's Certificate in Palliative and End-of-Life Care (PELC) and her DSW from the New York University Silver School of Social Work. She is a clinician and supervisor with 15 years of experience in medical and palliative social work.

Peleya Patterson, DSW, LCSW is a forensic social worker with over 15 years of experience working with youth and families in BIPOC communities across New York City. In her current role as Vice-President of Mentoring Initiatives, she supports a portfolio of mentoring programs for vulnerable and court-involved youth using a credible messenger model.

Grace Cosachov Protos, DSW, LMSW is the Executive Director of Work Life at New York University. She spearheads a focus on improving organizational health and wellbeing and being the institutional voice for work–life values. Grace holds a Master's Degree in Social Work from Columbia University and a Bachelor of Arts from St. John's University.

Renee Rosiecki, DSW, LCSW, LCADC holds her BSW and MSW from Rutgers University and her DSW from New York University. Renee is a Clinical Supervisor at a county jail specializing in trauma-informed care for incarcerated people and victims of domestic and sexual violence.

Benjamin R. Sher, DSW, MA, LMSW serves as director of continuing education for a metropolitan university. Previously, Ben worked in a behavioral healthcare agency where he directed residential programs for people with serious mental illness and conducted staff training and development. His area of professional interest is disability justice for college students with disabilities.

Laura A. Smith, DSW, LCSW is a DSW graduate from New York University Silver School of Social Work. Laura has experience working within youth diversion programs providing services to the vulnerable youth population and their families.

Carol Tosone, PhD, LCSW is Professor at New York University Silver School of Social Work, recipient of the NYU Distinguished Teaching Award, Founding Director of the DSW Program in Clinical Social Work, Distinguished Social Work Scholar in the National Academies of Practice in Washington, DC., and recipient of the American Association of Psychoanalysis in Clinical Social Work Lifetime Achievement Award.

Carmen Villavicencio-Hein, DSW, LCSW-R, MSW, MSEd co-founded a central-based social work initiative delivering multi-tiered support to New York City Public Schools. As an immigrant and English Language Learner, she is committed to improving the delivery of accessible, equitable, and culturally responsive services to vulnerable communities.

Amy C. Wilkerson, DSW, LCSW is a DSW graduate from New York University Silver School of Social Work. Amy has over 25 years of experience managing programs for children and families in the areas of juvenile justice, residential treatment, foster care prevention, clinical support in schools, and youth development.

Eboni Wooley, DSW, LSW is a psychotherapist at a community-based mental health agency in the South Bronx. Eboni's work focuses on examining the intersectionality of race, poverty, and mental health in order to enhance current therapy practices for under-resourced clients.

Chapter 1
Introduction

Carol Tosone

How does an idea for a book come about? An individual may feel a burning desire to entertain, inspire, provoke, or contribute their voice to a given topic. In this instance, we have a chorus compelled to educate beginning social workers about the realities of contemporary clinical practice, attendant to the needs of vulnerable populations they serve while being acutely aware of their own positionality and its impact on the clinical process. The idea for this volume spawned from the contributors' experiences as social work instructors and supervisors, with many lamenting the limitations of existing educational resources for their students. These contributors, mostly recent New York University (NYU) DSW graduates and members of the communities they serve, found existing texts limited in their descriptions of agency-based praxis from a positionality standpoint and without appreciation for the interrelationship between the mezzo- and macro-level institutional systems that impact micro-level practice. If this book had a subtitle, it would be "What I wish my MSW education had taught me."

The sheer number and successes of books on anti-oppressive practice (AOP) speaks to the hunger for texts demonstrating ethically sound, culturally responsive practice through a social justice lens. Existing books tend to approach the topic from a generalist perspective and are replete with definitions and emphasis on white clinicians empowering clients of color. By contrast, *Reframing Social Work with an Anti-Oppressive Lens: A Guide for Beginning Practitioners* applies an anti-oppressive, liberatory social justice lens to working with Black, Indigenous, People of Color (BIPOC) and other clients who are experiencing societal oppression. This volume provides beginning social workers with examples from social work practitioners-academics who model self-assessment steeped in deep reflection,

C. Tosone (✉)
Silver School of Social Work, New York University, New York, NY, USA
e-mail: ct2@nyu.edu

C. Tosone et al. (eds.), *Reframing Social Work with an Anti-Oppressive Lens*, Essential Clinical Social Work Series,
https://doi.org/10.1007/978-3-031-91391-4_1

lived experience, and the complexity of professional-personal identity in a therapeutic organizational context.

The Council on Social Work Education (CSWE) (2020), in *Social Work Profession: Findings of Three Years of Surveys of New Social Workers*, reported the demographic composition of recent graduates (2017–2019): Nearly 90% were women, 58% were white, 22% were Black/African American, 14% were Hispanic/Latino, and 13% were LGBTQ identified. These statistics reflect a steady but modest decrease in the number of white graduates and a steady increase in the number of graduates of color over the past decade (Zippia, 2024). As Saba et al. (2023) have suggested: BIPOC social workers can better empathize with marginalized and oppressed clients due to their own experiences of societal injustice.

In contrast to other mental health professions, social workers are generally attracted to the field because of its hallmark person-in-environment perspective, and emphasis on social and economic justice. BIPOC and other persons who have experienced injustice based on their age, abilities, ethnicity, gender identity, race, religion, sexual orientation, socioeconomic status, and other potential "isms" can appreciate how the larger social environment has affected them internally and their interactions with others. In providing a positionality statement—a self-reflective expression for locating one's identities in the social order and in interaction with others (Tien, 2019; Zeno, 2023), each contributor demonstrates a keen awareness of how their life experiences, whether of privilege or oppression, impact their perceptions of and work with clients, especially those from similar backgrounds or who have experienced shared social injustices. The composition of the contributors reflects the increasing diversification of the field, coupled with a growing appreciation of lived experience as an effective didactic tool. In this volume, voices often muted in academia, offer descriptions of pragmatic, skill-laden, ethical practices and thought-provoking questions for readers to consider.

Consistent with the existing 16 books in the *Essential Clinical Social Work Series*, this edited work concludes each chapter with reflection questions intended to foster the reader's critical exploration of their positionality, as well as offers discussion points for instructors and supervisors to facilitate enhanced learning. It behooves all readers, wherever they are in the academic or supervisory hierarchy, to (re)examine long-held beliefs about the client populations discussed in these chapters. Each contributor is an expert in working with their client group in an agency setting and is keenly aware of the organizational and personal biases their clients face daily. The contributors offer an anti-oppressive, liberatory social justice perspective, consistent with the most recent Educational Policy and Accreditation Standards (EPAS) and ethical principles from the Council on Social Work Education (CSWE) to the understanding of agency-based work in the dominant fields of practice: child welfare, education, health, mental health, youth justice, carceral systems, substance use, intimate partner violence, racial and other traumas, palliative care, world of work, and older adults. More specifically, whenever their role permits, the standards the contributors advance include the ability to: 1) demonstrate ethical and professional behavior; 2) advance human rights and social, economic, and environmental justice; 3) engage in antiracism, diversity, equity, and inclusion (ADEI) practice; 4) consider research-informed practice and practice-informed research; 5) take into account the impact of policy in practice; and 6) engage, 7) assess, 8) intervene, and 9) evaluate individuals, families, groups, organizations, and communities (CSWE EPAS, 2008, p. 3).

Additionally, each contributor, when discussing their approach to anti-oppressive practice, considers the following: 1) the history of social work in their practice setting; 2) an overview of the current research in the area and relevant past research where applicable; 3) the predominant evidence-based practice approach(es) being used in their area; 4) the role(s) of the social worker in the specific setting; 5) how anti-oppressive and ethical clinical practice is demonstrated in their agency; 6) an extensive case example and discussion, inclusive of the clinician's reflections and countertransference reactions; 7) practice and supervisory wisdom offered by the chapter authors as how to negotiate the organizational system to best benefit their clients; 8) the evolving nature and future direction of the practice area; and as discussed, 9) reflection questions for students, instructors, and beginning clinicians to ponder in working with this population or in this problem area. By the contributors' adherence to an internal structure, readers can compare practice approaches and take an in-depth look at intersubjective practice with the client populations, all while being mindful of their own preconceived notions about the clients being presented.

My co-editors, Kirk "Jae" James and Linda Lausell-Bryant, are award-winning teachers in the ADEI area. Jae was the recipient of the 2020 NYU Dr. Martin Luther King, Jr. Faculty Award and serves as Director of the DSW Program in Clinical Social Work and Chair of the Diversity, Race, Oppression, and Privilege (DROP) curricula area at NYU Silver School of Social Work. Formerly incarcerated, Jae has dedicated his life to creating liberatory spaces to heal and dismantle systems of oppression for all people. Linda Lausell-Bryant is Associate Dean for Academic Affairs and Clinical Associate Professor at NYU Silver. She also directs the Adaptive Leadership in Human Services Institute at NYU Silver, while serving as the Katherine and Howard Abel Executive-in-Residence. She was the past Director of the DSW program at Silver. She is the recipient of the Latino Social Work Coalition's 2021 Lifetime Achievement Award and the 2022 Martin Luther King, Jr. Faculty Award. Since a chorus provided the impetus for this project, Jae and Linda are the featured soloists and my co-conductors. I could not conceive of this book without their erudition and lived experience voices.

Reframing Social Work with an Anti-oppressive Lens: A Guide for Beginning Practitioners commences with their voices, and that of our fellow colleague, Juhi Malhotra. Each provides important liberatory, anti-oppressive practice frameworks: Jae for all practitioners, Linda for academic and organizational leaders, and Juhi for social work students. Specifically, Jae offers the B.I.G. didactic framework to foster self-awareness, active listening, and unlearning of inherent biases. B.I.G. stands for the examination of *B*iases, operationalization of *I*ntention and brave spaces, and the setting of *G*round rules for praxis, referring to the co-creation of a living document that reflects evolving theories of change and the demonstration of values in action. As an abolitionist and formerly incarcerated person, Jae calls for decolonization and the dismantling of systems of white supremacy as an ongoing professional commitment. Linda advocates for anti-oppressive practice on an organizational level through the examination of leadership frameworks with liberatory potential and adherence to core social work values. Recognizing the constraints of social work management in regard to funding priorities, billing policies, and other workforce challenges, Linda suggests that adaptive leadership requires strong business and legal skills, in addition to the consistent application of social work skills and values, such as empathy, self-reflection, and attention to systemic and organizational dynamics. Clients are viewed as key stakeholders and potential change makers who have much to contribute to the conversation; this perspective challenges traditional views of authority as managers as the sole possessors of the power and skills to bring about change. Linda draws from her experiences as an Afro-Latina child growing up in Puerto Rico to emphasize the importance of going beyond the status that those in power ascribe to others. It speaks to the importance of personal agency and appreciation for all perspectives in moving from oppression to liberation. Juhi proposes an anti-oppressive framework for students called the *Power of the Pause*, an exercise embedded within a preparatory lab designed to help students employ critical reflection as they embark on the uncertainty of their practicum settings. A case example demonstrates the importance of critical self-reflection to find alternative meaning to the power sources and structures that impact the supervisory and client relationships. In addition to critical race theory and intersectionality, these reflective prompts help students navigate existing power structures while developing essential self-awareness skills.

Following these antiracist explanatory frameworks tailored for social work academics, administrators, leaders, practitioners, students, and supervisors, we consider critical lifecycle and mental health issues impacting clients in a variety of clinical settings: colleges, community mental health, hospitals, and schools. We begin the section on anti-oppressive lifecycle practice with Fengtao Huang's chapter on perinatal mental health, referring to mental health issues that can arise during pregnancy and postpartum. While common problems, disparities remain in the access to and the provision of perinatal mental health services for BIPOC mothers and their newborns. Fengtao calls for the adoption of culturally responsive and trauma-informed treatment, and the integration of perinatal mental health care into primary care settings. She also stresses the importance of providers examining their own stereotypes and implicit biases.

Work with children and adolescents requires the clinician to have self-awareness and an in-depth understanding of trauma-informed and anti-oppressive practice and can take place in a myriad of settings. Daisy Lopez, for instance, traces the development of the Child Advocacy Centers (CAC) in their efforts to better serve the needs of survivors of sexual and physical abuse and their families. Social workers have played a critical advocacy role in shaping the trauma-informed, anti-oppressive practices taking place in CACs and helping families negotiate the potentially traumatic and daunting child welfare system. Amy Wilkerson, in discussing her work with youth of color, aptly notes that BIPOC youth are disproportionately represented in child welfare, law enforcement, and homelessness services. These institutions, intended to help youth of color, often perpetuate oppression and systemic racism and potentially foster intergenerational trauma. From her extensive clinical experience, Amy has observed that many of these youth report negative experiences that can extend to the family system.

Educational institutions, from primary to secondary to graduate level, are prime settings for preventative and anti-oppression practices. Carmen Villavicencio-Hein discusses the multifaceted role of school social workers as advocates, clinicians, community activists, and strategic planners. In these roles, social workers in New York City (NYC) primary and secondary schools incorporate culturally responsive and sustaining practices to an ethnoculturally and racially diverse student body. These interventions are student-centered and take place on micro, mezzo, and macro levels. Susan Koenig focuses her attention on the needs of sexually- and gender-diverse (SGD) adolescents in high school settings. She incorporates trauma-informed approaches to help assuage the damage caused by marginalization, microaggressions, and other forms of violence. Influenced by the liberatory pedagogy of Paulo Freire (1970), Susan stresses the importance of critical consciousness in helping SGD adolescents create new narratives of strength, agency, and collective action. Rather than passive victims of oppression, SGD youth can critically analyze and challenge these oppressive, inequitable societal systems. Ben Sher turns our attention to the importance of disability studies in social work education, noting that disability justice is consistent with the mission of the social work profession. As social work curricula emphasize anti-oppressive and social justice practice, he posits that disability studies and the ethical use of lived experience need to be central to that endeavor.

Eboni Wooley applies an anti-oppressive practice (AOP) framework to the understanding of individual symptomatology as a manifestation of structural factors in the client's larger environment. Stated differently, ongoing oppression and effects from poverty negatively impact the client's life in a myriad of ways, including the development of mental illness. Through the case of a middle-aged Latina woman in a community mental health setting, Eboni adapts AOP principles to empower the client, provide effective coping strategies, and counter systemic oppression and social injustice. Like Eboni Wooley, Phara Gladden considers treatment provided to BIPOC clients in community settings and implores clinicians to be mindful of implicit and unconscious biases that may interfere with optimal treatment that BIPOC clients deserve. Members of marginalized communities can experience negative health outcomes and Phara recommends trauma-informed interventions to improve outcomes and reduce clinician bias.

Of the many social work practice areas, the criminal justice system offers clinicians the opportunity to work in a variety of settings: from prevention and alternative programs for youth to incarceration and postprison programs. The section on anti-oppressive practice in the criminal justice system begins with an overview chapter from Jae and Erin Leigh George who provide an overview of the carceral system from the time of the Founding Fathers to mass incarceration and its modest decline, highlighting the Rockefeller drug laws as consequential in increasing the number of incarcerated persons. Citing James and Smyth's (2014) staggering statistic that the United States has 25% of the world's prison population, many of whom are Black descendants of slaves, Jae and Erin call on social workers to embrace abolition as a viable theory of change. Peleya Patterson, in discussing the role of forensic social work with BIPOC clients, notes collaboration is necessary among multiple systems: child welfare, community mental health, education, and probation. She incorporates restorative practices to build relationships and community bonds; neighborhood leaders with lived experience in the criminal justice system serve as credible messengers to engage BIPOC youth. Evidence-based approaches, such as Cognitive Behavior Therapy (CBT) and Trauma-Focused Cognitive Behavior Therapy (TF-CBT), are also used with youth justice populations.

Laura Smith introduces readers to youth diversion programs, created with the intention of court-involved youth avoiding further legal system involvement. She educates beginning clinicians as to what to expect and how to navigate within this system to identify the best course of action for clients stigmatized by the legal system and society. She encourages social workers to be mindful of internal biases and the preconceived notions perpetuated in the larger society about the populations they serve.

Women in the carceral system are exposed to oppression as are others in criminal justice settings, with the added burden of living in a patriarchal society. Allison McCullough examines the misogynistic and classist views through which women's behavior has been controlled in the prison system. She notes the high rates of trauma experienced by incarcerated women, particularly women of color. Anti-oppressive practice, she asserts, requires social workers to challenge the structural inequities and oppressive systems in which they work. She maintains that manualized CBT used in prison systems decontextualized the circumstances leading to women's incarceration; gender, race, and other cultural and systemic factors are not considered. She also observes that in states where prison nurseries exist, the carceral system determines which women can participate and which are separated from their babies based on their charges and previous involvement in the child welfare system. Renee Rosiecki also noted the disproportionate representation of women of color in the prison systems, many of which are domestic and sexual abuse survivors, and are retraumatized during incarceration. She advocates for a trauma-informed, anti-oppressive approach for incarcerated women.

In addition to carceral settings, comprehensive social work education also involves addressing anti-oppressive practices in hospitals, homeless shelters, and innovative work settings. Heather Menzer, for example, outlines the core responsibilities, challenges, and dilemmas of palliative social work. Using the composite case example of a sexual- and gender-diverse older adult (SGDOA) requiring the appointment of a surrogate decision maker, she discusses the importance of empowering patients, as well as colleagues and the systems in which they work. Caitlin Krenn turns the readers' attention to a critical analysis of the shelter system and homelessness services in New York City (NYC). Existing policies and regulatory practices, intended to benefit clients' lives, can have profound negative outcomes. Using the example of a dialysis patient requiring a transplant, she noted that gaps in services and among conflicting institutional policies prevented the client from getting the necessary treatment, and he died consequently. She also notes that competing funding regulations and underresourcing can place undue burden on social workers, potentially leading to burnout and high staff turnover. Many of these regulations can limit the client's right to self-determination and conflict with core social work aims. Lastly, Grace Cosachov Protos describes the evolution of the social work role in the employee assistance programs which were largely focused on drug and alcohol treatment and often outsourced to independent mental health providers and organizations. More recently and partially in response to the global pandemic and other collective traumatic events such as racial and political violence, the workplace environment has responded to the mental health needs of employees, especially those from oppressed groups. Cosachov Protos suggests that social workers have a unique skill set to address employee burnout, turnover, decreased work engagement, and other problems common to the work environment. As systems experts, they can address the interrelationship of workplace issues and interpersonal dynamics, leading to an effective application of their knowledge and skills. Bringing social work's values and unique systems perspective to the for-profit sector is the profession's next frontier.

Whether you are a beginning student or a seasoned clinician, my co-editors and I hope you will benefit from the collective 200+ years of dedication and practice wisdom imparted in the pages to come.

References

Council on Social Work Education. (2008). *Educational policy and accreditation standards.* Council on Social Work Education.

Freire, P. (1970). Pedagogy of the oppressed (50th Anniversary Edition). Bloomsbury Academic.

James, K., & Smyth, J. (2014). Deconstructing mass incarceration in the United States through a human rights lens: Implications for social work education and practice. In Advancing human rights in social work education. CSWE Press.

Saba, J., Nestor, D., Hernandez, N., & Brade Stennis, K. (2023). The shoe on the other foot: Considering oppression for BIPOC social workers. *Journal of Ethnic & Cultural Diversity in Social Work*, 1–8. https://doi.org/10.1080/15313204.2023.2291657

Tien, J. (2019). Teaching identity vs. positionality: Dilemmas in social justice education. *Curriculum Inquiry, 49*(5), 526–550. https://doi.org/10.1080/03626784.2019.1696150

Zeno, M. (2023). Big 8 identities workshops offer an introduction to social identities. Elon University Newsletter. https://www.elon.edu/u/news/2023/09/27/big-8-identities-workshops-offer-an-introduction-to-social-identities/#:~:text=Eight%20major%20social%20identities%2C%20often,sexual%20orientation%20and%20socioeconomic%20status.

Zippia. (2024, April 5). Social worker demographics and statistics in the US. Zippia.com. Retrieved August 11, 2024, from https://www.zippia.com/social-worker-jobs/demographics/.

Part I
Anti-oppressive Practice Frameworks

Chapter 2
BIG: Tools for Decolonization and Abolitionist Praxis in the Omnipresence of White Supremacy

Kirk "Jae" James

Introduction

We are at *war* with ourselves, each other, and Mother Earth. And as I write these words, I have little doubt that "our collective future—or its possibility—very much depends on our willingness to individually and collectively acknowledge, heal, and dismantle the vestiges of racism (and white supremacy) in our ideologies, institutions, interpersonal ways of being, and internalized self (Brock-Petroshius et al., 2022, p. 10). However, I am well aware—through history, lived experience, and the current state of this world—that the work to dismantle white supremacy is arduous and does not have the *imminent* impact we desire. But like past freedom fighters, I know we must never give up or drop the ancestral baton of *hope* for a world where every human being can self-actualize safely.

For this chapter, I discuss decolonization and abolition while sharing my evolving praxis in service of a world free from the shackles of white supremacy. Further, I share with fellow practitioners "BIG."—an evolving liberatory framework and toolbox amalgamating theory, reflection, and my practice experience centered around bias, intention, and grounding praxis (formerly ground rules).

K. J. James (✉)
Silver School of Social Work, New York University, New York, NY, USA
e-mail: kirkajames@nyu.edu

C. Tosone et al. (eds.), *Reframing Social Work with an Anti-Oppressive Lens*, Essential Clinical Social Work Series,
https://doi.org/10.1007/978-3-031-91391-4_2

White Supremacy!?

How do we dismantle and liberate the world from the shackles of colonialism and white supremacy? It's a question that nonwhite, marginalized, and oppressed people have intellectually massaged and given their lives to actualize for centuries (Dettlaff, 2024; Fanon, 1963; Freire, 1996). However, in the current global landscape fraught with sociopolitical upheavals, genocides, wars, and environmental challenges, it's imperative that *all* people who believe in the possibility of a better world ask themselves and their communities *the* question.

Before proceeding, allow me to introduce myself and share the impact of white supremacy on my life. For brevity, I am a black man, a descendent of stolen African slaves born in Jamaica —a former British colony left *rich* in white-supremacist ideologies and practices but economically poor upon its theoretical independence in 1962. In the mid-to-late 1970s—shortly after my birth—Jamaica, like many black and brown diasporic colonies, was further destabilized by American foreign policy (Reaganomics) and their fear of Jamaica aligning with Cuba and adopting Democratic Socialism as a means of governance (Harrison, 1988).

At only ten years old, political violence, food shortages, and the perpetual scarcities instigated in the name of American Democracy forced my family and me to migrate to the United States in February 1986—where, for the first time, I experienced freezing temperatures and the pain of leaving my country, home, family, and friends behind. A stranger in a strange land, I quickly became acquainted with misdiagnosed depression, forced acculturation, racism, classism, school pushout, and ultimately mass incarceration—when, at 18 years old, I was entrapped, arrested, and charged under the Rockefeller Drug Laws before being sent to Rikers Island without bail. I had no prior arrests or convictions, but this was the era of neoliberalism, tough-on-crime, and the height of the carceral genocide euphemistically termed mass incarceration. So, six months after my arrest, the white judge looked me in the eye and spoke to me for the first time, informing me that he was doing me a favor by *only* sentencing me to a life term in prison—with the possibility of parole after seven years (James, 2021).

My story is not an aberration. I came of age in the era of the "Central Park Five"—where one in three black men were under the carceral system, where politicians committed to "tough on crime" negated social determinants of behaviors or the empirical validity of their practices in favor of sensationalized media accounts labeling black boys *superpredators*—to instill fear of black criminality and to justify astronomical spending on the carceral apparatus in the form of police, jails, and prisons leading to "a system of social control unparalleled in world history" (Alexander, 2010, p. 7).

Further, for the last 500 years, ideas and practices of white supremacy through colonial, imperialistic, and capitalistic measures have continuously robbed, raped, murdered, imprisoned, and *legally* destroyed black and brown communities within the United States and throughout the world (Mauer, 2017). The sole pursuit of self-aggrandizement inherent in white supremacist systems is now threatening to destroy planet Earth by similarly normalizing and commodifying the exploitation of natural resources without any regard for environmental safety or future generations (Tetreault, 2017).

The best way to understand the impact of white supremacy is to juxtapose it with a highly contagious and infectious disease—that shapes and impacts our concept of self, ideas of the world, interpersonal ways of being, institutions, internalized behaviors, and *every aspect of life*. Further, it's a disease not confined by race, hue, or class—in fact, billions of people across the planet are infected. However, many are unaware, while others have been led to believe that the perceived benefits of these diseases to a few outweigh the danger they pose to humanity and planet Earth (Cole, 2018; M Beliso-De Jesús & Pierre, 2020).

As activists and people with power, positionality, and unwavering belief in the possibility of a better world, how do we heal from the disease of white supremacy when its ideas and practices are as ubiquitous and axiomatic as the air we breathe?

As a social work educator with multiple positions of oppression and privilege, I am keenly aware that the lens through which I view and engage with the world can *often* be colluded by the sea of white supremacy in which I was born (James, 2021; Seawright, 2014). And by white supremacy, I am not just talking about political, social, and economic systems that benefit white people; I am also referring to the more insidious white supremacist, colonial-rooted, ever-evolving educational indoctrination utilized to justify the perverse order of the world (Huber et al., 2008).

Decolonization

Colonization, rooted in the ideas of white superiority, religion, revisionist history, and Western-centric ideologies, has destroyed, stolen land, subjugated, murdered, waged war, and perpetuated genocides against non-white, black, and Indigenous populations for more than 500 years on planet Earth (Fanon, 1963; James, 2021).

Unbeknownst to many liberatory practitioners, colonization influences contemporary theory, practitioner understanding or dissonance, research methods, and varied approaches to ameliorating social ills. Additionally, colonization has disrupted indigenous knowledge systems, mutual aid, and community practices, leading to the marginalization and erasure of traditional bonds and healing methods—in favor of tools and approaches befitting capitalism and the status quo. Laenui (2000) states, "Colonialization and decolonization are social processes even more than they are political processes. Governance over people changes only after the people themselves have sufficiently changed" (p.1).

Ioakimidis and Trimikliniotis (2020) argue that "With colonialism, the development of social work was invariably seen as a 'soft' approach to perpetuating colonial rule through social control and reconfiguration of socio-cultural institutions" (p.6). The authors demonstrate through a historical analysis that social work, rooted in a colonial lens, has been utilized by military regimes and governments such as Nazi Germany to perpetuate genocide and eugenics, destroy families, steal children, and make bearable oppression for marginalized people in the United States and throughout the world.

Decolonization is not a place or label but a commitment—in practice—to undo the varied impacts of colonization on people, societies, and the world. It is committed to reclaiming indigenous practices, cultures, histories, and governance not rooted in scarcity, othering, and domination (Fanon, 1963). Decolonization requires us to go to the root of white supremacy—"the systemic privileging (independently of their beliefs) of the white population, as manifested in social, economic, and political structures" (Mills, 2000, p. 449). Decolonization seeks to understand how white supremacist ideas inform our understanding of history, religion, norms, education, racism, sexism, patriarchy, settler colonialism, slavery, racial capitalism, and most of the varied oppression we seek to dismantle. Decolonization liberates human possibilities from the shackles of white supremacy (Fanon, 1963). But how do we decolonize? What are our tools?

Abolition

Abolition, a theory of change born in resistance to chattel slavery, is aimed at the complete eradication of oppressive ideologies, systems, and practices. "The speeches and writings of … Frederick Douglass, Wendell Phillips, and William Lloyd Garrison, as well as the examples of active resistance offered by figures such as Harriet Tubman, Nate Turner, and John Brown, provided abolitionism with its foundational ideas" (Toraif and Mueller 2023, p. 2).

Abolition is not just eradication. It is imagining new possibilities and "building the new institutions and systems that will maintain freedom from oppression" (Dettlaff, 2024, p. 2). Abolition can be seen as a tool of decolonization—especially when we examine the history of carceral systems—rooted in colonial ideologies and practices that perpetuate racialized violence and exploitation predominately against black and brown communities. Abolition operationalizes the praxis of decolonization by challenging institutions such as social work—which profess values of liberation but often uphold colonial power dynamics through its support of the carceral system—which in turn perpetuates racialized violence and oppression against black, Indigenous, and other marginalized communities under the illusion of safety and justice.

Abolitionists seek to disrupt and dismantle ideas and systems of control and punishment with colonial roots—and as such, abolitionists believe in a world without police, jails, and prisons. A world where every human can have the resources and safety to live their best life. However, the ideals of capitalism, racism, meritocracy, neoliberalism, and antiquated concepts such as good and evil have normalized oppression and "crime" by making it about the individual *other*—and thus negating a critical analysis and accountability of our social systems. Richie and Martensen (2020) state, "a critique of the expansion of the carceral state hinges on an understanding of how crime is more of a social construction rather than an absolute phenomenon" (p.13).

Abolition is the key to unlocking the propaganda, dissonance, shackles of fear, otherness, and scarcity in which oppression thrives. I often use anti-oppressive practice (AOP) and abolition interchangeably. I believe it is an oxymoron to identify as someone committed to anti-oppression and not be against abolishing a racialized, economically exploitive, and carceral system with roots in colonial America that has destroyed millions of black and brown communities (James, 2021).

Abolition is again a colonial theory of change hundreds of years old—originating with free slaves and critically conscious people—many of whom were white men and women who understood that their humanity and values were also being destroyed by racism and slavery. A prominent abolitionist, Fredrick Douglas believed abolition was not just the end of slavery and the destruction of systems that do not benefit collective humanity but a radical reimagination of societies and governance not rooted in an ethos of oppression (Dettlaff, 2024).

Abolition is rooted in the oneness of humanity, intersectional and recognizes that there are no "single issue issues"—and that people and their varied social identities and histories drive their behavior (Crenshaw, 1989; Rodriquez, 2018; Salvatici, 2020). Abolition is not a band-aid but an elixir that goes to the root, knowing that healing and accountability can only happen when we reckon with the epistemology of white supremacy and America.

Rasmussen and Kim (2024) state, "Abolition is not only working towards the absence of oppression but towards realizing the presence of well-being" (p .42). I am an abolitionist who hails from a background littered with trauma and oppression. And while I have given my life to healing and dismantling the perpetuity of trauma inflicted by white supremacy, it does not mean that I am not infected or have reached *some* promised land—a place where I no longer create harm or have to do the daily work because of my race, religion, sexuality, lived experiences, or the articles, videos, books, and courses I have taken, read or written.

Professing to be abolitionist, anti-oppressive, anti-racist, social justice-oriented, or any other semantic term indicating your commitment to building a better world for humanity—means you are committed to applying theory, reflection, and action (praxis) in all aspects of your life. I love the word *praxis* as it considers the constant evolution of life and reminds its adherents that there is no mountaintop and the promised land does not exist—at least not as a fixed place one can arrive at. In *Pedagogy of the Oppressed*, Paulo Freire (1996) warns us of the dangers inherent in any perceived hierarchy of liberatory consciousness when he states, "At the point of encounter there are neither yet ignoramuses nor perfect sages; there are only people who are attempting, together, to learn more than they now know" (p. 90)

Suppose, again, that white supremacy and all manners of oppression are diseases; then abolition is an adaptogen—a constantly evolving praxis—ensuring individual and collective health for all people. Abolition, rooted in the oneness of humanity, by its nature, is somewhat amorphous yet constantly curious in its awareness that it does not know all the answers but is confident that by asking questions for ourselves and our communities while committed to critical dialogue, we can hope, imagine, and co-create solutions together (Zurn, 2021). However, my journey tells me that no matter my identification, decolonization, healing, and undoing of oppressive ideologies and practices are laborious—and we need better tools to prepare for that process.

Abolitionist Praxis

Rodríguez (2018) states, "The long historical praxis of abolition is grounded in a Black radical genealogy of revolt and transformative insurgency" (p. 1576) toward dismantling oppressive ideologies and practices through community building, introspection, and collective action. Liberatory scholars such as Freire (1996) and Hooks (1994) have lauded the "classroom" for its potential to actualize praxis and conscientization. However, in any community, abolitionist praxis will require *constant* labor to question, reflect, unlearn, and practice the right action—labor that can be exhausting, hurt and trigger us, and disable our ability to make critical decisions in honor of our values. It's a message I share within liberatory communities, and one I *really* learned during a course on "Mass Incarceration" half a decade ago.

The class, overregistered due to its content, took place in a predominantly white institution experiencing immense racial tensions. It began curiously in a small room, with us unable to sit in a circle—an Indigenous practice I often utilize to share power and build community (Salsbury, 2021). While the diversity was initially welcomed, many black students soon became distrustful of the white students, their role in the class, and their potential for harm while working within carceral communities.

The racial tensions within the school and class ultimately culminated in what Brock-Petroshius et al. (2023) terms: "racial battle fatigue—a draining, excessive psychosocial stress response that has been associated with negative educational and health outcomes" (p. 346). To make matters worse, many black students were distrustful of me and my willingness to see and support them in their struggle against the institution I represented—tensions that played out for weeks and made the pressures of class each week terrifyingly overwhelming.

One week, during a guest presentation, the tension reached a tipping point as the black students, all dressed in black, protested the class by remaining silent throughout. I was shocked, had no frame of reference, no one to talk to, and didn't know what to do. However, after class, a black female student whom I mentored and who had been incredibly supportive of me throughout the process asked to speak with me in my office, which at the time was no bigger than a small New York City closet. So, I was pretty surprised when my meeting with the student turned into a meeting with all the black students.

I lit some Palo Santo, took a deep breath, and listened as the students expressed how they felt harmed and unseen within the classroom—I was struggling to hold despite my best intentions. Much of what they said was hard for me to hear, but I remained silent, practiced active listening, and did my best not to personalize their complaints, which, after hearing and processing, made me realize we needed an intervention.

In the following weeks, I canceled the formal class and held voluntary restorative circles—another Indigenous tool utilized for understanding and accountability that everyone attended (Salsbury, 2021). And for the first time, beginning with myself, I apologized and took accountability for how I contributed to harm. I also shared a bit of my humanity with the class by discussing my pending divorce, which seriously impacted my capacity to show up as my best self. The students also shared their experiences, reflected collectively, and took accountability when necessary.

The struggles with my class were a powerful teaching and learning moment. I felt happy to salvage what could have been a *bad* semester. Still, the process took a toll on me, and I began questioning my commitment to the labor required of liberatory pedagogy. However, after a few weeks of restoration in Jamaica, I began to reread many of the books that inspired my educational journey in search of tools—and while there were many, the one thing that kept coming up was the necessity of friction, tensions, and often fractures in any critical or liberatory process. bell Hooks (1994) theorized that it was in these breakdowns that we had the greatest potential for growth and the process of becoming more human, which she termed "conscientization."

Examining my own life, I slowly began to accept the labor, weight, and potential of fractures inherent in growth. Yet, as an athlete, I felt some synergy between football training—specifically, the need to utilize heavyweights to isolate and break down specific muscles for growth and the labor of liberation. But there was one key difference—in football training, we would not get into the gym and begin to lift *any* weight without warming up and getting the muscle ready to be broken down and built back up. However, in liberatory spaces, we ask students and participants to bench-press centuries of internalized and normalized oppressive conditions and biases without warming them up and providing tools for success (Hammond, 2021; Farrington, 2021). Recognizing a gap in practice, I developed and began to utilize an AOP framework centered around bias, intention, and grounding praxis, otherwise known as "BIG." It is a framework and toolbox amalgamating my personal and professional experiences, liberatory, clinical, and neuroscience research into an accessible tool for decolonization and abolitionist praxis.

Bias

I introduce BIG in liberatory spaces by asking participants "Who is the greatest rapper?" and "How can you prove it?" My questions usually elicit laughter, mitigate tension, build community, and warm up practitioners for the labor of anti-oppressive work. After things begin to settle, I throw up a picture of the late great Christopher Wallace, aka the King of New York, aka The Notorious B.I.G.—and try to put into words just how much he and his music meant to my generation and why I chose to honor him in this way.

My question regarding the greatest rapper also prepares participants for my next question: *How do you know what you know*? *And who benefits*? They are questions that I ask myself and just about everyone I share space with. They are questions aligned with Socratic thought that recognize and question the pervasive impact of white supremacist indoctrination and collective bias even in spaces deemed liberatory. Essentially, *bias* for *all* humans is what water is to the fish—an invisible, omnipresent force that we swim in unbeknownst to most of us. Research has shown the prevalence of bias in race, gender, and the diagnosis of psychological disorders, all aspects of the carceral system, and just about any subject matter you can think of (Dee & Gershenson, 2017; Garb, 2021; Moriearty, 2009).

As a black man with varied oppressed identities, working and living in predominantly white spaces, I am very aware of the scrutiny and bias I experience daily by way of my status as a formerly incarcerated person, my complexion, bald head, dress, and speech. I am also aware of my *infection* and how I have misused my power and positionality—like demonstrating intellectual bias (prioritizing one style of writing, learning, or reasoning), gender bias, ageism, sexual bias, and varied forms of unconscious bias.

To illustrate unconscious bias, I often share a story of traveling to Turkey post-9/11 and becoming anxiety-riddled hearing Arabic being spoken on the plane. And while I was ashamed of this feeling, it demonstrated how easy and unbeknownst to me it is to be indoctrinated within a societal zeitgeist often equating Arabic, Islam, and terrorism. However, research and the recognition of bias inherent on so many personal and systemic levels have not thus far led to a more reflective society. Often, opinions fueled by bias win, not by critical inquiry and collective reasoning but by positionality, power, and violence (Keltner & Robinson, 1997).

Freire (1996) and Hooks (1994) insist that our educational systems are not predicated on critical thought; instead, they reasoned that we exist in what Friere terms a "banking system of education," where education (what we learn in school or varied social spaces) is a series of information to memorize. This information is then stored and regurgitated for exams, conversations, and varied spaces that reward us for being *smart*. Banking systems of education are a preeminent tool of white supremacy and purported Democracies to create fear, siloed thinking, and alignment with nationalistic, political, fascist, and oppressive ideologies and practices (aka conformance with the status quo).

The white-washed revisionist history we learn within early American childhood education, which speaks to the greatness of the founding fathers and our democracy and which culminates with a pledge of allegiance, is an excellent example of how the banking system works (Banks, 2002). I often ask students to consider the *empirical and factual* history of genocide on which the United States was built before asking them if they would still pledge allegiance.

Recognizing bias as a product of conditioning and social determinants vs. good and evil is essential. Thus, it is crucial to remember that what is learned can be unlearned. However, the perceived benefit of the bias to the individual (or communities) will often determine their willingness to examine it and make change—which Critical Race Theory terms "Interest Convergence" (Bell 1995).

If we are all, in some way, infected by the banking system of education—a polarized politized tool of white supremacy that fosters separation, revisionist history, and regurgitation, are we then willing to examine our bias? Give up our power and privilege? And ask the *why* of ourselves, others, and the systems we exist in?

"Dissonance is aroused when people are exposed to information inconsistent with their beliefs" (Harmon-Jones & Mills, 2019, p.6). Decolonization, unlearning, and conscientization will be complex for many reasons. However, a primary one is that our brains, like computers, are wired to seek cognitive consistency—meaning, like a computer, we want to believe and run the program we have been given. And will thus reject and defend it against new information. A neurological process psychologist, Leon Festinger, termed "cognitive dissonance" in the 1950s.

Franz Fanon's 1963 book, *The Wretched of the Earth*, and much of his work explored the psychological impact and dissonance of people living under oppressive ideologies and systems. Fanon believed that understanding oppression's psychological and cultural implications was essential. He reasoned that understanding, or lack thereof, impacted how we conceived and moved toward liberation.

Understanding cognitive dissonance and the psychological impact of oppression illuminates the neurological processes and tensions people experience within critical education and subsequently informs our approach and tools within its praxis. So, for example, when someone says something I disagree with, I don't immediately reject what they say and offer my opinion (which often provokes cognitive dissonance). Instead, I demonstrate curiosity, call them in, and seek to get to the root of the belief (or at least plant a seed of critical inquiry) by asking, "Why?" or "Why do you believe that?"

Why, a powerful cognitive disruptor, allows students, teachers, and learners to reflect critically on axiomatic beliefs. It also honors the stages of the change model, which posits that people learn in stages, beginning with precontemplation—"the stage in which there is no intention to change behavior in the foreseeable future. Most individuals in this stage are unaware or under-aware..." of a bias before moving to contemplation—where they begin to consider the possibility of such (Prochaska & Norcross, 2001, p. 443).

Why is a question most people, products of the banking system and/or biased, are rarely asked to answer or consider, which makes it an ideal tool and provocateur of contemplation. I like this curious approach to challenging bias as I know most people, including myself, at various points in my life will push back (aim to seek cognitive consistency) when told their positions, no matter how apparent, are wrong.

To wrap up this section, I often ask participants: Is there anyone who does not have bias? Again, this usually elicits laughter, but there are no challengers! I follow up the question with a picture of a man looking out into the world with glasses and the word "bias" spelled into the lens. I let the image sink in before asking them, as I ask you now: How is your bias impacting your work to dismantle white supremacy?

Intention

I often tell my students that shame in recognizing bias is natural, but shame will not dismantle bias. In recognizing bias, we must intentionally shift from "safe" to "brave" space, which acknowledges the labor and discomfort of liberatory pedagogy. Brave space, co-created and operationalized by participants, requires that we intentionally name and define our collective values and move away from safe conversations and being right (having our beliefs reaffirmed) in favor of understanding—the synthesis of many *truths*.

Brave space "…implies that there is indeed likely to be danger or harm—that requires bravery on the part of those who enter. But those who enter the space have the courage to face that danger and to take risks because they know they will be taken care of" (Cook-Sather, 2016, p. 1). In the context of a "brave space," distinguishing between safety and discomfort is essential for fostering productive and meaningful dialogue. A brave space encourages participants to get out of their comfort zones, engage in difficult conversations, challenge their perspectives, and confront uncomfortable truths, all while ensuring that the environment remains respectful, supportive, and safe.

Before establishing a brave space, participants must all be transparent about their intentions and values, which I often describe as a north star that will guide us when things get dark (aka when fractures and breakdowns occur). In centering our collective intention, I often highlight a quote from *The Autobiography of Malcolm X,* which states: "I'm for truth, no matter who tells it. I'm for justice, no matter who it is for or against. I'm a human being, first and foremost, and as such I'm for whoever and whatever benefits humanity as a whole" (p. 400).

The quote from *Malcolm* demonstrates his ability to recognize his bias and grow from a pro-black nationalist to a human rights advocate committed to finding *truth* in service of all humanity. A commitment to recognizing bias (ourselves/ideologies/systems, etc.) and having clear intentions toward dismantling that bias in service of humanity is crucial for liberatory work. However, it's not enough to state your values and intentions; we must co-create and operationalize them in practice and service of a better world.

Grounding Praxis

On the perpetual journey of liberation within ourselves and our communities, we will experience fractures and harm. Grounding Praxis (GP) is our co-created, operationalized, ever-evolving theory of change, intention, reflection, and values in action.

GP is not a destination but a living document/agreement that guides how we decolonize from white supremacist ideologies—individually and within a shared community of practice (Brock-Petroshius et al., 2022). GP recognizes that the labor involved in critical and liberatory justice work frequently brings us face-to-face with deep-seated injustices and traumas, both personal and collective—exposure which can challenge our emotional resilience and cognitive clarity, making it difficult to remain grounded in our values.

GP is a social/community contract similar to the Constitution of the United States. The primary difference is that white men created the US Constitution for white men, while GP is made by and for *all* people. Social contracts (explicit or not) are everywhere—whether at work, home, or how we operate in public spaces. However, without intentional co-created social contracts, we often have people with the most power deciding what we define as right or wrong. Social contracts (legal or not) without the input of ALL PEOPLE are again oppressive and often serve to maintain the numerous examples of *legalized* systems of oppression, such as chattel slavery, black codes, convict leasing system, Jim Crow Laws, Chinese Exclusion Act, Internment of Japanese Americans, Redlining, School segregation, Immigration Policies, etc. (Seabrook & Wyatt-Nichol, 2016).

In a letter to James Madison dated 1809, Thomas Jefferson, a key author of the US Constitution, argued that social contracts should be viewed as living documents to avoid imprisoning future generations. Jefferson's letter reflects his understanding of the ever-evolving nature of people, communities, and the world. However, it also reveals the extent of his bias as a slave owner and father to Black children, who were dehumanized by the very ideas and laws he helped create (Onuf, 2000)

Jefferson's warning appears almost prophetic today, with varied Supreme Court decisions not honoring the people's needs but rather archaic *laws* and ideas designed to benefit white men. Grounding human and liberatory praxis within a social contract allows all community members to co-create a living document/agreement that reflects and guides their collective intention and values in action. Some examples I utilize to cultivate GP in my work are:

1. Community check-ins: As a starting point for liberatory work, we must acknowledge, respect, and be curious about all members of humanity, our communities, and the world.
2. Respect entry points: Social work promotes seeing people in their environment. However, it is often assumed that people committed to liberatory work have the same starting point and are not similarly shaped by their environment, thus requiring grace in their change process.
3. Trauma is drama: The labor of liberatory work will trigger and initiate the war button within our brains, specifically the Amygdala—our automated defense system which only knows flight, flight, or freeze and is incapable of critical thought, which then impacts our cognitive balance, window of tolerance, and varied biological functions. Trauma affects our ability to show up critically and as our best selves, which often leads to *drama* in our bodies, minds, and communities. Somatic awareness and a commitment to restorative practices allow us to mitigate trauma, remain in our window of tolerance, honor our values, and act in the most informed way.
4. Commitment to humanity and human language: Most systems of oppression begin with an idea of the other—reinforced through dehumanizing (and

desensitizing) language. We can combat that by evolving from nationalistic and myopic ideals to a greater vision inclusive of a collective humanity rooted in oneness. We can utilize people-first language, like formerly incarcerated people, people who struggle with substance use, and people I am of service to vs. clients. A commitment to shared humanity moves us from allyship into solidarity toward dismantling harm anywhere humans exist.

5. Calling in vs. calling out: When we can regulate our trauma responses, it is possible to challenge someone willing to be accountable by inviting them to critical discourse about their beliefs. This is particularly important since we all have biases and sometimes require a teaching moment to unlearn.
6. Love: We do not often speak of love as a tool of liberation, but many liberatory scholars rank it as the most important. Paulo Freire (1996) states, "If I do not love the world, if I do not love life, if I do not love people, I cannot enter into dialogue" (p. 63).
7. Praxis: Again, my favorite word honors each community member's commitment to restorative practices, brave space, and the utilization of critical theory, reflection, and action toward collective liberation *now* and in all aspects of their lives.

Closing

White supremacy has superimposed itself onto our consciousness programming to create and justify ideologies and practices that have positioned much of planet Earth on the brink of war, destabilization, genocide, famine, and all measures of inhumanity. To get free, we must first recognize our collective bias and know there is no promised land where we will all miraculously get along. Colonized human beings can only be free through decolonization and the perpetual praxis of liberatory theory, reflection, and action between themselves and the world—a laborious process made more daunting by cognitive dissonance and the shackling of our minds to possibilities beyond the present.

Again, in the now, labor and tension of praxis, we have the greatest possibilities for growth and the actualization of a liberatory world—decolonization, abolition, and BIG are tools I utilize in classrooms, training, prisons, nonprofits, and with people around the globe committed to the labor of dismantling "White-Supremacist Capitalist Patriarchy." BIG honors that wisdom, knowledge, understanding, and people are not static and are in perpetual states of evolution through relations with self, each other, and the world.

BIG in any community of practice is as simple as: 1. We all have a bias. 2. To understand bias, we must be transparent with our intentions: *Are we here to have our beliefs reaffirmed or seek understanding?* 3. If we recognize bias, intentionally conditioned through the banking systems of white supremacy, and we intend to decolonize from that bias, while utilizing theories espousing a liberatory future for all humanity, then let us co-create together the grounding praxis to guide our vision, engagement, and action toward its actualization in the *now*!

BIG is a tool toward the promised land, which again is not a physical place we will ever arrive at, but exists within our shared humanity, co-created values, and the perpetuity of praxis—of knowing and unknowing, of curiosity, of love with ourselves, each other, and every form of life on our planet.

I identify primarily as an abolitionist to honor all my ancestors, who, for centuries, have died fighting for collective liberation. However, I am not wedded to labels, nor should you!

My commitment is, and will forever be, as long as oppression exists, to give my all to actualizing a liberatory world. But my fellow activists, co-conspirators, and freedom fighters, please remember that the liberation we seek is not outside of us, as we are the instruments of liberation. However, the efficacy and health of our instruments have been compromised by the pandemic of white supremacy.

Our collective liberation begins at the root, with awareness of the varied impact of white supremacy; it starts with an intentional commitment to vanguard collective humanity, truth, healing, and planet Earth, which is being destroyed by myopic and capitalistic greed. We must move beyond *labels* and practices that have existed before us, will exist after us, and do not truly benefit *everyone*.

If *you* count yourself among the vanguard, then WE "must, like lovers, insist on, or create, the consciousness of the others - do not falter in our duty now, we may be able, handful that we are, to end the racial nightmare, and achieve our country, and change the history of the world (Baldwin, p. 16)."

Reflection Questions

1. How does bias impact your practice?
2. What are your tools to mitigate bias?
3. What can you take from BIG for your practice?

References

Alexander, M. (2010). *The New Jim Crow: Mass incarceration in the age of colorblindness*. New Press.

Banks, J. A. (2002). Race, knowledge construction, and education in the USA: Lessons from history. *Race Ethnicity and Education, 5*(1), 7–27.

Beliso-De Jesús, A. M., & Pierre, J. (2020). Anthropology of white supremacy. *American Anthropologist, 122*(1), 65–75.

Bell, D. A. (1995). Who's afraid of critical race theory? *University of Illinois Law Review, 1995*(4), 893–910.

Brock-Petroshius, K., Garcia-Perez, J., Gross, M., & Abrams, L. (2023). Colorblind attitudes, empathy, and shame: Preparing White students for anti-racist social work practice. *Journal of Social Work Education, 59*(2), 346–360.

Brock-Petroshius, K., Mikell, D., Washington, D. M., Sr., & James, K. (2022). From social justice to abolition: Living up to social work's grand challenge of eliminating racism. *Journal of Ethnic & Cultural Diversity in Social Work, 31*(3-5), 225–239.
Cole, K. (2018). Thinking through race: White racial identity, motivated cognition and the unconscious maintenance of White supremacy. *Politics, Groups, and Identities, 6*(2), 181–198.
Cook-Sather, A. (2016). Creating brave spaces within and through student-faculty pedagogical partnerships. *Teaching and Learning Together in Higher Education, 1*(18), 1.
Crenshaw, K. (1989). Demarginalizing the intersection of race and sex: A black feminist critique of antidiscrimination doctrine, feminist theory, and antiracist politics. *University of Chicago Legal Forum, 1989*(1), 139–167.
Dee, T. S., & Gershenson, S. (2017). *Unconscious bias in the classroom: Evidence and opportunities*.
Dettlaff, A. J. (2024). The unrealized dream of abolition. *Human service organizations: Management, leadership & governance*.
Fanon, F. (1963). *The wretched of the earth*. Grove Press.
Farrington, C. A. (2021). Equitable learning and development: Applying science to foster liberatory education. In *The Science of Learning and Development* (pp. 198–214). Routledge.
Freire, P. (1996). Pedagogy of the oppressed (revised). *New York: Continuum, 356*, 357–358.
Garb, H. N. (2021). Race bias and gender bias in the diagnosis of psychological disorders. *Clinical Psychology Review, 90*, 102087.
Hammond, Z. (2021). Liberatory education: Integrating the science of learning and culturally responsive practice. *American Educator, 45*(2), 4.
Harmon-Jones, E., & Mills, J. (2019). An introduction to cognitive dissonance theory and an overview of current perspectives on the theory.
Harrison, F. V. (1988). Capitalism: A perspective on Jamaican posses in the US. *Vine*, 10.
Hooks, B. (1994). *Teaching to transgress*. Routledge.
Huber, L. P., Lopez, C. B., Malagon, M. C., Velez, V., & Solorzano, D. G. (2008). Getting beyond the 'symptom,' acknowledging the 'disease': Theorizing racist nativism. *Contemporary Justice Review, 11*(1), 39–51.
Ioakimidis, V., & Trimikliniotis, N. (2020). Making sense of social work's troubled past: Professional identity, collective memory and the quest for historical justice. *The British Journal of Social Work, 50*(6), 1890–1908.
James, K. J. (2021). Black lives, mass incarceration, and the perpetuity of trauma in the era of COVID-19: The road to abolition social work. In C. Tosone (Ed.), *Shared trauma, shared resilience during a pandemic: Social work in the time of COVID-19* (pp. 281–290).
Keltner, D., & Robinson, R. J. (1997). Defending the status quo: Power and bias in social conflict. *Personality and Social Psychology Bulletin, 23*(10), 1066–1077.
Laenui, P. (2000). *Processes of decolonization. Reclaiming Indigenous voice and vision* (pp. 150–160).
Mauer, M. (2017). Incarceration rates in an international perspective. In *Oxford research encyclopedia of criminology and criminal justice*.
Mills, C. W. (2000). Race and the social contract tradition. *Social Identities, 6*(4), 441–462.
Moriearty, P. L. (2009). Framing justice: Media, bias, and legal decisionmaking. *Maryland Law Review, 69*, 849.
Onuf, P. S. (2000). Every generation is an "Independent Nation": Colonization, miscegenation, and the fate of Jefferson's children. *The William and Mary Quarterly, 57*(1), 153–170.
Prochaska, J. O., & Norcross, J. C. (2001). Stages of change. *Psychotherapy: Theory, research, practice, training, 38*(4), 443.
Rasmussen, C., & Kim, M. E. (2024). Abolition and the welfare state: Implications for social welfare. *Affilia, 39*(1), 42–58.
Richie, B. E., & Martensen, K. M. (2020). Resisting carcerality, embracing abolition: Implications for feminist social work practice. *Affilia, 35*(1), 12–16.

Rodríguez, D. (2018). Abolition as praxis of human being: A foreword. *Harvard Law Review, 132*, 1575.
Salsbury, E. (2021). Restorative justice: Dismantling structural racism within the US criminal justice system through decolonization (Doctoral dissertation, The Ohio State University).
Salvatici, S. (2020). Saving humanity, abolishing slavery. In *A history of humanitarianism, 1755–1989* (pp. 20–34). Manchester University Press.
Seabrook, R., & Wyatt-Nichol, H. (2016). The ugly side of America: Institutional oppression and race. *Journal of Public Management & Social Policy, 23*(1), 3.
Seawright, G. (2014). Settler traditions of place: Making explicit the epistemological legacy of white supremacy and settler colonialism for place-based education. *Educational Studies, 50*(6), 554–572.
Tetreault, D. (2017). Capitalism versus the environment. In *The essential guide to critical development studies* (pp. 341–350). Routledge.
Toraif, N., & Mueller, J. C. (2023). Abolitionist social work. In *Encyclopedia of social work.*
Zurn, P. (2021). Abolition is a kite-idea. *Building abolition.*

Chapter 3
Adaptive Leadership in Support of Anti-oppressive Practice in Social Work Organizations

Linda Lausell Bryant

Anti-oppressive practice (AOP) is "a form of social work practice which addresses social divisions and structural inequalities in the work that is done with people whether they be users ('clients') or workers and which aims to provide more appropriate and sensitive services which respond to people's needs regardless of their social status." Anti-oppressive practice is person-centered, grounded in egalitarian values and focused on mitigating the harmful impacts of structural inequalities on people's lives and empowering people (Dominelli, 1993 as cited in Gray et al., 2012). Garcia and Van Soest (2021) add that "dismantling oppression is bigger than a practice; it is not a status but an ongoing, never-ending personal process of learning, changing, and growing. Anti-oppression practice requires learning about and comprehending what oppression is and how it works, as well as its patterns, dynamics, and consequences" (p. 4). Those patterns, dynamics, and consequences are likely to manifest in organizations, yet Strier and Binyamin (2014) note a dearth of studies that document the implementation of anti-oppressive practice in service organizations. Karabanov (2004) says that the academic debate around anti-oppression has remained within the confines of pedagogy and/or practice (p. 57). He argues that anti-oppressive organizations should attempt to build safe and respectful environments for marginalized populations (p. 58) and describes characteristics of anti-oppressive organizational behavior that emerged from his study with service providers and youth living on the streets in Canada and Guatemala. These characteristics include less bureaucratic and more democratic and participatory structures and a focus on the mission of the organization's services. Clients should feel like human beings, whose identities are not defined by the problems for which they are seeking help. In addition, a systemic, holistic frame should

L. Lausell Bryant (✉)
Silver School of Social Work, New York University, New York, NY, USA
e-mail: linda.lausellbryant@nyu.edu

C. Tosone et al. (eds.), *Reframing Social Work with an Anti-Oppressive Lens*, Essential Clinical Social Work Series,
https://doi.org/10.1007/978-3-031-91391-4_3

undergird the understanding of the presenting problem, including social, economic, and other factors related to the problem. Karabanov also notes that "active participation, notwithstanding its difficulties in relation to implementation and coordination, allows for feelings of 'being accepted' and belonging" (p. 55). These characteristics create an organizational experience that supports clients in feeling human, empowered, engaged, and valued. In this chapter, I suggest that service providers also benefit from feeling human, empowered, engaged, and valued and that can be supported by leadership practices that are aligned with anti-oppressive social work values.

Reflections on Positionality and Anti-oppression

My own history and positionality reflect a common struggle with oppressive perspectives and the importance of active resistance to internalizing and perpetuating those perspectives in practice. As an experienced social work manager with almost forty years of experience, I have come to appreciate the importance of theoretical and practice frameworks and tools that hold liberatory potential, by which I mean that they are able to support a strong sense of agency and an understanding of one's inherent value, in defiance of whatever value may have been ascribed on the basis of their identity or socio-economic standing. I am the second generation in my Puerto Rican family to be born in the mainland United States. My mother was one of seven children, born to parents who migrated to New York City from Puerto Rico in the late 1920s. My mother grew up in poverty, but with high expectations to fulfill the American dream. My father, born in Puerto Rico, was the eighth of nine children and grew up in extreme poverty, with the quest for a daily meal defining his childhood. I was raised with high expectations to defy the negative stereotypes that were commonly applied to Puerto Ricans. My family's message was clear and consistent: We must prove that we are good, clean, and decent people in order to overcome pervasive perceptions to the contrary. Proving our worth depended upon the opinions of the white people in power, who controlled most of what we needed, whether access to apartments, jobs, credit, and social standing. This struggle was compounded for me as an Afro-Latina child. I learned early on that my olive skin tone, tightly coiled hair, full lips, and broad nose were markers of Blackness and considered unattractive by white people. As a child, I was subjected to many attempts to 'repair' these features, like getting my first chemical hair straightening at the age of six. This was a source of shame for me; however, I focused on doing well in school, having internalized the importance of education. I became the first person in my extended family to get a college degree. I began learning about the African diaspora in college and began to understand and appreciate my African ancestry and Latin ethnicity. These experiences helped me understand the toll of a pervasive worldview that reinforces the superiority of some groups (mostly white people) who have the power to bestow (or not) acceptability onto others. The fallacy of these ideas gave rise to my fierce commitment to work toward all people having the opportunity to pursue, develop, and live in their full humanity. My experiences shaped my attunement to people who are invisible or restricted in their full participation in society. It has centered the struggle, the quest for equity and inclusion, in all my work. In my roles in middle, senior, and executive management, I navigated the conundrum of being in positions of authority while trying to avoid replicating oppressive dynamics. Freire (1968) noted that "reality which becomes oppressive results in the contradistinction of men as oppressors and oppressed" (p. 51). Moen (2017) suggests that conscientization is an antidote: "A democratic formative culture will need a higher level of consciousness and humanization to be established which can be achieved through conscientization" (p.24). Relatedly, Freire (1968) posited, "Through critical reflection upon the very condition of existence inside the context of a situation, the individual can see their situation as an 'objective-problematic situation" (p. 109). This is a description of the work of conscientization. Anti-oppressive practice involves the work of conscientization, of moving toward critical consciousness and action to change the reality of oppression. I appreciate that the struggle to not perpetuate oppressor/oppressed dynamics is real within the social work profession. I submit that leadership practice that is grounded in values-aligned frameworks can help us become more conscious of the struggle and more intentional in our efforts to embody anti-oppressive values in our individual and organizational practice.

Social Work Leadership: A Work in Progress

A walk through most American bookstores reveals tomes on leadership written by successful business titans, sharing their leadership wisdom, practices, and outcomes as gospels that can be applied in any setting. Their narratives highlight outcomes such as growth in revenue, scale, acquisitions, and even the ubiquity of their products and services, much like Microsoft was instrumental in placing a computer on virtually every desk. In business, this metric of impact and success makes intuitive sense when placed in the context of what business does. Generally, businesses seek to make products or provide services that can be monetized, allowing the business to make a profit, and if it benefits society in some way, that is a bonus. A business's success, however, is measured more in its profits and dominance in the marketplace. The value of its leadership practices is in creating and supporting the conditions, circumstances, efficiencies, innovations, and other key factors to achieve the goal of making a profit and sustaining the company's dominance in the marketplace.

Social work has different goals from corporate businesses; however, there are far fewer books and articles written by social workers about how their leadership practices have helped them make progress in addressing pressing social issues. Sullivan (2016) references social work's lack of a generally accepted definition of leadership, let alone our own models. While social work can take a page from some of the corporate business leadership approaches to increase efficiencies and develop innovations that can help us do our work better, we must be cognizant of social work's different purpose. Social work provides services without the goal of making a profit, and in fact, if we are successful in our work, we would put ourselves out of business, having addressed the need for our services so thoroughly and completely. Imagine a social work organization that successfully develops and implements interventions that result in eradicating hunger. There would no longer be a need for this organization to exist. Of course, the organization could reinvent itself and adapt its mission; however, the point is that social work's purpose is distinct, and therefore, its leadership practices would serve social work better if they were aligned with its purpose. It may be helpful for the social work profession (or any profession for that matter) to periodically interrogate its purpose and whether it is still operating in service of it.

Hopefully, this chapter will spark vigorous dialogue on the question of social work's purpose, but for argument's sake, let's consider social work's purpose to be supporting human development and protecting human rights, so that all people are able to thrive, free of oppression from individuals and socioeconomic, sociopolitical structures, with special attention to those who are not thriving. This is consistent with the Council on Social Work Education (CSWE's) view of social work's purpose, described as "promoting human and community well-being which is achieved by promoting social and economic justice, preventing conditions that limit human rights for all people, and helping people of all backgrounds overcome their unique challenges" (CSWE, 2015, p. 5). The fulfillment of this purpose takes place predominantly in organizations, which are increasingly complex, intervening in some of our most pressing and rapidly changing social challenges, while responding to ever-shifting forces within the larger marketplace in which they exist. Their work is influenced, impinged upon, and often constrained by shifts in funding priorities, billing policies, managed care, and emerging needs and workforce challenges, especially in the postpandemic landscape. Social work managers need to embody social work values and also possess finance, legal, and other business skills. It is crucial for social workers to be equipped with needed leadership and managerial capacities in order to simultaneously steward social work agencies as businesses and steward the integrity and impact of the profession. There is a tension between fulfilling social work's purpose to advance social transformation toward justice and the need to comply with the rules of the marketplace that seek containment of social problems and reward organizations that can do that at the lowest cost. Social work organizations are expected to operate in similar ways as corporate businesses in the context of market-based pressures. Samimi (2019) astutely describes how nonprofit organizations must compete for government or foundation funding to survive, forcing them to focus on maintaining their funding sources rather than the missions guiding their work. In a recent book, Coltoff and I argue that

> The social services nonprofit sector has always had a symbiotic relationship with Wall Street and with corporate America. It depends on corporate America for trustees, funding, volunteers, and all forms of in-kind support. In symbiotic relationships, partners can adopt the values, perspectives, and strategies of one another. These things happen organically, often imperceptibly, and it helps to do a "gut-check" to make sure that our identity and values as a social services sector are still strongly aligned with the values and perspectives that should drive the work (Lausell Bryant & Coltoff, 2021, p. 7).

Notably overlooked in this tension are the service users and how they are affected by the forces that affect the agencies. Despite these tensions and dilemmas, social work organizations have redoubled their efforts to engage as agents of social transformation, embracing anti-oppressive frameworks and practices. They have been at the forefront of social impacts stemming from demographic shifts, whether helping new immigrants to acclimate and survive or helping long-time residents to deal with being priced out of their communities due to gentrification. They have helped countless families process the impacts of incidents of police brutality where the victims were people from minoritized communities. Social work organizations navigate the worlds of their true missions as advocates for social change and businesses constantly struggling to stay in business.

The Leadership Framework Matters

What kind of leadership framework and practices would align with social work values and purpose? Unfortunately, we lack the guidance of social work research to address this question. In fact, social work leadership research has not yet linked the applicability of extant leadership models to social work practice and research (Peters, 2018). This is an important area for social work contributions to research.

Let us come back to the issue of social work's purpose and values. Integrity is one of our core values, and we can keep it sharp by consistent self and organizational interrogation of our purpose and values. Are our values being translated into action? Are we having the impact intended in our organizational missions? Is social work really helping to transform the social systems and conditions that oppress some people, or are we keeping oppressed people functioning just adequately enough within their oppressed situations? Imagine coming across a group of people stuck in a ditch. How should we intervene? We can send food, water, and other necessities down to the people in the ditch, a necessary intervention, but is it sufficient? Are we also working to get the people out of the ditch, and to close the ditch so that others will not fall in? Peters (2018) notes that "a mismatch between the leadership theories used in social work and core social work values may make subtle, but significant, contributions to leadership challenges in social work practice" (p.33). For example, we could (and unfortunately do) "sweep" homeless people off the streets but are we working to address the human rights of all to have a place to live? Anti-oppressive social work values direct us to challenge and go beyond the functions of social control and problem management and to work to advance social justice.

From the definition of anti-oppressive practice (AOP) referenced earlier, AOP requires social workers to critically reflect on their values, beliefs, and biases and actively work to challenge, disrupt, dismantle, and eliminate oppressive systems and practices. Let's engage in a brief "gut-check" reflection. What efforts is your organization engaged in to challenge and disrupt systemic oppression? Is the practice of leadership replicating oppressive systems, with people in power directing without meaningful input or participation from those who understand the challenges best, and are most affected by them, like the clients and providers that work with them? Are the leadership frameworks and practices in your social work organization primarily focused on social change or working within the existing systems and structures to comply with funding mandates and program outcomes, helping people to function better within their oppressed conditions? This is not a matter of "either-or," rather it is "both-and," in that social work organizations must comply and meet goals to remain viable, and yet social work's values call on us to advocate for social justice, which can only happen on a systemic level. Is this tension candidly acknowledged and discussed within the organization? How would you describe the leadership practices and how they contribute to or detract from building an anti-oppressive organizational culture? These questions are presented to encourage you to reflect on the challenges of embodying our professional values and your own thoughts about the role you can play in contributing to change. Identify the values that are in tension and the systemic and structural factors that are contributing to specific social challenges. Consider what leadership practices can look like when aligned with anti-oppressive social work values.

Organizational Leadership and Anti-oppressive Practice

During the great recession of 2008, I had the opportunity to learn about a leadership framework that I have found to be aligned with anti-oppressive practice in some key ways. I was the CEO of a nonprofit youth agency that helped pregnant and parenting young women in foster care. I was at a meeting with a funder, Caroline Williamson, who was the CEO of the B. Robert Williamson, Jr. Foundation. Ms. Williams courageously recognized that funders can use their power to direct programs and services and can override the people who know the needs of communities better than they do, even inadvertently. Ms. Williams resisted the familiar pull to fund her own vision, instead asking me and other potential grantees what we really needed in those difficult times. We needed help "holding" our teams through the prolonged uncertainty of that recession, where changes were coming at us at a fast and furious pace. We needed support to develop our leadership capacities in those turbulent times, and we needed our staff to bring their best ideas and approaches. It was this funder's courageous and inclusive approach, engaging her grantees to identify what it needed most, that led to the opportunity to learn about and bring adaptive leadership to my organization. Adaptive leadership is a framework developed at the Harvard Kennedy School by Ronald Heifetz and Marty Linsky and became known as a leadership theory with the 1994 publication of Heifetz's book *Leadership Without Easy Answers* (Harvard Kennedy School of Government (n.d.). I piloted the implementation of adaptive leadership in the agency, with the help of Marc Manashil, an adaptive leadership consultant, and years later, I brought it to New York University, inviting Marc to work with me. I became aware of how many of adaptive leadership's concepts and practices were aligned with social work and anti-oppressive values. While this chapter is not a comprehensive overview of the entire adaptive leadership framework, it is an introduction to some of its key concepts in relation to anti-oppressive social work practice.

Key Concepts in Adaptive Leadership

In the adaptive leadership framework, leadership is distinguished from authority, and these concepts are commonly conflated. Leadership is defined as a *practice* to mobilize people to work on a problem, one that requires new learning (Heifetz, 2019). It is *not* defined as position, role, or power. In fact, it's irrespective of position. "We view leadership as a verb, not a job" (Heifetz et al., 2009, p. 24). Verbs connote action, so think about leadership as action. Note how Heifetz describes leadership and how it is linked to a purpose, which is mobilizing people to work on a problem that requires new learning. Authority, on the other hand, is related to role and position, and its purpose is to provide protection, direction, and/or order. Authority can be formal (holding a formal position or role) or informal, but in either case, the authority is given or granted. A CEO can have tremendous authority in a company and yet exercise minimal, if any, leadership. It is also possible for someone without any title or rank to exercise leadership. Does anyone come to mind? A key point is that leadership, being about action and practice, is not located in the *person* who is called "leader". An understanding of leadership as uncoupled from role or position means that anyone could take up leadership. Personally, as an Afro-Latina woman of color, who grew up in the 1960s and 1970s, when most "leaders" were white men, I found this to be a radical and exciting concept, for it democratizes the exercise of leadership for anyone who wants to engage in its practice. Most importantly, there's an opportunity to leverage the potential diversity of perspectives and creativity that may exist among the organization's team members, which can help advance stronger practice and outcomes. Typically, leadership has been conceptualized as the ability, skill, and often position that someone uses to get people "on board" with a perspective or a direction that the person known as "leader" has deemed is the right way to go. Peters (2018) says that

> leadership training should not focus on specific skills, behaviors or characteristics, but instead on changing how individuals approach their work and their professional relationships in order to create the potential for cultural shifts. Conversely, a focus on personal traits and characteristics can preclude the identification of individuals based on personality traits or cultural background (Peter, 2018, p. 42).

The adaptive framework's concept of leadership, uncoupled from position or role, frees our thinking from traditional notions that people in positions of authority are the only ones who have the power, intelligence, skill and/or, experience to bring about change. We can engage the contributions of others, including ourselves, irrespective of position or status. Consider the example of Rosa Parks, who lacked formal power or authority, title, or office, yet her actions were instrumental in advancing civil rights. She challenged the status quo by refusing to give up her seat on the bus. Harriet Tubman also exercised leadership, taking enormous risks to get enslaved people to freedom. Social work surely has modern-day Rosa Parks and Harriet Tubmans (and perhaps you are one of them) taking risks, speaking truth to power, and mobilizing people for change. Heifetz et al. (2009) also note that leadership is a risky and dangerous activity. When we exercise leadership to bring about change, we are challenging the status quo and that is not always welcomed.

Anyone can exercise leadership to help bring about change, and that means that a lack of power or authority does not have to constrain our ability to work for change. We need not wait for power, position, or permission. This conceptualization of leadership is potentially anti-oppressive and empowering, a tool that can help us to mobilize to do the risky and hard work of challenging and dismantling oppressive practices, policies, laws, and systems. It is an unshackling of the ideas of leadership as being for the few, the special, the powerful. The opportunity to exercise leadership is there for us all.

Getting to the "Root" of the Problem

The adaptive leadership framework acknowledges different kinds of challenges—those that are addressable through knowledge and expertise (technical challenges) and those that are reflective of conflicts in values or perspectives (adaptive challenges) (Heifetz et al., 2009). Social work challenges are often those that have no easy answers and are manifestations of conflicts in values and perspectives. America is one of the wealthiest nations, yet we have many people who experience food insecurity. It is a social problem that could be addressed as a technical problem by leveraging existing knowledge of food resources and financial resources. Seems straightforward, however, this is not a challenge that can be addressed with only technical approaches. There are adaptive aspects to this challenge, which Heiftez et al. (2009) describe as "elephants" in the room, and they recommend that these elephants be named (p. 167). The "elephants" are the root issues and can include a range of underlying perspectives. Sometimes the elephant may be the issue of racial or socio-economic differences that may make some people feel uncomfortable. People who experience hunger, while we do not, may trigger a range of emotions, perhaps discomfort, guilt, or helplessness to name a few, any of which can be unconscious. The thrust of the adaptive leadership framework is that to make progress on adaptive challenges, we must get to the root of the underlying issues. With social problems, we commonly see the application of technical solutions to what are, in essence, adaptive challenges. Building shelters is a technical solution to homelessness that does not address the need for stable and affordable housing nor the root issues that keep us, as a society, from pursuing more effective remedies. Adaptive leadership's typology of challenges can be useful for social workers trying to address the root issues of complex social challenges and recognize that adaptive work takes time and is not conducive to quick fixes. In anti-oppressive practice, we also want to get to the root issues, and there is a recognition that oppression is not a challenge that can be simply or easily addressed. Adaptive work involves self-reflection and also attention to system dynamics, consistent with social work and anti-oppressive practice.

Systems Thinking

Adaptive leadership recognizes that we operate in systems. Families are systems, organizations are systems, nations are systems, and *we* are systems. As such, when we are trying to make change, we need to understand the systems that we are a part of and the system(s) that the challenge we want to address is embedded in. Heifetz et al. (2009) have conceptualized the need to *diagnose the system* (p. 49) so as to understand the values of the stakeholders in the system, as well as their loyalties, because this is often where resistance to change is rooted. We also assess the potential losses that stakeholders may face if change happens. What would some stakeholders stand to lose if we actually solved racism and it no longer existed? As a practice, when we surface a variety of perspectives, we open up the potential for innovation that comes with new and different ideas. Progress depends on innovative thinking, and diversity in perspectives can be a strength, even if we tend to be more comfortable with familiar perspectives. Simultaneously, we need to negotiate the potential discomfort that comes with new ideas. This is an interesting practice for social workers because it supports inclusion of diverse perspectives, recognizing that we are stronger for it and encouraging us to do the hard work of creating space for different perspectives. It also recognizes that hidden perspectives can be very "active" and influential in a system, when not surfaced. In the adaptive framework, difference is perceived as a strength. This framework also recognizes that humans are commonly uncomfortable with change, even when it is desired, because we tend to associate change with loss. This allows us to actively engage "resistance," rather than quash it. This can lead to mobilizing people to engage in change work. In AOP, we seek to understand the perspectives of those who are engaging in oppressive behaviors so that these insights can help us determine how we will engage in change work. In social work practice, understanding the person in their environment, the person in their systems, allows us to intervene with a more comprehensive appreciation of their situation.

Getting on the Balcony, Stepping Away from the Dance Floor, and Getting Perspective

Heifetz et al. (2009) introduce the notion of getting on the balcony, a metaphor for repositioning yourself (sometimes literally but often metaphorically) so as to be able to see the big picture (from the perspective of the balcony) in a way that you can't see from the dance floor. Getting on the balcony allows you to see the problem or challenge from a different vantage point and gain new perspectives. In terms of AOP, the practice of getting on the balcony allows us to metaphorically put ourselves in the shoes of another and try to understand what things are like for them. This allows us the opportunity to build empathy and to bring a stronger appreciation for their humanity.

Applying Adaptive Leadership Concepts to Advance Anti-oppressive Practice

Here are a few suggestions for advancing organizational anti-oppressive practice through some adaptive leadership concepts. These can be used by people who have roles of authority to practice in a more adaptive and anti-oppressive manner in organizations. They can also be used by people who don't have positions of authority, because you can exercise leadership without formal authority.

Make Space for Self and Organizational Reflection (Get on the Balcony)

From the balcony, we can see things from a different perspective than the view we would have from the dance floor. Be intentional about getting on the balcony, and invite your team to do the same. This could manifest as intentional reflection time and can include guided activities or questions to support reflection. Try putting yourself into the shoes of others, including your clients, to practice understanding their experiences and circumstances. Organizationally, this begins to convey value for reflection and the perspectives of others.

Observe the Practice of Leadership in the Organization

If you are in a position of authority, observe where you see leadership happening in your organization. Who are the people thinking out of the box, anticipating change and taking risks to push for innovation and change? Communicate that the organization welcomes and values ideas, even when they are different from the mainstream. If you are not in a position of authority in the organization, remember that you can contribute to culture shift and change by introducing an idea or raising a question that may help mobilize others to consider engaging in change work. Be mindful of what risks may be involved for you, and consider who can serve as allies for you in this effort. Leadership is not a solo activity. Change work is collective work.

Consistently Reconnect with the Organization's Purpose

Explore the impact you want your work to have, and how it could contribute to dismantling oppression. Examine whether the impact is being achieved. This is a good time to reference the questions outlined earlier in this chapter in the section titled "The Leadership Framework Matters." How can the organization's mission and goals drive your work, beyond complying with stakeholder mandates or expectations?

Create Opportunities to Surface Other Perspectives

Pay attention to whose voices (and perspectives) get heard. Consider whose voices are rarely heard and why that might be. How can you engage those voices to be heard? How can you use your voice? People's differences (race, ethnicity, gender, educational, cultural background, and life experiences) may result in some expressing their opinions and suggestions at work and others holding back. Are the ideas of people in authority the ones that get all the traction? Are the men doing most of the talking? Whether you are in a role of authority or not, just observe who tends to speak up more, less, or not at all. The workplace may be losing out on valuable ideas, insights, and perspectives that could potentially help advance its work. More perspectives can translate into more ideas that can spur innovation and fewer voices can reinforce the impression that only some people's perspectives have value. Anti-oppressive practice values inclusion and not just the valuing of some.

Help People Identify (and Celebrate) Progress

Adaptive challenges rarely have an answer, but progress can be made. It helps teams to learn to see the progress being made, even if small. Every big win is made up of many small ones. Acknowledge the small wins and celebrate them.

Remember Your Clients as Key Stakeholders

Recognize that the service users (clients) are one of your most important stakeholders. To understand service user experiences without their input reinforces their oppression by withholding the opportunity for service users to use their voice to share their experiences and opinions (Ramsundarsingh & Shier, 2017).

Conclusion

Adaptive leadership concepts and approaches represent a shift toward a more collective and inclusive leadership approach, which is aligned with anti-oppressive social work practice. We would be better equipped to address the challenges of racism, and the social disparities it creates, by practicing leadership in a way that does not replicate the same assumptions that a select, few people can take us to a better future. Instead, adaptive leadership engages our collective intelligence, experience, and wisdom to create innovative approaches toward meaningful progress on the pressing social problems that social work aims to address. In this way, leadership can become a tool that helps us move toward liberation from oppression.

Reflection Questions

1. How do you identify an oppressive practice occurring in an organization?
2. What criteria are you using to identify oppressive organizational practices?
3. What does anti-oppressive leadership practice mean to you?
4. How could you intervene as a manager to encourage the surfacing of perspectives or voices that are rarely heard?
5. In what ways can your leadership practice align more with anti-oppressive values?
6. How could you mobilize people to shift organizational policies or protocols to be more anti-oppressive? Which policies or protocols come to mind as ripe for change?
7. How can you "get on the balcony" as a regular leadership practice for yourself and any people you work with?

References

Council on Social Work Education Commission on Accreditation. (2015). *Educational policy and accreditation standards.*

Freire, P. (1968). *Pedagogy of the oppressed.* Seabury Press.

Dominelli, L. (1993). Anti-oppressive practice. In M. Gray, J. Midgley, & S. A. Webb (Eds.), *The SAGE handbook of social work* (1st ed.). Sage. https://search.credoreference.com/articles/Qm9va0FydGljbGU6MzE2MTcwMQ==?aid=237298.

Garcia, B., & Van Soest, D. (2021). *Social Work Practice for Social Justice: From Cultural Competence to Anti-Oppression*. VA., CSWE Press.

Gray, M., Midgley, J., & Webb, S. A. (2012). *The SAGE handbook of social work* (1st ed.). Sage. https://search.credoreference.com/articles/Qm9va0FydGljbGU6MzE2MTcwMQ==?aid=237298

Harvard Kennedy School of Government. (n.d.). *HKS authors*. Harvard Kennedy School. https://www.hks.harvard.edu/publications/practice-adaptive-leadership-tools-and-tactics-changing-your-organization-and-world#citation.

Heifetz, R. A. (2019, April 26). *On leadership*. Harvard University, [Video]. YouTube. https://www.youtu.be/ioocNc-HvTs.

Heifetz, R. A., Grashow, A., & Linsky, M. (2009). *The practice of adaptive leadership: Tools and tactics for changing your organization and the world*. Harvard Business Press.

Karabanov, J. (2004). Making Organizations Work: Exploring Characteristics of Anti-Oppressive Organizational Structures in Street Youth Shelters. *Journal of Social Work, (4)*(1), pp. 47–60. https://doi.org/10.1177/1468017304042420

Lausell Bryant, L., & Coltoff, P. (2021). *Social work: A call to action—a time of reflection and reckoning*. New York University Silver School of Social Work.

Moen, D. (2017). The leader-investigator: Using leadership studies as a model for conscientization through adaptive leadership, the four frames approach, giving voice to values, and the competing values framework. *Journal of Thought, Fall-Winter*.

Peters, S. C. (2018). Defining social work leadership: A theoretical and conceptual review and analysis. *Journal of Social Work Practice, 32*(1), 31–44. https://doi.org/10.1080/02650533.2017.1300877

Ramsundarsingh, S., & Shier, M. L. (2017). Anti-oppressive organisational dynamics in the social services: A literature review. *British Journal of Social Work, 47*, 2308–2327.

Samimi, J. C. (2019). Funding America's Nonprofits: The Nonprofit Industrial Complex's Hold on Social Justice. *Columbia Social Work Review, 8*(1), 17–25. https://doi.org/10.7916/cswr.v8i1.1967

Strier, R., & Binyamin, S. (2014). Introducing Anti-Oppressive Social Work Practices in Public Services: Rhetoric to Practice *British Journal of Social Work, 44* 2095–2112. https://doi.org/10.1093/bjsw/bct049

Sullivan, W. P. (2016). Leadership in social work: Where are we? *Journal of Social Work Education, 52*(S1), S51–S61. https://doi.org/10.1080/10437797.2016.1174644

Chapter 4
The Power of the Pause: Preparing Students for Critical Reflection

Juhi Malhotra

Positionality Statement

The author of this chapter is a Sikh-American, cisgendered, heterosexual, mother of three children, who is a faculty member within the Department of Practicum Education and Community Partnerships in a school of social work. My previous practice history includes almost two decades of clinical social work and administrative roles in hospital psychiatry. The case example is a composite of common student situations that occurred in the practicum setting and in the coordination process. I recognize that due to my insider status in the operations of this department, and my previous history as a hospital social worker, this carries influence regarding my conceptualization of the student challenges, but also demonstrates my connection with a closer understanding of the hierarchical structures within hospital corporations.

Introduction

Critical Reflection is an integral part of the development of the professional social worker's identity (Fook, 2016; Morley & O'Bree, 2021; Rankine, 2018; Theobald et al., 2017). Jan Fook is one of the leaders in writing about critical reflection tools (Milner & Wolfer, 2023; Theobald et al., 2017). Though reflection has been well documented in the literature, scant attention is given to the concept of critical reflection in the practicum (or field) education literature (Theobald et al., 2017).

J. Malhotra (✉)
Silver School of Social Work, New York University, New York, NY, USA
e-mail: ju218@nyu.edu

C. Tosone et al. (eds.), *Reframing Social Work with an Anti-Oppressive Lens*, Essential Clinical Social Work Series,
https://doi.org/10.1007/978-3-031-91391-4_4

Additionally, the *critical* part of reflection typically needs to be addressed early and with greater intentionality within practicum education (Theobald et al., 2017). In practicum education, the critical reflection process is key to understanding the nuances in the relationships between the student, the agency supervisors, the clients, and the entire organizational system (Mehrotra et al., 2023; Morley & O'Bree, 2021; Nayak, 2022; Robinson & Macfarlene, 2021; Theobald et al., 2017). This chapter introduces the historical roots and definitions of reflection and critical reflection, discusses the state of practicum education and anti-oppressive practice, introduces an accessible anti-oppressive tool to be utilized in practicum education, and examines at length a composite case study of a former master of social work (MSW) student during their praxis journey. The chapter will reconceptualize critical reflection to include *an intentional pause.* This tool will illuminate how its *power* (Power of the Pause) can be effectively applied by students, faculty, and community partners. The tool will reveal that critical reflection is the cornerstone in preparation for anti-oppressive praxis in practicum education. With the benefit of hindsight, the *Power of the Pause* (POP) will be used to analyze a case composite to identify how it can be implemented to prevent common challenges in practicum education. Practice wisdom and reflections will be included to demonstrate the missed learning opportunities, the increased risk of further bias and assumptions, and the overall potential for further harm to clients and communities when we don't pause. Finally, the discussion will conclude with reflection questions for students, clinicians, and educators to consider how the *Power of the Pause* could be applied within their own practices.

Reflection and Critical Reflection

Reflection can be defined as a process that involves detailed thinking a person undergoes about an event or experience, and the new perspective or knowledge one gains as a result of this process (Bruce, 2013; Carroll, 2011; Ferguson, 2018; Rankine, 2018; Schon, 1983). Two early educational philosophers who are associated with reflection and reflection practices are John Dewey and Donald Schon. Dewey is known for his insistence on a questioning stance, especially when faced with difficult situations (Dewey, 1933). Schon was more focused on clinicians' ability to think quickly, and so he is known for the phrases, reflection-in-action, and reflection-on-action, which is described as individuals having reflective dialogue within themselves, in hopes of having a quicker impact (Schon, 1983).

In social work practice, self-reflection and self-awareness are also important aspects of the reflective process (Ferguson, 2018; Finch et al. 2019; Rankine, 2018; Redmond, 2006; Ruch, 2002; Sheppard, 2007). The ability to look inward, evaluate recent interactions, and process our thoughts and feelings about them is crucial to the development of the social work professional self. MSW students in practicum education are asked to reflect (with guidance from their practicum instructors) during ongoing supervisory dialogue and to engage in reflective writing for the purposes of connecting their experiences within an agency setting, and to their own personal thoughts and feelings. If a reflective process is encouraged and supported adequately and the student engages fully, the learner will ultimately have new knowledge about themselves as well as the individual, community, and agency in which they are engaged in practice.

Critical reflection includes the process of looking inward and finding a deeper meaning to experiences, but also scrutinizing power structures that impact relationships (Brookfield, 2009; Morley & O'Bree, 2021; Rankine, 2018; Robinson & MacFarlane, 2021; Theobald et al., 2017). For social workers, this process is important as it supports practitioners in examining biases and assumptions that are crucial to understanding their work through a more meaningful, and more anti-oppressive, lens (Fook & Gardner, 2007; Gray & Webb, 2013; Rankine, 2018). For example, if a social work student identifies as a White, cisgendered female, married to a man, and she is being supervised by a Black, single mother of four children, the reflection process will need to include a process of deconstructing the individual, social, political biases and stereotypes associated with Black, single mothers, and the privilege and power associated with White women.

Social work students must learn and practice reflection and critical reflection to become critical thinkers (Ruch, 2002; Shea, 2020). It has also been documented that critical reflection has been defined differently. According to Theobald et al. (2017), one of the major differences in definitions is in the understanding of the word *critical* in critical reflection. Many people use the word critical to be synonymous with analytical, with the capacity to think conceptually and systematically (Theobald et al., 2017). While an important skill in social work practice, it doesn't include the values of social justice including understanding social power and identity dynamics that social workers are charged with within their service to vulnerable communities. The concepts of reflection and critical reflection have different meanings depending on context and practice, and this can be confusing for students and educators (Watts, 2019). Perhaps the various interpretations of the word critical contribute to the inconsistent way students are prepared for practicum education.

Reflective practice encourages the theory to practice integration by looking at one's actions for ongoing learning and improved practice (Schon, 1983). Curry and Epley (2022) studied the effects of engaging in a reflective practice framework and how this impacted clinicians' self-care process. Their findings suggested that it is crucial for higher education to implement these frameworks as many of the participants in the study reported that without reflective tools and frameworks, their practice was more "reactive" (Curry & Epley, 2022, p. 301). In essence, participants remarked that their experience with students and practitioners who include a reflective practice framework are often less reactive and describe themselves as a healthier professional.

Practicum disruptions occur for a variety of reasons, including insufficient resources in the agency structure, lack of quality supervision, student unpreparedness, and overwhelming clinicians with increased daily responsibilities (Parker, 2010). Consequently, these challenges make it difficult to provide an optimal learning experience for students (Ayala et al., 2018; Bogo et al., 2017; Gushwa &

Harriman, 2019 Kourgiantakis et al., 2019). When disruptions occur within the practicum setting, students are often asked to write a reflection paper to understand the reasons for the disruption and to encourage the critical reflexive process. The critical reflexive process calls for a deeper understanding of the intersections of systems, identities, and power. Later in this chapter, a case composite will be analyzed of a student who struggled with the critically reflective process when a disruption occurred. The case analysis will expose the challenges experienced by all the stakeholders within this practicum experience.

Practicum Education and Anti-Oppressive Practice

Practicum education has been referred to as the signature pedagogy of social work education (CSWE, 2015). Though the National Association of Social Workers (NASW) and the Code of Ethics have always called for social justice within social work, many revisions have occurred since its creation in 1960. The revisions include the language evolving from cultural awareness to cultural competence and cultural humility (National Association of Social Workers, 2021). In 2022, the Council on Social Work Education (CSWE) revised its competencies to include antiracism, diversity, equity, and inclusion (ADEI), in which the third competency states, "social workers understand how racism and oppression shape human experiences and how these two constructs influence practice at the individual, family, group, organizational, and community levels…" (CSWE, 2022, p. 9). According to Garcia & Van Soest (2021), anti-oppressive practice in social work necessitates clinicians to examine power dynamics in relationships and to see the dimensions of oppression in organizations and society. However, it is still unclear as to how these practices are being taught within the various social work curriculum areas (Beasley et al., 2022; Kishimoto, 2018; Lee et al., 2022). Certainly, the start of the COVID-19 pandemic and racial uprisings of 2020 ignited social work academies to quickly transition to anti-racism and equity-focused curricula. The literature reveals that millennial incoming students are more racially aware; however, few are comfortable with engaging in this dialogue due to feelings of anxiety, guilt, and shame (Beasley et al., 2022; Hamilton-Mason & Schneider, 2018; Wagaman et al., 2019). Also, given the hierarchical structures in the academies that are buttressed by oppressive values and practices, the message remains unclear (Beasley et al., 2022). The impact of the pandemic has left agencies with fewer resources, including less qualified supervisors. Agencies were forced to focus on workplace safety, thereby leaving student training by the wayside (Davis & Mirick, 2021). Additionally, there is a paucity of literature on best practices for preparing students for anti-oppressive and antiracist praxis within practicum education. This scarcity of best practices in the literature can explain the learning gap between student learning in the classrooms and agency practice (Drolet, 2020). Even more troubling is the fact that at times the practicum instructors will depend on the students for informing them of current research and best practices (Mantulak et al., 2020). Practicum instructors should not be relying on students to teach them current best practices and pedagogical approaches, as this could result in more microaggressions and harmful behavior, which ultimately may contribute to more disruptions within the practicum setting.

Social justice pedagogy is also being questioned in social work education. For example, many have criticized that schools of social work are still focused on diversity and cultural humility (Blackdeer & Ocampo, 2022). Furthermore, the discussions around oppression are still focused on individual experiences rather than attention to the systemic causes (Blackdeer & Ocampo, 2022; Craig et al., 2021). This is reminiscent of the early twentieth-century debates around case versus cause with respect to the imbalance of micro and macro social work teaching in social work education (Abramovitz & Sherraden, 2016). The results of the rise in neoliberal forces, such as the emphasis on consumerism, have made it more difficult to tackle the growing inequities and social challenges in the twenty-first century (Abramovitz & Sherraden, 2016). While the profession is still figuring out the language and how to convey consistent messaging uniformly, schools of social work are compelled to develop their own approaches to operationalizing anti-oppressive praxis within the curriculum (Atterberry-Ash et al., 2021). This makes it more difficult to have a consistent pedagogical approach to anti-oppressive practices in practicum education.

Beasley et al. (2022) conducted a systematic review focusing on equity-mindedness and antiracism within practicum education. In this review, these studies examined student experiences regarding racism within the school structure, pedagogical models, and the curriculum in social work programs. The findings suggest that many programs rely on outdated pedagogical models while students are experiencing racism throughout the school, including their practicum areas. Furthermore, students need experiences that will assist in deconstructing racism, and learning how to process injustices (Beasley et al., 2022; Swick et al., 2021). Essentially, the authors implore social work schools to infuse equity within the structures, and regular norms and policies to make practicum education a better experience (Beasley et al., 2022).

Lee et al. (2022) conducted a scoping review on the various pedagogical methods of how social justice is being taught in social work programs. In their review, they found seven predominant teaching methods that schools utilize to promote social justice within their curricula. These methods include intergroup dialogue, online synchronous discussion boards, simulation and role play, written reflection and experiential learning, and community engagement. A major recommendation from this study is that social work educators must consider integrating social justice perspectives within the community itself and not only within the classroom.

Many agency structures are also complicit in systemic racism and implicit bias. Social work educators should also direct their efforts to improve the practicum experiences within the agency setting. Some settings are drivers of oppressive forces and practicum instructors can also be significant contributors to negative experiences for students (de Bie et al., 2021). For example, in a study conducted by McDermott et al. (2021), the findings suggested that while most agreed that racial equity is a human rights issue, and this needs to be emphasized in practicum education, challenges remain to operationalize this due to the paucity of resources, time, and expertise to promote this change.

Additional studies have been done to understand the experiences of minoritized students as very few studies have historically included perspectives of Black, Indigenous, People of Color (BIPOC) students (Gooding & Mehrotra, 2021). Gooding and Mehrotra (2021) concluded in their qualitative study of BIPOC students and BIPOC practicum instructors that race in the practicum setting is crucial to addressing race and equity issues in the curriculum. Furthermore, there is essentially no research published on race and identity issues from the perspectives of BIPOC practicum instructors as it relates to the student-supervisor relationship (Mehrotra et al., 2023).

Rationale for More Critical Tools

As stated earlier in this chapter, minimal research has been done to fully understand how schools of social work are preparing students for practicum learning. Some scholars have explored students' abilities in critical reflection with respect to the practicum. For example, according to Giles and Pockett (2013), their studies revealed two notable challenges for students. The first was that students struggled with their abilities to step outside of a situation or experience, and the second was their understanding of power in relationships. Students were more aware of their own powerlessness instead of considering narratives of other perspectives (Giles & Pockett, 2013). In my own experience as a practicum educator, community partners have often reported that students are not ready to start working with vulnerable communities. Students are often unsure about how to approach their clients and the agency environment through an anti-oppressive lens. Calling on my own observations as an educator in the practicum learning area, many students are often making hasty assessments and judgments leading to quick decisions without employing tools that would capture a more critical focus. Many students appear to be unaware of what it means to have a critical focus and how this is necessary for their own professional development and their client's well-being. For example, many White students report high levels of anxiety when they are faced with the possibility of commuting to an unfamiliar (typically Black and Brown populated) neighborhood. Due to this discomfort, some students will immediately request to be placed in areas that are familiar to them through their family, friends, or peers, to avoid these feelings. This reaction, often void of any critical process, has ethical implications on how the vulnerable become even more marginalized.

Disruptions in practicum occur because of various factors: conflict within the supervisory relationship, challenges with ethical practices, and marginal performance with the core competencies (Parker, 2010). Sometimes these disruptions can be managed through a reflective process and with interventions by school practicum advisors. However, other times these disruptions lead to abrupt terminations from the agency. Some cases can be quite complex as many intersectional variables, including, race, ethnicity, gender expression, and age, are often at play, and they are not considered when disruptions are brewing. Additionally, the supervisors and other co-workers can also be complicit in reacting without being purposeful and engaging in a critically reflective capacity.

The social work landscape is changing, and students and clinicians must engage in a way that demonstrates both the capacity and tolerance to critically reflect when challenges arise. Students and practitioners need tools to help better prepare for sustaining their relationships and caring for marginalized communities that lend their trust to practitioners.

The Power of the Pause

Practicum education has many nuances and complexities that call for critical reflexivity during the student learning experience. It is for these reasons that one school of social work in the Northeastern area of the country collected anecdotal support to emphasize the importance of critical reflection by piloting a preparatory lab. The lab was designed to introduce anti-oppressive frameworks and tools that students will need before beginning their practicum experiences with clients and communities. In the modules, concepts including critical reflexivity, location of self, intersectionality, and others were introduced via videos, case examples, and simulative tools that highlighted prototypical client interactions. More specifically, to illuminate the iterative process of critical reflexivity, the *Power of the Pause* (POP) was created by the authors of the labs. The POP is a running theme throughout the modules to introduce the idea of slowing the entire process down by thinking more intentionally and critically. For example, case vignettes were presented in the modules that demonstrated commonly known barriers that students sometimes encounter before and during the practicum experience. The POP consisted of reflective prompts that encouraged students to think more intentionally about the proposed challenges presented within the case vignette. The questions were designed to promote a reduction in reactive interventions, and a more intentional approach utilizing the theoretical concepts as guideposts. The repetitive nature of this exercise was created to embrace the process of considering one's own positionality as it relates to whom they are working with and in what context, as well as to consider alternative perspectives, to become more prepared to practice.

Although the POP was initially thought of as a tool for assisting students to critically reflect on their experiences and challenges, this applied tool may benefit new practitioners, faculty, and ultimately clients, as they interact with each other. In fact, this tool could be employed by seasoned clinicians who may need a new way of looking at understanding how identities and systems intersect with one another. This is evidenced by many of us in the practicum department who often casually remark about how we need to *pause* and think more intentionally when faced with student issues and agency complexities. Locating ourselves, identifying the power differentials, naming the vehicles of oppression, and considering all the intersectional variables that collide within our lived experiences will help new practitioners develop alternate pathways in building empowerment and strength (Nayak, 2022). The following is an example of a case composite of an MSW student and their experience within the practicum setting. The case will highlight the challenges that the student and the agency were managing, the disruption that inevitably occurred, and how the reflection process could have been more meaningful if the POP was considered by all the individuals involved.

Case Study

Conner is a 25-year-old White, cis-identified male, able-bodied, single student entering his specialized practice year for his practicum placement at a very busy city hospital during the first year of the COVID-19 pandemic. The student chose this site as his first choice and felt that he was very much suited for busy, crisis-oriented work within an inpatient psychiatric setting. Conner came from a family of mental health professionals and communicated this to the practicum coordinator as the primary reason for his being qualified for a busy hospital. During the placement process, Conner requested multiple meetings with the placement coordination team to emphasize his practice interests, and his non-interests, and to ensure that the Department of Practicum Learning was aware of his family's professional status. While it is typical to schedule meetings with rising second-year MSW students prior to placing them, it is unusual to have multiple meetings at this early stage of the placement process. It is also important to note that the student was persistent about a specific hospital, and not just any city hospital. Oftentimes, during these meetings, Conner would appear to be overwhelmed and would sometimes cry. When asked about the reason for his apparent distress, his response would be "I just want to be placed at this hospital so badly."

During the first month of the internship, just after the initial peak of the first COVID-19 wave, the student was attending his placement three times a week in person at the city hospital that he requested. In this month, he expressed generalized anxiety about interning in a hospital during a pandemic. These anxious feelings only worsened over time. Conner frequently expressed concern and frustration that his colleagues at his internship were making jokes regarding patient interactions and were sometimes observed to be more relaxed about wearing their masks. Due to the escalation in his anxiety, the student participated in meetings with the university faculty advisor and with the practicum supervisor to understand the challenges, barriers, strengths, and possible resolutions.

The hospital supervisor was a Black, cis-identified female, in her forties, and had been working in this role for 10 years. The other co-workers included professionals from other disciplines including nurses, case managers, other social workers, doctors, and support staff. The agency supervisor expressed multiple concerns relevant to Conner's behavior, professional attitude, and performance. Specifically, the supervisor communicated that Conner had made some derogatory comments about other co-workers on the unit, often had difficulty receiving constructive feedback and self-regulating in a professional capacity, and ultimately was unable to meet the competencies required in his intern role. The student was terminated from the agency by the end of the first semester.

After the termination occurred, Conner was asked to complete a written reflection assignment to examine the deeper meaning of his experience as an intern in a hospital during a public health crisis. The student had difficulty reflecting in a critical capacity and rather insisted that the termination had very little to do with him. Conner believed that the supervisor was being too harsh and that the rest of the hospital team simply didn't like him.

Conceptualizing Conner's Case and Applying the Power of the Pause

To conceptualize the case of Conner, it is important to deconstruct the process from the onset of the placement process. The next section will describe how the POP could have been applied through a critically reflective process in interaction with the placement coordinator, the engagement with the agency environment and stakeholders involved, and by considering the socio-political context at that time. Theoretical frameworks, including critical race theory (CRT) and Intersectionality, will also be discussed as the underpinnings of these reflections.

Reflection, Positionality, and Self-Awareness

The POP would begin with reflective questions that promote self-awareness and understanding one's own positionality. For example, in the labs, the students would observe videos and case vignettes and afterward respond to POP reflective questions such as:

> *How might it be helpful to learn how to practice reflection-in-action? How have your life experiences impacted your path toward anti-racism? How will your positionality inform your work in your practicum placement? What are your first impressions about your own identities and those of the people you will be working with and learning from?*

Once an understanding of self-awareness and social location has been reached, then the questions would look a little closer at utilizing critical theories such as critical race theory, and specifically intersectionality to help deconstruct some of the overt and less overt tension. For instance, those questions were:

> *Using the theoretical frameworks discussed earlier, how might you begin to understand and interact within a micro, meso, and macro lens? Who seems to benefit from the social structures in the agency? What are your intersecting identities that may be influencing your*

initial feelings? Now that you have taken a pause, how can you use your own understanding of your identities to respond versus reacting?

In the case of Conner, if we look at the entry point from the very beginning of the placement process, we can start to examine some of the dynamics that occurred when Conner was meeting with the practicum coordinator.

We might recall that Conner requested multiple meetings with the practicum coordinator to present himself as qualified and very interested in this specific hospital. Along with this plea to be placed in the hospital, were many tears shed to reinforce this message. If we begin with a reflective stance on our self-awareness and social location, we need to look closely at verbal and non-verbal cues. The placement coordinator is also the author of this chapter. I identify as a Brown female, cis-gendered, able-bodied, in my mid-forties, with two decades of professional experience in hospital social work.

Self-awareness should evolve naturally from self-reflection because it taps into our ability to assess how we react to the external environment (Finch et al., 2019). Self-awareness is an integral part of a social worker's personal and professional development, and it is achieved by identifying thoughts and feelings that may arise in response to a situation. By becoming more self-aware we gain a better understanding of how these thoughts and feelings can potentially affect our ability to interact with others (Bruce, 2013). The consistent practice of self-awareness, becoming more attuned to self, can also increase our awareness of the ways we *otherize* people and act on biases due to our own internalized beliefs (Finch et al., 2019). Using the POP within the first few meetings between Conner and myself could have slowed the process down by exploring the dynamics at play between us. For example, although Conner verbally communicated that he is qualified and ready for this role primarily due to his family's professional status as mental health providers, his frequent tears might suggest otherwise. The *pause* here could have ignited a reflective approach for both of us to consider this dichotomy. Although I did ask the student about his crying, the exploration could have directed the student to look at what he is verbally communicating and what his body language is saying. If I had directly communicated my observations about the ambivalence that was coming from him, and the power of the tears, perhaps this would have been a step toward promoting a conversation around self-awareness and positionality. I was aware that the tears could also have symbolized other relational dynamics and conflicts, but I was being cautious about addressing the tears in depth. My role was to be an educator, not a therapist.

The POP could also be emphasized through a critical reflection approach. For example, in this early phase, we could see nuances in the power and privilege that were operating in this dialogue. I could have further slowed this process by probing questions about how power, privilege, race, and positionality shaped our conversation about his placement requests. For example, I could have directly asked him, *What is it like for you to be working with an Indian woman? Where do you see any power nuances within our relationship? Where do you have privilege here, and where do I? How does this impact how we work together?* I presume that it was unintentional that the student used his Whiteness and his family's professional status to influence my perception, attitude, and behavior. The message I heard through our interactions was *I'm qualified because my family has determined this, and this is powerful, and if you don't grant me my placement you will be alone in this decision and there may be consequences*. The dialogue about this impact is important and can provide a teachable moment.

Critical Race Theory and Intersectionality

Once the student arrived at the agency that he specifically requested, the challenges only became more complicated. Conner has already received the message that his power and privilege have been successful, and he can continue using this approach to meet his goals. At this stage, the racial dynamics only intensified with multiple people involved within the supervisory team. Given that the practicum instructor was a Black woman with multiple years of experience in this setting, the power became more nuanced and complex. The *pause* here could have been a conversation about what Conner's thoughts were about their varying identities between them, their degrees of power within an organizational context, and how this shapes and informs their work together. The identities of the co-workers in the hospital were also important to the overall discussion on power differences.

If we use the POP within the supervisory relationship, we could use critical race theory and intersectionality to help inform the critical reflective process. Critical race theory is a theoretical framework that examines power structures that maintain racial inequities and seeks to empower voices that have been traditionally marginalized (Daftary, 2020). Rooted in legal theory, the original attempts of this postmodern perspective were to unpack oppressive parts of society to create societal transformation (Daftary, 2020; Ortiz & Jani, 2010). For example, according to Kolivoski et al. (2014), critical race theory maintains that racism has been normalized in the United States and that is perpetuated through social structures and institutions (Bell, 1992; Kolivoski et al., 2014). Furthermore, it is mostly agreed that hierarchical structures govern political, economic, and social spheres, yielding to Whites as being privileged and non-Whites as socially constructed as others (Decuir & Dixson, 2004: Kolivoski et al., 2014). Critical race theory has many more tenets to its framework, however, if we look at just this first one, there is much to consider within a hospital infrastructure. If the POP were used in this respect during supervision, reflective prompts and assignments (as mentioned earlier) could have been encouraged to examine how the structures in a hospital setting might complicate the balance of power, and the oppression of social workers of color and their dynamics while supervising a White student. Finally, how does this influence the quality of care provided to clients?

Rooted in black feminist theory, Kimberle Crenshaw termed intersectionality to describe the interactions between conflicting identities including race, class, gender, and sexual orientation, that individuals are composed of, and these identities can hold privilege and/or marginalization (Crenshaw, 1991; Daftary, 2020; Mattsson, 2014). If we use intersectionality to help further understand some of this tension, we could use the POP to engage in dialogue about the various social categories and identities that interconnect and collide within an oppressive hospital system (Daftary, 2020). In essence, Conner's social identities, the practicum instructor's social identities, and other co-workers' social identities on the inpatient unit were all intersecting and creating experiences that were unique to them, and yet the privileges and marginalization needed further discussion. A deeper pause could have been enacted to consider how these multiple forces work together within an organizational system that is built to negate this.

Trauma and Racial Reckoning

The challenges that Conner faced during his internship were certainly not unique to him. Considering the socio-political context of the pandemic, notably the racial reckoning that was occurring at the time, there were numerous external stressors that may have impacted the teaching and learning experience. During the pandemic, students expressed a range of emotions including anger, fear, sadness, and confusion, which were not unlike what students had reported after experiencing the traumatic events of September 11, 2001 (Dempsey et al., 2021; Tosone et al., 2003). This is another point at which a *pause* to reflect on shared trauma from the pandemic and the events of 2020 may have impacted Conner's capacity to engage in critical reflection, as well as my own. During this period, hospital social workers were on the front lines and had multiple demands on them, both physically and emotionally (Craig et al., 2022). Many of our community partners reported anxieties related to their own safety but didn't feel they had the power or the choice to voice these concerns within their organizations. A POP approach here could have also been useful in discussing the common anxieties that all employees and students were collectively feeling.

The racial reckoning and the impact that was occurring post-George Floyd were also alive in the room but not addressed within the context of the student and supervisor relationship. The POP approach here would call for a discussion on justice, rights, historical traumas, and how these all connect to potential obstacles when addressing challenging situations.

Power of the Pause Is a Useful Anti-oppressive Tool

There is power in the Power of the Pause. Utilizing critical race theory, intersectionality, and other frameworks grounded in anti-oppressive practice, can assist stakeholders in the process of slowing down potential ruptures in student practicum learning, thereby increasing critical reflexive development. This applied tool has the capacity to be transformational if it is utilized more collectively and through an engaged pedagogical approach (Hooks, 2010). Students, practitioners, and educators working collaboratively, being vulnerable, and taking risks to pause and reflect will model this practice for clients and communities. This collaborative process inevitably shifts power differentials within these relationships and offers a more inclusive approach. It supports new clinicians as they develop their own professional style of practice and can help reframe the problem-solving process for even the most experienced social worker.

Practice Wisdom and Reflections from a Practicum Coordinator

The student depicted in this chapter was ultimately replaced in a different setting for the remainder of his final year of the MSW program. Since graduating from the program, he has been practicing in a different state and recently communicated with this practicum coordinator. In this conversation, the student was able to reflect on this experience in a more profound capacity. He explained that at the time, he did not understand why he was being asked to critically reflect on his experience and to consider alternate perspectives, including what he could have done differently. He stated that he was so sure he was right in every *accusation* that was made against him. However, since he has started working within a very busy residential setting that houses individuals with substance use challenges, he has been connecting some of his internship experiences with his current practice. Specifically, he has reflected on some of the racial dynamics and his privilege and power that he was unable to acknowledge at that time. When asked what helped him gain this new knowledge, he reported that he had time to pause and reflect.

In higher education, faculty and administrators are often compelled to comply with what is referred to as neoliberal agendas (Robinson & Macfarlane, 2021). Students are consumers and therefore faculty must maintain the status quo and keep the economic peace. As faculty, these implications weigh heavily as ethical considerations are sometimes ignored to sustain the economic objectives of universities (Robinson & Macfarlane, 2021). In Conner's case, he was unable to fully participate in the learning process during his internship. This has implications for how clients are receiving services, and ultimately more at risk of being harmed. Often in practicum education, when students have disruptions, some faculty try to engage them in a critical reflexive process, but many times students are resistant to this process. Students often claim that this process is somehow oppressive and punitive in nature. The reasons for this resistance could be due to inconsistency in the encouragement of critical reflexive pedagogy across the curriculum areas, as discussed earlier in this chapter (Beasley et al., 2022). Students and faculty are handling multiple competing demands and often this critical process is not fully developed, leaving faculty, students, practitioners, and ultimately clients at a disservice. Faculty need more support as they manage the continuing evolving social work practicum landscape. Engaging in critical conversations through the utility of applications such as the *Power of the Pause* can be part of anti-racist pedagogy training within the multi-level organizational system. Various curriculum areas can benefit from convening, collaborating, and presenting a unified vision for this message to permeate through the student collective.

Practicum education department faculty are charged with the successful connection between students and their agency placements. In fact, this is a very complicated and nuanced process. Some have also referred to practicum coordination as the *negotiated pedagogy* (Asakura et al., 2018). The practicum coordination process is complex, requiring collaboration, diplomacy, reflection, and patience. Students are often making assumptions about the "perfect placement" and are expecting the practicum coordinators to also be "perfect" (Morley & Dunstan, 2013, p. 146). Many times, students who are unaware of their own social position and the coordinators' positionality can inadvertently engage in microaggressions or inflict their power as a student who is paying large tuition dollars in hopes of receiving exceptional education in return. In my own anecdotal experience, it is this *exceptional education* that seems to be debatable today. Many students do not perceive a disruption in their agency placement as a potential for a deeper learning experience. As a result, they will simply insist on a replacement without a more detailed educational process. As the practicum coordinator for Conner, it was often difficult to be present in the same room and to model patience, collaboration, and diplomacy. His tears spoke loudly, and my reaction was to adhere to his requests or else face the consequences of a displeased White student in a private university. Upon reflection, the Power of the Pause could have helped me too. If I intentionally slowed down the process and engaged the student to actively reflect on his own behaviors, thereby raising his self-awareness, location of the self, and capacity for critical thinking, and seeing it through an anti-oppressive lens, perhaps a different outcome would have been achieved.

Reflection Questions

The following reflection questions can be applied to students, new practitioners, faculty, and instructors as they consider how the POP can be applied in their practice.

1. How have you used CRT, Intersectionality, and Critical Reflection in your practice? How has using one or more of these perspectives helped you? What barriers have you faced when using one or more of these perspectives?
2. What challenges have you encountered when supervising students or working with clients? How could you use the Power of the Pause to have a more meaningful learning experience?
3. Consider Conner's case and think about a time when you were 1) in a position of power and 2) when you were not, and how this impacted a relationship. Now add

the intersections of race, ethnicity, age, gender expression, and ability. What questions would you ask yourself and why?
4. Reflecting on Conner's case, are there any additional dimensions of critical reflection that you think could have been vital in this process?
5. How can students, faculty, and community partners work more collaboratively within an anti-oppressive capacity?

References

Abramovitz, M., & Sherraden, M. S. (2016). Case to cause: Back to the future. *Journal of Social Work Education, 52(51)*, 589–598. https://doi.org/10.1080/10437797.2016.1174638

Asakura, K., Todd, S., Eagle, B., & Morris, B. (2018). Strengthening the signature pedagogy of social work: Conceptualizing field coordination as a negotiated social work pedagogy. *Journal of Teaching in Social Work, 38(2)*, 151–165.

Atteberry-Ash, B., Nicotera, N., & Gonzales, B. (2021). Walk the talk of power, privilege, and oppression: A template analysis. *Journal of Social WorkEducation, 57(1)*, 7–15. https://doi.org/10.1080/10437797.2019.1661917

Ayala, J., Drolet, J., Fulton, A., Hewson, J., Letkemann, L., Baynton, M., Elliott, G., Judge Stasiak, A., Blaug, C., Gérard Tétreault, A., & Schweizer, E. (2018). Field education in crisis: Experiences of field education coordinators in Canada. *Social Work Education, 37(3)*, 281–293. https://doi.org/10.1080/02615479.2017.1397109

Beasley, C. C., Singh, I. M., & Drechsler, K. (2022). Anti-racism and equity-mindedness in social work field education: A systematic review. *Journal of Ethnic & Cultural Diversity in Social Work, 31(3-5)*, 173–185. https://doi.org/10.1080/15313204.2021.1991868

Bell, D. A. (1992). *Faces at the bottom of the well: The permanence of racism*. Basic Books.

BlackDeer, A. A., & Ocampo, M. G. (2022). # SocialWorkSoWhite: A critical perspective on settler colonialism, white supremacy, and social justice in social work. *Advances in Social Work, 22*(2), 720–740.

Bogo, M., Lee, B., McKee, E., Ramjattan, R., & Baird, S. L. (2017). Bridging class and field: Field instructors' and liaisons' reactions to information about students' baseline performance derived from simulated interviews. *Journal of Social Work Education, 53(4)*, 580–594. https://doi.org/10.1080/10437797.2017.1283269

Brookfield, S. (2009). The concept of critical reflection: Promises and contradictions. *European Journal of Social Work, 12(3)*, 293–304. https://doi.org/10.1080/13691450902945215

Bruce, L. (2013). *Reflective practice for social workers. A handbook for developing professional confidence*. Open University Press.

Carroll, M. (2011). Supervision: A journey of lifelong learning. In R. Shohet (Ed.), *Supervision as transformation: A passion for learning* (pp. 14–28). Jessica Kingsley.

Council on Social Work Education. (2015). *Educational policy and accreditation standards*. Author.

Council on Social Work Education. (2022). *Educational policy and accreditation standards*. Author.

Craig, S. L., Kourgiantakis, T., Kirkland, A., Muskat, B., & Sur, D. (2022). Riding the wave: Pandemic social work in hospitals. *Social Work in Health Care, 61(5)*, 323–337. https://doi.org/10.1080/00981389.2022.2085232

Craig, S. L., McInroy, L. B., Goulden, A., Eaton, A. D., Kourgiantakis, T., Bogo, M., Adamson, K., Iacono, G., Gagliardi, L., Krasovec, T., & Small, M. (2021). The health social work competency rating scale: Development of a tool for education and practice. *Social Work Education, 40(7)*, 928–941. https://doi.org/10.1080/02615479.2020.1768233

Crenshaw, K. (1991). Mapping the margins: Intersectionality, identity, and violence against women of color. *Stanford Law Review, 43*(6), 1241–1300.

Curry, A., & Epley, P. (2022). "It Makes You a Healthier Professional": The impact of reflective practice on emerging clinicians' self-care. *Journal of Social Work Education, 58*(2), 291–307. https://doi.org/10.1080/10437797.2020.1817825

Daftary, A. (2020). Critical race theory: An effective framework for social work research. *Journal of Ethnic & Cultural Diversity in Social Work, 29(6)*, 439–454. https://doi.org/10.1080/15313204.2018.1534223

Davis, A., & Mirick, R. G. (2021). COVID-19 and social work field education: A descriptive study of students' experiences. *Journal of Social Work Education, 57(supl)*, 120–136. https://doi.org/10.1080/10437797.2021.1929621

de Bie, A., Chaplin, J., Vengris, J., Dagnachew, E., & Jackson, R. (2021). Not 'everything'sa learning experience': Racialized, Indigenous, 2SLGBTQ, and disabled students in social work field placements. *Social Work Education, 40*(6), 756–772.

DeCuir, J. T., & Dixson, A. D. (2004). "So when it comes out, they aren't surprised that it is there": Using critical race theory as a tool of analysis of race and racism in education. *Educational Researcher, 33*, 26–31.

Dempsey, A., Lanzieri, N., Luce, V., de Leon, C., Malhotra, J., & Heckman, A. (2021). Faculty respond to COVID-19: Reflections-on-action in field education. *Clinical Social Work Journal*. https://doi.org/10.1007/s10615-021-00787-y

Dewey, J. (1933). *How we think: A restatement of the relation of reflective thinking to the educative process* (2nd ed.). D.C. Heath.

Drolet, J. (2020). A new partnership: Transforming the field education landscape intersections of research and practice in Canadian social work field education. *Field Educator, 10*(1) https://fieldeducator.simmons.edu/wp-content/uploads/2020/05/Conversation_10.1-1.pdf

Ferguson, H. (2018). How social workers reflect in action and when and why they don't: The possibilities and limits to reflective practice in social work. *Social Work Education, 37(4)*, 415–427. https://doi.org/10.1080/02615479.2017.1413083

Finch, B. J., William, F. O., Mondros, B. J., & Franks, L. C. (2019). *Learning to teach, teaching to learn: A guide for social work field education*. Council on Social Work Education.

Fook, J. (2016). *SocialWork: A critical approach to practice* (3rd ed.). Sage.

Fook, J., & Gardner, F. (2007). *Practicing critical reflection*. Open University Press.

Garcia, B., & Van Soest, D. (2021). *Social work practice for social justice from cultural competence to anti-oppression*. CSWE.

Giles, R., & Pockett, R. (2013). Critical reflection in social work education. In J. Fook & F. Gardner (Eds.), *Critical reflection in context* (pp. 208–218). Routledge.

Gooding, A., & Mehrotra, G. R. (2021). Interrupting white supremacy in field education. experiences of microaggressions in placement settings. *Advances in Social Work, 21*(2/3), 311–330.

Gray, M., & Webb, S. A. (Eds.). (2013). *The new politics of SocialWork*. Palgrave Macmillan.

Gushwa, M., & Harriman, K. (2019). Paddling against the tide: Contemporary challenges in field education. *Clinical Social Work Journal, 47*, 17–22. https://doi.org/10.1007/s10615-018-0668-3

Hamilton-Mason, J., & Schneider, S. (2018). Antiracism expanding social work education: A qualitative analysis of the undoing racism workshop experience. *Journal of Social Work Education, 54*(2), 337–348. https://doi.org/10.1080/10437797.2017.1404518

Hooks, B. (2010). *Teaching critical thinking: Practical wisdom*. Routledge.

Kishimoto, K. (2018). Anti-racist pedagogy: From faculty's self-reflection to organizing within and beyond the classroom. *Race Ethnicity & Education, 21(4)*, 540–554. https://doi.org/10.1080/13613324.2016.1248824

Kolivoski, K. M., Weaver, A., & Constance-Huggins, M. (2014). Critical race theory: Opportunities for application in social work practice and policy. *Families in Society, 95(4)*, 269–276. https://doi.org/10.1606/1044-3894.2014.95.36

Kourgiantakis, T., Sewell, K. M., & Bogo, M. (2019). The importance of feedback in preparing social work students for field education. *Clinical Social Work Journal, 47*, 124–133. https://doi.org/10.1007/s10615-018-0671-8

Lee, E., Kourgiantakis, T., Hu, R., Greenblatt, A., & Logan, J. (2022). Pedagogical methods of teaching social justice in social work: A scoping review. *Research on Social Work Practice, 32*(7), 762–783.

Mantulak, A., Bullen, A., & Arundel, K. M. (2020). Generational learning in social work: Is it them or us? *Field Educator, 10*(1).

Mattsson, T. (2014). Intersectionality as a useful tool: Anti-oppressive social work an critical reflection. *Journal of Women and Social Work, 29*(1), 8–17. https://doi.org/10.1177/0886109913510659

McDermott, C., Stafford, J. D., & Johnson, S. D. (2021). Racial equity as a human rights issue: Field agency practices and field instructors' knowledge and attitudes. *Journal of Human Rights and Social Work, 6*, 14–20. https://doi.org/10.1007/s41134-020-00155-9

Mehrotra, G. R., Gooding, A. R., & Bormann, O. K. (2023). Race/ism in field education: Narratives of BIPOC field instructors. *Journal of Teaching in Social Work, 43*(2), 135–154. https://doi.org/10.1080/08841233.2023.2176033

Milner, M., & Wolfer, T. A. (2023). Using the reflective judgment model to understand and appraise effective reasoning by social work students. *Journal of Social Work Education, 59*(1), 78–90.

Morley, C., & Dunstan, J. (2013). Critical reflection: A response to neoliberal challenges to field education? *Social Work Education, 32*, 141–156. https://doi.org/10.1080/02615479.2012.730141

Morley, C., & O'Bree, C. (2021). Critical reflection: An imperative skill for social work practice in neoliberal organisations? *Social Sciences, 10*(3), 97.

National Association of Social Workers. (2021). *Code of ethics*. https://www.socialworkers.org/About/Ethics/Code-of-Ethics/Code-of-Ethics-English.

Nayak, S. (2022). An intersectional model of reflection: Is social work fit for purpose in an intersectionally racist world? *Critical and Radical Social Work, 10*(2), 319–334. https://doi.org/10.1332/204986021X16555682461270

Ortiz, L., & Jani, J. (2010). Critical race theory: A transformational model for teaching diversity. *Journal of Social Work Education, 46*(2), 175–193. https://doi.org/10.5175/JSWE.2010.200900070

Parker, J. (2010). When things go wrong! Placement disruption and termination: Power and student perspectives. *British Journal of Social Work, 40*, 983–999. https://doi.org/10.1093/bsjw/bcnl49

Rankine, M. (2018). How critical are we?: Revitalising critical reflection in supervision. *Advances in Social Work and Welfare Education, 20*(2), 31–46.

Redmond, B. (2006). *Reflection in action*. Ashgate.

Robinson, K., & Macfarlane, S. (2021). 'Resistant to change?': Using critical reflection to analyse positionality within a neoliberal academic environment. *Critical and Radical Social Work, 9*(3), 437–450.

Ruch, G. (2002). From triangle to spiral: Reflective practice in social work education, practice, and research. *Social Work Education, 21*(2), 199–216. https://doi.org/10.1080/02615470220126435

Schon, D. A. (1983). *The reflective practitioner: How professionals think in action.* (p. 1983). New York: Basic Books.

Shea, E. S. (2020). Field note—engaging social work interns in reflective practice: A specialized training series for field instructors. *Journal of Social Work Education, 56*(1), 193–200. https://doi.org/10.1080/10437797.2019.1633973

Sheppard, M. (2007). Assessment: From reflexivity to process knowledge. In J. Lishman (Ed.), *Handbook for practice learning in social work and social care* (pp. 128–137). Jessica Kingsley.

Swick, D. C., Dyson, Y. D., & Webb, E. (2021). Navigating a pandemic, racial disparities, and social work education through the lens of the NASW code of ethics. *Reflections: Narratives of Professional Helping, 27*(1), 84–93.

Theobald, J., Gardner, F., & Long, N. (2017). Teaching critical reflection in social work field education. *Journal of Social Work Education, 53*(2), 300–311. https://doi.org/10.1080/10437797.2016.1266978

Tosone, C., Lee, M., Bialkin, L., Martinez, A., Campbell, M., Martinez, M. M., et al. (2003). Shared trauma: Group reflections on the September 11th disaster. *Psychoanalytic Social Work, 10*(*1*), 57–77.

Wagaman, M. A., Odera, S. G., & Fraser, D. V. (2019). A pedagogical model for teaching racial justice in social work education. *Journal of Social Work Education, American Academy of Social Work & Social Welfare, 55*(2), 351–362. https://doi.org/10.1080/10437797.2018.1513878

Watts, L. (2019). Reflective practice, reflexivity, and critical reflection in social work education in Australia. *Australian Social Work, 72*(*1*), 8–20. https://doi.org/10.1080/0312407X.2018.1521856

Part II
Anti-oppressive Lifecycle Practice

Chapter 5
Perinatal Mental Health: Addressing Service Gaps and Advancing Anti-Oppressive Practice

Fengtao Huang

Positionality Statement

It is important to acknowledge that an author's positionality is shaped by their personal and professional experiences. I am a first-generation Chinese immigrant, cisgender female social worker, psychotherapist, and program leader with previous experiences working in the creative art and media field. My previous academic and work experiences in the creative and media field helped me to form a habit of observing individuals through their community dynamic. They also expanded the opportunities for me to practice analyzing events from informed perspectives. Being a female, cisgender individual, I am attuned to gender-related disparities that can influence mental health issues. I also recognize that the perinatal period can be especially challenging for LGBTQ2S+ families due to the gendered nature of the pregnancy and childbirth process (Kirubarajan et al., 2022). Many barriers and inequities exist in these individuals' childbearing and childbirth process, and related studies are limited in scope and depth. I strive for openness to learning from diverse perspectives and experiences. In the case study, I will demonstrate how my personal insights as an immigrant and perspective as a social worker helped me navigate the unique cultural factors and complexities of perinatal mental health issues that may impact help-seeking behaviors within the Chinese community and provide culturally sensitive treatment to the clients. I believe my positionality also presents certain limitations, and it is an ongoing process to understand myself and others. I am committed to continuous learning, self-reflection, and embracing cultural humility as essential components of my clinical practice, research, and teaching.

F. Huang (✉)
Silver School of Social Work, New York University, New York, NY, USA
e-mail: f.huang@nyu.edu

C. Tosone et al. (eds.), *Reframing Social Work with an Anti-Oppressive Lens*, Essential Clinical Social Work Series,
https://doi.org/10.1007/978-3-031-91391-4_5

Introduction

"They instantly become 'daddy, grandpa, grandma' with your first cry. They welcome your birth with laughter and joy, but no one mentioned how mommy experienced the bone-opening delivery process with the world's greatest pain. In the days that followed, everyone praised you for being well-behaved, but they did not know how many sleepless nights mommy endured. Mommy has seen the stars at every hour of the night and has cried alone, forcing herself to heal at the same time when she broke down. Yes, she is tired, but she dares to say it, afraid that others will say she is being overly dramatic… it seems like being a mother is something that a mother should do alone. Everyone's lives have not changed; only mommy's has. 'Mommy' is enough for me to have no friends, no job, and to be a babysitter for a lifetime…"—Amanda from the author's treatment cohort talked about her experiences going through postpartum depression on her social media in Mandarin, with permission to translate and use.

Perinatal mental illness refers to mental health disorders that are prevalent during an individual's pregnancy and/or postpartum period (O'Hara & Wisner, 2014). Although the exact timeframe of postpartum is debatable, ranging from several months to 2 years after childbirth, there is consensus about the variety of mental health disorders that may occur during the perinatal period. Some common perinatal mental health conditions include depression, anxiety, obsessive-compulsive disorder (OCD), psychosis, bipolar disorder, and trauma-related disorders.

Perinatal mental health disorders are highly prevalent in the United States (US) and worldwide. Recent reports from the Centers for Disease Control and Prevention (CDC) (2020) indicate the prevalence rate of postpartum depression symptoms is 13.2% and 12–15% for anxiety in 2018. The incidence of depression exceeded 20% for women who encountered other adverse experiences such as domestic violence, substance use, history of depression, and other mental health issues (Bauman et al., 2020; Zhou et al., 2019). Zhou et al. (2019) estimated that 43–45% of women suffer from depression and are also affected by anxiety. Another large-scale study involving more than ten thousand participants confirmed the high comorbidity rate. As high as 66% of study participants suffered from depression and anxiety disorders in their postpartum period (Wisner et al., 2013). Severe mood disorders such as acute mania and psychosis affect about 1–2 individuals in every 1000 childbirth (Perry et al., 2021).

The impact of perinatal mental health issues is more severe among the underserved communities. Wisner et al. (2013) indicated a significantly higher rate of postpartum mental health disorders among African Americans, the younger population, the less educated, those lacking social support, and those involved in the Medicaid healthcare system. Another national research found that unmarried White and Native American women with low income/education had the highest rates of depression (Ertel et al., 2011). It also indicated that Black and Latinx mothers who suffer from depression are less likely to receive services. During the immediate postpartum period, Asian women are nearly nine times more likely to report suicidal ideation than their White peers (Tabb et al., 2020).

In this chapter, the author will explore the perinatal mental health disparities from a social justice lens using a case example of providing treatment based on social determinants of health to a mothers' group from an underserviced immigrant community.

Perinatal Mental Health Disparities

Impact on Maternal Mental Health and Wellbeing

Mothers with perinatal mental health issues often experience difficulties in their daily functioning, sometimes even disabling conditions, which can disrupt the mother–infant relationship and bonding, impact a child's development, and lead to more stress, anxiety, and guilt in the mother. Paris et al. (2009) found that mothers who experienced higher levels of postpartum mental illness symptoms reported higher levels of suicidality. Muzik and Borovska (2010) explored the harmful medical and psychological impact of perinatal depression and indicated that mothers with psychiatric illness report decreased ability to hold daily functions such as self-care, seeking support, poor eating habits, substance use, and relationship difficulties with partners.

Impact on Child Development and Outcomes

A considerable amount of research studied how perinatal depression impacts a child's developmental outcomes. Schetter and Tanner (2012) pointed out that depression, anxiety, and stress are directly associated with preterm birth, low birth weight, and negative neurodevelopment outcome for the child. According to Paris et al. (2009), mothers are less sensitive to their baby's cues when suffering from mental disorders. They tend to demonstrate fewer positive interactions and bonding with their babies, leading to low maternal self-esteem and more parenting-related stress. Goodman (2019) also indicated that children are at higher risk of cognitive and emotional problems if exposed to perinatal depression. Impacts on children can range from disorganized eating and/or sleeping during infancy to behavioral problems and mood disorders in childhood and adolescence.

Barriers to Access Care

Many barriers can set back an individual's help-seeking behavior and prevent them from accessing care. These barriers all contribute to the underutilization of perinatal mental health treatments, and addressing these multifaceted factors is crucial to ensure all individuals' access to care. On the individual level, a lack of literacy and awareness about perinatal mental health can deter individuals from seeking help (Howard et al., 2014; Oates, 2003). The presence of bias, stigmas, and cultural beliefs and practices can make people reluctant to disclose their symptoms and admit the need for mental health treatments (Chung & Bemak, 2002; Howell et al., 2009). For individuals with limited English proficiency, their needs are often misinterpreted or overlooked due to inadequate assessment and communication, leading to difficulty accessing resources. Financial constraints, which are often accompanied by adding a new family member, may restrict an individual's ability to obtain care at an appropriate level or in a timely manner (Flynn et al., 2004; Lancaster et al., 2010). Moreover, Flynn et al. (2004) pointed out that limited mobility and lack of transportation during the perinatal period may discourage individuals from attending their appointments.

Racism and discrimination in perinatal care, such as ableism, ageism, neurodivergence, homophobia, and transphobia, can perpetuate disparities among marginalized populations (Bauer et al., 2016; Admon et al., 2018). Admon et al. (2018) found significantly higher rates of maternal morbidity and mental health disorders in every racial and ethnic minority group during the birthing process compared with the non-Hispanic White group.

From a systemic perspective, the scarcity of specialized perinatal mental health services restricts access to care, especially in underserved communities. Despite many windows of opportunity that come along with prenatal and postnatal physical care, studies found that patients still report a lack of accessibility to perinatal mental health services (Wisner et al., 2013; Masters et al., 2020). This is caused by inadequate screening and assessment due to a lack of training, tools, and protocols in the healthcare system, which makes it difficult for healthcare providers to miss early intervention opportunities.

Perinatal Mental Health through a Social Justice Lens

The author would like to examine this problem from a social justice lens. Social justice refers to "unfair treatment or inequalities that have resulted from racism, sexism, socioeconomics, sexual orientation, religion, ableism, and other 'isms,' all of which affect the quality of life" (Chung & Bemak, 2012, p. 26). When people in power positions define the problems that underserved communities are experiencing, their prejudicial beliefs, cultural differences, and stereotypes can consciously and unconsciously interfere with the process and cause harm (Chung & Bemak, 2012, p. 29). Chung and Bemak point out that the motivations for the powered group can range from maximizing their benefits to maintaining the status quo, rather than making changes to improve the quality of life for others. The unequal distribution of power can lead to severe injustice in the perinatal mental health issue.

Perinatal mental health problems have always been defined by an elite group of medical and mental health providers. Perinatal mental health disorders were first recognized by a French psychiatrist Louis-Victor Marcé in the mid-nineteenth century, where he published comprehensive articles regarding identifying and treating perinatal-related mental health issues (Trede et al., 2009). However, these issues did not draw much attention until recent decades, when more and more individuals in powerful positions started to report their struggles, which raised societal attention. Today, the *Diagnostic and Statistical Manual of Mental Disorders* (DSM) was developed by a small group of selected individuals who are in powered positions. DSM-5-TR was developed by 200 people, of which 60% of them were psychiatrists and 25% were psychologists (APA, 2022). Clinical social workers, which are the largest group of mental health providers in the United States, do not have enough representation in defining perinatal mental health problems. Until today, the DSM does not adequately capture perinatal-related mental health issues and does not recognize perinatal mental health disorders as a separate category with its unique traits. For example, perinatal depression is categorized under Depressive Disorders as a specifier of "with peripartum onset." Antenatal depression was not recognized until DSM-5 came out in 2013. Furthermore, the diagnostic criteria also required the onset of symptoms within 4 weeks following the delivery, excluding many individuals who did not recognize postpartum depression symptoms until much later. There is also a lack of cultural perspective for childbearing and birth-giving individuals, especially those from the underserved community.

On a legislative level, we have seen increased attention focusing on perinatal mental health issues (Rhodes & Segre, 2013). More depression screenings have been rolled out universally since early 2000, which prompted more initiation to treatment among mothers who suffer from perinatal depression. On the federal level, the Mom's Opportunity to Access Health, Education, Research and Support (MOTHERS) Act was finally passed as part of the Affordable Care Act (ACA) in 2010, almost 10 years after the tragic death of Melanie Blocker-Stokes, who suffered from postpartum psychosis. It recommended more research on different levels to focus on the perinatal mental health field, increased access to health care, and encouraged universal screening of pregnant and new moms for depression. Several years after ACA passed, a study that focused on the impact of ACA on pregnant and reproductive-aged individuals found a significant decrease in uninsurance and increased rates of Medicaid and nongroup private coverage utilization. The study also indicated that ACA was also associated with a 1.5% decline in cost-related barriers to medical care (Daw & Sommers, 2019). Another study also found increased postpartum treatment participations, which was directly associated with Medicaid expansion (Steenland & Trivedi, 2023).

Case Study

This case study examines the experiences of 13 Chinese immigrant mothers with perinatal mental health issues using Dahlgren and Whitehead's (1991, 2021) social determinants of health model. The author provided 6-month intensive interventions to the cohort at a community mental health clinic that specializes in perinatal mental health treatments. The study will explore the unique social and cultural determinants that impact the mothers' mental health and highlight the intervention strategies that provide comprehensive support to address their needs and improve overall wellness. This cohort includes 13 mothers aged between 25 and 42 years old who were born in Mandarin-speaking regions in East Asia and have lived in the US for several months to 10 years. Upon the time of admission, five of them were at different stages of their pregnancy, and seven gave birth within the last year.

In the case study, Dahlgren and Whitehead's (1991, 2021) model of health determinants and World Health Organization (WHO) (2014) social determinants of health frameworks are used to conceptualize the case study and analyze contributing factors to mothers' mental health and the interventions provided. Figure 5.1 demonstrated how proximal and distal risk factors and protective factors impacted clients' mental health outcomes through five social determinant domains, which are biopsychological, economic and education, family and cultural, community and societal, and policy and environmental. Bronfenbrenner's (1979) ecological system theory is also used to help organize the domains of the framework. Bronfenbrenner observed that a complex interplay of distal and proximal factors influences human development and mental health (Fig. 5.1). Distal factors such as childhood experiences, genetics, and cultural background occur earlier in life. In contrast, proximal factors, such as acute stressful events, social support, and individual coping mechanisms, occur more immediately. Studies over the past decade found that negative distal and proximal factors, such as childhood trauma, maltreatment, and stress, were associated with an increased risk of depression, anxiety, and other mood disorders, while positive factors such as social support and proper coping strategies can protect an individual against mood disorders (Fleischman et al., 2022; Heim & Binder, 2012; McLaughlin et al., 2014; Nurius et al., 2015).

Biopsychological Domain

The perinatal period can be a time of significant biopsychological changes for any birthing person, and many factors may contribute to mental health distress. Similar to what many people go through during pregnancy, the frequently reported proximal factors from this group of mothers during the prenatal period are unplanned or unwanted pregnancy, fears and worries when bearing a child, and physical discomforts such as constipation, rashes and aching, and urinary incontinence. The cohort has several afterbirth factors in common, including difficulties with breastfeeding, poor sleep quality, physical pain related to the birthing process, and unwanted changes in appearance, such as weight gain, stretch marks, and decreased energy level. Various traumatic experiences such as domestic violence, immigration trauma, and childhood trauma are the most reported contributing distal factors that trigger mental distress. This cohort of mothers reported an average of two items on their Adverse Childhood Experiences (ACEs) screening, with emotional abuse and

Social Determinants for Perinatal Mental Health Outcome

	Proximal & Distal Risk Factors	Protective Factors
Biopsychological Domain	• Unplanned or unwanted pregnancy • Physical discomforts and pain • Breastfeeding • Poor sleep quality • Changes in appearance • Traumatic birthing experiences • Adverse Childhood Experiences • History of depression and anxiety	• No obesity and overweight • Health lifestyle • No substance uses • "Zuo Yue Zi" • Healthy eating • Resting
Economic and Education Domain	• Economic recessions • Low income and poverty • Unstable Housing • Financial strain & debt • Unemployment • Food insecurity • No access to education	• Family financial support • Access to resource • Stable Employment
Family and Cultural Domain	• Family history • Interdependence and collectiveness • Decreased sense of autonomy • No social support networks • Culture expectations • Underreported pain • Delayed help-seeking actions	• Interdependence and collectiveness • Close family Relationship with supports from extended families
Community and Societal Domain	• Neighborhood deprivation • Safety and security • Gentrification • Overcrowding and low housing quality • Community trauma • Isolation • Pollution • Asian-hate crimes	• Lives in the Chinatown area with easier access to services in their preferred languages
Policy and Environmental Domain	• National, state laws and local regulations not inclusive to low-pay workers or undocumented individuals	• Access to insurance • Government child-care voucher

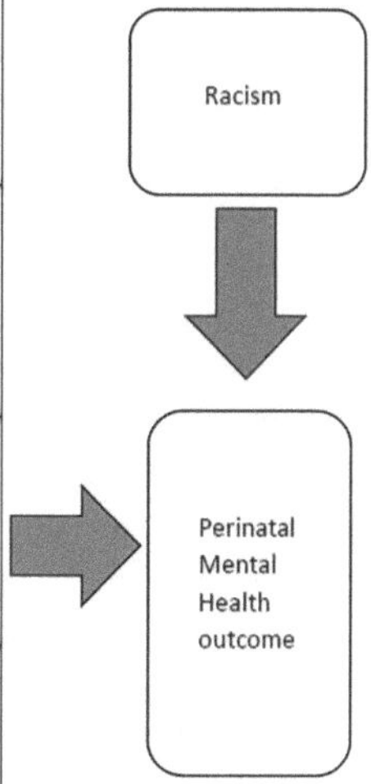

Fig. 5.1 Social determinants for perinatal mental health outcome based on Dahlgren and Whitehead (2021), Lund et al. (2018), Tomlinson et al. (2021)

neglect as the most selected categories. Mothers described that bearing and raising a child brought back some painful memories of how they were mistreated when they were little, which can cause emotional disturbances. Other commonly reported adverse distal biopsychological factors are having a history of depression and anxiety during a previous pregnancy or in earlier life, chronic physical issues, and a family history of mental health disorders.

On the other hand, the mothers recognized some protective biopsychological characteristics that could mitigate postpartum symptoms and reduce the risk of developing mental health disorders. For instance, they acknowledge that maintaining healthy lifestyle practices such as managing body weight, healthy eating habits, and no substance use can reduce the risk of complications and health problems for both mother and child (Blomberg, 2013; Santos et al., 2019). The Chinese cultural postpartum confinement, or "Zuo Yue Zi," which all the mothers from the cohort practiced during the first month after giving birth, involves many activities emphasizing physical health, such as eating nutritious food, resting as much as possible, and taking herbal remedies (Chang Hall et al., 2018).

Economic and Education Domain

Research has shown that even in a universal healthcare system, economic barriers can lead to inadequate prenatal care, increased birth complications, and mother's physical health issues (Kim et al., 2018). Generally speaking, for immigrants who have moved to a new country with limited language proficiency, education can positively impact their personal and professional development (Lueck, 2018). According to a national study, there is a positive relationship between education level and earnings (National Center for Education Statistics, 2023). However, many new immigrant mothers face various difficulties on their educational journey. In the case of the 13 mothers, they come from different socioeconomic and educational backgrounds, with most of them finishing high school or equivalent education in their country of origin. All of them expressed the need and willingness to obtain an advanced degree or increase English proficiency after emigrating to the United States. However, due to financial and family burdens, only about a quarter of them had an opportunity to take classes or work toward their educational goals, and only one of them finished her degree. Moreover, compared with White women, Asian American women who came to the United States after high school are more likely to be unemployed, less likely to be promoted, and have fewer earnings (Kim & Zhao, 2014). Besides the mother who finished her degree and identified as middle-income, the rest of the mothers all reported financial strain and stress related to an increased risk of depression and anxiety. Some of the reported economic risk factors that are impacting mothers' mental health from the cohort are poverty, food insecurity, and unstable housing. Since many of the mothers and their family members are working in service industries—restaurants, stores and supermarkets, nail and hair salons, car service, and travel agencies—the economic recession associated with the COVID-19 pandemic has taken a serious toll on their living conditions. In the meantime, the cohort recognizes attaining financial stability can bring a great sense of security for their families, especially when at least one of the family members has stable employment or access to resources.

Family and Cultural Domain

Research has shown that Chinese families tend to strongly emphasize interdependence and collectiveness, which can play both protective and adverse roles (Shao et al., 2021). On the one hand, it is naturally expected for family members such as spouses, parents, parents-in-law, and relatives to be actively engaged during a person's pregnancy and the postpartum period. This higher level of family engagement, cohesion, and support has been found to mitigate postpartum distress and mental health issues (Shao et al., 2021). On the other hand, the strong beliefs about filial piety and the family unit may lead to mothers' decreased sense of autonomy and hesitations to discuss their own needs when the quality of support is low. Several of the mothers from the group reported that during the postpartum confinement period, they had to stay with family members who added more stress in the name of "helping out," leading to more family conflicts and mental health issues. Other mothers who reported having close relationships with their husbands and extended families were more likely to recover from their perinatal mental health symptoms.

Despite the common cultural practices on support, not all mothers have access to a sufficient support network due to various reasons. Building a social circle is especially hard for individuals who came to the United States in the past few years without any family and friends due to the COVID-19 pandemic. Several mothers in the group have spouses who had to work in a different state and only return home on weekends or when there is an urgent issue. In addition, many families and subcultural groups expect women to be the primary caregiver and take most of the childcare responsibilities. Being in a family that has an absentee spouse, usually means a mother is raising a child 24/7 and going through perinatal challenges alone, even though they have a spouse who can potentially be helpful. Some mothers became overwhelmed by the obligations, feeling stuck and unempowered, which can cause significant emotional implications.

Cultural factors also shape mothers' interpretation and expression of mental health symptoms and their attitudes toward seeking help. A commonly reported mindset from this cohort is stoicism which showed up as underreporting pain and suffering, with the belief of "I should just bear with it." This can result in reluctance and delayed actions in seeking professional help, further exacerbating maternal mental health issues.

Community and Societal Domain

The majority of this cohort lives in one of the Chinese immigrant communities; they can have easier access in their preferred languages to medical, educational, religious, and social services, as well as participate in daily life activities. On the other hand, due to language barriers, cultural differences, and, in recent years, fear of discrimination, living in such segregated neighborhoods may contribute to a slower acculturation process, causing hesitations and fears about going out and hindering interactions with individuals from diverse cultures. These neighborhoods tend to have dense populations and living spaces with noise and light pollution, which may create more stress during the perinatal period. More than half of the mothers in the cohort reported sharing their living space with other roommates due to affordability, which is often in unregulated rental units. Gee et al. (2011) pointed out the concerning issue of lack of quality affordable housing in Asian immigrant communities. According to Gee et al., approaching 30% of Asian renters live in an overcrowding or severe overcrowding household, which is the highest rate among all ethnic groups in New York City. They also shared concerns about fire hazards and unsafe living conditions in these shared housing situations, which can be even more worrisome for a pregnant or postpartum individual to live in.

Since the COVID-19 pandemic, the surge in anti-Asian hate crimes has caused the immigrant population to develop feelings of helplessness, fear, anxiety, powerlessness, and frustration (Gover et al., 2020). Many of the mothers reported heightened vigilance in public spaces, avoidance behaviors, and overprotection toward their children. Several of the mothers presented posttraumatic stress symptoms after experiencing or witnessing violence and discrimination in the community.

Policy and Environmental Domain

Several laws and legislations on federal and state levels aim to expand access to perinatal mental health services. The Mental Health Parity Act and Addiction Equity Act of 2008 requires health plans to provide unlimited coverage for both mental health and substance use treatment. The Affordable Care Act (ACA) of 2010 ensured more resources for treatment and professional training.

Compared with people living in other states in the United States, living in New York State can be a protective factor for mothers. The Maternal Depression Screening Bill, passed in 2017, requires more access to maternal depression screening and treatments in multiple settings, from pediatricians' office to hospitals with health plan coverage. In New York City, all pregnant women, undocumented immigrants included, are eligible to have Medicaid with free full perinatal mental health coverage. Mothers from the cohort stated feeling more comfortable utilizing their insurance knowing the laws in New York State (NYS) are more relaxed and will not need to disclose their immigration status when they use insurance.

Although the New York State Paid Family Leave Law of 2018 allows workers to use paid time off to care for a newborn and receive perinatal mental health treatments, none of the mothers in the cohort are eligible to use this benefit because of their limited job opportunities.

Racism

Dahlgren and Whitehead (2021) suggested not to include racism as a determinant of health but rather view it as a significant "driving force" that shapes all domains of determinants. This can help to interpret the intricate layers of racism that this group of mothers experienced. On individual and community levels, mothers reported feeling isolated and excluded from the larger society due to their immigrant status and cultural differences, even for those who have language proficiency. A commonly reported obstacle to accessing perinatal mental health treatment is experiencing discrimination and microaggressions from healthcare, educational, and social service providers. Several mothers reported internalizing racism, having symptoms such as self-rejections of their culture and values, deceased sense of control and competence, feeling embarrassed, and blaming themselves for not being able to assimilate into the mainstream culture fast enough. Looking through institutional and structural aspects, providers and agencies may have held biases or stereotypes toward Chinese immigrants and not have enough culturally sensitive interventions, leading to delays in seeking help, misdiagnosis, and inadequate treatments. Furthermore, a lack of representations of female Chinese immigrants in leadership further perpetuates the disparities in accessing mental health care.

Additionally, due to institutional racism, this cohort of mothers struggles to find a job and are more likely to work in low-paying and long-hour positions with limited access to paid leave and benefits, making it difficult for them to take time off for medical appointments, self-care, or recuperate after giving birth. All these factors can influence and contribute to chronic distress, financial pressure, and overall poor perinatal mental health outcomes for these mothers. These observed phenomena are all consistent with research findings on how structural racism and discriminatory systems reinforced the inequity in perinatal health (Bailey et al., 2017).

Culturally Sensitive Interventions

Recruitment through Community Education

During the start of the program, the author noticed that despite the disabling struggles that occurred during the perinatal period, Chinese immigrants who go through perinatal mental health issues hesitate to seek help because of their limited understanding of perinatal issues, lack of familiarity with the mental health system, and embarrassment or shame to admit the mental health issues. Efforts must be made to educate potential participants and change their views regarding mental health issues. Accordingly, the author led her team to develop culturally appropriate recruitment approaches in the community. The recruitment and community education period lasted about a year.

When translating the flyers and promotional materials of the program, the author and her team modified the language to plain and simple wording and spread the promotion through many channels. For example, using "孕产期 (pre- & postnatal period)" instead of its formal translation "围产期 (the perinatal period)," as it can be easily understood and identifiable to the target audience. Several key community partners who focus on health care, parent–child relationships, and social services in the Chinese community were identified to help promote treatment and build trust among potential participants. The team hosted a press conference with major Chinese media, local legislators, and community partners and made many media appearances on TV programs, newspapers, radio stations, and social media. There were five online and in-person workshops on the topics of perinatal mental health, infant social-emotional development, attachment, postpartum depression, infant first aid, and CPR provided in Mandarin Chinese free of charge. The workshops together attracted around two hundred participants from the community. The team also provided free mother–baby dyadic groups collaborating with other community organizations providing services to the perinatal population.

All the outreach efforts helped to provide education and destigmatize perinatal mental health issues, build trust and rapport with the targeted population, and help to normalize help-seeking behaviors for mental health treatments. Several mothers from the Chinese cohort described their process of gradually feeling more comfortable and motivated to begin treatment after attending several outreach events and talking to the staff members individually. One of the mothers began to follow the program's work during her pregnancy and finally had the courage to reach out when her child turned one.

Culturally and Linguistically Appropriate Treatment

As demonstrated in Fig. 5.2, the cohort received two whole-day treatments weekly with four groups each day during phase I for the first 3 months, then transitioned to one whole-day treatment with four groups during phase II for another 3 months. During the recruitment period, surveys were conducted to potential participants to determine the most needed areas of treatment. The group topics covered four areas: behavioral skills, parenting and family relationships, mother–baby dyadic intervention, and relaxation and personal growth. Behavioral skills incorporate

Sample Treatment Schedule

Treatment Phase I (3 Months)

Time	Day 1	Day 2
10:00 - 10:30 AM	Breakfast	Breakfast
10:30 - 11:30 AM	Bright beginnings	Mother-baby reading time and activities
11:30 - 12:30 PM	CBT for pregnancy and postpartum anxiety	Parenting journey I
12:30 - 01:00 PM	Lunch	Lunch
01:00 - 02:00 PM	Scrapbooking	Parenting journey II
02:00 - 03:00 PM	Pregnancy support group	Personal growth group

Treatment Phase II (3 Months)

Time	Day 1
10:00 - 10:30 AM	Breakfast
10:30 - 11:30 AM	Mother-baby dyad group
11:30 - 12:30 PM	Emotional regulation and anger management
12:30 - 01:00 PM	Lunch
01:00 - 02:00 PM	Positive parenting
02:00 - 03:00 PM	Personal growth and creative activities

Fig. 5.2 Sample treatment schedule

evidence-informed interventions such as dialectical behavior therapy (DBT) skills groups, mindfulness, and cognitive behavioral therapy (CBT), which have proved to be effective in targeting perinatal mood disorders symptoms (Nillni et al., 2018; Cooper et al., 2003). These interventions all have been used in treating Chinese Americans and showed positive results when adopted with culturally sensitive strategies (Bercean et al., 2020; Yang et al., 2020). Parenting and family relationships included two curriculums of Positive Discipline and Parenting Journey, which the group facilitators had prior experiences in conducting the groups with Chinese immigrant population. Bright Beginnings is a well-liked mother–baby dyadic group curriculum that was developed by the Ackerman Institute to enhance the parent–child relationship and strengthen children's social, emotional, and cognitive development (Ackerman Institute, 2022). Team members who facilitated the group received ongoing training and supervision from Ackerman Institute to ensure the fidelity of the intervention. Relaxation and personal growth groups provided psychoeducational topics with creative activities incorporated, such as scrapbooking, crochet, art-making, and sensory toy building, to help mothers explore and practice more coping strategies. Individual and family therapy related to each mother's personalized care plan was also provided, as was transportation assistance to expand accessibility.

One of the unique approaches for this cohort is to build group cohesion and treat the group as a whole, which is culturally more effective and particularly suitable for short-term, compacted interventions because of the collectiveness in Chinese culture. Li et al. (2020) found that putting participants in a group setting is more effective since group members were able to provide diverse perspectives and insights. Li and colleagues indicated that participants feel more encouraged to express themselves with peer encouragement and are able to build on each other's ideas, leading to more in-depth discussions. Group cohesion is extremely helpful in every phase of group development. In the beginning, the group helped the mothers in the normalization of their experiences and struggles. It allowed them to develop self-compassion and reduce the sense of isolation. As mothers started to bond, the group's social connections helped them build a sense of belonging. This cohesion helped the group members to support each other in providing a safe environment for open conversations, boosting their learning process, and reducing stigma that related to their mental health symptoms. The power of shared learning experiences helped mothers absorb new information quickly within a short time. As the group relationship got stronger, the author noticed that group members started to provide motivation and accountability for each other's progress and goals. When a group member gives birth or is going through stressful events, others will act as a collective source of motivation and support, offering emotional and material support to the one in need and helping each other to reify their commitment to treatment and personal goals. Toward the end of the treatment period, mothers had already formed strong social connections and friendships. The cohort had several successful occasions where they supported a group member in getting through their distress and organized several social events together. The cohort is taking a step further with the goal of working together to open a daycare center. With the heart of helping more families in the community who are going through a perinatal period, the cohort decided to provide services for children from birth through age 3. They applied for a grant that emphasized community impact and established a business plan.

Strengthen Protective Factors

The treatment team implemented several strategies to help mothers strengthen their protective factors by expanding access to financial support, healthcare, childcare, and education. To enhance this cohort of mothers' economic stability and alleviate financial stressors, the treatment team collaborated with another program that provides direct cash assistance and helps build peer-driven support. To participate in this program and qualify for a $200 monthly unrestricted cash incentive, mothers meet monthly to discuss their personal and family goals and support each other in achieving these goals. Through these meetings, mothers gradually evolved their own ways of providing mutual support, sharing experiences, brainstorming, problem-solving, exchanging resources and knowledge, practicing financial planning, and fostering a sense of community empowerment.

In order to support the mothers' acculturation process and help them build a sense of belonging, many activities were implemented, such as holiday celebrations that emphasize both US and Chinese holidays, baby showers, trips with components of cultural promotion, and educational workshops related to healthcare, social and educational systems. There were also workshops and individual sessions designed to support them in obtaining childcare vouchers, community resources, and work opportunities according to their individual needs. The program also provides free breakfast and lunch for attendees.

Anti-Oppressive Practices for Closing the Service Gaps

The pervasive impact of perinatal mental health problems makes it a significant public health issue that demands more attention and resources. The perinatal period can also be seen as an opportunity for family interventions to increase access to health care and insurance. Therefore, the author proposed changes on different levels to address the need for perinatal mental health treatments.

Expand Treatment and Services at Community Level

On the state and city levels, CDC suggested to implement screening and treatment with programs like Head Start, home visiting programs, and existing grants to address perinatal mental health issues (2020). Guintivano et al. also pointed out that providers should ensure robust assessments as clinical screening is the best tool for identifying women who are at risk of Postpartum Depression (2018). This should include grants to projects and programs that establish, operate, and coordinate to deliver essential services to individuals and their families at risk for postpartum conditions. Other than traditional routine screening, diagnostic assessment with treatments, child-focused early interventions, and mother–child dyadic and family interventions should also be provided. Other supportive services that can help with the unique needs of perinatal experiences, such as transportation, homemaker services, respite services, and financial assistance, should also be increased.

Expand Research Opportunities

In a recent CDC (2020) report regarding postpartum depression, only about half of the states in the United States have perinatal mental health data. It is still unclear how this issue is influencing the general population nationwide. Studies have indicated a higher rate of postpartum mental health disorders among the Black, Indigenous, and People of Color (BIPOC) communities; but there is not enough research to understand how to address these health disparities, and how to provide modified treatment to support perinatal individuals (Mollard et al., 2021; Collins, 2023). Perinatal mental health–related risk factors, screening and diagnostic tools, and treatment methods are all in need of development, especially among underserved communities.

Update Diagnostic Tools

As mentioned previously, the current diagnostic tool that has been used in the United States, the DSM-5-TR, does not recognize perinatal-related mental health issues as a separate category. Perinatal mental health disorders have their unique variety and features, which should be studied separately for a better understanding. Consumer mothers, social workers and other front-line providers such as nurses and doctors, early-intervention specialists, and educators who work with the population should all be included in the development of these tools.

Emphasize Public Education

Educational programs and campaigns should be implemented targeting the general population to raise awareness of perinatal mental health disorders. Education curriculums need to be designed for the targeted population instead of a direct translation from its official English version. Education programs should be implemented in obstetrics and gynecology, primary care settings, and hospitals to ensure families expecting or with a new baby have access to the resources. Services providers, schools, and programs need to have knowledge of local resources for referral to treatment and follow-up.

Training Programs for Health Professionals

According to a CDC reproductive health report, about 20% of women who attended a prenatal visit were not screened for depressive symptoms, which means that healthcare providers are missing opportunities to ask about prenatal mental health conditions. Some providers may not have the knowledge and tools to screen or do not recognize the importance of perinatal mental health issues. Training and continuing education should be provided to medical and mental health professionals in all settings, such as individual offices, inpatient and outpatient programs, case management, and programs that provide benefit access to the perinatal population.

Explore New Intervention Methods

Studies have shown that when treating perinatal mental health disorders, it is crucial to address them from a holistic approach which can prioritize the well-being of both mother and infant (Nillni et al., 2018; Allen et al., 2014). Therefore, we need new interventions that are culturally modified and can address maternal mental health needs, ameliorate adverse effects on infants, and increase mother–baby bonding. Treatment should address all aspects of the client's social determinants with a combination of interventions such as individual therapy, parenting skills coaching, relaxation activities, child development education, and support network building.

Conclusion

In conclusion, perinatal mental health has gained attention in recent years with the growing recognition of its impact on birthing individuals, infants, and their families. Nevertheless, disparities in identifying and accessing treatment are very prevalent, especially in disadvantaged communities, requiring attention from healthcare and mental providers, policymakers, community organizations, research institutions, and media. This chapter utilized social determinants of health model and ecological system theory to exam the treatment experiences of a group of Chinese immigrant mothers with perinatal mental health issues. Moving forward, research and practice must utilize a comprehensive approach with targeted anti-oppressive practice strategies aimed at expanding access and diminishing inequity in perinatal mental health.

Reflection Questions

1. Why do you think the perinatal mental health problem persists despite policies that have been implemented to address it?
2. Approach a couple of people in your social network, and ask them what they think about perinatal mental health issues. How does their positionality impact their view of the issue?
3. You are in the position of developing a treatment program for individuals with perinatal mental health issues in your community. How would you design the program?
4. Consider the treatment model presented in the case study, what are some of the interventions you would like to keep, and what are some changes you would like to make?
5. Consider the World Health Organization (WHO)'s (2014) social determinants of health frameworks,
   (a) Apply the framework on yourself, or a client of yours. Identify each domain of social determinants to see how they impact your thoughts, behaviors, socioemotional well-being, and daily living.
   (b) Examine a community issue with this framework. Identify how you can improve the issue by applying targeted solutions in each domain.

References

Ackerman Institute. (2022). *Developing child and family. Ackerman institute for family*. Retrieved on June 22, 2023, from https://www.ackerman.org/research/developing-child-and-family/

Admon, L. K., Winkelman, T. N. A., Zivin, K., Terplan, M., Mhyre, J. M., & Dalton, V. K. (2018). Racial and ethnic disparities in the incidence of severe maternal morbidity in the United States, 2012-2015. *Obstetrics and Gynecology, 132*(5), 1158–1166. https://doi.org/10.1097/AOG.0000000000002937

Allen, J., Balfour, R., Bell, R., & Marmot, M. (2014). Social determinants of mental health. *International Review of Psychiatry, 26*(4), 392–407. https://doi.org/10.3109/09540261.2014.928270

American Psychiatric Association (APA). (2022). *The people behind DSM-5-TR*. Retrieved from https://www.psychiatry.org/File%20Library/Psychiatrists/Practice/DSM/DSM-5-TR/APA-DSM5TR-ThePeopleBehindDSM.pdf

Bailey, Z. D., Krieger, N., Agénor, M., Graves, J., Linos, N., & Bassett, M. T. (2017). Structural racism and health inequities in the USA: Evidence and interventions. *Lancet (London, England), 389*(10077), 1453–1463. https://doi.org/10.1016/S0140-6736(17)30569-X

Bauer, A., Knapp, M., & Parsonage, M. (2016). Lifetime costs of perinatal anxiety and depression. *Journal of Affective Disorders, 192*, 83–90. https://doi.org/10.1016/j.jad.2015.12.005

Bauman, B. L., Ko, J. Y., Cox, S., D'Angelo Mph, D. V., Warner, L., Folger, S., Tevendale, H. D., Coy, K. C., Harrison, L., & Barfield, W. D. (2020). Vital signs: Postpartum depressive symptoms and provider discussions about perinatal depression–United States, 2018. *Morbidity and Mortality Weekly Report, 69*(19), 575–581. https://doi.org/10.15585/mmwr.mm6919a2

Bercean, A.-V., Breen, L. J., McEvoy, P. M., Yeak, S., & Rooney, R. (2020). Improving the cultural sensitivity of cognitive-behavioral therapy for Chinese migrants with depression: Community members' and clinicians' perspectives. *Professional Psychology: Research & Practice, 51*(6), 613–622. https://doi.org/10.1037/pro0000326

Blomberg, M. (2013). Maternal obesity, mode of delivery, and neonatal outcome. *Obstetrics and Gynecology, 122*(1), 50–55. https://doi.org/10.1097/AOG.0b013e318295657f

Bronfenbrenner, U. (1979). *The ecology of human development: Experiments by nature and design*. Harvard University Press. https://doi.org/10.2307/j.ctv26071r6

Centers for Disease Control and Prevention (CDC). (2020). *Identifying maternal depression, missed opportunities to support moms*. Retrieved April 25, 2023, from https://www.cdc.gov/reproductivehealth/vital-signs/identifying-maternal-depression/index.html

Chang Hall, W. A., Campbell, S., & Lee, L. (2018). Experiences of Chinese immigrant women following "Zuo Yue Zi" in British Columbia. *Journal of Clinical Nursing, 27*(7–8), e1385–e1394. https://doi.org/10.1111/jocn.14236

Chung, R. C., & Bemak, F. P. (2012). *Social justice counseling: The next steps beyond multiculturalism*. SAGE Publications. Incorporated.

Chung, R., & Bemak, F. (2002). The relationship of culture and empathy in Cross-cultural counseling. *Journal of Counseling & Development, 80*(2), 154–159.

Collins, L. H. (2023). Risk, race and racism in maternal mental health. *Counseling Today, 65*(9), 14–17.

Cooper, P., Murray, L., Wilson, A., & Romaniuk, H. (2003). Controlled trial of the short- and long-term effect of psychological treatment of post-partum depression: I. Impact on maternal mood. *The British Journal of Psychiatry, 182*(5), 412–419. https://doi.org/10.1192/bjp.182.5.412

Dahlgren, G., & Whitehead, M. (1991). *Policies and strategies to promote social equity in health*. Institute for Future Studies.

Dahlgren, G., & Whitehead, M. (2021). The Dahlgren-Whitehead model of health determinants: 30 years on and still chasing rainbows. *Public Health, 199*, 20–24. https://doi.org/10.1016/j.puhe.2021.08.009

Daw, J. R., & Sommers, B. D. (2019). The affordable care act and access to Care for Reproductive-Aged and Pregnant Women in the United States, 2010–2016. *American Journal of Public Health, 109*(4), 565–571. https://doi.org/10.2105/AJPH.2018.304928

Ertel, K. A., Koenen, K. C., & Rich-Edwards, J. W. (2011). Maternal depression in the United States: Nationally representative rates and risks. *Journal of Women's Health, 20*(11), 1609–1617. https://doi.org/10.1089/jwh.2010.2657

Fleischman, E. K., Connelly, C. D., & Calero, P. (2022). Depression and anxiety, stigma, and social support among women in the postpartum period. *Nursing for Women's Health, 26*(2), 95–106. https://doi.org/10.1016/j.nwh.2022.01.008

Flynn, H. A., Davis, M., Marcus, S. M., Cunningham, R., & Blow, F. C. (2004). Rates of maternal depression in pediatric emergency department and relationship to child service utilization. *General Hospital Psychiatry, 26*(4), 316–322. https://doi.org/10.1016/j.genhosppsych.2004.03.009

Gee, P., Nam Le, D., Lee, R., Yoo, J.-A., & Kui, C. (2011). The struggle for quality affordable housing in New York City: Asian Americans for equality. *Asian American Policy Review, 21*, 9–17.

Goodman, J. H. (2019). Perinatal depression and infant mental health. *Archives of Psychiatric Nursing, 33*(3), 217–224. https://doi.org/10.1016/j.apnu.2019.01.010

Gover, A. R., Harper, S. B., & Langton, L. (2020). Anti-Asian hate crime during the COVID-19 pandemic: Exploring the reproduction of inequality. *American journal of criminal justice: AJCJ, 45*(4), 647–667. https://doi.org/10.1007/s12103-020-09545-1

Guintivano, J., Manuck, T., & Meltzer-Brody, S. (2018). Predictors of postpartum depression: A comprehensive review of the last decade of evidence: A comprehensive review of the last decade of evidence. *Clinical Obstetrics and Gynecology, 61*(3), 591–603. https://doi.org/10.1097/grf.0000000000000368

Heim, C., & Binder, E. B. (2012). Current research trends in early life stress and depression: Review of human studies on sensitive periods, gene–environment interactions, and epigenetics. *Experimental Neurology, 233*(1), 102–111. https://doi.org/10.1016/j.expneurol.2011.10.032

Howard, L. M., Molyneaux, E., Dennis, C. L., Rochat, T., Stein, A., & Milgrom, J. (2014). Non-psychotic mental disorders in the perinatal period. *Lancet (London, England), 384*(9956), 1775–1788. https://doi.org/10.1016/S0140-6736(14)61276-9

Howell, E. A., Mora, P. A., DiBonaventura, M. D., & Leventhal, H. (2009). Modifiable factors associated with changes in postpartum depressive symptoms. *Archives of Women's Mental Health, 12*(2), 113–120. https://doi.org/10.1007/s00737-009-0056-7

Kim, C., & Zhao, Y. (2014). Are Asian American women advantaged? Labor market performance of college educated female workers. *Social Forces, 93*(2), 623–652. https://doi.org/10.1093/sf/sou076

Kim, M. K., Lee, S. M., Bae, S. H., Kim, H. J., Lim, N. G., Yoon, S. J., Lee, J. Y., & Jo, M. W. (2018). Socioeconomic status can affect pregnancy outcomes and complications, even with a universal healthcare system. *International Journal for Equity in Health, 17*(1), 2. https://doi.org/10.1186/s12939-017-0715-7

Kirubarajan, A., Barker, L. C., Leung, S., Ross, L. E., Zaheer, J., Park, B., Abramovich, A., Yudin, M. H., & Lam, J. S. H. (2022). LGBTQ2S+ childbearing individuals and perinatal mental health: A systematic review. *BJOG: an International Journal of Obstetrics and Gynaecology, 129*(10), 1630–1643. https://doi.org/10.1111/1471-0528.17103

Lancaster, C. A., Gold, K. J., Flynn, H. A., Yoo, H., Marcus, S. M., & Davis, M. M. (2010). Risk factors for depressive symptoms during pregnancy: A systematic review. *American Journal of Obstetrics and Gynecology, 202*(1), 5–14. https://doi.org/10.1016/j.ajog.2009.09.007

Li, Q., Xue, W., Gong, W., Quan, X., Li, Q., Xiao, L., Caine, E. D., & Poleshuck, E. L. (2020). Experiences and perceptions of perinatal depression among new immigrant Chinese parents: A qualitative study. *BMC Health Services Research, 21*. https://doi.org/10.1186/s12913-021-06752-2

Lueck, K. (2018). Socioeconomic success of Asian immigrants in the United States. *Journal of Ethnic & Migration Studies, 44*(3), 425–438. https://doi.org/10.1080/1369183X.2017.1320940

Lund, C., Brooke-Sumner, C., Baingana, F., Baron, E. C., Breuer, E., Chandra, P., Haushofer, J., Herrman, H., Jordans, M., Kieling, C., Medina-Mora, M. E., Morgan, E., Omigbodun, O., Tol, W., Patel, V., & Saxena, S. (2018). Social determinants of mental disorders and the sustainable development goals: A systematic review of reviews. *The Lancet Psychiatry, 5*(4), 357–369. https://doi.org/10.1016/S2215-0366(18)30060-9

Masters, G. A., Li, N., Lapane, K. L., Liu, S. H., Person, S. D., & Byatt, N. (2020). Utilization of health care among perinatal women in the United States: The role of depression. *Journal of Women's Health (2002), 29*(7), 944–951. https://doi.org/10.1089/jwh.2019.7903

National Center for Education Statistics. (2023). *Annual earnings by educational attainment. Condition of education*. U.S. Department of Education, Institute of Education Sciences. Retrieved on June 19, 2023, from https://nces.ed.gov/programs/coe/indicator/cba

McLaughlin, K. A., Sheridan, M. A., & Lambert, H. K. (2014). Childhood adversity and neural development: Deprivation and threat as distinct dimensions of early experience. *Neuroscience and Biobehavioral Reviews, 47*, 578–591. https://doi.org/10.1016/j.neubiorev.2014.10.012

Mollard, E., Kupzyk, K., & Moore, T. (2021). Postpartum stress and protective factors in women who gave birth in the United States during the COVID-19 pandemic. *Women's Health, 17455057*, 1–10. https://doi.org/10.1177/17455065211042190

Muzik, M., & Borovska, S. (2010). Perinatal depression: Implications for child mental health. *Mental Health in Family Medicine, 7*(4), 239–247.

Nillni, Y. I., Mehralizade, A., Mayer, L., & Milanovic, S. (2018). Treatment of depression, anxiety, and trauma-related disorders during the perinatal period: A systematic review. *Clinical Psychology Review, 66*, 136–148. https://doi.org/10.1016/j.cpr.2018.06.004

Nurius, P. S., Green, S., Logan-Greene, P., & Borja, S. (2015). Life course pathways of adverse childhood experiences toward adult psychological Well-being: A stress process analysis. *Child Abuse & Neglect, 45*, 143–153. https://doi.org/10.1016/j.chiabu.2015.03.008

Oates, M. (2003). Perinatal psychiatric disorders: A leading cause of maternal morbidity and mortality. *British Medical Bulletin, 67*, 219–229. https://doi.org/10.1093/bmb/ldg011

O'Hara, M. W., & Wisner, K. L. (2014). Perinatal mental illness: Definition, description and aetiology. *Best Practice & Research Clinical Obstetrics & Gynaecology, 28*(1), 3–12. https://doi.org/10.1016/j.bpobgyn.2013.09.002

Paris, R., Bolton, R. E., & Weinberg, M. K. (2009). Postpartum depression, suicidality, and mother-infant interactions. *Archives of Women's Mental Health, 12*(5), 309–321. https://doi.org/10.1007/s00737-009-0105-2

Perry, A., Gordon-Smith, K., Jones, L., & Jones, I. (2021). Phenomenology, epidemiology and Aetiology of postpartum psychosis: A review. *Brain Sciences, 11*(47), 47. https://doi.org/10.3390/brainsci11010047

Rhodes, A. M., & Segre, L. S. (2013). Perinatal depression: A review of US legislation and law. *Archives of Women's Mental Health, 16*(4), 259–270. https://doi.org/10.1007/s00737-013-0359-6

Santos, S., Voerman, E., Amiano, P., Barros, H., Beilin, L. J., Bergström, A., Charles, M. A., Chatzi, L., Chevrier, C., Chrousos, G. P., Corpeleijn, E., Costa, O., Costet, N., Crozier, S., Devereux, G., Doyon, M., Eggesbø, M., Fantini, M. P., Farchi, S., Forastiere, F., et al. (2019). Impact of maternal body mass index and gestational weight gain on pregnancy complications: An individual participant data meta-analysis of European, north American and Australian cohorts. *BJOG: An International Journal of Obstetrics and Gynaecology, 126*(8), 984–995. https://doi.org/10.1111/1471-0528.15661

Schetter, C. D., & Tanner, L. (2012). Anxiety, depression, and stress in pregnancy: Implications for mothers, children, research, and practice. *Current Opinion in Psychiatry, 25*(2), 141. https://doi.org/10.1097/YCO.0b013e3283503680

Shao, H.-H., Lee, S.-C., Huang, J.-P., & Hwang, L.-C. (2021). Prevalence of postpartum depression and associated predictors among Taiwanese women in a mother-child friendly hospital. *Asia Pacific Journal of Public Health, 33*(4), 411–417. https://doi.org/10.1177/10105395211001172

Steenland, M. W., & Trivedi, A. N. (2023). Association of Medicaid Expansion with Postpartum Depression Treatment in Arkansas. *JAMA Health Forum, 4*(2), e225603. https://doi.org/10.1001/jamahealthforum.2022.5603

Tabb, K. M., Hsieh, W.-J., Gavin, A. R., Eigbike, M., Faisal-Cury, A., Hajaraih, S. K. M., Huang, W. D., Laurent, H., Carter, D., Nidey, N., Ryckman, K., & Zivin, K. (2020). Racial differences in immediate postpartum depression and suicidal ideation among women in a Midwestern delivery hospital. *Journal of Affective Disorders Reports, 1*, 100008. https://doi.org/10.1016/j.jadr.2020.100008

Tomlinson, M., Hunt, X., Daelmans, B., Rollins, N., Ross, D., & Oberklaid, F. (2021). Optimising child and adolescent health and development through an integrated ecological life course approach. *BMJ British Medical Journal, 372*. https://doi.org/10.1136/bmj.m4784

Trede, K., Baldessarini, R. J., Viguera, A. C., & Bottero, A. (2009). Treatise on insanity in pregnant, postpartum, and lactating women (1858) by Louis-victor Marcé: A commentary. *Harvard Review of Psychiatry, 17*(2), 157–165. https://doi.org/10.1080/10673220902891802

World Health Organization (WHO) & Gulbenkian Global Mental Health Platform. (2014). *Social determinants of mental health*. World Health Organization. Retrieved April 29, 2023, from https://apps.who.int/iris/bitstream/handle/10665/112828/9789241506809_eng.pdf

Wisner, K. L., Sit, D. K. Y., McShea, M. C., Rizzo, D. M., Zoretich, R. A., Hughes, C. L., Eng, H. F., Luther, J. F., Wisniewski, S. R., Costantino, M. L., Confer, A. L., Moses-Kolko, E. L., Famy, C. S., & Hanusa, B. H. (2013). Onset timing, thoughts of self-harm, and diagnoses in postpartum women with screen-positive depression findings. *JAMA Psychiatry, 70*(5), 490–498. https://doi.org/10.1001/jamapsychiatry.2013.87

Yang, X., Liu, D., Wang, Y., Chen, Y., Chen, W., Yang, C., Zhang, P., Ding, S., & Zhang, X. (2020). Effectiveness of Zhong-Yong thinking based dialectical behavior therapy group skills training versus supportive group therapy for lowering suicidal risks in Chinese young adults: A randomized controlled trial with a 6-month follow-up. *Brain & Behavior, 10*(6), 1–14. https://doi.org/10.1002/brb3.1621

Zhou, J., Ko, J. Y., Haight, S. C., & Tong, V. T. (2019). Treatment of substance use disorders among women of reproductive age by depression and anxiety disorder status, 2008-2014. *Journal of Women's Health, 28*(8), 1068–1076. https://doi.org/10.1089/jwh.2018.7597

Chapter 6
Child Advocacy Centers: A Multidisciplinary Approach to Trauma-Informed Care

Daisy Lopez

Unfiltered questions from curious children are the norm at a Child Advocacy Center (CAC). "Do you sleep here? And how much does the government pay you?" I don't recall all the responses I've given over the years, but I do distinctly remember breathing a sigh of relief during these interactions. These innocent questions meant, even if for a moment, children were focused on something other than the abuse allegations that brought them to the CAC.

Prior to the 1980s, lacking law enforcement and child welfare practices sparked a movement to better support child abuse victims. Poor communication and siloed efforts burdened child victims, non-offending caregivers, and siblings (Bai et al., 2009; Herbert & Bromfield, 2016). Children and their families were tasked with navigating numerous agencies to initiate the investigative process. As a result, children were often subjected to multiple distressing interviews in different settings, increasing the traumatic nature of investigations. Low prosecution rates and too few children engaging in psychological services post disclosure also contributed to the demand for a more streamlined approach (Newman et al., 2005).

The development of the CAC model, introduced in 1985, brought about a paradigm shift in the investigation, prosecution, and therapeutic treatment of child abuse. CACs, national community-based organizations offering a trauma-informed, culturally responsive, multidisciplinary team approach in response to child abuse allegations, restructured former practices (McNees, 1987; Jenson et al., 1996; Lalayants & Epstein, 2005). Multidisciplinary teams (MDTs) are individuals from diverse agencies and areas of expertise who come together to collaboratively review cases. As noted by Herbert and Bromfield (2016), this new system brought together a team of professionals, including law enforcement officers/detectives, child

D. Lopez (✉)
Silver School of Social Work, New York University, New York, NY, USA
e-mail: dl4811@nyu.edu

C. Tosone et al. (eds.), *Reframing Social Work with an Anti-Oppressive Lens*, Essential Clinical Social Work Series,
https://doi.org/10.1007/978-3-031-91391-4_6

protective services workers, child abuse pediatricians, district attorneys, forensic interviewers, mental health providers, and victim advocates. With the MDT approach gaining prominence as the new norm, child maltreatment was regarded as a multilayered community problem requiring timely and comprehensive support (Hochstadt & Harwicke, 1985; Krugman, 2012). Since 1985, CACs have grown to over 1,000 centers across the United States using this model (National Child Traumatic Stress Network, 2021).

Allegations of abuse are referred through multiple channels, including reports into the Statewide Central Register of Child Abuse and Maltreatment (SCR), a "hotline" or database that houses reports of abuse and maltreatment. CACs receive cases of physical and sexual abuse allegations with alleged offenders ranging from caregivers to extended family members to strangers, or persons unknown to the victim. A protocol of an MDT premeeting to conduct intake and review CAC practices with any nonalleged caregiver is followed by a forensic interview with the reported victim. Wraparound services, including mental health, case management, and medical examinations, ensure families receive substantial support. Though every CAC is modeled from the initial 1985 center, evidence-based interventions and organizational practices vary across centers. There is currently no literature exploring the range of therapeutic interventions across CACs (Lalayants & Epstein, 2005). New York City (NYC) CAC social and mental health workers have three rotating roles of forensic interviewer, trauma-focused therapist, and case manager or family advocate.

In doing this work I am mindful of the privilege I hold. I am also at the forefront of activism against abuse and exploitation of children and families. But to overlook the ramifications of partnering with systems that have historically caused harm to marginalized and vulnerable groups makes advocates complicit in perpetuating cycles of oppression and racism. Our well-intentioned efforts may cause more damage to families we have pledged to defend. The lessons and case vignettes presented in this chapter are unique to a New York City CAC setting and from the perspective of a social worker balancing these complexities. The hope in doing this is twofold: highlighting the strengths of a CAC setting while also presenting a realistic picture of its struggles and debates.

Lesson 1: Honor Lived Experience

For social workers in agency settings, evidence-based practices, that is, any practice that is deemed effective through scientific research based on specific criteria, remains the favored intervention approach (Drake et al., 2001). New York City CACs use the Child and Family Traumatic Stress Intervention (CFTSI), an evidence-based intervention to support children and their nonoffending caregivers after disclosures of abuse. This model, developed at the Yale Child Study Center, is a brief intervention of five to eight sessions for children aged 7–18 years. The two major goals include increasing communication between the caregiver and the child concerning the child's stress reactions and developing coping skills for a caregiver to use with the child in response to trauma reactions. CFTSI is an effective intervention to offset posttraumatic stress disorder when implemented within 30–45 days of an event or disclosure (Stover et al., 2022). The success of CFTSI is based on the child and caregiver reporting fewer reactions and lowered scores across measurements (Epstein et al., 2017). These practices, when used with integrity, improve client outcomes (Drake et al., 2001).

The more formal and scientific forms of knowledge are not to be disregarded, but trauma is a subjective experience. The emotional and cognitive impact of an event is shaped by how an individual experiences these events. It is distinguishing between having experienced a traumatic event versus being traumatized by that event (van der Kolk, 2014). CACs can appreciate the validity of formal knowledge *and* incorporate other approaches, such as lived experience, to help clients find the words to meaningfully interpret their experiences. Lived experience refers to first-hand accounts gained through personal experience. It is a phenomenological approach within qualitative research examining the meaning people assign to personal events and experiences (Finlay, 2009).

I'm reminded of a former family who engaged in CFTSI and sparked the conversation of lived experience. Mark, a Mexican American and 12 years old, disclosed sexual abuse by his maternal grandfather. He was placed in the custody of his father, Mr. L, during the investigation phase. Mr. L. emigrated from Mexico to the United States in his early twenties, and Mark was born soon after. They reported having a stable relationship despite some differences. Mark is bilingual but prefers to speak English, while Mr. L. speaks primarily Spanish. Mr. L. is a man of few words and has not had any experiences with therapy. Mark had a few sessions with a school counselor and appears more at ease with the idea of continued therapy. They had not spoken about the abuse.

The National Association of Social Workers (NASW) encourages the incorporation of clinical experience, client preferences, and culture into the development and delivery of services (Clark, 2013). With approximately 301 Latino or Hispanic families starting CFTSI in 2021, the year Mr. L. and Mark arrived at the CAC, remaining mindful of these points became especially important. CFTSI can accommodate more than one participating caregiver. In cases with no primary caregiver present or cases with the caregiver listed as the alleged offender, an appropriate substitute, such as a foster parent, is acceptable. Mark primarily lived with his mother and grandfather, but now sought his father's guidance as his mother struggled to process the allegation.

A brief description of each session highlights the process this family engaged in: The first session provided psychoeducation, gathered caregiver trauma history, and collected the caregiver's assessment of his child's coping post disclosure. The second session collected the child's perception of the experience and current trauma reactions. A series of self-report measures, including Weathers et al.'s (1993) Post Traumatic Stress Disorder Checklist Civilian Version (PCL-C), Green's (1996) Trauma History Questionnaire (THQ), Pynoos and Steinberg's (2015) Post Traumatic Stress Disorder Reaction Index (PTSD-RI), and Costello and Angold's

(1988) Mood Feelings Questionnaire (MFQ), were used throughout CFTSI to measure how child and caregiver were coping with the aftermath of abuse and disclosure. Session three focused on comparing measurement responses of child and caregiver and discussed discrepancies and areas of agreement. Communication was then facilitated between child and caregiver concerning areas of challenge and grouped into categories of avoidance, intrusive, and hyperarousal symptoms. Coping skills were then discussed as a proactive measure in anticipation of future trauma reactions. Sessions four and five reassessed child and caregiver's trauma responses using the series of measurements from sessions one and two. Coping skills were then modified as needed. CFTSI success is currently measured by lowered scores across measurements, indicating the frequency and intensity of a child's reactions have decreased (Epstein et al., 2017).

While family support serves as a primary protective factor for children exposed to a traumatic experience, other factors should be considered (Kliewer et al., 2004; Epstein et al., 2017). CFTSI relies on a solid foundation of communication and trust between child and caregiver. Skills such as active listening, clarifying statements, and responding with curiosity are essential to creating interactions that can withstand vulnerability and discussion of difficult topics. This type of communication style is not the generational norm or the standard for all families. Many families have traditional roles parents and children must adhere to, which interferes with the rich level of emotional sharing asked of them. First-generation children may also find it difficult to connect with caregivers if family values are not compatible with the communication CFTSI requires (Aviles, 2015).

As we got deeper into the sessions, it became clear both father and son were uncomfortable and distant toward one another. Unfortunately, the standardized format and structure of CFTSI made it difficult to integrate any reflections on the intersection of trauma and culture. Social workers must support clients in addressing needs through avenues that are mindful of individual differences and diversity. The CFTSI model weakens this principle with its inflexible structure promoting epistemic oppression. Epistemic oppression refers to persistent exclusion blocking a person's ability to contribute to knowledge resources. Qualitative data invites families and practitioners to learn from lived experiences and narratives that cannot be measured through statistics (Dotson, 2014).

Mark and Mr. L. benefited from a deeper examination of their hesitations, and with that, we essentially modified the definition of "success" in this case and uncovered an area we could focus on for the remaining time: psychoeducation. I used the assessments to guide discussions with Mark and his father, separately. Empathy, respect, acceptance, and positive regard, aspects of a positive therapeutic alliance, created a stronger connection between Mark and Mr. L. I learned about Mr. L's upbringing in Mexico and the guilt he felt as the head of the household from not protecting his son. The term "trauma" is not readily used in Mexico, and the series of assessments felt overwhelming. Mr. L. was still trying to grasp the psychoeducation provided and felt he was failing his son again throughout this process.

Mr. L: Mark lives a different life than I did growing up. Things like this stayed in the family, and we relied on one another and our community. I tell him some things in life are hard, but we can't dwell on that. I'm angry about what happened. Had I been there things would've been different. I get up early on the days I feel it building and go running. My father would drink, and I just don't want to be that person.

Mr. L.'s words were a reminder to filter experiences through the lens of clients. Mr. L. understood the seriousness of the matter but leaned toward reason and logic to cope. Family and cultural values also emphasize *familismo,* reliance on family and clergy connections rather than formal helping systems. Machismo may exist as a protective factor, as men are taught to honor and take responsibility for their families. Mr. L. was not aware of the abuse and could not serve as his son's protector (Bermúdez et al., 2010).

Mark spoke about his sexual abuse, not only as a male but as a Mexican American male. Mark describes an upbringing of opportunity and cannot identify with his father's childhood and the sacrifices he made to emigrate to the United States.

Mark: My dad doesn't really talk about growing up in Mexico. I know he's made a lot of sacrifices. He's a proud person too. He works all the time and never takes breaks.

He also spoke about avoiding in-depth conversations about sensitive topics because he knows his father is of a different generation and isn't sure how he would react to the vulnerability. According to Hochschild (1979), this scenario presented an example of "feeling rules" or the cultural rules binding clients to feel and respond a certain way to situations. Without intent to minimize a child's experience, this may subconsciously shape a caregiver's expectations for a child. Feeling rules manage emotional responses and may potentially cause a child to withhold reactions that may be culturally unacceptable. These conversations, without the limitations of assessments, revealed the barriers we needed to address before moving forward.

Mr. L. and Mark came together and with facilitation, exchanged thoughts from their individual meetings. Mr. L. needed more psychoeducation to understand the nature of trauma and Mark needed to hear that his father was accustomed to coping through reason and logic but was receptive to learning ways to communicate with him. The outcome of this case may not be considered a "win," but it gave Mark and Mr. L the foundation to start building a more emotionally connected relationship.

Lesson 2: Beware of Bias

On a mid-fall evening, I met a 7-year-old boy, M.C., in the waiting room. He was brought to the CAC for an allegation of sexual abuse by his father. He disclosed touching by his father "all over" to his teacher. M.C.'s mother, mostly absent from his life, was incarcerated. The disclosure prompted a call to the State Central Registry (SCR), and the case was flagged as an Instant Response Team (IRT), indicating a child in potential immediate risk and requiring immediate contact. M.C. is excited by the games and books in the waiting area, possibly unaware of the coordination happening around him. MDT members: Child Protective Specialist (CPS) from the Administration for Children's Services (ACS), Special Victims Squad (NYPD), District Attorney of New York (DANY), and I (CAC Social Worker), discussed the case in a premeeting to prepare for the forensic interview. ACS shared M.C. was placed in foster care for approximately 6 months when his mother left him in the care of a friend and never returned. M.C.'s father was located, and M.C. has been in his care for the last year. M.C. also has a diagnosis of Attention-Deficit Hyperactivity Disorder (ADHD) with the date of diagnosis unknown. The Child Protective Specialist (CPS) assigned to the case conducted a preliminary interview with M.C., per ACS guidelines. M.C. denied the allegation when asked about the disclosure. M.C.'s teacher mentioned M.C.'s history of lying but never concerning any serious subject such as sexual abuse. CPS also added M.C. understands why he is at the CAC today.

Forensic interviewing is one component of a child abuse investigation, and its purpose is to gather information from an alleged abuse victim in a developmentally appropriate manner. This is an opportunity for children to narrate their stories to a trained and neutral person in a child-friendly space. Forensic interviewing techniques minimize suggestive or leading questions and can help MDT partners focus on areas needing further investigation and exploration. As research expands, interviewers gain more insight of how to maximize a child's potential to narrate their experiences (Newlin et al., 2015).

Following the premeeting, MDT members gathered in a room equipped with audio and video to watch the interview. I introduced myself to M.C. in the waiting room, and he consented to the interview. A portion of M.C.'s forensic interview:

Interviewer: (Entering the interview room followed by M.C). M.C., could you sit in this chair for me please?

M.C. (looks around the bare room while he takes his seat).

Interviewer: M.C., my name is Daisy, and my job here is to talk to kids. We're going to spend some time together, and I'm going to ask you questions so I can get to know you. First…remind me how old you are.

M.C.: I'm 7.

Interviewer: Ok, thank you for that. M.C., before we start, I want to tell you a little bit about this room. Do you see those boxes in the corners of the room? (M.C. nods). Ok, those are cameras, and they're in the room because I have team members next door watching. They can see and hear us, but it will be just the two of us in this room, ok? They're watching to help me ask you questions. Sometimes I may leave the room to check in with them, but I will always let you know before I do that. Do you have any questions?

M.C. Team members? Is my dad watching? Can I see them? Can I come with you to visit them? (Walks around the room and waves at the cameras). Can they see me now?

Interviewer: Yes, they can see and hear both of us. Your dad isn't watching either. Just my team members who are helping me tonight.

M.C. was more interested in learning about the team members than engaging in the interview. I made a mental note to be mindful of any signs of avoidance or resistance since he questioned whether his father, the alleged, would also be watching. I transitioned into rapport-building, a phase of forensic interviewing when attempts to build a trusting relationship with a child are made. This period also allows the interviewer to better gauge a child's developmental level, verbal capabilities, and legal credibility through narrative practice, open questions probing a neutral topic or area of interest to the child (Newlin et al., 2015).

Interviewer: Tell me some things you like to do.

M.C. Well, I like Roblox...going to the park...today I saw a dog outside and wanted to pet it, but he wasn't friendly.

Interviewer: Oh, ok...thanks for letting me know about that. You like going to the park? Tell me about the last time you went to the park.

M.C.: (Walks around the room before answering) um, I rode a bike...and...do you live here? This room is so empty.

Interviewers make a judgment of when and if to introduce Play-Doh or paper and markers into the room. Some children relate easier when given an activity while others are distracted. I decided to instead move forward with the substantive phase of exploring information related to the allegation.

Interviewer: What are you here to talk to me about tonight?

M.C.: I don't know.

Interviewer: Well, who brought you here tonight?

M.C.: Some ACS lady who came to my school.

Interviewer: Tell me about the ACS lady coming to your school.

M.C: I don't know.

Interviewer: Is it that you don't know or that you don't want to talk about it?

M.C.: Ugh, I don't know...how come this room doesn't have any snacks?

Interviewer: I'm sorry we don't have any snacks, but thank you for sitting with me. You told me the ACS lady went to your school. What happened when she got there?

M.C.: She just asked me all these questions, but I don't want to talk about this anymore.

Interviewer: Ok, what makes you not want to talk about it?

M.C.: I just don't.

Interviewer: What do you think might happen if you do talk about it?

M.C.: (Silence).

The interview was now moving past 8:00 p.m., and it was evident M.C. was tired. Probing further could elicit more information, or it could further disengage him from the entire process. I told M.C. I need to check in with my team. Our check in debated differing opinions:

CPS: He needs to be confronted and asked why he told his teacher he was abused.

Interviewer: Confronting him will only shut him down if he thinks he's in trouble. He also didn't bring up his father, and I cannot suggest that to him first. Plus, he's tired and isn't focused.

DANY: We don't have anything right now, so he will have to come back for another attempt. I don't have a sense of his credibility.

I was exhausted and battled with self-doubt. Did I allow the premeeting reports of lying and a possible recantation influence how I engaged M.C.? Did I explore all avenues or was I overly concerned with not overwhelming him at the late hour? It was late and processing it all required too much energy. A decision was made to schedule another interview.

The following day I reflected on the previous night and came to several conclusions. First, as a social worker or mental health professional, it's crucial to value your expertise in this space. Our experience spans beyond forensic interviewing techniques, and our knowledge of child development, trauma reactions, assessment, and diagnosis is critical in building rapport and gaining trust.

Second, M.C. has faced a lot of adversity in his few years. While some may see a disruptive and easily distracted child, a closer look may reveal something deeper: underlying trauma masked by an ADHD diagnosis. Children from marginalized populations have higher rates of ADHD misdiagnosis than other groups. This can be attributed to several factors, including bias within the healthcare system and inadequate assessments from underqualified practitioners (Ford & Connor, 2009).

Third, recantation is a common occurrence that is shockingly not thoroughly explored in the realm of child welfare. M.C.'s interview wasn't considered a recantation, but it would be explainable had he recanted. Children are more likely to recant when they do not have a support system validating their disclosure. Also, children who have previously experienced the foster care system may use the defense mechanism of identifying with their aggressor to cope with the trauma by expressing positive feelings for their abuser (Frankel, 2018). A similar outcome may occur when a child wants to protect a nonoffending caregiver. Caregivers with chronic or ongoing trauma may be too overwhelmed to tend to a child's needs, creating an opening for a child to deny an allegation. As a result, a child may compensate with denial to not upset the caregiver further (Bernardon & Pernice-Duca, 2010). In these cases, it is especially important to steer away from any confrontational language as this will remove any trust the child has in the interviewer.

Lastly, children who have been victims of abuse or witnessed violence may lack expression or emotion, or they may have an emotional response that is disconnected from their narrative. M.C. was notably excited during his interview, and assumptions cannot be made to explain his affect. The memories of children who have suffered extreme trauma may be impaired or distorted, and an inability to clearly recollect events is not an indication of deceit. Specifically, recounting details of time, place, and occurrence are especially difficult for these children. (Feiring & Tasca, 2005).

Lesson 3: Learn More, Question More

Macro-level challenges make CACs vulnerable to practices and policies that may not align with their mission. CACs are typically funded by federal funding, grants, and donations. This transaction, like any transaction, indicates grantees have grantor requirements to fulfill. Securing funding can be challenging, but questioning the organizational impact is vital to preserve self and professional integrity (Faller & Palusci, 2007).

Questions to consider:

1. Are there staffing requirements? A grantor may stipulate the hours and days a CAC operates and the number of staff members they deem appropriate. This impacts the distribution of workload and the propensity for burnout.
2. What deliverables are expected from these interventions, and who decides the interventions implemented? Like lived experience, CAC workers have first-hand knowledge of the complexities involved in this setting and the needs of families. As such, discuss who is regarded as a qualified decision-maker. Interventions can be grounded by theory while also incorporating different knowledge sources into practice and evaluation. Medina (2017) supports this by arguing that epistemic resistance positions those with privilege to assume they know more, which invalidates a person's social and historical background. The "actively ignorant" group dictates what counts as knowledge and who counts as a knowledge contributor. Medina discusses the usefulness of active ignorance in consciously supporting the privileged in maintaining power. As a result, social workers' ethical responsibility to meaningfully contribute to research and evaluation is significantly reduced. Thyer (2008) discusses the importance of balancing intentions and outcomes with evidence-based practices. He argues evidence-based work is vulnerable to focusing too much on measurable results rather than immeasurable gains. From this outlook, success may be regarded in terms of client gains relative to their baseline knowledge at the onset of treatment. Developers may not accept this feedback as scientifically meaningful and acceptable to forming truths, but practitioners can continuously grow a resource library of learning to benefit future clients.
3. Do you know the policies, protocols, and legislation impacting your work? Are they advancing anti-oppressive efforts? Within the child welfare system, reporting statistics highlight the disproportionate number of black and brown families affected. In 2022, approximately 92,000 SCR intakes were recorded in NYC. Of that number, 38% were children in African American/Black non-Hispanic households, while 44% belonged to Hispanic/Latinx households. White non-Hispanic households only made up 7% of SCR intakes. In 2022, legislation also went into effect that changed how New York State's Statewide Central Registry (SCR) operates. The bill raised the standard of evidence required for the system to register an indicated case, meaning a case now required more than "some credible evidence of abuse or neglect" (New York City Administration for Children's Services, 2022).
4. How do we address partner protocols and guidelines that interfere with our best practices? As an example, using the previous vignette, M.C. had a preliminary interview with a child protection specialist at his school. Forensic interviewing best practices recommend repeat interviews should be prohibited due to concerns that a child may not appear credible if they provide statements during the

formal interview that are inconsistent with the initial interview. How do we approach partner agencies to address policies and procedures that are not aligned with client-centered practice?

Lesson 4: Acknowledge Anger

Anger is a natural emotion often portrayed as threatening and dangerous. But while anger can sometimes lead to destructive behavior, it can also motivate action and social change. Anger signals to us that we may have been wronged, mistreated, or invalidated. It is the outcome of threats against personal values and principles (Lambert et al., 2019). It's not surprising when families present anger. For many CAC families, anger is a survival mechanism and serves a self-protective role against vulnerability and feeling powerless. Consider these situations:

> Mary, age 8, and her mother, Ms. H., have arrived at the CAC for the third time in the past 2 years. An anonymous allegation reported physical abuse by Mary's mother. Previous investigations were unfounded after a process of interviews, home visits, and exams by child abuse pediatricians. Mary's mother believes an ongoing dispute with her neighbor is behind these calls as her neighbor has threatened to report her in the past. Ms. H. is Chinese American and indicated this neighbor's harassment and insults have only increased since COVID. She is angry about the countless hours spent investigating this allegation and the lack of consequences for repeat reports.

> Sean's (age 6) school called in a report for suspected physical abuse after noticing what appears to be a burn on his arm. Sean's mother, Ms. C, was called and denied abusing him. She reported leaving him alone momentarily to change her infant daughter, and Sean grabbed her hair iron during this time and accidentally burned himself. Ms. C. also claims she told the school about the incident and is upset about the call. Ms. C. aged out of foster care and fears the same for her children. As a result, she does not want Sean interviewed and a dispute escalates between Ms. C. and MDT.

MDT members may have differing opinions on the above situations, but this doesn't change the frustration and anger felt by these mothers. System inequalities have created an imbalance, giving only a select few the permission to feel angry. Ms. C. has the right to decline a forensic interview and to receive notification of her full rights. Ms. H. has explained the harassment from her neighbor and is still subjected to an investigation despite no past indications of abuse.

If we explore the child welfare space and reporting practices closely, anger is an understandable reaction. In 2021, the United States state and local child protective services received an estimated 4 million child maltreatment referral reports with a bias toward Black, Indigenous, and People of Color (BIPOC) (US Department of Health and Human Services, 2021). To not bear witness to anger means abandoning clients when they're most vulnerable. In this process, we are not condoning abuse or judging the validity of allegations but simply extending respect to clients who are often threatened when voicing anger. It signals we can tolerate distress and hold space for the painful emotions that are often clients buried or silenced.

Become comfortable with your own anger too when faced with situations reinforcing racism, sexism, and other forms of oppression. As an MDT partner, we are committed to advocating for those who continue to deal with oppressive systems and to confront the negative labels placed on them. Other experiences may challenge our capacity to sit with our own difficult emotions. Consider this situation:

> Samantha, 12 years old, arrives at the CAC accompanied by her mother, Ms. B., and younger siblings. Samantha disclosed ongoing sexual abuse by her maternal grandfather to her teacher. She also reported being told to "try and not be alone with him" when she disclosed the abuse to her mother weeks ago. Samantha, sobbing and covering her face, again discloses the abuse in detail during the forensic interview. She takes deep breaths to ground herself as she explains her mother initially calling her a liar before advising her not to be alone with her grandfather.

What are your reactions to this scenario compared to the previous two situations? What are your initial feelings about Samantha and Ms. B? As you reflect on these questions, I will share how I grappled with a case of similar elements during my early months as a forensic interviewer. As the forensic interviewer, I sat across from a sobbing teen as she recounted in vivid detail sexual abuse by a family member. I could hear her voice wavering as she answered "many times" to my question of whether the abuse happened one time or more than one time. I struggled to soothe my inner tension and could feel my muscles tighten as she described disclosing to her mother and the lack of protection that followed. "It just kept happening," she said sadly. I ached for the burden she carried. Despite my professional role and training, I was human, and I was angry. A mother not protecting her child was and still is inconceivable.

With the support of my supervisor, I sat and acknowledged these reactive thoughts post interview. Having a nonjudgmental space to feel all the emotions was crucial. Emotions aren't the issue. They are neither good nor bad, they are simply what they are. It's the resistance against being fully present with these emotions and avoiding reflection that will hinder our own growth and self-awareness. This profession relies on emotional exchanges, and it is through this process that we understand ourselves better and accept the moments that make us human.

Conclusion

Prior to this work, I was a preventive worker for families referred by ACS. My first family, Ms. S., had three children. She casually opened her refrigerator and cabinets once I stepped into her home for the first time and waved me over. I was confused for a moment and then realized she was accustomed to this routine with child protection specialists. I also felt guilty. This was a conditioned response, and it emphasized an unequal power dynamic. I couldn't make space for Ms. S. without acknowledging the price of any vulnerability she shared with me. Emotional safety is an illusion in these situations, but I needed to have some grace for myself too. Change takes time. Ms. S. slowly stopped opening her cabinets the moment I arrived. We came to an understanding. I was still a preventive worker and mandated reporter, but also a social worker wanting to undo the damaging experiences she's had in the past. Our work with clients may last a day, a week, or more, but the impact—positive and negative—will likely last a lifetime. Whether you are a seasoned or rising social worker, challenges are constant, but so are opportunities to influence one another to create a more empathetic experience for our clients. Finally, make time for the innocent questions and moments. Families will have more than their fair share of difficult conversations.

Reflection Questions

1. How can you formally and informally honor the lived experiences of the families you serve?
2. How can you approach partner agencies to address policies and procedures that are not aligned with client-centered practice?
3. How can you navigate your role as an advocate while also partnering with systems that have historically oppressed vulnerable populations?

References

Aviles, E. H. (2015). *Experiences of multilingual social workers: Trauma therapy in Spanish and English.*

Bai, Y., Wells, R., & Hillemeier, M. M. (2009). Coordination between child welfare agencies and mental health service providers, children's service use, and outcomes. *Child Abuse & Neglect, 33*(6), 372–381.

Bermúdez, J., Kirkpatrick, D. R., Hecker, L., & Torres-Robles, C. (2010). Describing Latinos families and their help-seeking attitudes: Challenging the family therapy literature. *Contemporary Family Therapy, 32*, 155–172.

Bernardon, S., & Pernice-Duca, F. (2010). A family systems perspective to recovery from posttraumatic stress in children. *The Family Journal, 18*(4), 349–357.

Children's Bureau, Administration On Children, Youth And Families, Administration For Children And Families, U. S. Department Of Health And Human Services. (2021). *National child abuse and neglect data system (NCANDS) Child File,* Child Maltreatment | The Administration for Children and Families (hhs.gov)

Clark, E. J. (2013). National association of social workers. In *Encyclopedia of social work.*

Costello, E. J., & Angold, A. (1988). Scales to assess child and adolescent depression: Checklists, screens, and nets. *Journal of the American Academy of Child and Adolescent Psychiatry., 27, 726.*

Dotson, K. (2014). Conceptualizing epistemic oppression. *Social Epistemology, 28*(2), 115–138.

Drake, R. E., Goldman, H. H., Stephen Leff, H., Lehman, A. F., Dixon, L., Mueser, K. T., & Torrey, W. C. (2001). Implementing evidence-based practices in routine mental health service settings. *Psychiatric Services, 52*(2), 179–182.

Epstein, C., Hahn, H., Berkowitz, S., & Marans, S. (2017). The child and family traumatic stress intervention. In *Evidence-based treatments for trauma related disorders in children and adolescents* (pp. 145–166). Springer.

Faller, K. C., & Palusci, V. J. (2007). Children's advocacy centers: Do they lead to positive case outcomes? *Child Abuse & Neglect, 31*(10), 1021–1029.

Feiring, C., & Taska, L. S. (2005). The persistence of shame following sexual abuse: A longitudinal look at risk and recovery. *Child maltreatment, 10*(4), 337–349.

Finlay, L. (2009). Exploring lived experience: Principles and practice of phenomenological research. *International Journal of Therapy and Rehabilitation, 16*(9), 474–481.

Ford, J. D., & Connor, D. F. (2009). ADHD and posttraumatic stress disorder. *Current Attention Disorders Reports, 1*(2), 60–66.

Frankel, J. (2018). Psychological enslavement through identification with the aggressor. In *Ferenczi's influence on contemporary psychoanalytic traditions* (pp. 134–139). Routledge.

Green, B. L. (1996). Trauma history questionnaire. In B. H. Stamm (Ed.), *Measurement of stress, trauma, and adaptation* (pp. 366–369).

Herbert, J. L., & Bromfield, L. (2016). Evidence for the efficacy of the child advocacy center model: A systematic review. *Trauma, Violence & Abuse, 17*(3), 341–357. https://www.jstor.org/stable/26638130

Hochschild, A. R. (1979). Emotion work, feeling rules, and social structure. *American Journal of Sociology, 85*(3), 551–575.

Hochstadt, N. J., & Harwicke, N. J. (1985). How effective is the multidisciplinary approach? A follow-up study. *Child Abuse & Neglect, 9*(3), 365–372.

Jenson, J. M., Jacobson, M., Unrau, Y., & Robinson, R. L. (1996). Intervention for victims of child sexual abuse: An evaluation of the children's advocacy model. *Child and Adolescent Social Work Journal, 13*, 139–156.

Kliewer, W., Cunningham, J. N., Diehl, R., Parrish, K. A., Walker, J. M., Atiyeh, C., et al. (2004). Violence exposure and adjustment in inner-city youth: Child and caregiver emotion regulation skill, caregiver-child relationship quality, and neighborhood cohesion as protective factor. *Journal of Clinical Child & Adolescent Psychology, 33*(3), 477–487.

Krugman, S. D. (2012). Multidisciplinary teams. In C. Henry (Ed.), *Kempe: A 50 year legacy to the field of child abuse and neglect* (pp. 71–77). Springer Netherlands.

Lalayants, M., & Epstein, I. (2005). Evaluating multidisciplinary child abuse and neglect teams: A research agenda. *Child Welfare, 84*, 433–458.

Lambert, A. J., Eadeh, F. R., & Hanson, E. J. (2019). Anger and its consequences for judgment and behavior: Recent developments in social and political psychology. *Advances in Experimental Social Psychology, 59*, 103–173.

McNees, P. A. (1987). *Child advocacy: Today's answer for child abuse prevention.*

Medina, J. (2017). Epistemic injustice and epistemologies of ignorance. In *The Routledge companion to philosophy of race* (pp. 247–260). Routledge.

National Child Traumatic Stress Network. (2021). *History.* Retrieved December 10, 2022, from www.nationalcac.org/history/

Newlin, C., Steele, L. C., Chamberlin, A., Anderson, J., Kenniston, J., Russell, A., & Vaughan-Eden, V. (2015). *Child forensic interviewing: Best practices* (pp. 1–20). US Department of Justice, Office of Justice Programs, Office of Juvenile Justice and Delinquency Prevention.

Newman, B. S., Dannenfelser, P. L., & Pendleton, D. (2005). Child abuse investigations: Reasons for using child advocacy centers and suggestions for improvement. *Child and Adolescent Social Work Journal, 22*, 165–181.

New York City Administration for Children's Services. (2022). *Demographics of children and parents at steps in the child welfare system.* Retrieved from https://www.nyc.gov/assets/acs/pdf/data-analysis/2022/demographics-children-fy-2022.pdf

Pynoos, R. S., & Steinberg, A. M. (2015). *The University of California, Los Angeles, post-traumatic stress disorder reaction index (UCLA PTSD index) for the diagnostic and statistical manual of mental disorders* (5th ed., p. DSM-5). University of California.

Stover, C. S., Hahn, H., Maciejewski, K. R., Epstein, C., & Marans, S. (2022). The child and family traumatic stress intervention: Factors associated with symptom reduction for children receiving treatment. *Child Abuse & Neglect, 134*, 105886.

Thyer, B. A. (2008). The quest for evidence-based practice?: We are all positivists! *Research on Social Work Practice, 18*(4), 339–345.
van der Kolk, B. A. (2014). *The body keeps the score: Brain, mind, and body in the healing of trauma*. Viking.
Weathers, F. W., Litz, B. T., Herman, D. S., Huska, J. A., & Keane, T. M. (1993). The PTSD checklist (PCL)*: Reliability, validity, and diagnostic utility*. In *Paper presented at the annual meeting of the International Society for Traumatic Stress Studies*.

Chapter 7
Working Alongside Multiple System-Involved Youth of Color

Amy C. Wilkerson

Introduction

Youth of color are disproportionately involved in social service systems and overwhelmingly involved in child welfare, criminal justice, and homelessness settings. The overrepresentation points to racism, bias, and structural and systemic oppression. Working with this population requires anti-oppressive social work practice, which calls for social workers working in settings with these youth to challenge the oppressive policies and procedures within their organizations and the larger mezzo and macro systems by engaging in culturally appropriate practice, evidence-informed practice, advocacy, and activism. Anti-oppressive practice is necessary to best meet the needs of individuals and bring about social change, promote equity, and end the imbalance of power that maintains disparities.

This chapter will discuss drivers of overrepresentation for youth of color in child welfare, juvenile justice, and homeless youth systems. The history of the three systems and relevant research will be covered to enhance understanding of this population. The information provided will allow readers to better support multiple system-involved youth. The intersectionality and crossover from one system to another is an important consideration for supporting system-engaged youth of color. Research supports the use of trauma-informed evidence-based practice to better meet the needs of the youth. Clinical interventions that are proven effective with this population will be reviewed. The composite case study of Jonathan is introduced to provide experiences of ways to work alongside multiple system-involved youth.

A. C. Wilkerson (✉)
DSW, LCSW, Silver School of Social Work, New York University, New York, NY, USA
e-mail: amyc.wilkerson@gmail.com

C. Tosone et al. (eds.), *Reframing Social Work with an Anti-Oppressive Lens*, Essential Clinical Social Work Series,
https://doi.org/10.1007/978-3-031-91391-4_7

Racial Disproportionality among System-Involved Youth

People of color experience higher rates of poverty, high school dropout, and poor health, as well as involvement in child welfare, carceral, homeless, and other systems (Jones, 2016; Olivet et al., 2021; Hirsch et al., 2018). Racism and systemic oppression fuel the widespread negative well-being outcomes for people of color in America (Hirsch et al., 2018). Racial inequities are the result of systemic and overt racism and oppression, which creates trauma that is passed along generationally (Fortuna et al., 2022).

Carter's Race Based Traumatic Stress (2007) and Degruy's (2005) posttraumatic slave syndrome explain the serious impact on emotional health due to racism and oppression. Both identify symptoms similar to posttraumatic stress disorder (PTSD), including cognitive disruption, depression, anxiety, sleep disturbance, and lowered self-esteem (Carter, 2007; Degruy, 2005). The trauma from historical and ongoing racist acts and systemic inequity is transmitted generationally, impacting physical, psychological, and social domains (Isobel et al., 2019). The trauma infiltrates family systems, creating stress that can impact family functioning, living conditions, outcomes, and overall mental health (Williams & Williams-Morris, 2000).

The impact of race-based trauma and systemic inequity is evident in the system involvement of youth of color. Black children make up 14% of the population but 23% of children in foster care (Duffin, 2022). More than 50% of Black minors will be involved in an abuse or neglect investigation before turning 18 years old (Ross, 2022). Forty-one percent of youth in the juvenile justice system are Black (Duffin, 2022). They are five times more likely to be arrested for person-related crimes and nine times more likely to receive an adult prison sentence as compared to White youth involved in similar crimes (Jones, 2016). Black youth aged 13–25 experience homelessness at almost twice the rate of White youth (Berger-Gonzalez et al., 2021). Ninety percent of youth involved in the juvenile justice system may have previous child welfare involvement (Campie et al., 2015); they are considered crossover youth because they moved from one system to the next (Baglivio et al., 2016).

The crossover between child welfare and youth homelessness is strong as well; studies found that on average between 11% and 37% of youth exiting foster care became homeless (Snyder et al., 2016). In one study conducted by Narendorf et al. (2020), 66% of youth who exited foster care became homeless within 6 months. The same crossover exists with homelessness and incarceration. A study conducted with homeless youth in eleven US cities found that 44% had been in a jail, prison, or juvenile detention center and almost 62% had been arrested at some point in their lives (Britton & Pilnik, 2018).

Youth in each of these systems also participate overwhelmingly in the mental health system (Modrowski et al., 2021). Social workers have historically supported youth receiving child welfare, juvenile justice, and homeless services and provide mental health support.

History of Social Work in Child Welfare, Juvenile Justice, and Youth Homeless System

Child Welfare System

The safety and protection of children have always been a part of American society, with the first documentation in 1655. According to Watkins (1990), a caregiver was found guilty of the death of a child in his care. Despite not having actual laws in place, he was punished by burning his hands and stripping off his finances.

In 1735, the first law was created that allowed for abused and maltreated children to be removed and placed in suitable family homes; children were taken away from parents only in instances of extreme abuse and neglect (Williams, 1983). Once removed, they were apprenticed or indentured to work for individuals or in institutions (Watkins, 1990). As a result, the removed children's lives were not much improved until the thirteenth amendment abolished slavery, which also ended the indenturing of abused or neglected children in 1865 (Watkins, 1990). The early attempts at child welfare were driven by public advocacy, not the authority's investigation (Williams, 1983).

A formal system of child welfare and protection did not occur until the public rallied around the case of a particular abused child. In the 1870s, a child named Mary Ellen was being harshly abused by her caretakers, who were brought forward by a concerned neighbor (Watkins, 1990). Due to inconsistent laws and no system to intervene in abuse cases, The Society for the Prevention of Cruelty to Animals got involved, which led to the creation of the first child protection agency in the United States—the New York Society for the Prevention of Cruelty to Children (NYSPCC) (Watkins, 1990; Williams, 1983). Mary Ellen was eventually removed and placed in a voluntary foster home, and the investigation and removal process was born (Williams, 1983). NYSPCC's practices became the model for child protection.

Abusive parents were given casework services to stop the abuse and neglect of their children (Williams, 1983). The casework supported parents with their needs to strengthen their ability to care for their children. It used the philosophy that children should only be removed from their parents when necessary, which is the cornerstone of child welfare today (Watkins, 1990; Williams, 1983). Social workers led the way and continue to champion child protection practices.

Juvenile Justice

According to Brownell and Roberts (2002), until the early 1800s, children were tried in criminal court, and if convicted they were sentenced to prison or even to death. This was applicable to children 7 years and older, but those under the threshold were presumed unable to form criminal intent (Brownell & Roberts, 2002). The first juvenile court was established in Chicago Illinois in 1899 (National Research

Council, 2001). The goal was to divert children from the destructive punishments of criminal courts and encourage rehabilitation (Brownell & Roberts, 2002). At that time, it was assumed that children had a better chance at rehabilitation than adults and that their criminal behavior was created by inadequate rearing (National Research Council, 2001). It was recognized that children are developmentally different from adults and should not be criminally responsible for their actions (Brownell & Roberts, 2002). Juvenile courts assumed minors require intervention and guidance as opposed to punishment (National Research Council, 2001).

The pioneering social worker, Jane Addams, was at the frontline of the creation of the juvenile justice system advocating for rehabilitation for youthful offenders (Brownell & Roberts, 2002). She lobbied for the development of a system to prevent harsh punishment of minors who commit crimes (Brownell & Roberts, 2002). Throughout the history of juvenile justice intervention, social workers have been responsible for advocacy, reporting, and risk assessments (Donisch et al., 2016). Social workers provided and continue to provide mental health and substance abuse counseling, group therapy, community outreach, and employment advocacy for justice-involved youth (Brownell & Roberts, 2002).

The evolving system consists of many entities with competing objectives between public safety and rehabilitation, such as law enforcement, court, rehabilitation, and mental programs (Donisch et al., 2016). Social workers at times find upholding social work values difficult in this environment, but advocacy is a historic role for social workers that must be done.

Youth Homelessness

Youth homelessness has existed since the inception of America; in that era, youth left home and ventured to America on their own seeking opportunity and prosperity (Moore, 2005). American youth typically worked from very young ages and lived unhappy lives; the youth left home hoping for a better future (Libertoff, 1980). Youth workers were a significant part of the development of the original 13 colonies providing a reliable workforce (Libertoff, 1980).

In the 1800s, there was widespread poverty and homelessness among immigrant groups, and as a result, youth became an additional burden if they were unable to work to contribute to the family's financial needs (Smollar, 1999). Youth were discarded by families forcing them to live on their own or on the streets (Moore, 2005). The youth begged for money, stole items to survive, and even engaged in sexual activities to make money (Smollar, 1999). Society viewed them as a nuisance and a menace to society; but social workers of that time stepped in to create programs and support services for these youth (Smollar, 1999).

The 1960s brought a new homeless youth population that willfully ran away from home due to their rejection of family rules, norms, and expectations (Smollar, 1999). Programs for runaway and homeless youth were created which were staffed by social workers providing casework and other support to meet these youth's needs

(Libertoff, 1980). The Runaway and Homeless Youth Act of 1974 created federal legislation for the rights and protections of runaway and homeless youth (Smollar, 1999). As social, economic, cultural, and political change occurred, the runaway population grew, and so did the social services to support them (Libertoff, 1980).

Research on Multiple System-Involved Youth

Campie et al. (2015) conducted a systematic review focused on the well-being of youth receiving support in multiple systems, such as child welfare, juvenile justice, education, and public health systems. The review stresses the need for a cohesive coordinated approach to improve well-being outcomes for youth engaged in cross-system services. The research noted discrepancies in how each system operationalized well-being, supports well-being development, and trains individuals working with youth to support well-being.

The study indicates that to successfully meet the needs of these youth, systems must work together by sharing data, cross-training staff, and using a unified approach for advancing the outcomes of youth in care. Interventions should emphasize building resilience and support while developing competency and permanency (Campie et al., 2015).

Similarly, Martijn and Sharpe (2006) conducted a study of homeless youth to identify psychological and systemic challenges that lead to homelessness. The study identified five pathways to homelessness: (1) trauma and resulting mental health struggles without drug or alcohol use; (2) parental drug and alcohol use and mental health issues; (3) family issues leading to rejection; (4) parental drug and alcohol use with or without; and (5) trauma alone that accounted for the smallest amount of study participants. The study's findings were that trauma is the most common experience of youth before becoming homeless. Over 70% of the study's participants experienced physical or sexual abuse, resulting in ongoing trauma and posttraumatic symptomology. It found that youth engage in criminal activity more frequently post homelessness than before and that homelessness increases mental health concerns and substance involvement. The identified pathways to homelessness spotlight the complex relationship between child welfare and homelessness, which needs preventive interventions to reduce the likelihood of abused and neglected children becoming homeless youth and young adults (Martijn & Sharpe, 2006). This study's findings propose that service providers should build trauma-informed programs that reduce mental health symptoms resulting from trauma that address cross-system needs of youth involved in multiple systems.

A study was conducted by Courtney et al. (2019) to assess the impact of the YVLifeSet program, which was developed in 1999 by a nonprofit organization, Youth Villages in Memphis, Tennessee. The program provides individualized case management to young adults transitioning to adulthood from the child welfare and juvenile justice systems. The program supports independent living through life skills training, financial assistance, and counseling. The program is manualized and consists of comprehensive assessments, treatment planning, weekly individual sessions, and group social activities, as well as educational and vocational support and referrals to other needed services. The social workers assigned to the youth in the program are trained in evidence-based clinical techniques such as motivational interviewing and trauma-focused cognitive behavioral therapy. The study identified a positive impact of the program on employment, income, housing stability, economic hardship, and health and safety. The YVLifeSet program model's successes should be considered for replication in other programs serving multi-system involved youth. There are a few promising components that support this population: individualized case management, trauma-trained interventionist, and a hyper-focus on independent living skills building.

Hirsch et al. (2018) conducted a study with youth involved in the juvenile justice and child welfare system to test the hypothesis that educational risk and services referrals predict system involvement and recidivism. Outcomes for 131 dual system–involved youth were compared to justice-only or child welfare–only groups and tracked for a 6-year period. Educational assessments were used to determine education level and the participants' utilization of referrals to needed services such as mental health, substance use and were tracked.

The crossover youth were overwhelmingly male youth of color: 60.1% male, 47.3% Black, and 37.4% Latinx as compared to 9.9% White (Hirsch et al., 2018). The racial disparity is a representation of the systemic bias and oppression that exist in youth of color becoming multiple systems involved (Hirsch et al., 2018). Harsher punishment and policies coupled with less tolerance for behavioral infractions, which is disproportionately applied to youth of color, are seen as a pathway between the child welfare system and juvenile justice system for this group (Hirsch et al., 2018). The study found that despite higher risk, the crossover youth received less service referrals for education and other services. Subsequently, the youth had poorer engagement in those that were referred. The study cites two possible reasons— poor system coordination and lack of trauma-informed services and supports. It states that dually involved youth typically have several forms of trauma; trauma-informed, coordinated services are required to sustain engagement.

Snyder et al. (2016) conducted a study with homeless youth in New York to understand experiences, stressors, and risk factors that put this population at high risk for justice system involvement. The study purports that between 71.8% and 78% of homeless youth have been arrested and 60% have gone to jail (Snyder et al., 2016). These statistics showcase the huge intersection between youth homelessness and justice involvement for youth.

The study uses strain theory to explain the high risk of justice system involvement. Strain theory explains behavior as a result of environmental and social factors that are strains in their life that place youth at high risk. The high risk subsequently places youth on a path to persistent homelessness (Snyder et al., 2016). The strains identified include experiences of polyvictimization, multiple system involvement, and discrimination based on their identity. Polyvictimization is defined as exposure to multiple forms of violence, violent victimization, and discrimination that may result from an LGBT and racial identity. Also, homeless youth have advanced needs evidenced by previous involvement with child welfare, juvenile justice, mental health, and substance treatment systems; they have complex trauma with histories of child neglect, as well as sexual or physical abuse (Snyder et al., 2016). The study implications call for system coordination, trauma-informed intervention for homeless youth, prevention efforts, and training for providers on the complex needs of this population.

Narendorf et al. (2020) conducted a robust study capturing the experiences of 1426 young adults experiencing homelessness in seven cities in the United States. The study sought to compare risk and resilience among youth and young adults with exposure to child welfare and/or juvenile justice systems. The study found a large percentage of homeless youth had multiple system involvement: 20% foster care only, 18% juvenile justice only, and 18% both juvenile justice and foster care involvement. The researchers sought to explore if system involvement is associated with high-risk behaviors. The study found that youth with juvenile justice system exposure were at risk for substance use problems and arrest. Young adults with dual system exposure had a higher risk of high school dropout, prolonged homelessness, adverse childhood experiences, suicide, negative coping, engaging in sex work, and unplanned pregnancy. The young adults with any kind of system exposure had higher levels of adverse childhood experiences, substance use, and mental health diagnosis as compared to the no-system involvement group.

The results indicated that previous child welfare and juvenile justice involvement create an extremely high risk for homelessness, arrest, and substance use. The elevated risk for multiple system-involved youth points to the need for the juvenile justice and child welfare systems to work collaboratively. They must enhance collaboration to support the needs of youth jointly involved in their systems (Narendorf et al., 2020). Additionally, the findings indicate that providers of support to this population must provide trauma-informed services due to the high presence of past trauma.

Evidence Based Approaches to Working alongside Multiple System-Involved Youth

Working in settings that serve youth with previous child welfare, juvenile justice, and/or homeless youth system involvement is a challenge. Multiple system-involved youth most likely have endured many forms of trauma, physical or sexual abuse, rejection, and victimization. This population is overrepresented by youth of color, who most likely have endured systemic oppression, discrimination, and overt racism (Hirsch et al., 2018). Before system intervention, their educational, mental health, and other service needs may have not been met (Courtney et al., 2019). Social workers practicing with this population whether in detention, in a residential setting, or in the community have a huge role to play. Research states that practitioners working with youth involved in multiple systems must use evidence-informed, client-centered, trauma treatment and assessment that coordinates with other service providers (Wiig et al., 2013; Zettler, 2021; Courtney et al., 2019; Hirsch et al., 2018).

Social workers should offer routine and universal screening for trauma, conduct a comprehensive assessment, and provide evidence-based, trauma-informed treatment for all youth that encounter these systems (Zettler, 2021). It should incorporate family and community, screen for multiple system involvement, assess for trauma and other potential areas of need, and coordinate services being received from other providers (i.e., probation, child protection, education, and medical providers) (Wiig et al., 2013).

There are many screening tools that are available for use with youth in various system settings. Because youth with system involvement have endured complex trauma, screening must look for signs of trauma and mental health conditions such as PTSD, anxiety, and depression (Zettler, 2021). The most common mental health disorders found in this population are depression, anxiety, conduct disorder, bipolar disorder, ADHD, and PTSD; 93% of youth with PTSD also had a co-occurring psychiatric disorder (Kumm et al., 2020).

Zettler (2021) calls for routine screening for trauma history and suggests seven screening tools: Adverse Childhood Experiences Questionnaire, Massachusetts Youth Screening Instrument, Traumatic Events Screening Inventory, PTSD Reaction Index, Childhood Trauma Questionnaire, Trauma Symptom Checklist for Children, and PTSD Checklist for Children/Parent Report. Table 7.1 takes a closer look at the purpose and use of these screening tools that are effective in identifying symptoms that the justice and child welfare system–involved youth may be experiencing.

Justice system–involved youth are approximately three times more likely to report PTSD symptoms and two to three times more likely to report exposure to traumatic events (Rhoden et al., 2019). Children in foster care are three to four times more likely to be diagnosed with a mental health disorder, and approximately 60% continue to experience mental health disorders throughout their lifetime (Engler et al., 2022). As a result, social workers must universally screen for trauma and mental health symptoms upon intake into any setting youth encounter.

According to Zettler (2021), universal screening for trauma history and evidence-based trauma-informed treatment should be the core of any intervention with multiple system-involved youth. After a comprehensive assessment, social workers will be able to determine the most appropriate intervention using trauma-informed techniques. Research points to using cognitive behavioral-based interventions to reduce trauma and other mental health symptoms (Zettler, 2021).

Trauma-Focused Cognitive Behavioral Therapy

Cognitive behavioral therapy (CBT) is the most used and researched behavioral treatment modality (Alexander et al., 2013). CBT foundational principles are that thoughts inform behavior, cognition can be controlled and altered, and

Table 7.1 Effective screening tools

Assessment Tool	Usage	Focus Areas
Adverse childhood experiences questionnaire (ACEs) Felitti et al., 1998	Measures childhood trauma	Childhood abuse and household dysfunction
Massachusetts youth screening instrument (MAYSI-2) Grisso & Barnum, 2000	Assesses behavioral needs of youth 12–17 years old in juvenile justice settings	Alcohol and drug use, anger, depression and anxiety, suicidality, trauma
Traumatic events screening inventory (TESI) Edwards & Rogers, 1997	Assess exposure to traumatic events in children aged 8–18	Child abuse and neglect, environmental violence, disaster, and loss
PTSD reaction index (PTSD-RI) Kaplow et al., 2020	Measures trauma history and diagnostic and statistical manual [DSM] mental health disorders in school-aged children and adolescents	PTSD symptoms
Childhood trauma questionnaire (CTQ-SF) Bernstein et al., 1998	Identifies childhood trauma in adolescents and adults	Child abuse and neglect
Trauma symptom checklist for children (TSCC) Briere, 1996	Measures posttraumatic stress symptoms in children aged 8–16	Child abuse and neglect, violence, and trauma
PTSD checklist for (PCL-5/C/PR) National Center for PTSD	Assess children for symptoms of PTSD	DSM PTSD symptoms

desired behavior change is achievable through cognitive adaptation (Dozois et al., 2019). CBT treatment has three therapeutic divisions: coping skills therapies, problem-solving therapies, and cognitive restructuring methods (Dozois et al., 2019). CBT has been adapted many times to meet the specific needs of various populations.

The most used trauma-informed treatment for youth is trauma-focused CBT (TF-CBT). TF-CBT has proven effective in reducing PTSD symptoms in child welfare–involved youth (Esterer et al., 2023) and reducing negative psychological symptoms associated with trauma in youth involved in the justice system (Zettler, 2021). The intervention is evidence-based and usually consists of 8–20 individual sessions with the youth and their parent or caregiver if appropriate (Esterer et al., 2023). TF-CBT sessions focus on psychoeducation and skill building around relaxation, affect expression, and cognitive coping (Zettler, 2021). Using trauma narratives is a core component of TF-CBT, which alleviates the pain associated with traumatic experiences (Esterer et al., 2023).

Youth involved in multiple systems are well-researched for having experienced trauma and resulting mental health struggles. TF-CBT is a good fit for this population because it works to lessen the maladaptive behaviors that develop as a result of trauma. TF-CBT is adaptable to many ages and presenting problems; it is used widely in community and residential settings for impacted youth and adults (Zettler, 2021).

Functional Family Therapy

Functional family therapy (FFT) is an evidence-based treatment modality that combines cognitive behavioral and systemic theories to address behavioral issues with youth and their families (Robbins et al., 2016). FFT is a short-term, strength-based family intervention (Alexander et al., 2013) that provides a coherent theory to understand the family relationship patterns and identify the function of behaviors within the family system (Robbins et al., 2016). Families typically engage in 12 intensive sessions that last three to 4 months, and the treatment consists of five phases: engagement, motivation, relational assessment, behavior change, and generalization (Zettler, 2021).

FFT has been extremely successful in improving family functioning and reducing problem behaviors which in turn improves mental health outcomes (Alexander et al., 2013). An adaptation was created to specifically provide behavioral and mental health services to families in the child welfare system called FFT-CW (Child Welfare) (Robbins et al., 2016). It addresses a variety of mental health, behavioral, and family problems that may be present in child welfare settings (Zettler, 2021). There is also FFT-G to work with youth and their families who are involved in gangs in the juvenile justice system (Robbins et al., 2016). The original FFT and several of its adaptations have been implemented in a wide variety of community settings in the United States and internationally (Zettler, 2021). Studies show that FFT is a reliable and effective intervention for youth involved in multiple systems and their families.

Multisystemic Therapy

Multisystemic therapy (MST) is an evidence-based intensive family treatment model for children and adolescents that can be practiced in home and community settings (Stambaugh et al., 2007). MST is a short-term, time-limited intervention that lasts 3 to 5 months (Swenson et al., 2010). An assumption of MST is that caregivers are the key to positive outcomes for their children; the interventions focus on empowering parents and caregivers to obtain the resources and skills needed to more effectively parent and care for their children (Henggeler & Schaeffer, 2016).

MST recognizes that developmental and behavioral issues exist across many systems and uses an ecological approach to resolving family issues (Zettler, 2021). It proclaims that behavior is determined by the functioning of the systems that individuals are embedded in and the interaction between all of the systems (Faw Stambaugh et al., 2007). The treatment surrounds parents and caregivers with support from family, friends, and members of the community to achieve treatment goals (Swenson et al., 2010).

MST was developed as a treatment model for juvenile offenders, and it has been adapted for child welfare and other youth-serving settings (Swenson et al., 2010). MST has several adaptations; the child welfare adaptation is called MST-CAN (Child Abuse and Neglect) for physically abused youth and their families. Research has proven MST-CAN effective at reducing youth and parent mental health symptoms and risk of abuse and improving parenting and social supports (Swenson et al., 2010). MST is used in a variety of community settings to improve mental health and family functioning for youth involved in social service systems (Zettler, 2021). Social workers practicing with juvenile justice, child welfare, and other youth-serving systems often use this modality contingent upon program structure and funding. This evidence-based treatment model will be effective with multiple system-involved youth.

Anti-Oppressive Social Work Practice with Multiple System-Involved Youth

The child welfare, juvenile justice, and youth homelessness systems are intrinsically oppressive. In any given year, minorities make up well over half of the national homeless population (Page, 2016), and Black Americans have an 83% higher risk of homelessness in comparison to White Americans (Samuels et al., 2019). Homeless youth of color 18–24-year-olds have the highest overrepresentation of all homeless populations at 82% (Olivet et al., 2021). More than 50% of Black minors will be involved in an abuse or neglect investigation before turning 18 years old (Ross, 2022). Black youth are five times more likely to be arrested for person-related crimes and nine times more likely to receive an adult prison sentence when compared to White youth involved in similar crimes (Jones, 2016). Differential treatment explains that the overrepresentation is the result of Black youth being treated differently than White youth (Jones, 2016). They are the recipients of differential policies and enforcement practices (Jones, 2016). The most effective way to practice anti-oppressive social work in these settings is to use culturally appropriate, trauma-informed social work practices that coordinate resources to make sure multiple system-involved youth receive adequate, equitable, and unbiased support.

According to the literature, system coordination is one of the main components needed for youth entering systems to be more successful and prevent further system involvement. Howell et al. (2004) make a strong case to integrate mental health, child welfare, education, substance abuse, and juvenile justice system services. National data obtained for the study showed that 40% of emotionally disturbed youth received services from at least three systems, and it is uncommon for youth to access only one system (Howell et al., 2004). The overwhelming statistic supports the need for cross-system coordination and planning.

Multiple system-involved youth are vulnerable and need concurrent planning among their service providers to obtain positive outcomes. They are traditionally from underresourced communities with frequent exposure to community and familiar risk, which contributes to their multisystem involvement (Vidal et al., 2019). With that in mind, interventions and service coordination must acknowledge their probable trauma histories that contribute to the presenting problem that initiated the system participation.

Youth participating in juvenile justice programs, whether residential or community-based, need transition planning (Britton & Pilnik, 2018). Coordination of resources post engagement requires social workers to organize with the other systems that the youth may be involved with or may need to ensure success in the future efforts will help reduce recidivism and further engagement with homelessness or juvenile justice systems (Britton & Pilnik, 2018). Discharge coordination should include housing and employment, as well as ensuring youth have identifying documents, health care, benefits and entitlements, and connection with ongoing service providers, all of which need to be provided in a culturally appropriate, trauma-informed manner (Britton & Pilnik, 2018).

Hirsch and Mosher (2023) introduced using a model called system dynamics simulation. It is a decision-support tool that gathers stakeholders together from diverse service sectors, which allows them to see the system as a whole, explore how systems interact, test the impact of different intervention alternatives, and develop insights about coherent approaches.

Coordination of system resources is important to be anti-oppressive but the most prevalent issue impacting the majority of multiple system-involved youth is systemic racism and oppression. Racism and oppression fuel inequities and ineffective system functioning. Social workers working with this population must call out the everyday injustices in their places of work. Everyday policies and procedures are often entrenched in bias and systemic inequities.

Many social workers provide direct practice, supervisory, and managerial support in these systems. It is the responsibility of social workers to challenge micro-level injustices that fuel the oppressive system. Social workers must advocate for macro changes in local, state, and federal laws and policies in addition to their practice role. Social workers must find opportunities to participate in rallies, testify at hearings, write to elected officials, and more.

In the next section, a composite case is introduced to provide examples of the struggles of multiple system-involved youth. The case is not work done with any one person and should be used as a tool to understand the concepts of this chapter. A brief look at the treatment used and outcomes will be discussed.

Case of Jonathan

The following composite case is impacted by the unique positionality of this writer. The conceptual and clinical work is greatly shaped by the therapist's own intersectionality of race, class, gender, culture, sexual orientation, and beyond. This author is a descendant of Africans that were kidnapped and forced into slavery in America. Those descendants lived in Georgia and North Carolina with mixed Indigenousness American roots to the Cherokee and Muscogee tribes.

The author was born and raised in Brooklyn, New York in a middle-income family and is the youngest of two children. This author identifies as a Black American gender nonconforming lesbian. Over the past 25 years, this author has worked with children, youth, and families in a variety of social service settings, such as child protection, foster care, juvenile justice, educational, and homeless youth settings.

The lens by which this writer views Jonathan is through an empathetic understanding of his experience as a Black American who has been disenfranchised by the system. Despite the many differences in identities between Jonathan and the author, the connecting factor was race, which assisted in the development of a strong therapeutic relationship.

Jonathan was born to a Black American mother and a Haitian American father. Jonathan has a younger brother, 4 years his junior. Jonathan and his brother have different fathers. Jonathan's father and mother separated when he was a baby. Jonathan did not see his father again.

Jonathan first became involved with the system when his school called child protective services due to his chronic absenteeism in the first grade. Child protective services intervened and referred the family for services. Jonathan's mother was a frequent marijuana user and displayed periods of highs and at times low motivation and depressive behaviors. After a psychiatric assessment, Jonathan's mother was diagnosed with bipolar disorder. She was prescribed medication but rarely took it and self-medicated by using more marijuana and alcohol. The mother was mandated to substance abuse treatment and mental health services.

Jonathan's behavior in school deteriorated. By second grade, he became physically aggressive with other children and teachers as well. He began receiving mental health services, and it was discovered that he was being physically abused. He and his brother were placed in foster care due physical abuse, educational neglect, and parental substance use. They were placed together in a stable home.

In care, Jonathan's behavior worsened, he was aggressive toward the foster parents and the foster siblings. Jonathan bounced from home to home as each foster parent was unable to manage his behavior. He was placed in the most inclusive educational setting, prescribed medication for ADHD, and received in-school mental health support. Despite those efforts, Jonathan entered a residential treatment facility at 10 years old for more intensive mental health treatment. Over the years, he was diagnosed with ADHD, PTSD, conduct disorder, and intermittent explosive disorder. His core competencies in reading and math did not exceed the third-grade level.

He was freed for adoption at 12 years old but was never adopted, while his younger brother was adopted by his foster parents. He lived on the residential treatment campus until 18 years old when he signed himself out of care. Jonathan reported that he was tired of being "drugged up," "having no freedom," and "being treated like a child." Jonathan left foster care without an approved housing or transition plan. He joined the Crips Gang while in care and planned to live with a few of his friends.

He also met a girl on campus who he was in love with and called his wife. She was 3 months pregnant with Jonathan's child and living in a mother–child program. Their relationship was volatile with many episodes of intimate partner violence. After foster care, he collected several arrests in a short period of time for petty theft, assault, and robbery, resulting in a 5-year probation sentence. Eventually, Jonathan decided that he could not stay with his crew any longer. He wanted to change his life to be a good father for his unborn child.

Jonathan heard about homeless youth services from a friend. The friend brought him to the 24-h Drop-In Center to get housing assistance and support. Jonathan was assessed for a battery of mental health concerns, education, employment, and housing. Jonathan was diagnosed with ADHD, PTSD, depression, intermittent explosive disorder, and cannabis use disorder.

The behavioral indicators were distractibility when completing tasks, oversleeping, withdrawal from activities, risky sexual behavior, physically violent outburst, verbally aggressive outburst, anger, irritability, and restlessness. Jonathan used marijuana approximately five times per day. Jonathan's functional skills were extremely low as he struggled with hygiene, independent living skills, and completing daily tasks and was unable to work.

The social worker coordinated services among the system providers in Jonathan's life: child welfare, justice, and homeless youth. With Jonathan's consent, the social worker contacted the person assigned to his case in each system. The social worker worked with the other providers to ascertain Jonathan's history and current participation. The social worker took on the role of primary support professional and made sure Jonathan's needs were being met holistically. Jonathan's plan included vocational rehabilitation, housing assistance, legal, medical, and mental health services. Jonathan was receptive to all resources but was hesitant to receive any mental health services.

He reluctantly agreed to see the Clinical Social Worker at the Drop-In Center. The therapist started treating Jonathan with trauma-focused cognitive behavior therapy twice per week for 10 weeks. By using techniques to identify the antecedent, behavior, and consequence, Jonathan was able to pinpoint the thoughts that precipitated his violent outburst. In sessions, significant time was dedicated to reviewing events that occurred between meetings. Each time a difficult situation occurred that involved anger, violence, or a strong emotional reaction, the therapist and Jonathan completed an ABC worksheet (Table 7.2). The worksheet had three headings: Activating Event (what event triggered your negative thoughts), Beliefs (what were your thoughts), and Consequences (physical results of actions and emotional results of actions).

Table 7.2 CBT ABC worksheet

Activating Event	Beliefs	Consequences
My girlfriend doesn't want to move in together.	She is leaving me, she doesn't Love me, I will lose my family.	Fear, anxious, angry, sad, Abandonment, unloved, Damaged property, sprained Hand, police contact

The vast majority of Jonathan's violent outbursts were situations that created fear of abandonment. *Jonathan initiated a conversation with his girlfriend about living together. He wanted her to sign herself out of the mother–child program and go to the family shelter with him. His girlfriend felt she needed the help and support that the mother–child program offered. She did not want to move in with him. During the conversation, Jonathan became enraged. He started yelling and breaking things. He punched a wall and left two holes.*

Through treatment, Jonathan was able to recognize that his girlfriend's actions made him think that she did not love him and did not want to be with him. He thought that she was leaving him. The therapist identified cognitive themes of being unloved and abandoned. Jonathan was able to connect this to his childhood foster care experience. He was taken from his home and placed in foster care to never return to his family. He was freed for adoption, but no one wanted him. He felt unloved and abandoned by his mother, who left him in the foster care system, and his father, who left him as a child. Jonathan was carrying hurt, sadness, anger, and feelings of loss from his childhood.

The social worker worked with Jonathan to identify patterns of thoughts and feelings. Jonathan was given a journal and as homework, he was encouraged to write between sessions about things he thought and felt daily. Jonathan wrote about joy, aspirations, sorrow, and fears. He noted events that took place throughout the day that may have been triggers. The journal was reviewed together in sessions with the therapist, encouraging insight and praising effort. He worked with the therapist to recognize thoughts that triggered memories of abuse and neglect which brought on feelings of being hurt, unloved, and abandoned.

He worked on recognizing the feelings in his body. Jonathan was able to identify that when he felt hurt, his breathing would speed up and he would feel warm. Jonathan and the therapist worked together to build skills to relax in those moments and alter the negative cognition. Deep breathing techniques were practiced in session to be used when the physiological symptoms were felt outside of the therapeutic setting. Positive self-talk was used to reduce the intrusive negative thoughts. Jonathan chose to repeat "I am good, I am loveable" when he started thinking negatively. At the end of the twenty sessions, Jonathan's aggressive outbursts were reduced. His feelings of abandonment and being unloved diminished. Jonathan's marijuana usage was reduced as well. His behavioral symptoms of isolation, oversleeping, and irritability also greatly improved. The case of Jonathan shows: (1) how multiple system-involved youth move through systems, (2) how TF-CBT can help reduce mental health symptoms in people impacted by trauma, and (3) how multiple system involvement may lead to homelessness. TF-CBT is effective with individuals who have problematic behavioral symptoms associated with trauma. It was extremely effective with Jonathan.

The social worker was able to connect with Jonathan about being a Black American as well as experiencing abandonment in their past. The commonalities improved engagement and Jonathan's willingness to work. Jonathan often expressed that the social worker reminded him of his aunt who always loved and supported him. The social worker was able to empathize with Jonathan's multiple system involvement and was committed to working alongside Jonathan to obtain positive results in his life. For this social worker, assisting Jonathan and other youth and young adults like him is their duty. Giving back to their community and helping other people of color escape systemic oppression is the cornerstone of their practice.

Looking Forward to Better Practice

To best meet the needs of youth involved in multiple systems, social workers must understand the context by which each person enters the system. Creating an individualized, trauma-informed, and culturally appropriate intervention is paramount. Social workers should make adaptations to evidence-based practices to be inclusive of culture. Consideration must be given to religion or spirituality, belief systems, community norms, and any other factor that impacts an individual's development.

Social workers wear many hats working with this population. They act as case managers, therapists, care coordinators, intake workers, discharge planners, aftercare workers, court-appointed social workers, advocates, and more. In addition to these roles, social workers must engage in advocacy for change of bias, oppressive and inequitable laws, policies, procedures, and practice. Advocacy on this level can be uncomfortable and create countertransference and vulnerability.

Social workers need adequate supervision that provides space to share feelings, build skills, and strengthen their resilience. Research indicates that supervision is needed for effective therapeutic practice and professional growth of social workers (Tomlin et al., 2014). Supervisors must be available, supportive, empathetic, and knowledgeable. Reflective supervision is an essential model for building trust between supervisor and supervisee, enabling discussion and reflection on practice (Ravalier et al., 2022). Good supervision should be therapeutic, improve skills, and facilitate learning (Tomlin et al., 2014). Reflective supervision is a model every social work supervisor should be familiar with.

Reflection Questions

1. What is the role of social workers in upholding the value of social justice?
2. How are you able to use yourself to disrupt oppressive practices within child welfare, juvenile justice, and youth homelessness system–involved youth?

3. What unique standpoint or positionality are you able to leverage for systemic change?
4. How can social service systems integrate resources to meet the needs of multisystem-involved youth?
5. How do systemic racism and oppression impact the social-emotional well-being of communities, individuals, children, youth, and families?
6. Which micro, mezzo, and macro influences impact system-involved youth of color? How?
7. How does racial trauma impact outcomes for individuals, children, youth, and families?

References

Alexander, J. F., Waldron, H. B., Robbins, M. S., & Neeb, A. A. (2013). *Functional family therapy for adolescent behavior problems*. American Psychological Association.

Baglivio, M. T., Wolff, K. T., Piquero, A. R., Bilchik, S., Jackowski, K., Greenwald, M. A., & Epps, N. (2016). Maltreatment, child welfare, and recidivism in a sample of deep-end crossover youth. *Journal of Youth and Adolescence, 45*(4), 625–654. https://doi.org/10.1007/s10964-016-0462-1

Berger-Gonzalez, S., Morton, M., Patel, S., & Samuels, B. (2021). *Centering equity in youth homelessness: Youth of color disproportionately impacted by housing instability*. Chapin Hall at the University of Chicago.

Bernstein, D. P., Fink, L., Handelsman, L., & Foote, J. (1998). Childhood trauma questionnaire. In D. P. Bernstein & L. Fink (Eds.), *Assessment of family violence: A handbook for researchers and practitioners* (pp. 161–171). Springer.

Briere, J. (1996). Trauma symptom checklist for children (TSCC) [database record]. *APA PsycTests*. https://doi.org/10.1037/t06631-000

Britton, L., & Pilnik, L. (2018). Preventing homelessness for system-involved youth. *Juvenile and Family Court Journal, 69*(1), 19–33. https://doi.org/10.1111/jfcj.12120

Brownell, P., & Roberts, A. R. (2002). A century of social work in criminal justice and correctional settings. *Journal of Offender Rehabilitation, 35*(2), 1–17. https://doi.org/10.1300/J076v35n02_01

Campie, P. E., Pakstis, A., Flynn, K., & McDermott, K. (2015). Developing a coherent approach to youth Well-being in the fields of child welfare, juvenile justice, education, and health: A systematic literature review. *Families in Society, 96*(3), 175–184. https://doi.org/10.1606/1044-3894.2015.96.25

Carter, R. T. (2007). Racism and psychological and emotional injury: Recognizing and assessing race-based traumatic stress. *The Counseling Psychologist, 35*(1), 13–105. https://doi.org/10.1177/0011000006292033

Courtney, M. E., Valentine, E. J., & Skemer, M. (2019). Experimental evaluation of transitional living services for system-involved youth: Implications for policy and practice. *Children and Youth Services Review, 96*, 396–408. https://doi.org/10.1016/j.childyouth.2018.11.020

DeGruy, J. (2005). *Post traumatic slave syndrome*. Joy DeGruy Publications, Inc.

Donisch, K., Bray, C., & Gewirtz, A. (2016). Child welfare, juvenile justice, mental health, and education providers' conceptualizations of trauma-informed practice. *Child Maltreatment, 21*(2), 125–134. https://doi.org/10.1177/1077559516630623

Dozois, D. J., Dobson, K. S., & Rnic, K. (2019). Historical and philosophical bases of the cognitive-behavioral therapies. In D. J. Dozois, K. S. Dobson, & K. Rnic (Eds.), *Cognitive-behavioral therapies: A practitioner's guide* (pp. 1–26). The Guilford Press.

Duffin, E. (2022, December 7). Foster care in the U.S.: Number of children by race. *Statista.* https://www.statista.com/statistics/255404/number-of-children-in-foster-care-in-the-united-states-by-race-ethnicity/
Edwards, J. H., & Rogers, K. C. (1997). Traumatic events screening inventory: Assessing trauma in children. In G. K. Kantor & J. L. Jasinski (Eds.), *Out of the darkness: Contemporary perspectives on family violence* (pp. 113–118). Sage Publications. https://doi.org/10.4135/9781452231130
Engler, A. D., Sarpong, K. O., Van Horne, B. S., Greeley, C. S., & Keefe, R. J. (2022). A systematic review of mental health disorders of children in foster care. *Trauma, Violence, & Abuse, 23*(1), 255–264. https://doi.org/10.1177/1524838020926064
Esterer, M., Carlson, J. S., Roschmann, S., Kim, H., Cowper, A., Cranmer-Fosdick, H., & DeCicco, B. (2023). Exploring early termination patterns and effectiveness of trauma-focused cognitive behavioral therapy for children in foster care. *Children and Youth Services Review, 147*, 106841. https://doi.org/10.1016/j.childyouth.2023.106841
Felitti, V. J., Anda, R. F., Nordenberg, D., Williamson, D. F., Spitz, A. M., Edwards, V., & Marks, J. S. (1998). Relationship of childhood abuse and household dysfunction to many of the leading causes of death in adults: The adverse childhood experiences (ACE) study. *American Journal of Preventive Medicine, 14*(4), 245–258. https://doi.org/10.1016/S0749-3797(98)00017-8
Fortuna, L. R., Tobón, A. L., Anglero, Y. L., Postlethwaite, A., Porche, M. V., & Rothe, E. M. (2022). Focusing on racial, historical and intergenerational trauma, and resilience: A paradigm to better serve children and families. *Child and Adolescent Psychiatric Clinics, 31*(2), 237–250. https://doi.org/10.1016/j.chc.2021.12.004
Grisso, T., & Barnum, R. (2000). *Massachusetts youth screening instrument, second version (MAYSI-2): User's manual and technical report*. University of Massachusetts Medical School.
Henggeler, S. W., & Schaeffer, C. M. (2016). Multisystemic therapy®: Clinical overview, outcomes, and implementation research. *Family Process, 55*(3), 514–528. https://doi.org/10.1111/famp.12232
Hirsch, G. B., & Mosher, H. I. (2023). Using a system dynamics simulation model to identify leverage points for reducing youth homelessness in Connecticut. *Systems, 11*(3), 163. https://doi.org/10.3390/systems11030163
Hirsch, R. A., Dierkhising, C. B., & Herz, D. C. (2018). Educational risk, recidivism, and service access among youth involved in both the child welfare and juvenile justice systems. *Children and Youth Services Review, 85*, 72–80. https://doi.org/10.1016/j.childyouth.2017.12.003
Howell, J. C., Kelly, M. R., Palmer, J., & Mangum, R. L. (2004). Integrating child welfare, juvenile justice, and other agencies in a continuum of services. *Child Welfare, 83*(2), 143–156.
Isobel, S., Goodyear, M., Furness, T., & Foster, K. (2019). Preventing intergenerational trauma transmission: A critical interpretive synthesis. *Journal of Clinical Nursing, 28*(7–8), 1100–1113. https://doi.org/10.1111/jocn.14735
Jones, C. A. (2016). Is disproportionate minority contact improving? An exploratory analysis of the arrest, confinement and transfer stages in rural and urban settings. *Journal of Ethnicity In Criminal Justice, 14*(1), 40–57. https://doi.org/10.1080/15377938.2015.1052172
Kaplow, J. B., Rolon-Arroyo, B., Layne, C. M., Rooney, E., Oosterhoff, B., Hill, R., Steinberg, A. M., Lotterman, J., Gallagher, K. A., & Pynoos, R. S. (2020). Validation of the UCLA PTSD reaction index for DSM-5: A developmentally informed assessment tool for youth. *Journal of the American Academy of Child & Adolescent Psychiatry, 59*(1), 186–194.
Kumm, S., Mathur, S. R., Cassavaugh, M., & Butts, E. (2020). Using the PBIS framework to meet the mental health needs of youth in juvenile justice facilities. *Remedial and Special Education, 41*(2), 80–87.
Libertoff, K. (1980). The runaway child in America: A social history. *Journal of Family Issues, 1*(2), 151–164. https://doi.org/10.1177/0192513X8000100202
Martijn, C., & Sharpe, L. (2006). Pathways to youth homelessness. *Social Science & Medicine, 62*(1), 1–12.
Modrowski, C. A., Chaplo, S. D., & Kerig, P. K. (2021). Advancing our understanding of the risk factors associated with crossover youth in the child welfare and juvenile justice systems: A trauma-informed research agenda. *Clinical Child and Family Psychology Review*, 1–17.

Moore, J. (2005). *Unaccompanied and homeless youth review of literature (1995–2005)*. National Center for Homeless Education.
Narendorf, S. C., Brydon, D. M., Santa Maria, D., Bender, K., Ferguson, K. M., Hsu, H. T., & Petering, R. (2020). System involvement among young adults experiencing homelessness: Characteristics of four system-involved subgroups and relationship to risk outcomes. *Children and Youth Services Review, 108*, 104609.
National Research Council. (2001). *Juvenile crime, juvenile justice*. National Academies Press.
Olivet, J., Wilkey, C., Richard, M., Dones, M., Tripp, J., Beit-Arie, M., Yampolskaya, S., & Cannon, R. (2021). Racial inequity and homelessness: Findings from the SPARC study. *the ANNALS of the American Academy of political and social. *Science, 693*(1), 82–100.
Page, M. (2016). Forgotten youth: Homeless LGBT youth of color and the runaway and homeless youth act. *Northwestern Journal of Law and Social Policy, 12*(17).
Ravalier, J., Wegrzynek, P. A., Mitchell, A., McGowan, J., McFadden, P., & Bald, C. (2022). A rapid review of reflective supervision in social work. *The British Journal of Social Work*, 1–18.
Rhoden, M. A., Macgowan, M. J., & Huang, H. (2019). A systematic review of psychological trauma interventions for juvenile offenders. *Research on Social Work Practice, 29*(8), 892–909.
Robbins, M. S., Alexander, J. F., Turner, C. W., & Hollimon, A. (2016). Evolution of functional family therapy as an evidence-based practice for adolescents with disruptive behavior problems. *Family Process, 55*(3), 543–557.
Ross, J. (2022, April 20). One in ten black children in America are separated from their parents by the child-welfare system. A new book argues that's no accident. *Time*. https://time.com/6168354/child-welfare-system-dorothy-roberts/
Samuels, G. M., Cerven, C., Curry, S., Robinson, S. R., & Patel, S. (2019). *Missed opportunities in youth pathways through homelessness*. Chapin Hall at the University of Chicago. https://voicesofyouthcount.org/brief/missed-opportunities-youth-pathways-through-homelessness-in-america/
Smollar, J. (1999). Homeless youth in the United States: Description and developmental issues. *New Directions for Child and Adolescent Development, 85*, 47–58.
Snyder, S. M., Hartinger-Saunders, R., Brezina, T., Beck, E., Wright, E. R., Forge, N., & Bride, B. E. (2016). Homeless youth, strain, and justice system involvement: An application of general strain theory. *Children and Youth Services Review, 62*, 90–96.
Stambaugh, L., Mustillo, S. A., Burns, B. J., Stephens, R. L., Baxter, B., Edwards, D., & Dekraai, M. (2007). Outcomes from wraparound and multisystemic therapy in a center for mental health services system-of-care demonstration site. *Journal of Emotional and Behavioral Disorders, 15*(3), 143–155. https://doi.org/10.1177/10634266070150030201
Swenson, C. C., Schaeffer, C. M., Henggeler, S. W., Faldowski, R., & Mayhew, A. M. (2010). Multisystemic therapy for child abuse and neglect: A randomized effectiveness trial. *Journal of Family Psychology, 24*(4), 497–507. https://doi.org/10.1037/a0020324
Tomlin, A. M., Weatherston, D. J., & Pavkov, T. (2014). Critical components of reflective supervision: Responses from expert supervisors in the field. *Infant Mental Health Journal, 35*(1), 70–80.
Vidal, S., Connell, C. M., Prince, D. M., & Tebes, J. K. (2019). Multisystem-involved youth: A developmental framework and implications for research, policy, and practice. *Adolescent Research Review, 4*, 15–29.
Watkins, S. A. (1990). The Mary Ellen myth: Correcting child welfare history. *Social Work, 35*(6), 500–503.
Wiig, J. K., Tuell, J. A., & Heldman, J. K. (2013). *Guidebook for juvenile justice and child welfare system coordination and integration*. Robert F. Kennedy Children's Action Corps.
Williams, D., & Williams-Morris, R. (2000). Racism and mental health: The African American experience. *Ethnicity & Health, 5*(3–4), 243–268.
Williams, G. J. (1983). Child protection: A journey into history. *Journal of Clinical Child Psychology, 12*(3), 236–243. https://doi.org/10.1207/s15374424jccp1203_2
Zettler, H. R. (2021). Much to do about trauma: A systematic review of existing trauma-informed treatments on youth violence and recidivism. *Youth Violence and Juvenile Justice, 19*(1), 113–134.

Chapter 8
Culturally Responsive School Social Work Practice: A Case Study in an Urban School "CVH"

Carmen Villavicencio-Hein

Introduction

This chapter will inform the reader about the critical work and immense responsibility of school social workers (SSWer) who serve diverse children in urban educational settings. It is unlikely that this work can be done without ongoing self-reflection and a compassionate heart. The power of change a SSWer has in a community is boundless; their efforts can be seen and felt immediately by the child being served, yet their impact can extend far beyond their time at the school. This is not theory but, in this author's experience, a lived reality for many schools. Unfortunately, not all schools have a SSWer, and not all schools see SSWers as valuable and viable assets for their school community. The author writes this chapter with a deep commitment toward the goal of having a SSWer equitably accessible to all children in schools and for SSWers serving in these settings to feel valued and supported.

The SSWer's role is vital and indispensable in the lives of children and future generations, yet it is historically undermined, overlooked, and neglected (Essex et al., 2022). The chapter will begin with a critical analysis of the origins of school social work (SSW) in the early 1900s, and its involvement in helping a population then referred to as the "misfits" (Stone, 2015), as well as its role in century-long advocacy and activism to mitigate the persistent and reoccurring damage to vulnerable and marginalized populations imposed by highly bureaucratic education systems. The chapter will then explore current practices that aim to shift this paradigm, emphasizing culturally responsive interventions. Over 15 years of experience in urban educational settings, this author situates the culturally responsive-sustaining (CR-S) framework as an essential future direction in the field, as this comprehensive

C. Villavicencio-Hein (✉)
Silver School of Social Work, New York University, New York, NY, USA
e-mail: cv836@nyu.edu

C. Tosone et al. (eds.), *Reframing Social Work with an Anti-Oppressive Lens*, Essential Clinical Social Work Series,
https://doi.org/10.1007/978-3-031-91391-4_8

tool has the potential to uncover the complex system of biases and structural inequities rooted in the history of the United States.

The CR-S framework engrosses individuals in anti-oppressive and anti-racist practices firmly rooted in evolving and shifting mindsets from "individual deficit" thinking to harness the power of difference as an asset to our communities (Moll et al., 1992; Yosso, 2005; Gay, 2010). The chapter will uncover the case scenario of Miguel, a composite of multiple real-life student experiences, using his life circumstances to plan, develop, and implement culturally responsive interventions central to this student's and family's lived experiences. Miguel's multiple, intersectional identities impact his ability to navigate the school system and others, and the author invites you to take an active role as a reader by being critical, curious, and self-reflective to see beyond your own limitations. There will be specific prompts for you, the reader, to examine and reflect upon as you learn about Miguel. This is hard work as your vulnerabilities, blind spots, and privileges will play out; all critical components necessary for supporting this chapter's aim to strengthen your knowledge and application of anti-oppressive and culturally responsive practices. The chapter concludes with implications and recommendations for advancing this critical work and ways to combat our shared reality. A century later, we continue to struggle to meet the needs of diverse children and families.

The Visiting Teacher: Historical Origins of School Social Work and Implications for Current Practice

As you read the following paragraphs, the author invites you to identify blind spots and privileges of the SSW practice during its early stages of development. Are there similar blind spots and privileges experienced by SSW practice today?

At the turn of the twentieth century, the United States experienced monumental shifts in urbanization, industrialization, and yet another critical wave of immigration (Tyack, 1992; Charles & Stone, 2019). As a result, there was a mass enrollment of students into the public education system in primarily urban destination hubs such as New York City (Guz & Suslovic, 2023). Simultaneously, the United States' public education system was experiencing internal pressures that resulted in a seismic shift toward a more centralized and bureaucratic structure. Taken together, these outward and inward pressures created tensions, particularly around issues like mandatory attendance. These imposed requirements were unrealistic for some segments of the new student body, mostly notably immigrant youth. For many immigrant families, then and now, sending their children to school was a financial burden: one less person would be financially contributing to the family, assisting with younger children or elder care. The educational system's lack of understanding of the hardships and circumstances of these groups of students and their families led to the identified need to bridge the gap between home and school, giving rise to the Visiting Teacher Movement (VTM) and spurring the development of the school social work profession in the United States (Charles & Stone, 2019; Guz & Suslovic, 2023).

Originally referred to as visiting teachers, the role was developed to better understand a student‘s home life. The visiting teacher became a bridge from school to home; the intention was to inform parents about the importance of education while gathering information to share back with the school on barriers faced by the student at home. A missing piece was examining how systems and structures played a role in oppressing and marginalizing vulnerable populations. The visiting teacher's intervention took place outside the classroom, addressing the individual student deficiencies with little to no involvement from other school staff (Stone, 2015). Although the approach was well-intentioned and beneficial in some ways, there were limitations, assumptions, biases, and unintended outcomes. Scholars have documented that at the time, the students identified for VTM support were considered "misfits" and often belonged to a vulnerable or minoritized group (Charles & Stone, 2019; Stone, 2015). The intervention aimed to address and remedy academic failures but often involved other behavioral challenges such as truancy and defiance. Leading the work were educated, middle-class white women who had been inculcated with and adopted a framework of economic efficiency and social justice interests. Left unchecked, they also carried and reflected their biases, blind spots, and privilege upon the "misfits" (Guz & Suslovic, 2023).

The "misfits" were and continue to be primarily immigrant, working-class students and families, considered by the dominant culture as ignorant and neglectful for not meeting their imposed standards (Tyack, 1992). As these student sorting strategies expanded, they consequently furthered the stigmatization and labeling of a population already suppressed, devalued, and imperiled by multiple forms of oppression. Scholars have argued that a strategy to differentiate the "misfitting" youth from other school populations was directly tied to the bureaucratization of education under the guise of school reform (Tyack, 1992; Crutchfield & Eugene, 2022). This is a powerful argument to hold as we reflect on our work to ensure that harm is not transmitted through our current school social work practices. This historical frame also calls for unpacking potential systemic harm, not just for the sake of analysis, but to determine actionable steps to remove such harm in the present.

Nevertheless, history proves that well-intended measures can sometimes have unintended adverse outcomes, especially among historically marginalized groups. This critical point in educational reform is not exempt; however, it gave rise to valuable programs and services, such as free lunch programs, school health clinics, and school social work as known today (Tyack, 1992). Therefore, the VTM had both a positive and negative impact on immigrant families.

A "Host" Setting Leads to Silos

Is working in silos beneficial or detrimental to SSW practice and those we serve? Does your school community promote a culture of interdisciplinary collaboration or working in silos?

Social work is grounded in a multilevel approach, where knowledge and skills are developed in micro-, mezzo-, and macro-level work. A subfield of social work practice, SSW began as a bridge between home and school but later evolved into a primarily micro-level practice and was sustained this way for numerous decades (Ball & Skrzypek, 2020; Crutchfield & Eugene, 2022). Driven by the perception of being a "structural add-on" of school reform and servicing in a "host" setting, it resulted in inequitable funding and inconsistencies that directly influenced issues of visibility, viability, and valuing of the practice (Keller & Grumbach, 2022). These circumstances led to SSWers typically becoming isolated from essential segments of the school culture and climate since they often did not take part in daily school and classroom activities, were not present during arrival/departure time, and/or did not participate in school teams (e.g., crisis team, planning, and placement team-PPT); their participation in these activities would foment multidisciplinary collaboration with fundamental stakeholders rather than working in silos.

Furthermore, clear and concise accountability measures were often blurred because only a single SSWer was assigned to a school(s) or even a whole district. All these issues can be traced back to policies within the United States educational system, which neglected to implement appropriate support structures to assess the quality and impact of SSWers' interventions and to develop and elevate the SSWers' practice. Consequently, the practice has been highly critiqued by scholars for its failure to be evidence-based and outcome-driven. For example, limited evidence links SSW services to specific academic outcomes such as improving grades and graduation rates (Stone, 2015). By contrast, there is rich literature with anecdotal claims that school-based social-emotional learning programs positively correlate to academic outcomes (Durlak et al., 2011).

Additionally, the SSWer is commonly supervised by an administrator, such as a principal. Not only is the hierarchical dynamic problematic, but administrators typically need a more comprehensive understanding of the training and capabilities of a SSWer, ultimately hindering the professional growth of the SSWer. Seen as service providers, SSWers have confined themselves to meet the "role" assigned by their administrator, limiting their presence in administrative, leadership, and political roles. We need to change this narrative through collegial collaboration, advocacy, culturally adapted and evidence-informed interventions, and data-driven practices to assess and demonstrate outcomes, and impact. If we do not, our work will continue to be fragmented.

Advocacy and Policy Change: Collective Hurdles to Combat

A hurdle at the national level is that school counseling mandates vary from state to state, and SSWers are not required in schools. The National Center for Education Statistics (NCES) has conducted the School and Staffing Survey seven times between 1987 and 2011. Yet the cross-sectional design only allowed for a descriptive "snapshot" of public and private school districts. The last study (2011–2012) identified 31,030 social workers in schools with a ratio of 660 students per full-time equivalent social worker. The vast majority served in suburban public elementary schools, with an enrollment of less than 500, and less than 35% of the student population was approved for free or reduced-price lunches. The National Association of Social Workers (NASW) advocacy practice suggests that SSW services should be provided at a ratio of one SSWer servicing up to 250 general education students. Further, NASW recommends that when a SSWer provides services to students with intensive needs in schools and districts with a disadvantaged student population, a lower ratio, such as one SSWer for every 50 students, should be required. For example, in schools servicing high numbers of students in temporary housing, SSWers would need a lower student ratio to address this group's needs. Leadership and legislation advocacy are critical efforts in our practice.

More than ever, states have begun to recognize that the way to address these needs is through policy change. For example, in New York State (NYS), Bill S54 passed the Senate and the Assembly in the 2023–2024 Legislative Session. This Bill statesd that "every public school district in the state shall on and after July first, two thousand twenty-three must employ and provide access to at least one licensed or certified school social worker in each of the schools under their jurisdiction" (S54, Section 1, Line 7–10). This bill did not pass beyond the Senate Educational Committee.

Many school districts, especially those in large urban areas, face challenges to achieving equitable access to SSWers even with the passing of proposed Bills. For example, New York City (NYC) is the country's largest public school system; despite its size and complex population dynamic, regulations and policies are often imposed by entities that are non-representative of the student population. In this case, the NYS Education Department (NYSED), located in Albany, develops and enforces educational legislation and regulations for the NYS school districts. Approximately 150 miles from Albany, the NYC school district serves 42% of the total NYS student population.

As reported by New York City Public School (NYCPS) in 2021–2022, the NYC public school population is also incredibly diverse, with an ethnoracial population of 41.1%Hispanic, 24.4% Black, 16.6% Asian, and 14.7% White. In comparison, NYSED student demographics report 2,448,537 students in NYS, 41% White, 29% Hispanic or Latino, 16% Black, 10% Asian, 1% American Indian/Alaskan Native, and 3% multiracial. This data is critical in understanding that the NYS student demographic data does not reflect that of NYC. Furthermore, according to the National Center for Education Statistics (2022), for the first time in our history, students of color make up the majority of students enrolled in US public schools. It is, therefore, incumbent for policymakers to consider the diverse needs of the populations impacted by their policies and regulations. Although the proposed requirement by Bill S54 warranted one SSWer per school, addressing the needs of schools with a student population of 4000 would continue to be underserved and increase the already existing disparities in accessible and equitable services. While Bill S54 is a step in the right direction, the diversity and specific challenges of large urban school districts require more resources.

*As part of macro-level work, SSWers must engage in policy-making. Consider a few entry points: get involved with local politicians; stay current on research, policy changes, and relevant data; learn about school social work and local and national associations' legislative advocacy efforts; and become an active member of these associations (*e.g., *NASW & School Social Work Association of America-SSWAA).*

More than a Century of Challenges: Inequities, Disparities, and Harm

Over 100 years later, the education system continues to face similar challenges. Education providers, from administrators to teachers to social workers, have continued to strive and struggle to meet K-12 children's diverse academic and social-emotional needs. Equitable, inclusive, and quality services for children and families vary significantly across schools, districts, and states. The United States ranks relatively poorly in student academic performance on international reading and math achievement tests (Voight et al., 2015). These concerns are only magnified by the well-known and documented achievement knowledge gaps between low-income and ethno-racial minority students compared to their more affluent and white majority peers, including state and national standardized test and school dropout rates (Stone, 2015). The rooted inequities in the education system routinely confer advantages and disadvantages based on gender, race, ethnicity, linguistic background, and socioeconomic status (Voight et al., 2015).

The pressures are significant for schools to implement culturally responsive, evidence-informed interventions that are equitable and accessible and foster a school culture that is inclusive and supportive of all students. Federal reports such as the *US Surgeon General's Report on Protecting Youth Mental Health* (Office of the Surgeon General (OSG), 2021) and the *President's New Freedom Commission on Mental Health* (2002) and legislation (e.g., *Individuals with Disabilities Improvement Education Act of 2004*; *Every Student Success Act of 2015*) have identified students'mental health well-being as one of the top priorities of schools.

The Youth Risk Behavior Survey (YRBS) is a cross-sectional, school-based survey by the Centers for Disease Control and Prevention (CDC) conducted biennially since 1991. The survey collects surveillance data from a nationally representative sample of public and private school students in grades 9 to 12 in the 50 States and

10-year trends on adolescent health and well-being. The survey includes analyses of disparities among gender, race, ethnicity, sexual identity, and sex of sexual contacts. YRBS Data Summary and Trends Report 2011–2021 is the most recent report, showing an increase in nearly all indicators of poor mental health and suicidal thoughts and behaviors from 2011 to 2021. In 2021, 42% of students reported in the past year having experienced persistent feelings of sadness or hopelessness (an increase of 14% from 2011), with prevalence estimated highest among females (57%), multiracial (49%), Hispanic (46%), lesbian, gay, bisexual, questioning, or another nonheterosexual identity (LGBQ+) (69%), and students who reported having sex with any same-sex (78%). In the 2021 survey, a new variable was captured indicating that 29% of students experience poor mental health, with prevalence estimated highest among females (41%), multiracial (33%), American Indian or Alaska Native (31%), LGBQ+ (52%), and students who reported having sex with any same-sex (54%) (Lindsey et al., 2019).

Although efforts have been made to mitigate the generational multisystemic harm upon ethnocultural minority groups and immigrant populations, inequities, accessibility, and disproportionalities continue to brew in a system servicing one of the most vulnerable populations, namely, children. The collective investment of educators needs to act toward an educational revolution that moves all of our children's educational experiences forward. We need a body of professionals forging through with fidelity and commitment, no longer allowing for "pockets of work" without any serious responsibility for alignment and equitable scale efforts.

Think of the education system as one entity. Can you identify blind spots of the system channeling ongoing social injustices?

Our Evolutionary Journey Forward: The Future of School Social Work

School social work is transforming from a micro-centered approach into a multidimensional practice. SSW recognizes that meeting students' needs and supporting academic and social-emotional success requires a culturally responsive, comprehensive approach (Crutchfield et al., 2020; Hammond, 2015). To do this collectively, we must continue to pull ourselves out of the office and visibly demonstrate the impact and outcomes of the multifaceted practice, making us a valuable and integral part of the school community. In tandem, we must use our positionality to advocate for the inequities and disparities in our school system. As school social workers, we are finding our voice and elevating the voices of historically discriminated and marginalized students and families, formerly referred to as the "misfits." There is growing evidence that addressing the needs of diverse students requires a holistic approach. Research shows that when "presenting problems" are addressed individually, we ignore the environmental factors affecting every facet of students'lives (Crutchfield & Eugene, 2022; Hammond, 2018). It demands culturally responsive practices driven by understanding and moving from an approach of what's wrong with you to what happened to you.

Culturally Responsive-Sustaining Education (CR-SE) flourished from Dr. Ladson-Billings' research with successful teachers of Black students. In the mid-1990s, Dr. Ladson-Billings named three pillars of what she called Culturally Relevant Pedagogy, which remain at the heart of what is today known as CR-SE: academic success, cultural competence, and critical consciousness. In 2018, NYSED and a panel of expert stakeholders gathered their collective insights and developed the Culturally Responsive-Sustaining (CR-S) Framework from the ground up.

CR-S is a transformative approach aimed at changing schools, intended to support education stakeholders in developing a student-centered learning environment that affirms cultural identities, fosters positive academic outcomes, develops students'abilities to build connections across lines of difference, and elevates historically marginalized voices. Research has shown evidence of the positive impact of CR-S on students and school communities. Some of the findings include facilitating brain processing, motivating and engaging students, cultivating critical thinking and problem-solving skills, strengthening students' racial and ethnic identities, and promoting a sense of safety and belonging (Hammond, 2015; Hammond, 2018).

Embedded in CR-SE is the Ecological Systems Theory, which identifies home and school within a child's microsystem (Marraccini et al., 2022). Schools are uniquely positioned to promote a sense of belonging, community, and connection. Among school stakeholders, SSWers play a critical role in leveraging the CR-S Framework into their school communities. The role extends their work into the Multi-Tiered Systems of Support (MTSS), a framework adopted by many schools to deliver targeted support, with a strong alignment to SSWers training in micro, mezzo, and macro-level work. They are the ideal broker to infuse/infiltrate schools in moving toward a future that leverages cultural differences (i.e., race, social class, gender, language, sexual orientation, nationality, religion, and ability) as an asset for building community, instruction, and learning. SSWers are disruptors, grounding the work of human development, and that culture is instrumental in shaping what, how, and when we learn.

A Transformative Multitiered Approach: Implementing Culturally Responsive-Sustaining in School Social Work

Addressing the needs of our diverse children demands a multifaceted SSW role and services that cultivate a supportive learning environment where students'sense of belonging, dignity, connection, and inclusion is of utmost priority. SSWers should be equipped with the skills to provide multitiered direct and indirect services to students, families, and school personnel. SSW practices should promote and support students' academic and social-emotional readiness and success. With the right resources and training, SSWers infuse CR-S into their work with schools and communities by ensuring that children of all cultural identities (i.e., race, ethnicity, age, gender, sexual orientation, disability, language, religion, and socioeconomic background) are respected, affirmed, valued and that their lived experiences are used as vehicles for teaching and learning. This type of transformative practice offers an innovative and integrative approach toward critically reflective practice with multitiered interventions addressing the complex needs of urban school communities.

In the following section, the author will utilize the case scenario of Miguel to illustrate the understanding and application of anti-oppressive, culturally responsive, multitiered interventions delivering quality and equitable, evidence-informed interventions to prevent the emergence of mental health problems and promote social, emotional, and academic success.

The MTSS model consists of three tiers of support. Tier one interventions are universal supports offered across the entire school community. Tier two interventions are implemented for targeted students, and support is provided in a group setting. Tier three interventions support the needs of students struggling with significant acute and or chronic stressors. This is a layered approach; if a student receives a tier three level of support, they also benefit from tier two and tier one support. The approach is also deeply rooted in the SSW profession, which also envisions practices at the micro, mezzo, and macro levels. Each level informs the other, offering a comprehensive and integrative approach. In school settings, the macro level attempts to spark large-scale systemic change. At the very least, it includes the entire school but could ripple out into the entire school district or the national educational system. The mezzo-level work includes working with groups. In the school setting, this often translates into targeted group work with internal and external stakeholders and collaborators. The micro-level work is directed toward the specific needs of students and families. There are clear connections between the levels of social work practice and MTSS; understanding these connections is crucial to grasp the breadth of the scope of the work. Figures 8.1 and 8.2 illustrate culturally responsive SSW the alignment of SSW practice levels and the MTSS framework, facilitating an understanding of the differences and connections between the two.

The following case scenario illustrates the complex and intersecting dynamics between the support needed for Miguel and his family, the transition to a SSWer role, the exploration of one's biases and assumptions, the development of an understanding of the school culture, the navigation of the school system, and the understanding local, state, and national policies and the crafting of culturally responsive interventions and support. Undoubtedly a demanding undertaking, yet the sole route to ensure comprehensive and adequate services and support.

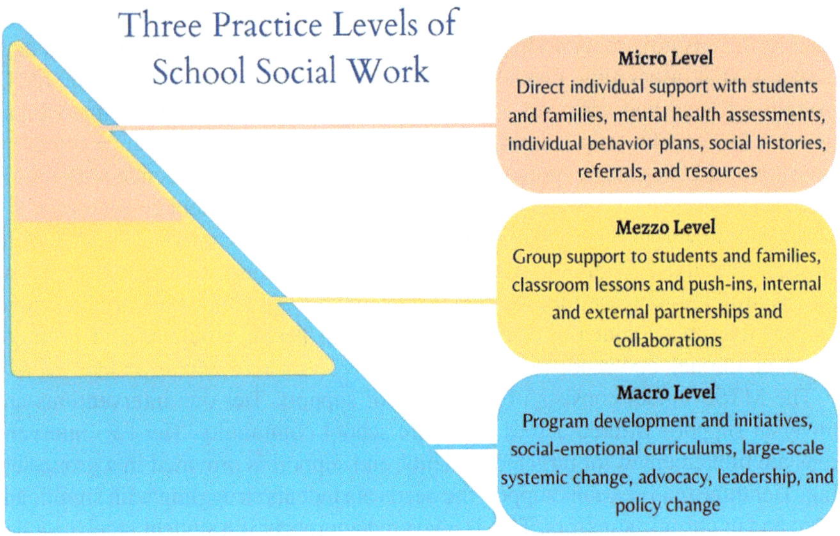

Fig. 8.1 Three practice levels of school social work

Case Scenario

Miguel arrived in the United States from Colombia 6 months ago. He immigrated with his mother and 8-year-old sister after a 2-month journey through Central America. He is a new enrollee at an urban public school, listed as a bilingual, Spanish-speaking student in temporary housing residing in a hotel. Miguel is 14 years old and identifies as a BIPOC bisexual male. Upon entering the educational system, he was placed in high school in a ninth-grade monolingual classroom. There were no bilingual classrooms in his school at the time of his enrollment. Reportedly, Miguel has had no formal schooling since the age of 11 due to the remote location of his native village and no access to online instruction during the COVID-19 global pandemic. Miguel is experiencing difficulties adjusting to school; he has, however, developed peer relationships with a few students who share a common language and recent immigration story. He frequently arrives late to school and is often observed to be withdrawn in the classroom.

It is mid-October, and imagine that you have recently been hired as the monolingual school social worker at the high school. The school's location has limited bus transportation and is a resource desert: there are no doctors, medical clinics, mental health services, or extracurricular activities within a minimum of a one-mile radius. You were provided with a list of 20 students new to the school and directed to assess and deliver at-risk support. You have been informed that there has been an influx of newly enrolled students since April of this year.

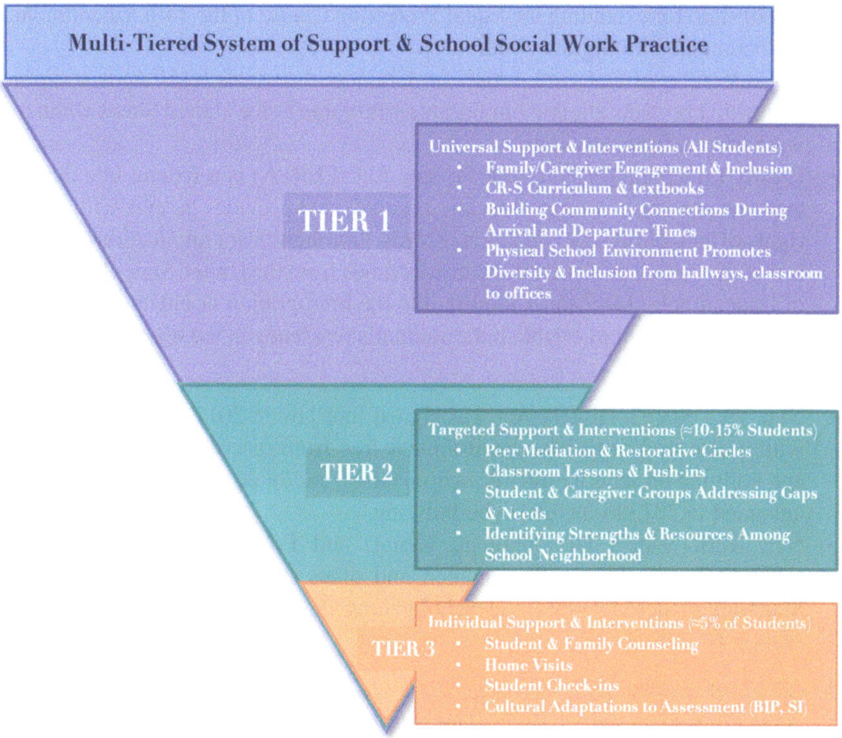

Fig. 8.2 Multitiered system of support and school social work

Macro-Level and Multitiered System of Support Tier One

The macro level of support grounds us in looking at policies and practices impacting Miguel and his family, such as immigration laws, education laws, local policies, and educational parental and student rights. This level of work is crucial in identifying gaps and areas that need to be addressed and the advocacy to promote systemic change and social justice, whether in the educational system, communities, governments, or other entities. This focal point allows us to grasp the intersectionality of the work and the need to address upstream factors affecting Miguel and his family. For example, the following are legislation and policies at the government, national, and local levels that would be important for the new SSWer to familiarize themselves with supporting Miguel and his family. We will reference the US Government, New York State, and NYCPS District to unpack the macro-level and MTSS tier 1.

Government Level

- The US Supreme Court ruled in Plyler vs. Doe (457 US 202 (1982) that undocumented children and young adults have the same right to attend public primary and secondary schools as US citizens and permanent residents. It holds schools responsible for extending the Equal Protection Clause of the 14th Amendment to undocumented immigrant children.

- Consideration of Deferred Action for Childhood Arrivals (DACA) is a national policy that protects eligible immigrants who came to the United States when they were minors from deportation.
- Family Educational Rights and Privacy Act (FERPA) is a federal law that protects the privacy of student education records and provides parents with specific rights to their children's education records. One significant implication of FERPA is that any school or district that receives funds from the United States Department of Education by law cannot inquire into the immigration or citizenship status of a student or parent to establish the student's residency in the district.

State Level

- New York State's Dignity Act was signed into law in 2012 to provide students with a safe and supportive environment free from discrimination, harassment, and bullying on school property, school buses, and/or at a school function. It was amended in 2013 to include cyberbullying.
- New York State's Development, Relief, and Education for Alien Minors (DREAM) Act gives undocumented and other students access to New York State-administered grants and scholarships that support their higher education costs.

Local Level

- NYC PS Student Bill of Rights and Responsibilities includes the right to a free public school education, a basic "student right" guaranteed to all children in NYC PS.
- Bill of Rights for Parents of English Language/Multilingual Learners provides critical rights concerning educational access and programming for English Language Learners (ELLs) and Multilingual Learners (MLs) and their parents.
- NYC PS' policy does not permit nonlocal law enforcement agents, including Immigration and Customs Enforcement (ICE) personnel, to enter schools except when absolutely required by law.

In response to assessing Miguel's needs, macro-level work aims toward large-scale systemic and social change by promoting structural solutions to systemic inequities and oppression. SSWers must contextualize their practice within the laws and policies that may directly create injustices, inequities, and disparities in the school context. Identification is the first step that drives crafting interventions, practice, program proposals, and policy change. The SSWer must inform the appropriate stakeholders of these findings and assist with developing evidence-informed interventions and supports. A recommended practice is to ensure that schools conduct annual needs assessments with a culturally responsive lens, which can be revised and referenced throughout the academic year. This practice would also catalog critical information on the school community's internal academic and social-emotional supports and list available community-based resources/referrals for students and families.

In Miguel's case, the SSWer must be able to communicate with the student and family. Given the language discordancy, accessible translation services will be critical. However, suppose the services offered by the school or district are inadequate. In that case, the SSWer must exercise their advocacy skills with due diligence; this includes conducting research, writing a letter to leadership, or developing a proposal, all to dismantle the identified barrier (e.g., lack of translation devices, long wait time for interpretation services). The SSW must also be deeply aware of how this linguistic barrier might compound other issues, such as information delivered electronically. For example, school districts typically have a website with a wealth of information, but it might only be offered in English. This, combined with issues of connectivity and ease of navigation, compounds the accessibility issue available to non-monolingual English students and their families. Often, even the district employees face challenges navigating these websites, and for caregivers, this can result in a prodigious barrier equivalent to the nonexistence of the information. Therefore, being mindful of how we share information and resources is critical.

Increasingly, SSWers can harness the power of school data to drill down on issues (e.g., attendance data, demographics of students in temporary housing, students with disabilities, English Language/Multilingual Learners, and school culture). Identifying trends, similarities, gaps, and disproportionalities are powerful quantitative tools that can quickly convey the level of need and aid in advocacy efforts to address these needs. Using Miguel's scenario, if the SSWer identifies 20 ELLs with the same home language in one grade and are not being offered a Bilingual Education Program, the SSWer would then advocate to the principal and educate the parents of their child's right under the Parent's Bills of Rights. This level of work explicitly embodies SSW's commitment to social justice, identifying inequities, and ensuring access to services and programs.

Mezzo-Level and Multitiered System of Support Tier Two

Mezzo-level work connects with MTSS tier-two support in working with groups and building multidisciplinary collaborations and partnerships with internal and external stakeholders. Let me introduce the concept of deficit thinking to highlight how this group work can be particularly difficult given Miguel's case scenario. Deficit thinking assumes that low-income and ethno-racial minority students and families are at fault for poor academic performance and unfortunately, it has been documented as one of the most prevalent forms of contemporary racism in schools (Yosso, 2005). It places the blame on the individual's cultural factors alone rather than exploring and understanding the individual's environment and impact. This environment includes students'learning contexts, such as the safety, inclusion, and comfort of a school, classroom, teacher, or SSWer and how lessons, ideas, and information are presented. It demands that students enter schools assimilated to the dominant and normative cultural knowledge and skills. It embodies a fixed mindset, brewing assumptions that parents do not care nor value their child's education, and places the cause for academic failures within the student's cultural group. In Miguel's school, we might hear comments such as "I cannot speak to that parent; they do not speak English," "Why is he always late? His parent must not care about his education," "I can never reach his parent, their number is always changing," or "That parent never shows up for their kid." SSWers must reflect on their beliefs and attitudes and those embedded within the school culture. In such instances, SSWers are encouraged to challenge these comments with curiosity and inquiry among their colleagues and self-reflection instead of defaulting to the status quo.

We are far from having effective and equitable school systems; therefore, it is unjust and detrimental to demand that students and families need to change and conform. Deficit thinking also extends to assumptions about communities and neighborhoods and prevents school staff and administration from harnessing naturally occurring forms of resiliency and tools embedded in every context. Urban schools are among the most impacted by deficit thinking, often because staff does not reside within local neighborhoods. It is heartbreaking to hear educators disparage a neighborhood, and worse when this is done in front of students. It is demoralizing to our students. To change this paradigm, SSWers are key champions in uncovering the strengths of neighborhoods. Yosso (2005) shifts the deficit view of communities of color as places of cultural poverty and disadvantages and instead conceptualizes community cultural wealth as an "array of cultural knowledge, skills, abilities, and contacts possessed by socially marginalized groups that often go unrecognized and unacknowledged" (p. 69). These rarely acknowledge cultural and social assets in Communities of Color, including aspirational, social, navigational, linguistic, resistant, and familiar capital. SSWers are essential allies in helping identify these multiple strengths and assets and ensuring that the school community understands the knowledge students bring from their homes and communities into the classroom.

In thinking of the case scenario presented, as a new SSWer to the school, you might not be well versed in the neighborhood's assets. Often, in urban settings, school staff do not reside within proximity to the school. If this is the case, consider key stakeholders who might know the neighborhood or can provide guidance, such as the parent coordinator or school counselor. Another helpful strategy is to collaborate in developing community mapping, an inventory of the types of local community resources, such as mental health clinics, faith-based organizations, extracurricular activities, and emergency food assistance providers. Lastly, community walks are incredibly helpful in uncovering hidden resources and seeing the neighborhood's strengths firsthand.

Now, let us turn back to Miguel; we know he identifies as a BIPOC bisexual male. This identity prompts a SSWer to hone in on their current knowledge. If little is known about the identity, SSWers are expected to take appropriate steps to learn more about the student and family. In-depth empirical research and data from reliable sources (e.g., academic journals, federal and state data) are critical in beginning to develop a thorough understanding. In this case, it would also be imperative to consider the intersection of identities beyond sexuality, to include gender, ethnicity, and socioeconomic and how they impact risk and protective factors. Research also indicates that lesbian, gay, and bisexual adolescents are two times more likely to report suicidal behaviors and attempts than their heterosexual peers. Transgender youth are four to five times more likely to attempt suicide than their cisgender peers (Ivey-Stephenson et al., 2019; YRBS, 2023). We know Miguel has developed relationships with a group of students, and fostering a sense of belonging and connection is a protective factor that can prevent suicidality. Developing a tier-two group intervention to foster student connection and belonging would be appropriate given the extensive work in and out of schools on the power of social networks (Marraccini et al., 2022; YRBS, 2023).

In considering a creating group intervention, engage in self-reflection when approaching this work. Critical questions to consider include: *How did I define the need for this group? Based on what information and data? Was it based on my perception and assumptions? Did students and/or parents have a voice? Does a type of group already exist? In developing a new group, how can I implement a participatory approach with students? Were group norms and objectives developed collectively? Am I blaming this group for the challenges they faced solely on my assumptions of their culture/identity group?*

Micro-Level and Multitiered System of Support Tier Three

School social work, on a micro-level, is the direct services provided to students and families in connection to tier-three interventions. In the case scenario of Miguel, assessing translation or interpretation services prior to outreach is critical in ensuring the family feels understood, valued, and acknowledged. We want to refrain from putting our students and families in a predicament where they feel even more unequipped to navigate an already complicated system. In establishing trust, the SSWer informs the parent and Miguel of their role, responsibilities, and expectations imposed by the education system and pertinent rights. Suppose the parent and Miguel are receptive to the SSWer support.

In that case, the family and student would benefit from a culturally responsive assessment. In regards to the family, learning about their current resources and strengths in navigating and adjusting to their new community and assessing needs (e.g., access to housing, healthcare, and social services), and for Miguel learning about his various cultural identities, (including but not limited to ethnicity, sexual orientation, economic background, religion, nationality, language, immigration status, and gender), experiences, strengths, and needs. If individual counseling is recommended, provide Miguel and the parent with psychoeducation to ensure mutual understanding and address possible cultural stigmatization toward mental health interventions.

In developing targeted interventions, SSWers ensure a participatory approach to crafting goals, time frames, and expected outcomes. Students play an active role in their intervention and assessment of progress. Based on the information provided by the scenario, presenting problems include his withdrawal observed in class, exploring the reasons for his frequent tardiness, language support, acculturation, and minority stress, and assessing his sense of belonging and connection among the various ecological systems. In brainstorming your clinical approach to interventions, assessment tools, and treatment goals, it is this author's experience that you should support space for exploring family dynamics (e.g., values, beliefs, religion/faith), stressors, trauma, political violence, discrimination, and feelings of loneliness. On the familial support system: *Is there an existing relationship with the father? From this gathering of information, what key findings might you uncover? Could Miguel be experiencing loss and grief above and beyond the often-painful process of acculturation most immigrant children experience? Or tension/conflict due to his sexual orientation? Does Miguel feel alone and disconnected from his school community or new neighborhood?* Studies indicate that suicidality is influenced by multiple risk factors and an individual's stress vulnerability. These stressors can be acute and chronic, present on various levels, and intersect: individual level (e.g., neurocognitive functioning deficits, self-perceived academic demands, knowledge and attitude toward suicide); family and friends level (e.g., adverse childhood experiences, family deportation, family history of suicide, childhood abuse, and maltreatment, problems in relationships with family and friends, the loss of someone important, family's stigmatized beliefs regarding seeking mental health supports); community level (e.g., persistent bullying, community violence, suicide contagion, accessibility to guns or other means of suicide, social rejection); and societal level (e.g., media portrayals reinforcing suicide, historical and generational trauma, economic deprivation, discrimination, racism, and marginalization). Clearly complex, these risk factors intersect and are associated with suicidality (Orozco et al., 2018; Vélez-Grau et al., 2022; Villarreal Sosa, 2019). But so do resiliency factors matter. In Miguel's case, a thorough assessment of both sources of vulnerability and resiliency is critical to determine and support his current mental health needs and overall well-being.

Additional areas in supporting Miguel are collaborating with his teacher to determine his academic strengths and weaknesses and identifying academic interventions to support his learning. The SSWer advocates for high expectations and rigorous instruction to prepare Miguel for rigor and independent learning while also considering the different ways Miguel learns. Discussions with his teacher to determine if the instruction is available in his native language, and if not, what resources are available to ensure he still benefits from rigorous instruction, opportunities to use critical reasoning, the ability to take academic risks, and leveraging a growth mindset to learn from his mistakes. If tardiness is due to dropping off his younger sister at school, then explore a flexible school schedule and assist the parent in identifying potential resources to assist in drop off and pick up. However, we must keep in mind that it may be just the three of them with no additional support.

Delivering direct student support is one of the most important and impactful services SSWers provide. This is a vulnerable place for our students, and we must be cognizant of how our power and positionality play out in direct student and family support. We must offer our students and families the best version of ourselves through a commitment to cultural humility and responsiveness. SSW training extends beyond the need to tether empathy and compassion to geographical and systemic boundaries. SSWers engage in ongoing self-reflection and self-awareness, as one must recognize one's positionality and be willing to dismantle assumptions, implicit biases, and blind spots to be an authentic champion of students. Self-reflection questions and journaling exercises are provided at the end of this chapter to harness and strengthen these skill sets.

Another layer of responsibility is ensuring we are up to date with our practices and that we are utilizing interventions that are evidence-informed. This can be achieved by committing to lifelong learning and ongoing professional learning rooted in the idea that teaching and learning are adaptive processes needing constant reexamination and inquiry and a critically conscious lens (Gay, 2010).

Conclusion

SSWers are an instrumental part of the school community. No longer seen as a "structural add-on" or in a "host" setting, the profession has come a long way. Over a century later, SSW has persevered over systemic barriers and fallen prey to injustices. The profession continues to evolve and cornerstone the multifaceted roles and responsibilities. The power of change motivates this profession; it fuels it with advocacy, activism, disruption, service delivery, policy-making, and leadership. SSWers promote structural solutions to systemic issues and inequalities. SSWers understand that, in essence, the whole school community is their caseload. Today, SSW is more visible than ever a pivotal moment in this practice's trajectory. This author leaves you with an ask: Channel your inner strength and find your superpower; you will need this in your work. You will be taking on servicing youth and families in their most vulnerable state. Rely heavily on harnessing human connection: From you they will seek comfort, validation, and support. A tremendous responsibility but one with invaluable impact. As early career SSWers, you are our future in this important specialized area of social work. Know you matter and that your work matters.

Self-Reflection Questions and Journaling

Think and reflect on your school community and your practice:

- How are your children? In particular, how are your Black, Indigenous, and Students of Color doing? How are your multilingual students, immigrant and refugees, LGBTQ+ students, and students with special needs and disabilities—how are they? Reflect on what you may know about the feelings, emotions, thoughts, and experiences your students have expressed; reflect on what you may not know.

- Is there any group of students that you avoid? Why? What steps can you take, both personal and professional, to dismantle this avoidance? How can you authentically get to know how they are doing?
- What areas of your practice, especially in family and community engagement, might reflect deficit thinking?
- What practices in your school are rooted in culturally responsive-sustaining education?
- Does the school culture foster inclusion, kindness, empathy, and compassion?
- What are the current barriers to delivering culturally responsive practices/interventions for the students you work with?
- What does cultural humility look like with your students and families and among the school culture?
- What would it look like if I were to walk into your office? Is it reflective of your students? Do they see themselves represented in your space? Is it inviting to all students?
- Cultural Responsiveness Continuum: Can you identify where your school is on this continuum? Can you identify where you are in this continuum?
  - Cultural destructiveness (e.g., forced assimilation, subjugation, rights and privileges for dominant groups only).
  - Cultural incapacity (e.g., racism, maintaining stereotypes, unfair hiring practices).
  - Cultural blindness (e.g., differences ignored, "treat everyone the same," only meeting the needs of the dominant groups).
  - Cultural precompetence (explore cultural issues, are committed, assess needs of organization and individuals).
  - Cultural competence.
  - Cultural proficiency.
  - Cultural humility.
  - Cultural responsiveness.
- Those who know each other treat each other better; it is harder to hate up close. What are your thoughts on this statement?

List of Resources

Ability
NYC public schools talking about disability • https://www.schools.nyc.gov/learning/special-education/help/talking-about-disability
Culturally responsive-sustaining education

Culturally responsive-sustaining education framework I new York State Education Department • https://www.nysed.gov/sites/default/files/programs/crs/culturally-responsive-sustaining-education-framework.pdf Culturally responsive-sustaining education facilitator's guide • https://educolor.org/wp-content/uploads/2022/02/Culturally-Responsible-Sustaining-Education-Facilitators-Guide.pdf Transforming our public schools: A guide to culturally responsive-sustaining education • https://static1.squarespace.com/static/5bc5da7c3560c36b7dab1922/t/5ed12955d45eb54e7a0854a3/1590765951611/CEJ_CRSEBook_v7.pdf Multilingual and immigrant Student support for NYC public schools • https://sites.google.com/schools.nyc.gov/ml-immigrantstudentsupport/home Internationally literacy association-list of children's books • https://www.literacyworldwide.org/blog/literacy-now/2021/03/10/why-children-need-to-see-themselves-in-books\\
Gender identity
NYC public schools LGBTQ+ supports • https://www.schools.nyc.gov/school-life/school-environment/LGBTQsupport • https://www.schools.nyc.gov/school-life/school-environment/guidelines-on-gender/guidelines-to-support-transgender-and-gender-expansive-students Resource center • https://www.myresourcecenter.org/give/out-for-safe-schools-ofss/#:~:text=What%20is%20Out%20for%20Safe,to%20be%20visible%20LGBTQIA%2B%20allies. Pronouns Graphic & Questions to consider • https://liveoutloud.org/wp-content/uploads/2022/08/School-Faculty-Guide-Being-an-Ally-for-LGBTQ-Youth.pdf GLSEN: • https://www.glsen.org/ The center • https://gaycenter.org/youth/
Implicit bias
Harvard's implicit association test (IAT) • https://implicit.harvard.edu/implicit/takeatest.html
Language
NYC public schools speak your language! • https://www.schools.nyc.gov/school-life/school-environment/hello NYC public schools language access policy • https://www.schools.nyc.gov/about-us/policies/language-access-policy
Race
NYC public schools guidance to Foster ongoing dialogue and action about race and equity • https://infohub.nyced.org/in-our-schools/programs/race-and-equity
Religious
EDUTOPIA-the December dilemma: Acknowledging religious holidays in the classroom • https://www.edutopia.org/blog/december-dilemma-religious-holidays-anne-obrien
Sexual orientation

NYC public schools guidelines to support transgender and gender expansive students • https://www.schools.nyc.gov/school-life/school-environment/guidelines-on-gender/guidelines-to-support-transgender-and-gender-expansive-students LGBTQ-INCLUSIVE LANGUAGE DOs and DON'TS • https://thesafezoneproject.com/wp-content/uploads/2018/09/LGBTQ-Inclusive-Dos-Donts.pdf . The 360 experience • https://liveoutloud.org/wp-content/uploads/2022/08/School-Faculty-Guide-Being-an-Ally-for-LGBTQ-Youth.pdf
Socioeconomic
APA-children, youth, families, and socioeconomic status • https://www.apa.org/pi/ses/resources/publications/children-families Social Indicators and Equity Report 2019 • https://www1.nyc.gov/assets/opportunity/pdf/SIER-2019.pdf

References

An act to amend the education law, in relation to requiring a licensed or certified social worker in each elementary, intermediate, middle, junior high and senior high school, S54. (2023). Retrieved on June 18th, 2023 from https://www.nysenate.gov/legislation/bills/2023/S54

Ball, A., & Skrzypek, C. (2020). School social work and the educational justice movement: A snapshot of practice. *Children and Schools, 42*(3), 179–186. https://doi.org/10.1093/cs/cdaa014

Centers for Disease Control & Prevention. (2023). *Youth risk behavior survey data summary & trends report: 2011–2021*. Retrieved on March 9th, 2023, from https://www.cdc.gov/healthyyouth/data/yrbs/pdf/YRBS_Data-Summary-Trends_Report2023_508.pdf

Charles, J., & Stone, S. (2019). Revisiting the visiting teacher: Relearning the lessons of the whole-child approach. *Social Service Review, 93*(4), 833–861. https://doi.org/10.1086/706788

Crutchfield, J., & Eugene, D. R. (2022). School racial climate and the ecosystems perspective: A model for anti-racist school social work practice. *School Social Work Journal, 46*(2), 1–22. http://proxy.library.nyu.edu/login?url=https://search-ebscohost-com.proxy.library.nyu.edu/login.aspx?direct=true&db=eric&AN=EJ1358808&site=ehost-live https://thedavidfollmergroup.com/school-social-work-journal/

Crutchfield, J., Phillippo, K. L., & Frey, A. (2020). Structural racism in schools: A view through the lens of the national school social work practice model. *Children and Schools, 42*(3), 187–193. https://doi.org/10.1093/cs/cdaa015

Durlak, J., Weissberg, R., Dymnicki, A., Taylor, R., & Schellinger, K. (2011). The impact of enhancing students' social and emotional learning: A meta analysis of school-based universal interventions. *Child Development, 82*(1), 405–432.

Essex, E., Yamano, N., & Massat, C. (2022). Chapter 20: Making school social work visible, viable, and valued. In M. Kelly, C. Massat, & Constable (Eds.), *School social work: Practice, policy, and research* (Vol. Pp, 9th ed., pp. 385–405). Oxford.

Gay, G. (2010). *Culturally responsive teaching: Theory, research, and practice*. Teachers College Press.

Guz, S., & Suslovic, B. (2023). "She must be experimental, resourceful, and have sympathetic understanding": Toxic white femininities as a persona and performance in school social work. *Affilia–Journal of Women and Social Work, 38*, 759. https://doi.org/10.1177/08861099231157337

Hammond, Z. (2015). *Culturally responsive teaching and the brain: Promoting authentic engagement and rigor among culturally and linguistically diverse students*. Corwin, a SAGE Company.

Hammond, Z. (2018). Culturally responsive teaching puts rigor at the center: Q&A with Zaretta Hammond. *Learning Professional, 39*(5), 40–43.

Ivey-Stephenson, A.Z., Demissie, Z., Crosby, A.E., Stone, D.M., Gaylor, E., Wilkins, N., Lowry, R., & Brown, M., (2019). Suicidal Ideation and Behaviors Among High School Students. Youth Risk Behavior Survey, United States, 2019. MMWR Suppl 2020; 69 (Suppl-1): pp. 47–55. http://dx.doi.org/10.15585/mmwr.su6901a6external icon.

Keller, J., & Grumbach, G. (2022). Chapter 1: The context of school social work: Historical background and current trends in schools. In *School social work: A skills-based competency approach*. Springer Publishing Company, LLC. https://10.1891/9780826163967

Lindsey, M. A., Sheftall, A. H., Xiao, Y., & Joe, S. (2019). Trends of suicidal behaviors among high school students in the United States: 1991-2017. *Pediatrics, 144*(5), e20191187.

Marraccini, M. E., Ingram, K. M., Naser, S. C., Grapin, S. L., Toole, E. N., Neill, J. C. O., Chin, A. J., Martinez, R. R., Jr., & Griffin, D. (2022). The roles of school in supporting LGBTQ plus youth: A systematic review and ecological framework for understanding risk for suicide-related thoughts and behaviors. *Journal of School Psychology, 91*, 27–49. https://doi.org/10.1016/j.jsp.2021.11.006

Moll, L. C., Amanti, C., Neff, D., & Gonzalez, N. (1992). Funds of knowledge for teaching: Using a qualitative approach to connect homes and classrooms. *Theory Into Practice, 31*(2), 132–141.

National Center for Education Statistics. (2022). Racial/Ethnic enrollment in public schools. *Condition of education*. U.S. Department of Education, Institute of Education Sciences. Retrieved [date], from https://nces.ed.gov/programs/coe/indicator/cge

NASW Highlights the Growing Need for School Social Workers to Prevent School Violence. (2018, Mar 27). Retrieved in April 20th, 2023 from https://www.socialworkers.org/News/News-Releases/ID/1633/NASW-Highlights-the-Growing-Need-for-School-Social-Workers-to-Prevent-School-Violence

New York City Public Schools Data at a Glance, Retrieved on May 5th, 2023. https://www.schools.nyc.gov/about-us/reports/doe-data-at-a-glance

New York State Education Department, NYSED Data, Retrieved on May 5th, 2023. https://data.nysed.gov/

Office of the Surgeon General (OSG). (2021). Protecting Youth Mental Health: The U.S. Surgeon General's Advisory. US Department of Health and Human Services.

Orozco, R., Benjet, C., Borges, G., Moneta Arce, M., Fregosto Ito, D., Feliz, C., & Villatoro, J. (2018). Association between attempted suicide and academic performance indicators among middle and high school students in Mexico: Results from a national survey. *Child Psychiatry Mental Health, 12*(9).

Stone, S. (2015). School social work in the United States: Current evidence and future directions. *Arbor, 191*(771), a201. https://doi.org/10.3989/arbor.2015.771n1003

Tyack, D. (1992). Health and social services in public schools: Historical persectives. *The Future of Children, 2*(1), 19–31. https://doi.org/10.2307/1602459

United States Department of Education, National Center for Education Statistics, Schools and Staffing Survey (SASS), "Public School Data File," 2011–12. Retrieved in April 20th, 2023 from https://nces.ed.gov/surveys/sass/tables/sass1112_027_s1n_04.asp

Vélez-Grau, C., Romanelli, M., & Lindsey, M. (2022). Adolescent suicide attempts in the United States: When suicide ideation and suicide capability interact. *Suicide Life-Threatening Behavior, 00*, 1–18.

Villarreal Sosa, L. (2019). Advocating for Latinx children's rights and supporting their healing from trauma: School social workers as nepantleras. *Children and Schools, 41*(4), 195–201. https://doi.org/10.1093/cs/cdz021

Voight, A., Hanson, T., O'Malley, M., & Adekanye, L. (2015). The racial school climate gap: Within-school disparities in students' experiences of safety, support, and connectedness. *American Journal of Community Psychology, 56*(3–4), 252–267. https://doi.org/10.1007/s10464-015-9751-x

Yosso, T. J. (2005). Whose culture has capital? A critical race theory discussion of community cultural wealth. *Race Ethnicity and Education, 8*(1), 69–91. https://doi.org/10.1080/1361332052000341006

Chapter 9
Beyond Binaries and Boxes: Anti-oppressive Perspectives on Clinical Social Work with Sexually- and Gender-Diverse Adolescents in School Settings

Susan B. Koenig

I remember sitting in my first clinical practice class, year one of my MSW program. The professor was talking about clinical work with children when another student asked about working in the school setting. Our professor made a dismissive snorting sound and said, "School social work isn't real social work." To this day, I can only speculate that she never worked in a school setting, with the myriad of ways that school social workers are engaged in the core competencies of our profession. Social workers have been working in school settings for over 100 years, in an evolving role that centers the relationship between students, families, the school, and the community (Allen-Meares, 2023). School social workers have expertise in multiple practice areas, such as advocating for the rights of students with disabilities, trauma-informed clinical practices, negotiating systems change within the school setting, case management, brokering community resources, and supporting and training staff, to name only a few. Social workers can also assume leadership roles in assessing student needs and creating programs to meet those needs. The school social worker is part of a support team that brings a systemic approach to solving disruptions in academic and social learning. In recent years following the pandemic, school social workers have been increasingly called upon for their clinical skills in ameliorating the effects of trauma and addressing chronic absenteeism and the increasing adolescent mental health crisis or the "fourth wave" of COVID (Villarreal Sosa, 2022).

However, our ethics go beyond the high school hallways. The International Federation of Social Workers invokes the language of liberation and engagement in their definition of social work practice

S. B. Koenig (✉)
Silver School of Social Work, New York University, New York, NY, USA
e-mail: sbk8058@nyu.edu

C. Tosone et al. (eds.), *Reframing Social Work with an Anti-Oppressive Lens*, Essential Clinical Social Work Series,
https://doi.org/10.1007/978-3-031-91391-4_9

> "Social work is a practice-based profession and an academic discipline that facilitates social change and development, social cohesion, and the empowerment and liberation of people. Principles of social justice, human rights, collective responsibility and respect for diversities are central to social work. Underpinned by theories of social work, social sciences, humanities and indigenous knowledge, social work engages people and structures to address life challenges and enhance wellbeing." http://ifsw.org/get-involved/global-definition-of-social-work/

These ethics of liberation inform our work with sexually- and gender-diverse (SGD)[1] youth at a critical time in the history of this country. The volume of anti-LGBTQ legislation has more than doubled this year alone (Choi, 2023). In supporting students who face challenges caused by systemic oppression, school social workers have a responsibility to critically examine our relationship with an educational system that is intricately linked to policies and legislation that perpetuate oppression. Furthermore, we are obligated to examine our positionality within this system by virtue of race, gender, ability, age, class, and so on. This anti-oppressive foundation is crucial in working with sexually- and gender-diverse (SGD) adolescents in the school setting. As social workers with a keen understanding of systems theory, we work with individuals, families, the school community, and the larger social environment to provide care and support to our students. This chapter will explore the premise of viewing adolescence not simply as a developmental stage, but as a dynamic culture. Furthermore, I will argue that without a framework of critical consciousness, we cannot create a transformed school community of safety and nurturance.

Current Research on SGD Well-Being and School Climate

School climate surveys and national statistics have paved the way to understanding SGD youth's lives in schools. Organizations such as GLSEN (Gay Lesbian Straight Education Network) provide local and national school climate surveys that report on a variety of factors, including the effects of a hostile school climate, and how the effects of feeling supported in school impact the lives of SGD students (GLSEN, 2022). These climate surveys also quantify the tragedies of self-harm, suicide, and homelessness among SGD youth. While the effects of discrimination and bullying are devastating and important to acknowledge, there is a danger of presenting a one-sided narrative of SGD youth only as victims (Pennell, 2017). As SGD youth gain more visibility by speaking out and embracing their SGD identities, there is an increased risk of harm. It is at this courageous intersection of vulnerability and visibility where support is needed most.

---

[1] A note on terminology. A deliberate choice was made to use the term "sexually and gender diverse" in this chapter. It reflects the expansive nature of sexuality and gender without trying to list or rank the gender and sexuality lexicon currently used and which, no doubt, will further evolve in the future.

School social workers can be instrumental in creating supportive school environments by advocating for gender-neutral bathrooms and other safe spaces to change for physical education classes. Gender-diverse students often experience dysphoria with their bodies, and choosing a bathroom can be emotionally challenging. Gender-neutral bathrooms or access to single-occupant restrooms lessens dysphoria and increases safety for gender-diverse students (Mangin, 2018). Policies that can be reevaluated for gender and sexuality inclusivity are social events centered around heteronormative gender roles, such as prom and homecoming king and queen, and graduation robe colors that are separated by gender.

Should school curricula address sexuality and gender explicitly? There is a current contentious debate about the appropriateness of expansive gender and sexuality education in schools and the effect of this education on students. German researchers Gegenfurtner and Gebhardt (2017) conducted a systematic review including studies from a variety of fields to answer three questions about the impact of LGBTQ+ pedagogy in schools: (1) What are the effects of teaching alternatives to heteronormativity? (2) What is the impact of SGD teachers on the behaviors of students? (3) Is nature or nurture the root cause of homosexuality and "transgenderism" [sic]? On these three points, the authors concluded first, teaching about SGD people makes schools safer for all students. Second, although the research on the impact SGD teachers have on students' behaviors is sparse, there appears to be no connection to impacting student behavioral choices. Lastly, SGD people are born this way. A critical look at this study and studies like it are warranted. If the findings showed that increased exposure to LGBTQ+ people or culture did impact one's choices to be in same-gender relationships or express nonbinary gender identity, would that impact our efforts to protect and nurture those children? Does it matter if SGD people are "born that way"?

This homophobic remnant exists because the construct of heteronormativity persists. Many years ago, I was providing training for new Licensed Mental Health Counselors (LMHC) on mental health issues impacting SGD clients. One of the newly minted LMHCs in the class asked me, "How do you get to the root of why?" I was confused, "Do you mean why your client would have mental health issues, like depression?" I asked. "No", she continued. "Why are they gay, what caused it? Was there trauma?" I don't remember the rest of the conversation verbatim because my nervous system kicked into protection mode. I do remember saying something about being gay was not pathology and asking her how she would "get to the root" of why someone is heterosexual. As a lesbian out for many years, I still felt defensive and simultaneously concerned for her future clients. SGD people are vulnerable in a society where their dignity and worth are marginalized and pathologized. This conflation of trauma with non-cisgender, non-heterosexual identities can have a destructive impact anyone, especially on school-age youth.

Trauma-informed approaches to counseling SGD students are called for due to the harm caused by discrimination, marginalization, and violence. In the educational setting, these approaches are gaining popularity and utility in stemming the tide of the adolescent mental health crisis. Many schools are using a trauma-informed positive-behavioral intervention approach or a three-tiered Response to

Intervention model (Allen-Meares, 2023). However, these models still focus on the maladaptive behaviors of individuals and largely ignore how the trauma caused by oppression impacts the student. Boylan (2021) outlines how the frameworks used in school social work need to adopt a critical orientation. Whereas the conservative approach centers on individual interventions, and the socially liberal approach aims to reform educational systems using anti-oppressive ethics of care, Boylan (2021) calls for a critical perspective that reinforces the agency of students utilizing relational-cultural therapy and social context.

Gender, like race, is a construct created to maintain hierarchical dominance. Valuing narratives created by individuals within the SGD community is paramount to developing critical consciousness. Using an SGD-affirming model created by SGD people creates a counternarrative to the hetero/cisgender normative story created by others (Wagaman, 2016). This is partially made possible when groups subject to discrimination are engaged in the process of reclaiming the language that is used to define them.

SGD-Affirming Language

Language is always emerging, and it is important to be mindful of the impact that words have on the people we support. It is also important to know that rarely will there be consensus on the terminology for any group of people. For that reason, when social workers engage in dialogue with SGD people, we want to engage with cultural humility. Language reflects culture, and cultures that do not value gender diversity (e.g., not acknowledging pronouns and resisting the use of the possessive plural "they" and "them" to refer to one person) are using language to reinforce marginilization of SGD people. "They" is commonly used to refer to a singular person when the subject's gender is unknown. Using neopronouns such as "ze" and "zir" is common in gender-diverse lexicon. The creation of new pronouns can be endorsed by entire countries. For example, Sweden added a gender-neutral pronoun "hen" to refer to nonbinary individuals (Neuman, 2015). In the 1950s, the term "homosexual" was widely used when discussing people with same-sex attractions (Drescher, 2009). Today calling someone "a homosexual' 'is widely seen as derogatory. Hiebert (2016) advocated for the replacement of the term "homophobia" with "homoppression" to emphasize a choice of action rather than attitude. The word "queer" has largely been reclaimed by younger SGD people, where one generation ago, this was considered a homophobic slur. Another term that requires sensitivity is "sexual and gender minority (SGM)." This is a commonly used term in research, and while it is true that LGBTQ+ people are less represented in the general population, "minority" connotes subordination or lack of status. The acronym LGBTQ+ typifies inclusivity of SGD people by including the terms "lesbian" "gay" "bisexual" "transgender" (note: NOT transgendered) "queer," and the "+" denotes those identities that are not named explicitly, such as asexual, intersex, and two-spirit. The best practice is to always ask what terms are preferred as teenagers rapidly reclaim and disclaim language.

Adolescence, Intersectionality, and Identity

Adolescence is a dynamic period of identity development. The notion that adolescent growth is solely contingent on developing agency and self-discovery is rooted in a Eurocentric, classist model (Schmitz & Tabler, 2021). Depending on each student's standpoint, there will be variation that impacts well-being. For example, a bisexual, cisgender boy who has a mother of Chinese descent and a father from Kenya will need support from a social worker who acknowledges and accommodates the complexity of his intersectional, cultural experiences. Velez and Spencer (2018) apply a critical approach to understand youths' identity formation vis-á-vis their phenomenological relationship to power and the ways they engage with it. From this place, social workers are not to make assumptions about the impact of the groups they belong to. They state, "An adolescent may belong to multiple discriminated social groups; however, to label them a priori as high risk—thus imposing additional marginalized criteria - neither does justice to their coping responses nor informs insights about how they understand the world" (Velez & Spencer, 2018, p. 86). This is where social workers need to employ a reflexive exploration of the meaning and value placed on identities. Historically, this has been problematic for our profession, with white social workers particularly. Assuming our role is to save the oppressed, without recognizing our role in that oppression or facing feelings of guilt in our complicity, gets us no closer to the transformation we claim to seek. "... paternalistic treatment of the oppressed, all the while holding them fast in a position of dependence, will not do" (Freire, 1970, p. 49).

Philosopher Iris Marion Young (2014) identified powerlessness, marginalization, exploitation, cultural imperialism, and violence as the "five faces of oppression." Mapping these "faces" onto the lived experiences of SGD youth is a tempting endeavor, and certainly, at first glance, it is clear how many of these faces apply to the lives of SGD youth. After all, heteronormative culture certainly marginalizes SGD youth through reinforcing the gender binary in classrooms. Acts of violence and bullying toward SGD youth in schools are well-documented. However, it does not empower the SGD students we work with to impose a narrative of oppression on them. How can we harness Young's faces of oppression powerfully and productively? Understanding these dynamics from an anti-oppressive perspective requires that the voices of those in groups experiencing discrimination tell us, the social workers, about how they perceive their relationship to their power and how they can use their power transformatively.

Adolescents and Critical Consciousness

It is this author's strongly held contention that anti-oppressive frameworks, in any domain of social work practice, will be ineffectual without a shift toward critical consciousness. The power of critical consciousness drives the transformative nature of social work, which has the potential to impact the well-being of individuals and society. Activist and educator Paulo Freire (1970) conceptualized this liberatory pedagogy to challenge inequitable systems. Critical consciousness allows abstractions regarding social justice to transcend the domain of the intellect to the realm of action (hooks, 1994). The impact of fostering youth critical consciousness has given deeper meaning to the experiences of youth living at the intersection of multiple identities (Godfrey & Burson, 2018).

Critical consciousness reconceptualizes oppression from happening to individuals or groups of individuals as passive recipients of maltreatment to an examination and analysis of the systems of marginalization and power. This analysis allows for the creation of a new narrative that focuses on strengths, agency, and collective action. In addition, critical consciousness demands that the lived experiences of our students are held with reverence as they create the interwoven narratives of their intersectional lives. Secondary school social workers are well situated at the intersection of educator and counselor. They can provide the opportunity to question the limiting categorical binary of sexual orientation and gender.

Deconstructing the Binary

Research on SGD mental health and well-being has evolved over the years using language and theories that mirrored the cultural zeitgeist regarding SGD people. From the earliest days when SGD people were viewed as psychologically disordered, researchers sought to explore why SGD people deviated from the cultural norms of the gender binary and heteronormativity. It is important to note that these norms are centered in a white supremacist hegemony. Many cultures and Indigenous groups before colonialism had expansive notions of gender and sexual orientation (Thomas et al., 2022; Vanita, 2013), Furthermore, criminalization for being SGD often coincided with colonial-era legislation and continues today in many countries previously colonized in Africa (Mkhize & Mthembu, 2023) and in the United States (Choi, 2023).

The theme of binaries is reinforced in Western culture as an outgrowth of the system of white supremacy. These binaries are marked by a power-over dynamic that is the basis of what relational-cultural theorist and clinician Maureen Walker calls "cultural pain" (2010). This cultural pain is the hallmark of a binary paradigm that attempts to reify the illusion of superiority (i.e., straight over gay, cisgender over transgender, white over Black, wealthy over poor, and citizen over immigrant, etc.). Anti-oppressive work requires social workers to critically examine our social identities and examine our power and privilege to prevent overshadowing the narratives of our students. Walker states, "Protected by its invisibility, the dominant group can impose its own story on relationship, set the definitional frames and terms of engagement with little or no accountability" (2010, p. 93). Walker is speaking here about the dynamic of relational connection necessary for an authentic therapeutic relationship, but this guidance also translates to cultivating student agency.

School social workers must understand the history and impact of homo/transphobia using a critical consciousness lens. The definitions of "disorder" and "normal" are subject to shifts in time and epistemology. The constructs of gender and sexual behavior that evolved in the West are tied to essentialism. The European physicians who determined homosexuality was pathological and gender-diverse people disordered set the stage for decades of violence and marginalization (Drescher, 2009). Today, remnants of these narratives remain. The Diagnostic and Statistical Manual (DSM) is not the volume of universal truths on human behavior; it is a collection of observations laced with culture and values that change with time. As adolescents are piecing together a cohesive narrative of themselves, school social workers are positioned to remind them that the representations that pathologize need not be taken at face value. Current research with SGD adolescents shows that self-identification is more expansive and empowered (Wagaman, 2016). Social workers who are not used to being reflexive regarding sexual orientation or gender may fall into the trap of assuming that SGD adolescents are feeling isolated and alone. Engagement with social media gives SGD adolescents access to support networks and information so that perceived isolation is decreased (Hulko & Hovanes, 2017). The mental health challenges of internalizing disorders such as anxiety, depression, and substance abuse in SGD youth have been explored extensively with the psychological model of comorbidity. This individual pathology model has given way to include the impact of discrimination and oppression on the well-being of SGD people. The most pervasive theory in research conducted to understand the mental health and well-being of SGD youth is the Minority Stress Theory (MST) (Diamond & Alley, 2022; Garcia et al., 2019; Goldbach et al., 2021; McDermott et al., 2021).

Minority Stress Theory

There is a plethora of research correlating negative health outcomes such as substance abuse, depression, anxiety, and suicidality with SGD youth and adults (Garcia et al., 2019; Mills-Koonce et al., 2018; Scroggs et al., 2020). For two decades, MST, proposed by Meyer in 2003, has been cited extensively as the primary model to understand negative health outcomes in the SGD population (Diamond & Alley, 2022). MST asserts that the cumulative burden of discrimination over time, on individuals experiencing racism, sexism, homophobia, and other oppressive forces, is detrimental to mental and physical health. The neuroscientific research on allostatic load coupled with the social narrative of oppression gives a broader view of the interconnection of externalized and internalized homophobia on physical health and well-being (Bruce et al., 2015). Negative health effects caused by stigma, concealment stress (being closeted), social isolation, loss of family support, misgendering, and ostracism for being SGD have all been explained by MST. However, the missing piece in this model is the impact of community, belonging, and resilience on SGD youth. This fact is borne out in the data. There have been inconsistent research findings regarding exposure to stress and the relationship to negative health outcomes for people who are members of groups that are marginalized and oppressed (Diamond & Alley, 2022). The finding that exposure to stress caused by oppression and the internalization of oppressive narratives is the root of reduced well-being does acknowledge the external impact of oppression on health; however, it does not explain the health and well-being of people who hold marginalized identities with little adverse effects. The meaning we create around our experiences carries weight and can modulate the influence of external stressors (McGonigal, 2016). Adapting a new neuroscience theory gives us a framework to understand the context of poor health correlates of SGD individuals by calling for a "critical shift from excess stress to insufficient safety" (Diamond & Alley, 2022, p. 5). This new model bridges the biological realm of the individual to the social realm of community.

Social Safety Theory

Slavich (2023) proposes a theory that the organizing function of the brain and the immune system is to regulate the biological need for safety by predicting the degree of social safety and threat in one's environment. Social Safety Theory (SST) has three components: social safety and threat, perceived social safety and threat, and the cognitive representations (schemas) of safety and threat related to the self, the world, and the future. This theory offers a social or person-in-environment view of how individuals perceive validation, belonging, and connection. The significance for school social workers is SST provides theoretical support to the data collected by the National School Climate Surveys. Creating opportunities for students to feel safety and connection is the domain of the school social worker.

Social Safety and Social Threat

Slavich (2023) defines a socially safe situation as one where inclusion, belonging, and authenticity are felt. These qualities are central themes in relational cultural theory and have an "evolutionary benefit" (p. 6). Social threat involves exclusion and devaluation (e.g., marginalization). In schools, social safety includes safe spaces, people, and policies that support the general health and well-being of SGD students. For example, visible safe space stickers, rainbow ribbons, and quotes by Queer activists are prominently displayed in hallways and classrooms. The curriculum includes a discussion of Queer themes, characters, art, and music. Social events encourage varied gender expression at dances. Social threat exists in schools where books with Queer themes are removed or absent from libraries. Other examples of social threat are observable characteristics in the school community, such as hearing homo/transphobic slurs in the hallways and witnessing the refusal of students and faculty to intervene in the presence of homo/transphobic behavior.

Perceived Safety and Threat

All human beings are vigilant in scanning for threats in our social environment. SGD people are acutely aware of the need to assess the safety of their surroundings. Past experiences shape the schemas created regarding safety and threat. The interpretation of social situations, whether perceived or actual, has a physiological similar impact (Diamond & Alley, 2022). Perceived safety includes the belief that you can walk down the hallway with your partner holding hands, or your family loves you and would support you no matter what. Perceived threat is the belief that your friends will abandon you once you come out, or your teacher will treat you differently if you ask to be called by pronouns consistent with your gender identity.

Social Safety Schemas

Social safety schemas are the stories we create about ourselves, our world, and our future as they relate to the sense of threat or safety we can expect based on past experiences (Slavich et al., 2023). This informs us how we move through the world and the impact we can expect to make on changing the world around us. Schemas can be altered based on interactions with others and an individual can have both safety and threat schemas simultaneously in different domains. For example, "I feel so sad about the anti-trans legislation being passed in my state" (threat/world) and "One day it will get better" (safety/future). When we can be an element of the safe schema for our students, they can experience nervous system co-regulation. When schools are culturally competent, students can attend to their academic, social, and motivational domains in the school environment (Osher et al., 2018). Social safety can be nurtured in the space of an active alliance of supportive students and adults.

Gender and Sexuality Alliances

Student groups such as the "Gender and Sexuality Alliance" (GSA) provide a school-sanctioned space to discuss issues that impact the well-being of SGD students and the allies who support them. The value of a GSA is multilayered and rooted in political action that is often not discussed. GSAs provide spaces for fostering emotional support and belonging, social engagement, increasing visibility, and advocacy for inclusive school policy (Garcia et al., 2019 & Poteat et al., 2021). The history of the GSA and the student-led effort to create these "safe spaces" has been largely whitewashed, and severed from its radical roots (Ventura, 2022). The first GSA is often credited to a private school in Massachusetts in 1993 with the "Safe Schools Program," which inspired GSAs in public and private schools across the state and then nationally (Johnson, 2007). However, the first student-led group to address the oppression SGD students faced in schools originated in 1972 in Washington Heights, New York City. Led by a young woman of color, Elle Lamadrid, the group wrote a list of demands that the city high schools of New York afford gay students the same rights as their straight peers, such as the right to form gay school groups and representation in classes on sexuality (Ventura, 2022). They used the language of human rights and dignity and called upon the power of other liberation movements of their time as their guide. This template is the link between providing support for SGD students and activism to ensure safety in the school system, and it is the embodiment of anti-oppressive work in schools.

The agenda and meeting structure are set by the students, empowering them to take leadership roles. GSAs are typically student-run clubs with an adult advisor. Social workers are ideal staff to fill this role. Working as the GSA advisor enables you to work closely with the SGD students and their allies, so they know you are a supportive adult in their school. The GSA is the space where policy ideas and program planning to address student safety issues are born. Being a familiar face at meetings and supplying community resources is essential to building rapport and trust with the students who need this safety net. Furthermore, it provides the opportunity for students to explore political action that impacts their lives as students. Educating GSA members as to the true origins of GSA is empowering as it highlights the intersection of social justice movements and places adolescents at the inception of this movement.

A Reflexive Exercise

For 10 years I was the Gender and Sexuality Alliance (GSA) advisor at the high school where I have worked for over 15 years. We weren't always the Gender and Sexuality Alliance. When I started, it was the Gay Straight Alliance. That change happened because the students recognized the need for a more expansive title. I think they also hoped that the club would grow and be able to discuss more political issues surrounding gender and society, as was the intended mission of the GSA. I loved witnessing these meetings. The students always took a leadership role in deciding the agenda and the activities to be discussed every other week after school on Tuesdays. I marveled as they shared their stories of courage in discovering a part of themselves that was rarely given permission to be spoken about. Many of the students were out to their friends, but not their families. And on the occasion, when a student would share that they had finally come out to their parents, regardless of their response, the students and I would clap and cheer.

But there I was, sitting in those meetings silent about my own sexual orientation. This was a struggle that I had with myself at every single meeting. My thoughts ranged from not wanting to overshadow their stories to the more insidious internalized homophobia that I still wrestled with. I decided I would never lie if I were ever asked if I were gay. And so, I never did, because I was never asked. I would share stories from pride parades of yesteryear and demonstrated an unusually thorough knowledge of LGBT history. When I took the GSA to a conference for LGBTQ youth, I just happened to know most of the adults in the room. It wasn't until 1 day during finals week that the president of the GSA, a tenacious young activist with amazing leadership qualities with whom I had a close relationship, came to see me in my office at the end of the day. "Ms. Koenig, can I ask you something? Either you are the most amazing ally ever or you're gay. Which is it?" I said, "It seems like this is important for you to know." She nodded. When I told her I was indeed a lesbian, she was overjoyed. "Thank you for telling me. Really. Thank you."

I think it's very important to hold space for young people to discover who they are and to celebrate whatever they discover. I am keenly aware that as a person who has been out for over 30 years, I'm still scanning for signs of safety and threat every day. The truth is we live in an ever-changing political climate, and depending on where you work and live will largely inform your decision on whether to come out if you are SGD. But overall, my schemas about myself, the world, and the future are overwhelmingly positive. With that security, I can hold feelings of threat when they arise, acknowledge them, and let them go. As Audrey Lorde's wise words, hanging on my office wall remind me and my students every day, "When I dare to be powerful—to use my strength in the service of my vision—then it becomes less and less important whether I am afraid."

Maintaining a Liberatory Frame

The simultaneous action of working against systemic oppression while supporting individuals' growth toward freedom is the heart of liberatory practice. Liberatory practice merges understanding the consequences of oppression on one's well-being with empowerment to make social change (Belkin Martinez, 2014). Supporting SGD youth in expressing their lived experiences as they make meaning of their realities is an essential component of liberation psychology (Almeida et al., 2019). There is not a singular technique to employ when intervening with SGD youth, because SGD youth have different standpoints and conceptions of the societal impact on their lives. Liberatory practices keep the focus on challenging the systems that inhibit freedom of expression and well-being. This can involve empowering youth to advocate for themselves or develop an action plan to engage in collective advocacy. From this framework, our work is not to solve a list of problems that are rooted in the individual's psychology. We are collaborating with our students through a process of deep listening to develop action steps for social change. For those who are still finding their voices and not ready to act, our role is to develop the students' awareness of the external pressures that exert an impact on their lives.

Eliminating bullying and harassment is one aspect of the work in schools with SGD students. However, providing attunement and presence is foundational in alleviating the trauma of marginalization. The lived experiences of SGD youth vary with respect to their internalized narratives created in relationship with others. We cannot assume that SGD youth are struggling with "coming out" or experiencing overt discrimination. We also cannot assume guiding a student toward coming out is the best intervention. Physical, emotional, and social safety is always the first concern. This requires discernment beyond biopsychosocial data collection. A liberatory approach requires that the students we connect with inform us of their readiness to engage in action toward systemic change, and that we honor that capacity (Belkin Martinez, 2014).

Case Example 1

Several years ago, a student I will call "Joshua" came to my office late in the day as the school year was ending. "So, I like guys." He announced quickly, looking away as soon as he said it. "That's great," I said with a smile. I continued to look at his face, wondering if he would return my gaze or bounce out of my doorway. Joshua was tall, lanky, and always in motion, like the "Winnie the Pooh" character Tigger personified. He was thoughtful and always kind to his peers, finding ways to encourage and compliment others in every social situation I witnessed. Peter was a gifted poet and enjoyed writing. I had known him for a year at that time, but our conversations had centered on schoolwork and organization. After a few beats of silence, he remained in the doorway. I asked him, "Have you told anyone else?"

As a Black teenager who lived in a conservative Christian family, Joshua assumed that at best, he would not be supported, and no one would speak of it again. At worst, he imagined he would be kicked out of the house. He had shared this piece of his identity with an online friend, but no one "in real life." I asked him how it felt to say it out loud to another person. He said it felt good to say it. Then he asked me about my summer plans and left. In the fall of the following year, Joshua came to see me again. We talked about his classes (most of which he didn't like), his job (which he did like, sometimes), and his dogs (which he loved). "Do you remember I told you I liked guys?" he asked. "Yep, I do," I said. "Ok good, I'll see you around." Joshua wasn't asking for advocacy or action. He was engaging in rapprochement, touching base, and going off into the school day. He would stop by occasionally to chat, and his sexuality rarely came up. He didn't ask for help to come out to his parents, he said he'd think about it when he was away at college. We talked about what it might feel like to share this part of himself with his friends.

By the Spring of that year, Joshua shared a poem he had written about a beautiful shell on a beach waiting for the ocean to reach it and pull it back into the water. I felt the emotions of longing and isolation in his words. I felt he was giving me an invitation to his world. "Is that how you feel Joshua? Like you're waiting on the shore, hoping to be a part of something bigger? Waiting to be pulled in?" His knee bounced up and down, but he met my eyes. "There are not many Black kids in this school, and I am definitely the only Black and Queer one." He was taking a huge risk talking about his lived experience as a Black, Queer teenager. This opened the door for a deeper connection. We talked about the impact of this isolation in this mostly white school and the challenges of not feeling able to share his sexuality or pursue a relationship. We talked about using writing to access his voice and I asked if he had read any books by Black Queer authors like James Baldwin or Julian Winters. My role as a social worker unfolded during these conversations, based on his needs, not on my projections of his needs. Joshua needed a space to be seen authentically, where the ocean reached the shore.

In my work with Joshua, I began by giving him the space to share about himself and followed his pace of sharing. As Joshua talked about his intersecting identities, I listened. Had I defended the "friendly school environment," I would have completely invalidated his feelings and shut down our connection. Suggesting reading the works of Baldwin and Winters, I hoped to offer Joshua a connection to other writers who he would resonate with and encouraged him to continue exploring his feelings through his writing. I reflected on my limitations to connect with Joshua as a white adult, who had chosen not to share my sexual orientation. There is sometimes a pull to share this aspect of myself with students or clients in my private practice who are newly identified as SGD. But this was his journey, and I could support him without decentering his experience by inserting mine. Joshua was not looking to get involved in political action, and connection to our local Queer youth organization was not an option for him at that time. But by graduation, he had come out to his close friends with happy results. In time he may opt to engage in community action, but Joshua has his whole life ahead of him to walk the path he chooses, knowing that he is not alone.

Case Example 2

Working in school systems, social workers can create a school environment that promotes safety for SGD students. One important issue is advocating for the proper usage of affirmed names and pronouns. Social workers can advocate for indicating affirmed pronouns on student records and databases so that students can focus on academics instead of worrying about the substitute teacher using their deadname (the name given at birth that doesn't accurately reflect their current identity). If your school is unwilling to make these adjustments, having an open dialogue about your efforts to change the system creates an alliance with your students. Teachers and other adults in school who reinforce stereotypes limit authentic engagement through negative interactions or are openly hostile can increase stress, leading to lower academic performance and health outcomes (Gómez et al., 2015; Osher et al., 2018).

I once had an interaction with a teacher who sought me out to complain about a transgender student's varying gender presentation. I had come to this white heterosexual, cisgender female teacher before to ask her to refer to the student using he/him pronouns. According to the student, the teacher was doing her best and was trying to be consistent. But on this day, the teacher came to find me. Visibly flustered, she complained that this transgender student had worn a skirt and earrings to school. "I mean, pick a lane!" she cried. "Do I use female pronouns today? She should make up her mind!" I assured my colleague he was still he, and we discussed how we all have different ways of expressing ourselves through clothing and accessories. I acknowledge that this could be confusing, but it is because we are taught rigid rules about gender expression, and then have certain expectations. She tried to engage me in a cultural debate about how we never had this type of thing when she began teaching 20 years ago. I took a deep breath and tried to connect with the compassionate part of me that saw this person struggling. "I hear you. But whether in a skirt or pants he still needs help to pass that algebra test."

Keeping Affirming Resources and Referrals

Referrals of current support services in the community, both local agencies and online, that are safe spaces for SGD adolescents are an essential part of your toolbox. Have an updated referral list of therapists who are dedicated to supporting SGD youth and their families, with a critical consciousness lens. I have had parents of gender-expansive young people tell me that their last therapist told them, "There's a 30% chance 'she'll' grow out of it." Many people in the mental health field have not explored their own biases about gender and sexuality, making it impossible to extricate themselves from hetero-cisnormative stories. It is necessary to explore expectations and fears with parents. However, delving into family historical narratives and dynamics around sexuality and gender is beyond the scope of the school social worker.

Conclusion

There is so much joy in the Queer community. There is music, art, theater, literature, poetry, and expansive freedom. For adolescents discovering who they are, who they love, and how they want to move in the world, living outside of cultural constraints is an act of transgression and liberation. Social workers who engage critical consciousness can nurture this becoming with individual students, as well as speak to the models of expansive gender and sexual identity by supporting systemic change within school systems. The problem is not within our SGD students, it is with the narrow and restrictive frame of the gender and sexuality binary. The problem is with the essentialist, biological deterministic model that keeps people in boxes, unable to express themselves with authenticity and joy.

Explore your own attitudes toward SGD people and feelings about your own sexual orientation and gender. Advocate for the well-being of SGD children with parents. The research shows that supportive parents contribute to happier, healthier SGD youth (Coolhart, 2018; Melton et al., 2021; Wigderson et al., 2019). Working with students whose parents are unsupportive can activate powerful countertransference. Because of our own histories, narratives, intersectional identities, and feelings about injustice as social workers, we need to be vigilant stewards of our embodied reactions and embrace them without judgment. In light of recent major changes to national policy affecting SGD students and the school professionals who support them, school social workers will need to stay vigilant, compassionate, and courageous as we navigate the impact these policies will have on our students. Familiarize yourself with current research and policy briefs that accurately reflect the current climate and the probable consequences to SGD youth and adults faced with a hostile and stigmatizing environment (e.g. https://williamsinstitute.law.ucla.edu/publications/deischools-eo-impact/).

Reflections for Your Consideration

Abraham Maslow's seminal *Hierarchy of Needs* was published after he spent time with the Blackfoot Nation on Siksika land in what is now called Alberta, Canada in 1938 (Ravilochan, 2021). According to Maslow, there is a stepwise process where we move toward "self-actualization" once we have satisfied our more basic needs (physiological, safety, love, belonging, and esteem). The Blackfoot and many other Indigenous Peoples around the world believe that we are innately self-actualized, and we work to sustain community actualization within a framework of living in connection to the land, all living beings, and the generations that have come before us and will come after (Ravilochan, 2021). Why are these teachings important to our work with SGD students in schools? Because all of us, especially people within groups that are marginalized by others, need to be able to see that we exist within communities that have come before and will continue after. That we are inherently worthy of love and belonging, and the narratives that have been taught to us about our place in the world are not universal truths. Sit with this concept and notice how you feel in your body. Using an anti-oppressive lens means working toward liberation for all. Just as intersectionality requires that social workers understand power and lived experiences from multiple cultural perspectives, anti-oppressive practice requires that we must work toward dismantling oppressive systems to achieve the goal of liberation.

Critical consciousness is not an intellectual exercise. We must understand how we take part in these systems as social workers and as individuals. It requires that we question how we participate as oppressors, and it requires that we speak up and act out in the service of creating a world where liberation is possible. Practicing social work from an anti-oppressive position is not a dispassionate exercise or a series of techniques. It requires a reflexive mindset with a willingness to engage in compassionate action. I urge you to explore the writings of liberation thinkers such as bell hooks, Paolo Freire, Lila Watson, and Audre Lorde to inspire and inform your work.

Reflection Questions

1. Reflect on the voices of your teachers, in and out of the classroom. Do they have different standpoints than you? How can you expand your learning to include other voices and disciplines to add to your liberatory toolbox?
2. What is your understanding of the binary models of gender and sexuality? How can you explore and confront this model? Can you verbalize how this binary model can harm everyone, not only SGD people?
3. How does theory impact our practice with SGD individuals? Consider how epistemology (how we come to know our beliefs, and where that knowledge comes from) causes us to interpret what we know about SGD people.
4. What are some ways you would engage critical consciousness in the school setting with SDG students?
5. How would you work with the student presented in the first example?

References

Allen-Meares, P. (2023). School Social Work. *Encyclopedia of Social Work*. Retrieved May 2, 2023, from https://oxfordre.com/socialwork/view/10.1093/acrefore/9780199975839.001.0001/acrefore-9780199975839-e-351

Almeida, R. V., Werkmeister Rozas, L. M., Cross-Denny, B., Lee, K. K., & Yamada, A.-M. (2019). Coloniality and intersectionality in social work education and practice. *Journal of Progressive Human Services, 30*(2), 148–164. https://doi.org/10.1080/10428232.2019.1574195

Belkin Martinez, D. (2014). The liberation health model: Theory and practice. In D. Belkin Martinez & A. Fleck-Henderson (Eds.), *Social justice in clinical practice: A liberation health framework for social work* (pp. 9–28). Taylor & Francis Group.

Boylan, M. (2021). Trauma informed practices in education and social justice: Towards a critical orientation. *International Journal of School Social Work, 6*(1). https://doi.org/10.4148/2161-4148.1071

Bruce, D., Harper, G. W., & Bauermeister, J. A. (2015). Minority stress, positive identity development, and depressive symptoms: Implications for resilience among sexual minority male youth. *Psychology of Sexual Orientation and Gender Diversity, 2*(3), 287–296. https://doi.org/10.1037/sgd0000128

Choi, A. (2023, April 6). Record number of anti-LGBTQ bills have been introduced this year | CNN politics. CNN. https://www.cnn.com/2023/04/06/politics/anti-lgbtq-plus-state-bill-rights-dg/index.html

Coolhart, D. (2018). Helping families move from distress to attunement. In C. Keo-Meier & D. Ehrensaft (Eds.), *The gender affirmative model: An interdisciplinary approach to supporting transgender and gender expansive children*. American Psychological Association.

Diamond, L. M., & Alley, J. (2022). Rethinking minority stress: A social safety perspective on the health effects of stigma in sexually-diverse and gender-diverse populations. *Neuroscience & Biobehavioral Reviews, 138*, 104720.

Drescher, J. (2009). Queer diagnoses: Parallels and contrasts in the history of homosexuality, gender variance, and the diagnostic and statistical manual. *Archives of Sexual Behavior, 39*(2), 427–460. https://doi.org/10.1007/s10508-009-9531-5

Freire, P. (1970). *Pedagogy of the oppressed (50th Anniversary Edition)*. Bloomsbury Academic.

Garcia, J., Vargas, N., Clark, J. L., Magaña Álvarez, M., Nelons, D. A., & Parker, R. G. (2019). Social isolation and connectedness as determinants of Well-being: Global evidence mapping focused on LGBTQ youth. *Global Public Health, 15*(4), 1–23. https://doi.org/10.1080/17441692.2019.1682028

Gegenfurtner, A., & Gebhardt, M. (2017). Sexuality education including lesbian, gay, bisexual, and transgender (LGBT) issues in schools. *Educational Research Review, 22*(22), 215–222. https://doi.org/10.1016/j.edurev.2017.10.002

International Federation of Social Workers. (n.d.). Global definition of social work. https://www.ifsw.org/what-is-socialwork/global-definition-of-social-work/

GLSEN. (2022). *The 2021 National school climate survey EXECUTIVE SUMMARY*. https://www.glsen.org/sites/default/files/2022-10/NSCS-2021-Executive_Summary-EN.pdf

Godfrey, E. B., & Burson, E. (2018). Interrogating the intersections: How intersectional perspectives can inform developmental scholarship on critical consciousness. *New Directions for Child and Adolescent Development, 2018*(161), 17–38. https://doi.org/10.1002/cad.20246

Goldbach, J. T., Rhoades, H., Rusow, J., & Karys, P. (2021). The development of proud & empowered: An intervention for promoting LGBTQ adolescent mental health. *Child Psychiatry & Human Development, 54*, 481–492. https://doi.org/10.1007/s10578-021-01250-2

Gómez, J. M., Lewis, J. K., Noll, L. K., Smidt, A. M., & Birrell, P. J. (2015). Shifting the focus: Nonpathologizing approaches to healing from betrayal trauma through an emphasis on relational care. *Journal of Trauma & Dissociation, 17*(2), 165–185. https://doi.org/10.1080/15299732.2016.1103104

Hiebert, D. (2016). Is it homophobia or homoppression? *Canadian Review of Sociology/Revue Canadienne de Sociologie, 53*(4), 488–492. https://doi.org/10.1111/cars.12131

hooks, b. (1994). *Teaching to transgress: Education as the practice of freedom*. Routledge.

Hulko, W., & Hovanes, J. (2017). Intersectionality in the lives of LGBTQ youth: Identifying as LGBTQ and finding community in small cities and rural towns. *Journal of Homosexuality, 65*(4), 427–455. https://doi.org/10.1080/00918369.2017.1320169

Johnson, D. (2007). "This is Political!" Negotiating the legacies of the first school-based gay youth group. *Children, Youth, and Environments, 17*(2), 380–387.

Mangin, M. (2018). Supporting transgender and gender-expansive children in school. *Phi Delta Kappan, 100*(2), 16–21. https://doi.org/10.1177/0031721718803564

McDermott, E., Eastham, R., Hughes, E., Pattinson, E., Johnson, K., Davis, S., Pryjmachuk, S., Mateus, C., & Jenzen, O. (2021). Explaining effective mental health support for LGBTQ+ youth: A meta-narrative review. *SSM – Mental Health, 1*, 100004. https://doi.org/10.1016/j.ssmmh.2021.100004

McGonigal, K. (2016). *The upside of stress: Why stress is good for you, and how to get good at it*. Avery.

Melton, T. N., Brehm, M. V., & Deutsch, N. L. (2021). Broadening the perspective on youth's systems of support: An ecological examination of supportive peer and adult relationships during adolescence. *Journal of Community Psychology, 49*(5), 1334–1357.

Mills-Koonce, W. R., Rehder, P. D., & McCurdy, A. L. (2018). The significance of parenting and parent–child relationships for sexual and gender minority adolescents. *Journal of Research on Adolescence, 28*(3), 637–649.

Mkhize, S. P., & Mthembu, A. (2023). Unpacking pervasive heteronormativity in sub-Saharan Africa: Opportunities to embrace multiplicity of sexualities. *Progress in Human Geography, 47*(3), 377–391. 03091325231166402.

Neuman, S. (2015, March 27). He, she or hen? Sweden's new gender-neutral pronoun. News. https://www.wgbh.org/news/post/he-she-or-hen-swedens-new-gender-neutral-pronoun
Osher, D., Cantor, P., Berg, J., Steyer, L., & Rose, T. (2018). Drivers of human development: How relationships and context shape learning and development1. *Applied Developmental Science, 24*(1), 6–36. https://doi.org/10.1080/10888691.2017.1398650
Pennell, S. M. (2017). Training secondary teachers to support LGBTQ+ students: Practical applications from theory and research. *The High School Journal, 101*(1), 62–72. https://doi.org/10.1353/hsj.2017.0016
Poteat, V. P., Fish, J. N., & Watson, R. J. (2021). Gender-sexuality alliances as a moderator of the association between victimization, depressive symptoms, and drinking behavior among LGBTQ+ youth. *Drug and Alcohol Dependence, 229*(Part B), 109140. https://doi-org.proxy.library.nyu.edu/10.1016/j.drugalcdep.2021.109140
Ravilochan, T. (2021, August 18). Could the Blackfoot wisdom that inspired Maslow guide us now? Medium. https://gatherfor.medium.com/maslow-got-it-wrong-ae45d6217a8c
Schmitz, R. M., & Tabler, J. (2021). Health services and intersections of care: Promises and pitfalls experienced by LGBTQ+Latino/a emerging adults. *Journal of LGBT Youth, 18*(1), 1–22. https://doi.org/10.1080/19361653.2019.1684416
Scroggs, B., Durtschi, J., Busk, M., Goodcase, E., & Jones, D. L. (2020). Within-minority group discomfort in lesbian, gay, and bisexual emerging adults of color: Implications for group identification and Well-being. *Journal of Gay & Lesbian Mental Health, 24*(2), 1–19. https://doi.org/10.1080/19359705.2019.1703869
Slavich, G. M., Roos, L. G., Mengelkoch, S., Webb, C. A., Shattuck, E. C., Moriarity, D. P., & Alley, J. C. (2023). Social safety theory: Conceptual foundation, underlying mechanisms, and future directions. *Health Psychology Review, 17*(1), 1–55. https://doi.org/10.1080/17437199.2023.2171900
Thomas, M., McCoy, T., Jeffries, I., Haverkate, R., Naswood, E., Leston, J., & Platero, L. (2022). Native American two-spirit and lgbtq health: A systematic review of the literature. *Journal of Gay & Lesbian Mental Health, 26*(4), 367–402.
Vanita, R. (Ed.). (2013). *Queering India: Same-sex love and eroticism in Indian culture and society*. Routledge.
Velez, G., & Spencer, M. B. (2018). Phenomenology and intersectionality: Using PVEST as a frame for adolescent identity formation amid intersecting ecological systems of inequality. *New Directions for Child and Adolescent Development, 2018*(161), 75–90. https://doi.org/10.1002/cad.20247
Ventura, A. (2022, June 24). The radical history of the first gay-straight alliance. Www.thenation.com. https://www.thenation.com/article/society/gay-liberation-high-school/
Villarreal Sosa, L. (2022). School social work: Challenges and opportunities. *Children & Schools, 44*(2), 67–69. https://doi-org.proxy.library.nyu.edu/10.1093/cs/cdac005
Wagaman, M. A. (2016). Self-definition as resistance: Understanding identities among LGBTQ emerging adults. *Journal of LGBT Youth, 13*(3), 207–230. https://doi.org/10.1080/19361653.2016.1185760
Walker, M. (2010). How therapy helps when the culture hurts. In J. V. Jordan (Ed.), *The power of connection: Recent developments in relational-cultural theory* (pp. 84–102). Routledge.
Wigderson, S., Lindahl, K. M., & Malik, N. M. (2019). Parental responsiveness toward GLB children: Impact on mental health two years later. *Journal of GLBT Family Studies, 15*(4), 326–341.
Young, I. M. (2014). Five faces of oppression. In *Rethinking power* (pp. 174–195).

Chapter 10
Nothing About Us, Without Us: The Importance of Disability Justice in Social Work Education

Benjamin R. Sher

Introduction

Living with or acquiring a disability is a universal human condition. All human beings, at one point in their life, can be affected by a disability. One in four Americans experience a disability in their lifetime (Taylor, 2018). Data from the US Census reports that 27.2% of all Americans (or 85.3 million) had a disability in 2014. Disabilities are an identity that any of us could acquire.

As a profession, social work addresses the human condition. Our discipline emphasizes advocacy and reduction of systematic forms of injustice to help the most marginalized of society. Social work students must be trained to combat all society's "isms," inclusive of those directed at people with disabilities. Yet, a content analysis study by Kristen and Krcek (2012) found that disability was mentioned as an educational focus area in only 7% of the top 25 schools of social work's curriculum across the country. The 2022 Educational Policy and Accreditation Standards (EPAS) of the Council on Social Work Education (CSWE) name disability and ability awareness as key intersectional components of an educational program focused on anti-racism, diversity, equity, and inclusion. The author's own experiences and anecdotal discussions with beginning clinicians in practicum placement evidence discomfort in helping people with disabilities. Students in social work school report feeling unprepared to serve individuals diagnosed with a mental health disorder, physical disability, intellectual challenge, or learning difficulty. Thus, though all of us could experience a disability in our lifetime, there is a disconnect in our schools of social work to prepare students to work with disabilities.

B. R. Sher (✉)
Silver School of Social Work, New York University, New York, NY, USA
e-mail: benjamin.sher@nyu.edu

C. Tosone et al. (eds.), *Reframing Social Work with an Anti-Oppressive Lens*, Essential Clinical Social Work Series,
https://doi.org/10.1007/978-3-031-91391-4_10

As schools of social work move toward a curriculum embedded in anti-oppressive and social justice–oriented practice, disability studies and disability justice must be a central part of this work. This chapter traces the historical work of social work practice with disabilities, centering on how this practice area must be connected to anti-oppressive and anti-racist work. It explores the current work being done to bring disability justice studies to social work pedagogy, as well as how accreditation standards have evolved over time to support implementation. The chapter continues with specific ideas for implementation practices to help develop a model for schools of social work to consider. A key component of this work is the facilitation of lived experience presentations on disabilities so that those closest to the problem can design an education program that captures a workable solution to teaching about disability justice. Ethical use of lived experience models in social work education on disability justice is a requirement of this curriculum design, and the chapter explores ideas on what will support this practice. The chapter offers some concrete examples for a curriculum on disability studies/justice in social work classes and posits some recommendations for future work. The chapter ends with a series of reflective questions for students and instructors to consider in bringing a disability justice perspective to social work pedagogy. The chapter assists schools of social work in preparing students for collaborating with people with disabilities.

Language Considerations and Definitions

As we begin our discussion on implementation of disability studies in social work education, it is important to frame relevant terms. According to the Americans with Disabilities Act (ADA), a disability is defined as a physical or mental impairment that limits one or more major life activities (Kimball et al., 2016). This is a reductionistic definition, in that it focuses only on the person. Glison and DePoy (2002) define disability as perceived impairments that are out of the norm of society. These become a challenge when a negative social meaning attaches to the concern, as well as when said issue is a barrier to participation in society. An example of this would be someone who uses a wheelchair due to a physical limitation, such as paraplegia. The use of a wheelchair is a disability because access barriers occur as a result; people who use wheelchairs may not be able to access all the buildings in a community if they can only be physically accessed by stairs.

Disabilities may be either visible or invisible. Invisible disabilities cannot be discerned by perception and include psychological conditions, learning difficulties, internal medical conditions, or intellectual challenges. An example of a visible disability would be a person in a wheelchair.

Language considerations are crucial as we discuss disabilities. Due to stigma and discrimination, naming someone as disabled could further exploit them. "Person-first" language (e.g., "person with mental illness") has become the appropriate language when addressing people. However, as social movements develop, groups have co-opted terminology that recognizes their experience as their own. For example, the Autistic community often prefers "Autistic" as opposed to "person with Autism." Though this language differentiation exists, this chapter will use "person-first" language to show respect and concern for people with disabilities.

Positionality

Important for this discussion is one's positionality. The author is writing this chapter from the perspective of a white cisgender male. I have had my own experiences with disabilities, which drives my commitment to this work. Disabilities have impacted family members and friends, as well as me. The author's understanding of privilege and oppression in relation to disabilities has evolved over time. For example, it was not until I worked in mental health that I learned the sharp dichotomy between access to quality care for someone using public health insurance as opposed to private. Clients who were on Medicaid were denied access to quality care and relied on the fragmented public mental health system for treatment.

It is through my interactions with students in practice that I am aware of how vital disability studies is to social work education, as well as how challenging it can be for students to experience exposure to it. This will be further addressed in the current state of social work education section of this chapter.

Historical Practices in Disability Social Work

Educational models for disability social work reflect the practice modalities directed toward this group. For a good part of the nineteenth and twentieth centuries, people with disabilities were institutionalized and separated from society. The moral model of care highly influenced social work services to this population. For example, beliefs that disabilities were limited led to social care models that reflected paternalism, control, and authority over individual goals. Deemed unable to make effective decisions for themselves, the moral model posited that authority figures "knew what was best" for people with disabilities and therefore managed all aspects of their lives. Social workers embraced this model and often played a significant role in limiting the rights of people with disabilities (Ben-Moshe, 2020).

As Civil Rights expanded in the twentieth century for many marginalized groups, so did it for people with disabilities. Deemed the "Civil Rights Act" for people with disabilities, the Americans with Disabilities Act (and its subsequent revisions) has assisted millions of people with access to employment, services, inclusion, and care. However, the medical and diagnostic model for social work practice with people with disabilities has prevailed into the twenty-first century (Glison & DePoy, 2002). Social workers have relied on the diagnosis of a disability as the primary form of treatment intervention, therefore placing emphasis on the disability as a problem within the person. This has been reflected in social work education courses, where human behavior and social environment classes are often focused on psychopathology and diagnostic determinism.

Social constructivist models of disability brought the environment into consideration. Challenging assumptions that the disability lived within the person, social construction noted that it was societal perspectives on what defined disability that influenced its treatment. For example, environmental barriers to universal access created the disability, rather than the person themselves. Criticism of the social constructivist model has arisen in recent years. Recognizing that not all disabling situations are created by environmental conditions, the practice has moved toward an interactionist model of working with people with disabilities. For example, because there are multiple forms of disabilities, and some do exist within the person, such as mental illness, an interactional model recognizes that both environment and biology play a role in the disability.

The evolution of the interactional model in work with people with disabilities lays the groundwork for disability studies and disability justice in social work education. Interactional models recognize that there are many truths to theory. This aligns with social work education's movement toward critical theory as its foundation. Critical theory emphasizes the multiple truths that are out there and that systems interacting with these perspectives influence how learning is gained. Just as we know that race and racism influence every aspect of American society, critical disability theory recognizes that our perceptions of people with disabilities influence our work with them.

Anti-oppressive and anti-racist social work education aligns with disability justice. Disability justice, like anti-oppressive and anti-racist social work education, focuses on the tenet that systemic factors have deeply harmed and impacted marginalized groups. Each poses a liberatory framework for people impacted by social problems. Anti-oppressive social work practice, like disability justice, promotes equity, inclusion, transformation, and social justice (Morgaine & Capous-Desyllas, 2023). Both ideas further support the lived experience as an influential aspect of learning. "Nothing about us without us" is the rallying cry of people with disabilities, and it is also echoed in other oppressed groups. The detached clinical "stance" of the medical and moral model in social work education has harmed the very groups we aim to support. Therefore, the timing for critical work in disability justice in social work education is right.

Current State of Disability Content in Social Work Education (SWE)

Oversight of curriculum in US schools of social work is provided by the Council on Social Work Education (CSWE). Accredited schools follow the Educational Policy and Accreditation Standards (EPAS), created by the Commission of Accreditation (COA) of CSWE. The EPAS is reviewed every 7 years. 2022 standards are currently being promulgated, and schools of social work are expected to be in full compliance with them by July 1, 2025 (CSWE, 2022a, 2022b).

In their analysis of disability content in social work schools, Kristen and Krcek (2012) point out that the EPAS did not mandate disability content in social work schools until 2001. This was reflected in the experience of this author, who received his MSW in 1994. At that time, I did not receive any formal curriculum on disability studies, though my area of specialization was mental health, which can be perceived as a form of disability. In a review of 1620 course titles and descriptions from the top 25 schools of social work, Bean and Krcek found only one course that explicitly described the Americans with Disabilities Act (ADA). Though this seminal legislation is seen as a form of emancipation for people with disabilities, it was not clear from Bean and Krcek's work that schools of social work are covering this topic.

Even an informal review of the curriculum of metropolitan NYC schools of social work supported this finding. Only one school of social work in the NYC area offered required courses in disability studies. It was also the only school to offer students a specialization in this area. Though this is a cursory review, and as Sherwood and Kattari (2023) Galambos (2004) emphasize, disability studies may be embedded in course content and not explicitly defined in the title of the course or its description.

This leads us to how disability studies are currently taught in schools of social work. According to Kristen and Krcek (2012), disability content may either be infused or dedicated, or a combination of both. Infused disability content is when information about disabilities is spread across the full curriculum of a program, and shows up in the full spectrum of practice, research, policy, and human behavior and the environment (HBSE) courses. Readings, assignments, and content in the infused model reflect the full range of disabilities in their pedagogy. Dedicated disability content assigns the study of disabilities to one or two courses, usually in courses on diversity and cultural awareness. The combination model reflects both infused and dedicated courses.

In their article on the assessment of integrating disability content into social work education, Ogden et al. (2017) pointed out that the MSW curriculum is already crowded. There is much to be covered in a school of social work, and the aim to prepare a professional social worker in both generalized and specialty practice is a challenge. The rigors of practicum placement, coupled with the demands of understanding evidence-based interventions for the communities social workers serve, have placed a heavy burden on faculty to prepare students for fields of practice. Accreditation standards, though crucial to the formalization of pedagogy, present a demand for schools of social work to address all aspects of practice.

A focus on the explicit and implicit curriculum has been one way to address this challenge. As defined in the EPAS (2022), the explicit curriculum in social work education is the formal education taught to students. It would include the required courses and elective courses that a student takes while in social work school. The implicit curriculum is the larger student learning experience placed in the context of their experience in the program. Because the process of professionalization for a beginning social worker is a developmental process, the implicit curriculum can be envisioned to be as crucial as what is taught in the classroom.

Building on suggestions from Ogden et al. (2017) and other authors, the CSWE Commission for Diversity and Social & Economic Justice, through the Center for Diversity & Economic Justice, published the *Curricular Resource on Issues of Disability and Disability-Competent Care: Diversity and Justice Supplement* (2018). This guide focuses both on the explicit and implicit curriculum in infusing disability content into social work education. Addressing each of the nine competency standards in the EPAS, the curricular guide crosswalks these standards with ways to infuse disability-competent care into social work education. For example, in the EPAS Competency 1: Demonstrate Ethical and Professional Behavior, the guide addresses the disability learning outcome of applying the dignity of risk. Dignity of risk, according to the guide, is related to the social work principle of self-determination and is focused on the ability of a person with disabilities to make choices that may go beyond of scope the comfort for a professional social worker. A person with mild intellectual disabilities who chooses to go bungee jumping after being educated on the risks and rewards of doing so is an example of dignity of risk. Beginning social workers may experience discomfort and paternalism with this choice, yet dignity of risk and social work self-determination means we accept the choices of the people we serve, even when we might not fully agree with them.

The *Curricular* guide offers specific educational resources to teach on such areas of dignity of risk. For example, the guide offers that a policy course can teach on the Olmstead decision from the Supreme Court that directs states to ensure people with disabilities can live in the least restrictive settings. It also suggests that students can be challenged to apply standards of dignity of risk in the practicum sites and discuss in practice classes how client choices can affect people positively and negatively.

There are multiple examples of how the guide can be used for the explicit curriculum in social work education. It also offers ideas for the implicit curriculum to support a culture of diversity and inclusion for people with disabilities. For example, schools of social work can be the standard bearer for ADA compliance at their universities and colleges. They can ensure all communications and coursework meet ADA standards. Technology and larger university resources, such as centers for disability inclusion or the disability services office, can collaborate with schools of social work to make this happen. Resources such as closed captioning for all online and alt text guides for images can be accessed. Assignments and course materials can be displayed in multiple formats, and clear standards on accessibility can be promoted by faculty.

Students with diverse learning styles can be embraced in the implicit curriculum at schools of social work. For example, a widespread practice can be to assess the learning style of a student as they begin their educational journey. For example, do they learn best by processing information through visual-perceptual pathways, or are they more comfortable in taking in what they learn through reading and digesting information? This author has established this standard with the students he supervises in placement. At the beginning of our work together, this author uses a standardized assessment tool as well as facilitated discussion to unpack the prominent learning style of the student. He then tailors his supervision and works with the student to meet these learning goals.

Through the implicit curriculum, schools of social work can host talks on disability-related issues. Offices of professional development at schools of social work can invite alumni who work in the field of disabilities to return to school to share their experiences. Prominent speakers with disabilities can be invited to school to talk about their lived experience and how (if at all) social work has impacted them Kristen & Krcek (2012).

Schools of social work can develop and promote groups for students with disabilities. They can embed them in the fabric of the school as a recognized organization or encourage students to join larger disabled student unions or affinity groups. At our university, a campus-wide Disability Inclusion and Accessibility working group is open to all students, both those who identify as disabled and those who do not. This group examines campus-wide issues around accessibility and has been instrumental in supporting policy, practice, and faculty development to integrate students with disabilities onto the campus. With a large budget at its disposal, this provost-recognized committee has dramatically enhanced the accessibility needs of students with disabilities. For example, all buildings at the university can be accessed through automatic doors, and each facility has accessible restrooms at every level.

Ogden et al. (2017) presented the challenges to addressing the explicit curriculum for disability studies in social work education. A survey sample of 300 CSWE members, mostly who were assistant professors (22.7%), reported about the curriculum challenges they faced in bringing disability studies to social work education. Common themes included institutional barriers, such as changes to curriculum requiring committee approval or a specific lack of knowledge, interest, expertise, or initiative on the development of disability studies in social work education. Sherwood and Kattari (2023) and Galambos (2004) suggest other barriers and address the issue of ableism in social work education. Ableism, as defined by Mackelprang and Salsgiver (2015), and Kattari et al. (2020) is the idea that people without disabilities are somehow better than those with disabilities, and like racism, it is systematic devaluing of this population. These articles speak to the challenges of bringing disability studies to the explicit social work curriculum and highlight the need for disability justice in social work education (Cox et al., 2021).

Disability Justice in Social Work Education

A disability justice (DJ) model is defined as a lived-experience-centered movement that supports access practices for all people involved, regardless of ability (Slayter et al., 2022). Developed in the arts professions, DJ centers the priorities and needs of the most historically excluded and marginalized, including (but not limited to) people with disabilities who are also women, Black, Indigenous, People of Color (BIPOC), immigrants, incarcerated, or Lesbian, Gay, Bisexual, Transgender, Queer, Intersex, Asexual, and Two-Spirit (LGBTQIAS2S+) (Slayter et al., 2022). With its focus on oppressed groups, DJ is a natural fit for anti-oppressive and anti-racist social work education.

Just as the social work curriculum has returned to its roots in social justice with a laser focus on anti-racist and anti-oppressive practices, so must the curriculum attend to disability justice practices. The two are complementary and intersectional, and the most vulnerable of all individuals with disabilities are the people social workers are committed to serving. This leads us to the intersectional lens of DJ work.

Oppressed people are seldom oppressed along one dimension (Dupre, 2012). Repeatedly, the most marginalized people with disabilities are Black, queer, female-identified, and poor. The intersectional model of critical theory lives in disability justice. It recognizes disability as an oppressed cultural identity, which leads our society to be the major perpetrators of disability bias (Slayter & Johnson, 2022). This fact, coupled with the almost universal reality that every human being could become disabled in their lifetime, necessitates why we must add a DJ frame to social work pedagogy.

Intersectionality requires us to be mindful of the multiple identities our clients bring to the table when they meet us in social workspaces. Students can be trained to apply the intersectional lens when serving people in their practicum sites. They can critically reflect on how a parent with an identified mental illness will be treated in the child welfare system. Students can discuss ways in which learning differences are or are not supported in public education spaces and the differential access to care for White families with a child with a learning exception as opposed to a Black family.

Faculty can build on this intersectional lens as well. When case examples are brought for discussion in practice courses, they can ensure they create a dimension of disability to the case. They can discuss the implications for this dimension and how it can impact the client system in diverse ways. Doing so embraces the systemic person-in-environment model that social work defines as its signature work. Rather than "adding on" to the explicit curriculum, as has already been found to be a challenge, bringing disability justice along with anti-oppressive/anti-racist social work education facilitates learning. An infused model for disability studies works best, as Kristen and Krcek (2012) found.

Ethical Standards

Ethical Standard #1 of the National Association of Social Workers (NASW) Code of Ethics (2021): Social Workers Ethical Responsibilities to Clients includes a subsection (1.05) on Cultural Competence:

> Social workers should obtain education about and demonstrate understanding of the nature of social diversity and oppression with respect to race, ethnicity, national origin, color, sex, sexual orientation, gender identity or expression, age, marital status, political belief, religion, immigration status, and **mental or physical ability** (Section 1.05 (d); emphasis added by the author).

Though the NASW Code of Ethics does not explicitly name obtaining education about disability, it can be implied from the above section that this is a crucial form of study. Social workers are required by our Code of Ethics to understand oppression as it occurs with all groups, and a later part of the Code (4.02), which addresses protection from discrimination, does explicitly state disability as one of the groups social workers should not discriminate against (Cheatham et al., 2015). This, along with the social worker's core value of respecting the dignity and worth of the person, emphasizes how disability studies and disability justice must become an element of the social work education curriculum.

Focusing primarily on people with intellectual and developmental disabilities, Laws et al. (2010) assert that people with disabilities are an oppressed group. People with disabilities have had their rights taken away from them, inclusive of sterilization and euthanasia. Because our profession dictates focus on ethical work with oppressed groups, people with disabilities need social workers to help navigate systemic challenges and discrimination. Poverty is also extant among people with disabilities, and our profession's foundation is to help the poor. Our core values, mission, and ethical standards require social workers to support people with disabilities. Schools of social work must uphold these standards by educating students about disabilities as they focus on anti-oppressive and social justice education.

Social work ethics falls against a dramatic changing backdrop in the way social services are provided to people. Managerialism, or the principle of driving service by outcomes and impact, has prevailed in social service agencies in the twenty-first century. Gone are the days in which block grants in social services are provided to assist communities. Every effort is now made to measure success for the people served and to ensure public dollars are being spent to ameliorate problems.

Deemed neoliberalism, these efforts have had a major impact on the ways social workers provide care, especially to oppressed groups such as people with disabilities. Social workers must account for their efforts and create outcomes for the people they serve, or they face the risk of seeing clients cut from service rolls or denied access in the first place. The medical model prevails in work with people with disabilities, often requiring this population to diagnostically demonstrate they have a service need before it is granted. Schools of social work must integrate this reality into their curriculum. They need to help students grasp the challenge of ethical practice in a managerialist social services frame. This lends credence to infusing social work education with disability studies and disability justice. Students must be educated in all aspects of human services work (e.g., policy, practice, research, and human development) to grasp the full tension of ethical social work standards and practice realities. Disability justice models, with their emphasis on allyship and elevation of the voice of people with disabilities, embraces this collectivist model. Social workers trained in disability justice work can become co-conspirators for people with disabilities. They can support their efforts to demand systemic change and equitable treatment. With this in mind, we turn to the ways we can implement a disability justice framework in social work education.

Implementing a Disability Justice Framework in Social Work Education

Bringing a disability justice framework to social work education requires a deep understanding of the self (Moyle, 2016). Beginning students in social work practice are developing their professional identities as social workers, and recognition of assumptions and bias is key. The author himself understands this work. His own frame of disability, both professional and personal, is evolving after 29 years as a social worker. Many mistakes and assumptions have been made along the way. This has occurred as recently as assumptions being made about supervising a student with a visible disability and what practice assignments they would want to engage in. A standard assignment for social work students assigned to our office is to create a conference to practice program planning skills. At the onset of placement, the author suggested that this student work on a conference that raised awareness about people with disabilities. This assumption fell flat, and the student quietly rejected this suggestion by not taking steps to work on this assignment. This action helped the author understand his own bias and error in judgement, and he instead explored with the students what *they* wanted to do in program planning. Knowing that our short-term study away courses (another part of our office's work) needed promotion, the student designed a series of video interviews with faculty and students to educate MSW students about these courses. Program planning around effective ways to raise this awareness led these students to suggest on their own a way to raise awareness of living with a disability. They engaged in making a video about their experiences of having a disability at the university. This video has become a tool for practice professors to help their students understand living with a disability, and the pride in ownership that this student feels about the video shows how self-determination is a crucial part of the work in disability studies in social work education. The author uses this example to emphasize that bringing a disability justice framework to social work education takes work and that awareness of judgments and bias is key to implementation success Moyle, (2016).

As stated above, this awareness relates to the skill of developing a differential sense of the self. A key component of professional social work education, a sense of self in practice is the combination of knowledge and skills gained in education intertwined with one's personal identity as a social worker, inclusive of traits, belief systems, life experiences, and cultural exposures (Dewane, 2006). Before the implicit and explicit curriculum can be defined, before we can create a model of infused or dedicated curriculum, we must help the beginning social work student to understand their attitudes and values toward working people with disabilities. Cheatham et al. (2015) have developed the *Social Worker's Attitude Towards Disability Scale*, a validated instrument that can be used as social work students begin their educational journey. It can also be used as a tool to assess students after their curriculum and practice have exposed them to work with people with disabilities.

An infused disability justice curriculum in social work education that is experiential, didactic, intersectional in its focus, driven by resources, and enables the student to critically reflect on working with this population will be successful (Kaushik, 2017). **Appendix 1** of this chapter offers some key components of this model (Table 10.1). Central to this model will be a Universal Design for Learning Approach (UDL), as suggested by Sherwood and Kattari (2023). UDL is a model borrowed from universal design architecture, where spaces and places are created such that

Table 10.1 Nothing about us, without us: the importance of disability justice in social work education

Didactic dimension	Ideas
Assess Student values	
Explore how the student experiences disabilities. Have them establish their attitudes, beliefs, and values about people with disabilities (PWD).	Administer *The Social Worker Attitudes Towards Disabilities Scale (Cheatham* et al., 2015*)* and discuss. Complete a relationship map that explores people in the student's lives and assess how similar/different it is for PWD.
Examine inherent bias in working with PWD.	Invite someone with lived experience to the class. Have them share +/− experiences with paid personnel.
Didactic[a]	
Definitions of disability.	Americans with Disabilities Act (ADA). Moral models, medical models, social models, constructivist ideas, invisible/visible disabilities
Policy.	Elementary and Secondary Education Act (ESEA), Individuals with Disabilities Education Act (IDEA), Education Rehabilitation Act (ERA), ADA, Improving America's Schools Act (IASA), No Child Left Behind (NLCB), Every Child Succeeds Act, Universal Design for Learning.
Historical & modern practice.	Social Diagnosis Model (Mary Richmond), Settlement House Model (Jane Addams), Moral treatment model., institutionalization/deinstitutionalization, rehabilitation model, social control.
Intersectionality	
What does it mean to possess multiple identities and be disabled?	Crip Justice, Anti-Black racism in disability work, Definitions of disability justice and social work intersections, Sins Invalid work.
Experiential	
Students build empathy by working with PWD.	Students reflect on a time when they needed help in their lives. What worked? What did not? Why? How does this relate to PWD?
Students grasp the lived experience of having a disability.	Lived experience presentation by a person with a disability.

[a] Key readings for this section include: (1.) Russell, M., & Stewart, J. (2001). Disablement, prison, and historical segregation. *Monthly Review*, *53*(3), 61–75. https://doi.org/10.14452/mr-053-03-2001-07_6. (2.) Beaulaurier, R. L., & Taylor, S. H. (2001). Social work practice with people with disabilities in the era of disability rights. *Social Work in Health Care*, *32*(4), 67–91. https://doi.org/10.1300/J010v32n04_04

anyone, regardless of ability or need, could take advantage of them. UDL would be applied to a disability justice frame in the following manner Kaushik (2017):

- Materials for learning are created in an accessible format and offered in advance to students attending the program.
- Training in accessibility standards for faculty will be made available.
- Multiple modes of learning assessment will be created for students, and creativity in assignment submission will be encouraged.
- All syllabi in the program will have a clear accessibility statement as well as a statement for students with disabilities. This will be reviewed and discussed in the first class.
- Personnel decisions will include hiring a diverse range of faculty, including faculty with disabilities.
- Other factors, such as technology (e.g., closed captioning) and physical plant (e.g., automatic door openers) issues, will be addressed and ameliorated prior to student commencement.

The Power of the Lived Experience in Disability Justice Work

"Nothing about us, without us"—though this statement has been associated with numerous lived experiences groups, the roots of this expression lie in work with people with disabilities. For most of their lives, people with disabilities have had other people dictate how they act, use their voice, engage in society, and choose services. Because of this, lived experience movements for people with disabilities have demanded that no policy, action, service, intervention, or choice be made without their explicit input. To do otherwise is to repeat patterns of patriarchy and paternalism toward this group.

This idea extends into work in disability justice in social work education. Just as lived experience models have become paramount for other marginalized groups, so must it for disability justice. Though self-disclosure should be a choice and never a dictation, Kiesel et al. (2018) argue that faculty with disabilities in social work should be recognized for their scholarly endeavors and supported in their ability to achieve promotion and tenure. Brown and Leigh (2018) devote considerable time discussing the lack of disability in faculty as a form of diversity in schools of social work. Advocates and co-conspirators of people with disabilities must feel empowered to support their colleagues and assist in negating the stigma of having a disability.

Careful steps must be taken to engage the lived experience in disability justice and social work education. As Knapp (2021) so aptly writes, we must be careful to avoid "inspiration porn." Knapp wrote this in relation to the Winter Paralympic Games, where athletes with disabilities were put on high pedestals for having a disability and for being a top-notch athlete. Paralympians want to be celebrated for being at the top of their game, just like any professional athlete would. Their disability does not define them, and it should not be the source of wonder and awe when being written about. This risk can run true in the lived experience model in disability justice in social work education. We can easily invite people with a lived experience to "share their story of hope and inspiration," which in turn further marginalizes and devalues their humanity.

Voronka and Grant (2022) write of one model to avoid this risk—co-facilitation and co-creation of the disability justice curriculum. Inviting guest speakers into the classroom to share their stories reinforces the power differentials that can lead social work students to focus on the problem and not the solution. People with disabilities must assist in creating the curriculum related to disability justice, either through advisory work or in faculty who are themselves open about their disability. Schools of social work can partner with local independent living centers and centers for diversity excellence to create their curriculums in disability studies. As Roulstone (2012) points out, most research and academic writing on people with disabilities is performed by nondisabled people. Just as schools of social work have advanced the diversity of voices in pedagogy, so must this happen in curriculum addressing disability justice.

As Dupre (2012) points out, schools of social work must engage with a culture of disability. Social work schools must create opportunities to embrace the diversity of people with disabilities and work to learn their norms, ways, and practices. The voice of people with disabilities must be an active one in schools of social work. The *Curricular Resource* guide from CSWE Center for Diversity and Social & Economic Justice discussed earlier in this chapter is an excellent tool for this work. Through careful study and implementation of its competency suggestions, work can be done to bring disability justice squarely into social work education.

Conclusions and Future Implications

Key to implementation of disability justice in social work education is *praxis*, or theory into action. Schools of social work must embody the principles that the beginning social worker learns best by critical thinking and by doing. An infused curriculum model that teaches all aspects of work to people with disabilities must be created. This includes a focus on the history of work with this population, social work's co-option of societal norms and attitudes toward people with disabilities, policies that have both opened and closed doors for this population, research that has created success for people with disabilities and that has failed them, and human development models that focused on both the challenges and strengths of this group. Central to this work is direct experience and exposure to people with disabilities, not as people to be gawked at and wondered over, but as human beings who experience joys, challenges, successes, and failures like all of us. This chapter began with the truth that all human beings could become a person with a disability in our lifetime, and this common frame speaks to the humanity of bringing disability justice to social work education. There must be a sense of safety and empathy for people in schools of social work to share their own lived experiences in this space, and to be embraced in ways we are aiming to do with all marginalized and oppressed groups. We must examine our own values and beliefs about what living with a disability means, and we must be open to examining our bias and misperceptions. These align with our core values and professional ethics. If schools of social work truly aim to be anti-oppressive, anti-racist, and social justice-driven, disability justice must be at the core of the praxis in which we engage. The intersectional aspect of living with a disability demands this.

Reflection Questions

1. What are your attitudes, beliefs, and values toward people with disabilities? Are they a marginalized group? Do schools of social work have a responsibility to teach disability justice?
2. What are some of the barriers to implementing a disability justice framework in social work education? How do we overcome these barriers?
3. Should people with a disability disclose their identity? What are the advantages? What are the disadvantages to doing so?
4. How do schools of social work break down barriers related to Universal Design Learning and become the apex of this model?

Appendix 1: Key Components of a Disability Justice Curriculum

References

Ben-Moshe, L. (2020). *Decarcerating disability*. University of Minnesota.
Brown, N., & Leigh, J. (2018). Ableism in academia: Where are the disabled and ill academics? *Disability & Society, 33*(6), 985–989. https://doi.org/10.1080/09687599.2018.1455627
Cheatham, L. P., Abell, N., & Kim, H. (2015). Development and validation of the social worker's attitudes toward disability scale. *Journal of Social Work Education, 51*(2), 379–397. https://doi.org/10.1080/10437797.2015.1012939
Council on Social Work Education (CSWE). (2018). Disability-competent care curriculum workgroup. Curricular resources on issues of disability and disability-competent care diversity and justice supplement. https://www.cswe.org/CSWE/media/Diversity-Center/Curricular-Resource-on-Issues-of-Disability-and-Disability-Competent-Care-11_6_18-FINAL.pdf
Cox, D., Cleak, H., Bhathal, A., & Brophy, L. (2021). Theoretical frameworks in social work education: A scoping review. *Social Work Education, 40*(1), 18–43. https://doi.org/10.1080/02615479.2020.1745172

CSWE. (2022a). 2022 educational policy and accreditation standards. Author. Retrieved from https://www.cswe.org/getmedia/94471c42-13b8-493b-9041-b30f48533d64/2022-EPAS.pdf
CSWE. (2022b). 2022 EPAS interpretation guide: For Baccalaureate and Master's Social Work programs (Version 12.22). Author. Retrieved from https://www.cswe.org/getmedia/a09930d0-bf14-4a47-8470-fba545ecd44a/2022-EPAS-Interpretation-Guide-v-12-2022.pdf
Dewane, C. J. (2006). Use of self: A primer revisited. *Clinical Social Work Journal, 34*(4), 543–558. https://doi.org/10.1007/s10615-005-0021-5
Dupré, M. (2012). Disability culture and cultural competency in social work. *Social Work Education, 31*(2), 168–183. https://doi.org/10.1080/02615479.2012.644945
Galambos, C. M. (2004). Social work practice with people with disabilities: Are we doing enough? *Health & Social Work, 29*(3), 163–165. https://doi.org/10.1093/hsw/29.3.163
Glison, S. F., & DePoy, E. (2002). Theoretical approaches to disability content in social work education. *Journal of Social Work Education, 38*(1), 153–165. https://doi.org/10.1080/10437797.2002.10779088
Kattari, S. K., Ingarfield, L., Hanna, M., McQueen, J., & Ross, K. (2020). Uncovering issues of ableism in social work education: A disability needs assessment. *Social Work Education, 39*(5), 599–616. https://doi.org/10.1080/02615479.2019.1699526
Kaushik, A. (2017). Use of self in social work: Rhetoric or reality. *Journal of Social Work Values & Ethics, 14*(1), 21–29.
Kiesel, L. R., DeZelar, S., & Lightfoot, E. (2018). Challenges, barriers, and opportunities: Social workers with disabilities and experiences in field education. *Journal of Social Work Education, 54*(4), 696–708. https://doi.org/10.1080/10437797.2018.1507365
Kimball, E. W., Wells, R. S., Ostiguy, B. J., Manly, C. A., & Lauterbach, A. A. (2016). Students with disabilities in higher education: A review of the literature and an agenda for future research. In M. Paulsen (Ed.), *Higher education: Handbook of theory and research* (Vol. 31). Springer. https://doi.org/10.1007/978-3-319-26829-3_3
Knapp, G. (2021, September 5). 'Inspiration Porn': Paralympians know it when they see it. *New York Times, CLXX*(59172), 24. http://proxy.library.nyu.edu/login?qurl=https%3A%2F%2Fwww.proquest.com%2Fnewspapers%2Fseptember-5-2021-page-24%2Fdocview%2F2580792877%2Fse-2%3Faccountid%3D12768
Kristen, F. B., & Krcek, T. E. (2012). The integration of disability content into social work education: An examination of infused and dedicated models. *Advances in Social Work, 13*(3), 633–647.
Laws, J., Parish, S. L., Scheyett, A. M., & Egan, C. (2010). Preparation of social workers to support people with developmental disabilities. *Journal of Teaching in Social Work, 30*(3), 317–333. https://doi.org/10.1080/08841233.2010.497128
Mackelprang, R. W., & Salsgiver, R. O. (2015). *Disability: A diversity model approach in human service practice* (3rd ed.). Lyceum.
Morgaine, K., & Capous-Desyllas, M. (2023). *Anti-oppressive social work practice: Putting theory into action (revised 2nd edition).* Cognella.
Moyle, J. (2016). Including disability in the social work core curriculum: A compelling argument. *Australian Social Work, 69*(4), 503–511. https://doi.org/10.1080/0312407X.2016.1216575
National Association of Social Workers. (2021). Code of ethics of the National Association of Social Workers. Retrieved from April 30, 2023, from https://www.socialworkers.org/About/Ethics/Code-of-Ethics/Code-of-Ethics-English/Social-Workers-Ethical-Responsibilities-to-Clients
Ogden, L., McAllister, C., & Neely-Barnes, S. (2017). Assessment of integration of disability content into social work education. *Journal of Social Work in Disability & Rehabilitation, 16*(3–4), 361–376. https://doi.org/10.1080/1536710X.2017.1392394
Roulstone, A. (2012). 'Stuck in the middle with you': Towards enabling social work with disabled people. *Social Work Education, 31*(2), 142–154. https://doi.org/10.1080/02615479.2012.644942

Sherwood, K. L., & Kattari, S. K. (2023). Reducing ableism in social work education through universal design for learning and policy. *Journal of Social Work Education, 59*(1), 119–132. https://doi.org/10.1080/10437797.2021.1997686

Slayter, E., & Johnson, L., Eds. (2022). Social work practice and the disability community: An intersectional anti-oppressive approach. Open Social Work Education. https://disabilitysocialwork.pressbooks.com

Slayter, E. M., Kattari, S. K., Yakas, L., Singh, R. C. B., Goulden, A., Taylor, S., Wernick, L. J., Simmons, L. D., & Prince, D. (2022). Beyond ramps, curb cuts, and captions: A call for disability justice in social work. *Social Work, 68*(1), 89–92. https://doi.org/10.1093/sw/swac045

Taylor, D. M. (2018). *Americans with disabilities: 2014, Current Population Reports, 70–152, U.S. Census Bureau*. Author.

Voronka, J., & Grant, J. (2022). Service user storytelling in social work education: Goals, constraints, strategies, and risks. *Social Work Education, 41*(5), 977–992. https://doi.org/10.1080/02615479.2021.1908251

Chapter 11
Anti-oppressive Practice in Community-Based Mental Health: Examining Current Research and Clinical Implications

Eboni Wooley

Introduction

There has been a growing movement in the social work profession to fight against systematic oppression; however, this is not a new challenge. Historically, oppressed societies can be traced back to as early as the 1600s with the start of colonization. The "discovery" of the new world resulted in inequalities brought against the Indigenous population (Burnette & Figley, 2017). Similarly, from the beginning of the slave trade to the well-documented bloodshed that occurred in 1965 on Alabama's Edmund Pettus Bridge, Black men and women have fought to be liberated from the shackles of oppression. This author grew up in Alabama, where the unsettled dust of Jim Crow laws still lingers. These prolific historical events eerily foreshadowed the more recent merciless killing of George Floyd, where calls from around the nation intensified for anti-oppressive policing. The revolutionary leader of the civil rights movement, Dr. Martin Luther King Jr., had the foresight to proclaim that freedom would not be merely given but demanded by the subjugated. He fervently stated that "oppressed people cannot remain oppressed forever. The yearning for freedom eventually manifests itself" (King, 1994, p. 4).

The primary goal of oppression can be found in its Latin root, *opprimere*. *Opprimere* means to suffocate, to crush, to worry, or to depress (Merriam-Webster, n.d.). The interconnection between poverty and oppression is overt. Poverty is the partial or general deprivation of basic human and social rights, often displayed in

E. Wooley (✉)
Silver School of Social Work, New York University, New York, NY, USA
e-mail: edw303@nyu.edu

C. Tosone et al. (eds.), *Reframing Social Work with an Anti-Oppressive Lens*, Essential Clinical Social Work Series,
https://doi.org/10.1007/978-3-031-91391-4_11

the inadequacy of education, housing, job opportunities, and healthcare (Creamer, 2020). Despite its collective wealth, the United States has one of the highest rates of poverty in the developed world (Hodgkinson et al., 2017). The burden of poverty falls disproportionately on the Black, Indigenous, and People of Color (BIPOC) community (Creamer, 2020). Poverty does not merely encompass being of low socioeconomic means. It impacts the individual's economic, physical health, and mental well-being, in addition to experiencing social exclusion based on systemic policies, practices, and behaviors (Beech et al., 2021).

An individual's mental health is formed by their social, environmental, and economic conditions in which they were born into, grow, work, and age. Poverty is a key determinant of a child's social and behavioral development, which in turn shapes their mental health as an adult (Francis et al., 2018; Knifton & Inglis, 2020). Even though people living in poverty have an increased risk for mental health issues, they are more likely to experience barriers when seeking treatment, due to stigma, cost, and access (Francis et al., 2018; Knifton & Inglis, 2020). In the United States, community-based mental health centers were developed by the federal government to aid in addressing these barriers to improve care in under-resourced communities. These agencies serve as "one-stop shops," where clients can receive help in accessing community resources, psychotherapy, and medication management at low to no cost (Garland et al., 2013). Community-based mental health centers primarily serve individuals who have Medicaid, a federal-funded health insurance for low-income individuals where the eligible limit for a single-person household is $14,580 per year (Daniel-Robinson & Moore, 2019).

As the number of community-based mental health clinics in our country continues to grow, mental health services are becoming more accessible, especially in underserved areas (Expanding Community-Based Mental Health Services and Support, 2021). Despite the increased access, few members of underserved communities receive high-quality mental health service (Hodgkinson et al., 2017). A 2023 study found that structural inequity, like poverty, is often ignored or minimized by the clinician in psychotherapy (Ballo & Tribe, 2023). Disregarding the catastrophic impact of poverty is a form of oppression. To address this barrier in treatment, we must take an anti-oppressive approach.

Anti-oppressive practice (AOP) is a theory and an approach that focuses on how larger systems create and protect the power that privileged groups have while also creating, maintaining, and upholding burdensome and unequitable conditions for marginalized communities (Baines, 2017). Utilizing an AOP framework in community-based mental health centers can improve the quality of care that individuals of lower socioeconomic stratum receive by centering their experience to help psychotherapy be more effective and beneficial. By focusing on how poverty has and continues to influence their lives, the clinician can aid the client in fostering resilience in coping with the stressors caused by poverty. To do so, we must take a deeper look at the intersectionality of poverty and its effects on mental health.

Intersectionality of Poverty and Its Effects on Mental Health

The mental health effects of poverty are comprehensive because it intersects with all other social determinants of health, including race/ethnicity, gender, education, community conditions, immigration status, access to healthcare, and the built environment, which encompasses the infrastructure, transportation structures, and distribution systems in which we live (Beech et al., 2021). To understand how poverty affects one's mental health, we must examine the immense evidence from a wide range of interdisciplinary studies that demonstrate a causal relationship between poverty and mental health (Ridley et al., 2020). While the intersection of poverty and mental health is garnering increased awareness, the following section will focus on the ways in which mental health of an individual is impacted by being born into, growing up, working, living, and aging while impoverished.

Born into Poverty

Experiencing poverty during one's pregnancy places one at a greater risk of multiple health issues, including mental distress. For example, inconsistent income, reliance on government programs, housing insecurity, food insecurity, and anxiety about paying bills are more likely to be found in childbearing people suffering from poverty (Doser, 2022). This increased stress leads to increased levels of cortisol, the primary stress hormone, which triggers one's fight or flight response. In triggering this response, it alters one's immune system, reproductive system, and growth process (Chu et al., 2023). Those experiencing consistent higher cortisol levels during pregnancy can trigger preterm birth, which is correlated with low birth weight. High cortisol levels can also damage a fetus' cortisol regulation system, making them at greater risk for toxic stress behaviors later in life that can trigger emotional distress. (Doser, 2022).

The increased strain on a childbearing person not only impacts the prenatal stage but the postpartum period as well. While the infant mortality rate in the United States has declined, it is still higher than most developed countries. The United States has the highest rates of death at term births, which are categorized as the loss of life at 37 weeks or higher. This stage of the pregnancy is considered "a period of heterogeneous risk." Studies have found that term deaths tend to occur in the post neonatal period, with assaults, accidents, and sudden infant death syndrome being the leading causes (Reddy et al., 2011). Deaths during this period are more likely to be associated with systemic socio-environmental factors such as housing conditions, infant sleep environment, access to healthcare, nutrition, and social services (Mohamoud et al., 2019).

Additionally, impoverished childbearing people are at greater risk of developing postpartum depression. If left untreated, postpartum depression is one of the most prevalent and debilitating perinatal mood disorders, if left untreated. While postpartum depression is a well-studied disorder, research on how this disorder impacts oppressed communities is lacking (Keefe et al., 2018). The prevalence rates of postpartum depression, which include mothers of diverse backgrounds, indicate that approximately 12% of White mothers will develop postpartum depression (Gaynes et al., 2005) and mothers of color will have more than triple the likelihood of developing postpartum depression at 38% (CDC, 2008). A 2015 study found that low-income women who live in urban areas have higher levels of depressive symptoms and post-traumatic stress disorder than their counterparts who were of higher socioeconomic means (Garfeild et al., 2015). When an infant is born into poverty, it can have a devastating impact on their childhood development beyond infancy.

Growing Up in Poverty

While children under the age of 18 account for only one-fourth of the US population, they are disproportionately impoverished. Approximately 16 million children live in families that have incomes below the federal poverty line (National Poverty Center, 2016). Of the 16 million children, 1.5 million families live in extreme poverty, defined as living on $2.00 or less per day, per family member (Ekono et al., 2016), at 50% below the federal poverty level (Beeber et al., 2014), or in a neighborhood where 40% or more of residents live below the federal poverty level (Ludwig et al., 2012). While most impoverished children are White, children from marginalized communities are disproportionately affected by poverty, particularly African American, American Indian, and Hispanic children (Jiang et al., 2015). African American and Hispanic children were three times more likely than White and Asian children to be poor, creating a greater possibility for minority children to suffer from behavioral problems.

Poverty has the potential to weaken the parent/child relationship and diminish the quality of parenting, which, along with environmental stressors, elevates the risk of child behavioral problems (Mary et al., 2017). These unmet social needs manifest into social-emotional difficulties that directly influence the way the child functions. Poverty in childhood is associated with lower school performance, poor cognitive, defiant behavior, attention-related outcomes, and higher rates of delinquency, anxiety, and depression disorders (Garland et al., 2013). However, the child's poor performance in school is generally blamed solely on the child's inability to follow "social norms" and not looked at as a direct result of poverty, despite the numerous studies that show that children who are impoverished are disadvantaged. Research suggests that children of low socioeconomic means are 2–4 times more likely to develop disruptive behavior disorders compared to children of a higher socioeconomic stratum (Gresl et al., 2016), which translates into approximately 30% of children in low-income communities evincing serious behavioral problems (Mary et al., 2017). Children who display socio-environmental problems are placed at a greater risk of suffering from emotional distress as adolescents.

Poverty can impact the quality of life for adolescents and their ability to adjust socially. Research suggests that adolescents who have an awareness of parental financial difficulties noted an increased risk for depression in adolescent girls, and adolescent boys were more likely to drink to the point of intoxication (Dashiff et al., 2009). This recognition of their family's economic hardship has also been associated with a reported sense of helplessness and feelings of shame and inferiority. Also, adolescents from low socioeconomic environments have a higher risk for teen suicide (Hoffmann et al., 2020), and exposure to violence experienced by adolescents living in impoverished neighborhoods has been associated with increased depressive symptoms, anxiety, and externalizing problem behaviors like criminal offending (Dashiff et al., 2009). Whether rapid or gradual, poverty creates a vulnerability during the major adolescent life changes that influence the working and living conditions they experience as adults.

Working and Living in Poverty

Adulthood represents the period in one's life where they are meant to reach their full physical and intellectual maturity. However, research suggests that poverty stunts an individual's ability to function and thrive. One study found evidence that shows poverty imposes a psychological burden so significant that impoverished individuals are left with little mental "bandwidth," showing that the constant stress from the anxiety of having little money to pay bills, suffering from food insecurity, living in unsuitable housing conditions, and experiencing the trauma of distressed neighborhoods leaves individuals with little cognitive function (Mani et al., 2013). This limited cognitive capacity makes it more difficult for the individual to make informed decisions that could benefit them and their families. Manhica et al. found that individuals who experience poverty are more likely to engage in drug use and drug-related crimes. While there have been no findings that can unmistakably say that poverty causes substance use disorders, the "working poor" have high levels of substance abuse (2021).

The relationship between poverty and the labor market is complex. Stable, high-paying wages and full-time employment can keep most individuals out of poverty. However, the stagnation of wages at the lower tier of the US labor market has led to many Americans being considered the working poor. Individuals who spend more than 27 weeks working or looking for work yet still fall below the poverty line are categorized as the working poor (Llosa et al., 2022).

According to the US Bureau of Labor Statistics, roughly 9.5 million individuals fall under the working poor guidelines. Women were found to be more likely than men to be among the working poor. Blacks and Hispanics are also much more likely than Whites and Asians to be among the working poor (2020). This only increases the risk of dealing with emotional distress for those who are barely able to get by, despite working regularly. A Gallup study found that the declining mental health of poor workers cost the US 4.8 billion dollars a year due to unplanned days off which impact productivity (Witters & Agrawal, 2022). Unstable employment leads to unstable wages which directly affects the housing options of the impoverished.

Employment and housing insecurity create a form of double precarity for under-resourced individuals. While homelessness is the most visible form of housing insecurity, millions of Americans live in unstable housing conditions. In 2020, at the height of the COVID-19 pandemic, 30–40 million people were at risk of losing their housing (Benfer et al., 2020). Evictions are now increasing and have surpassed pre-pandemic levels significantly (The State of the Nation's Housing, 2022). Housing assistance through the government is found at both the federal and state levels, to address housing affordability among the impoverished.

However, public housing has been associated with a wide range of health conditions, including respiratory infections, asthma, lead poisoning, injuries, and negative mental health outcomes. One study found that people who experienced housing instability were considerably more likely to have experienced anxiety attacks and other symptoms of emotional distress (Kim & Burgard, 2022). Additionally, research found that of impoverished people dealing with housing insecurity, 28% reported currently battling depression, 18% noted increasing substance use, and 8% reported suicidal ideation. This increasing burden of poverty does not dwindle throughout adulthood but only exacerbates as the individual ages.

Aging in Poverty

Aging is understood as the natural process of a decline in function of the senses and activities of daily life and increased susceptibility to disease, frailty, or disability (The National Institute on Aging, n.d.). However, aging only places one at a greater risk for staying in or falling into poverty. According to the US Census Bureau data, poverty among Americans over the age of 65 is the group that has seen an increase. Poverty rates rose from 8.9% in 2020 to 10.3% in 2021, totaling 6 million, remaining at one of the highest levels in the developed world (2022). The elderly who fall within marginalized groups are at an even higher risk of poverty. Four million elderly women are living at or below poverty, in comparison to the 2.8 million men. Additionally, the Supplemental Poverty Measure shows that Black, Hispanic, and Native American women are almost two times more likely to live in poverty than older White women (Older Women and Poverty, 2018).

Due to the increased vulnerability, with one's declining physical health impacting their mental health, being impoverished only increases the risk factors for emotional distress. One research study among older adults found evidence that those suffering from economic hardships were more likely to be depressed compared to older adults with fewer economic hardships (Spruha et al., 2017). There are several pathways that can explain why impoverished elderly individuals are at a higher risk of suffering from mental distress, one pathway being their limited mobility, making them more dependent on local services and relying on local sources of social support. Poor neighborhoods are more likely to lack the supportive social services and social engagement, such as community centers (White et al., 2009).

Another pathway to consider is that elders who live in impoverished neighborhoods are exposed to more stressful life events, such as direct events of victimization and witnessing violence (Spruha et al., 2017). These stressful life experiences have been directly connected to depression among older adults (Arean et al., 2010) due to fear and stress being known causes of depression. Lower levels of social cohesion, green space, and walkability and higher levels of crime and physical disorder have all been shown to increase the risk of depression in general and among older adults (Spruha et al., 2017).

Additionally, suicide among the elderly population is a growing concern. While older adults are around 12% of the population, they make up about 18% of reported suicides. One study found that impoverished elderly had a higher risk of suicide than those with a high income in the same age group (Choi et al., 2019). With increasing rates of depression and suicide, this continues to bring into question whether Medicare and Social Security are enough to meet the needs of one of its most vulnerable populations, the elderly (Creamer et al., 2022).

Despite findings that highlight the intersectionality of poverty and poor mental health outcomes, there are few studies that focus on how to address poverty in psychotherapy. These findings support the theory of social causation, which posits that there is an inverse relationship between poverty level and mental health; parents and children who are within the lowest income levels are at the highest risk for adverse mental health outcomes. This increased emotional distress can lead individuals to fall into an even lower socioeconomic stratum and unable to escape property (Mary et al., 2017).

Additionally, emerging research has shown that the impact of poverty is not just felt by the individual but possibly by generations to come. This is due to the exposure to stressors changing one's DNA, which has the potential to cause epigenetic alterations across generations (Hodgkinson et al., 2017). By highlighting the weathering effects of poverty and how it impacts nearly every facet of an impoverished individual's life is how we, as social workers, can take a step toward facilitating change. Approaching treatment with an anti-oppressive lens could strengthen the treatment outcomes for impoverished individuals by acknowledging their experience and empowering them to combat their emotional distress. Applying an AOP framework can be a valuable approach in psychotherapy with impoverished clients.

Anti-oppressive Practice in Psychotherapy

For under-resourced individuals, community-based mental health clinics are often the only available specialty treatment in their community, thereby making community-based mental health clinics the backbone of mental healthcare in low-income communities (Cummings et al., 2017). Currently, evidence-based practices are standard in most mental healthcare settings. Evidence-based practices are interventions that through extensive research have proven to assist clients in achieving their desired treatment goals (van Os et al., 2019). Taking into consideration the number of studies that have shown its ability to be effective with a wide range of mental disorders, cognitive behavioral therapy (CBT) is arguably the gold standard in psychotherapy (David et al., 2018). CBT teaches individuals to challenge their own thoughts and assumptions, as well as to change their emotions and behaviors.

CBT has shown that it can be effective when working with impoverished populations. Spiegel et al. found that utilizing CBT when working with families living in a homeless shelter helped reduce the trauma-related symptoms and the externalizing behaviors that were found in children (2022). However, despite its many strengths, CBT has been criticized by critical social theorists for its individualistic approach to treatment, which ignores forms of structural oppression (Payne et al., 2016). This can be limiting especially when working with impoverished clients who have been impacted by systemic oppression and unequal power dynamics (Windsor et al., 2015). Applying an AOP approach when using CBT with under-resourced clients can strengthen its effectiveness by exploring the impact of oppression on their mental health.

AOP focuses on how the larger system creates and protects the privilege and power that majority groups have while also creating, maintaining, and upholding the unequitable conditions for marginalized groups (Baines, 2017). This multi-disciplined theoretical framework draws on several different theories, including antiracism, decolonization, and feminist theory to assist in deepening one's understanding of the world and encourage critical thinking (Centre for Innovation in Campus Mental Health, n.d.). AOP in psychotherapy seeks to take a wider view of a client's presenting problem by exploring how structures and systems influence emotional distress. Therefore, when applying AOP to an intervention like CBT, the clinician is grounded in a nonjudgmental, strength-based, critical, reflective, and empowering philosophy that promotes equity (Rubin, 2020).

For the clinician to do this effectively, they must build critical consciousness by uniting reflection and action. Being critically conscious requires us to reflect on our practice and ask probing questions about how we impact those around us, particularly our relationship with clients, and then by taking action to improve our practice. By building one's critical consciousness, the clinician could incorporate the five principles of AOP into CBT or other evidence-based practices in a manner that is beneficial to the client. Table 11.1 briefly discusses the five principles of AOP (Healy, 2014) and provides tangible steps on how to incorporate them into psychotherapy with impoverished clients. The following action steps are based on the author's work in a community-based mental health setting.

The therapeutic alliance between the clinician and the client is a crucial element to the effectiveness of AOP. However, this alliance exists in the context of the social structures that surround it. This shift toward AOP requires us to move beyond a "one-size-fits-all" approach (Norcross & Wampold, 2018). The influence of poverty on one's mental health requires the attention of the clinician working with those of lower socioeconomic stratum, to be beneficial to the client. This form of social oppression is intertwined in their presenting problems and, if not addressed, could

Table 11.1 Applying AOP in psychotherapy with impoverished clients

AOP practice principles (Healy, 2014)	Action steps
Critical reflection on self in practice: Acknowledging the unequal power dynamic that exists between the clinician and the client to avoid recreating oppressive social relations in the therapeutic relationship	1. Asking one's self-reflective-based questions. For instance, "in what way does my role as a clinician create a position of privilege?" and "how does my own financial history influence my work with impoverished clients?" 2. Reflecting on one's social location, including both areas of privilege and oppression. Asking oneself, "in what areas of my life have I been oppressed and/or witnessed oppression?" and "how does this show up in my work?"
Critical assessment of service users' experiences of oppression: Understanding the diversity and intersectionality of oppression in the lives of our clients. Exploring how personal, cultural, and structural experiences each affect individuals' problems and the access they have to solutions	1. Critically analyze how race, gender, and class intersect in the client's life. For instance, "how do you believe race/gender influence your symptoms of depression?" this forms the groundwork to make connections toward macro level oppression 2. Understand how dialogue and language has been used as a tool to further oppress. It is important to be mindful of the language used when discussing their problems (e.g., avoiding terms such as "decompensating" or "lacking insight")
Empowering service users: Empowering clients on both an individual and institutional levels is the central theme of AOP. This process allows the client to grasp the structural influence of their emotional distress and use this to enhance change	1. Externalizing your client's presenting problems and/or symptoms of emotional distress. For instance, this can be achieved by reframing poverty as something to combat rather than personalizing it. In response to a client saying, "I can't properly provide for my family. I'm useless," perhaps try responding with "how does your financial situation change the way you view your self-worth?" 2. Clinicians promote and advocate for change at the institutional (agency, organization) level to enhance client control. For example, this can be achieved by providing psychoeducation to clients on their diagnosis and offering a detailed rationale for the proposed intervention
Working in partnership: The therapeutic relationship should be a collaborative effort while positioning the client as the expert of their own lives	1. As much as possible, the client should be included in the decision-making process. For instance, ensuring that the client's stated needs are a part of their treatment plan/goals 2. The relationship between the clinician and client is equitable and seeks to understand the structural factors, like poverty, that contribute to the individual's lived experience and mental health. For instance, asking the client, "how have your unsuccessful attempts to find stable housing impacted your symptoms of anxiety?"
Minimal intervention: Intervening in the least intrusive way possible in efforts to reduce the chances of furthering the oppression of a client. Emphasizing early intervention and preventive services to reduce the chances of further social control	1. The goal of AOP is not to teach clients how to learn to adjust to oppression; rather it seeks to understand the client's social reality and empower them. For instance, giving direct advice should be avoided as much as possible, due to the possibility of hindering growth 2. The clinician should intervene in a client's life in the least intrusive manner possible. For instance, honoring the client's goals while using a voluntary and short-term intervention model

lead to more harm. Based on the table above, this author will use a case study to demonstrate how to apply an AOP approach while using CBT when working with a client of lower socioeconomic stratum.

Case Study

Client History

Camila[1] was a 43-year-old married woman of Puerto Rican descent who sought treatment at her local community-based mental health center. Camila was encouraged to seek treatment from Child Protective Services, after having an active case with the agency, due to educational neglect. She is the mother of two children, a 17-year-old daughter and an 8-year-old son. Her daughter rarely attended school, and her son, who suffers from autism, was not enrolled in school at all. At her initial intake, Camila reported that she has had a long history of struggling with emotional distress and had been diagnosed with persistent depression disorder and bipolar II disorder in the past. She revealed that she has been hospitalized at least three times since her teenage years. Camila presented with a depressed mood, feelings of hopelessness, low energy, and little interest in former hobbies and did not engage in proper hygiene-related activities (e.g., taking showers, brushing teeth). Also, she described having periods of hypomania, where she suffered from racing thoughts, a decreased need for sleep, hypersexuality, and irritability. After her intake assessment, Camila was diagnosed with bipolar II disorder.

At the onset of treatment, Camila expressed that "something was always wrong" with her mental health since she "could remember." She reported that she was born into an impoverished family. She reported that her mom and dad migrated from Puerto Rico with her two older siblings when her mother was pregnant with her "in hopes for a better life." Camila expressed that her mom and dad worked several jobs, but they had little money to meet their basic needs. She reported that due to her parents' hectic work schedule, she was not able to properly bond with them. Camila expressed that she believes the stress of poverty and isolation from their support system in Puerto Rico led to the constant verbal and physical fights between her parents.

Camila reported that unlike her siblings, she found little solace in education. She reported performing poorly in school, leading to her placement in special education classes. She often felt anxious in school due to living in a neighborhood that had high rates of community violence. As a result of her community's high crime rate, Camila spent most of her time isolated at home. Later in treatment, she revealed that she suffered sexual abuse during her childhood and adolescent years from a

[1] This is a composite case example. The names have been changed to protect the identities of the clients.

neighbor that her parents trusted to watch her. She stated "now that I know what depression is, I know I was extremely depressed then too." She attempted to end her life at the age of 16, which led to her first inpatient hospitalization.

After graduating from high school, Camila married her husband, and they went on to have two children. Despite her best efforts, they did not make enough money to support their family. She worked at a grocery store, her husband worked as a janitor at a school, and they had to live in various shelters and other forms of low-income housing. The stress from having to rely on governmental agencies to provide aid only "made me more depressed." She noted that her depression symptoms became so severe that she was let go from her job due to missing too many days. The financial burden only got worse after losing her job, and her mental health continued to decline, causing further strain between she and her family. Her children appeared to be struggling emotionally as well, leading to behavioral problems. Camila reported that they refused to go to school and she "didn't have the strength to fight with them."

Due to her bipolar II disorder, Camila was recommended for weekly psychotherapy sessions and medication management services. After conducting her own research online prior to starting therapy, she expressed interest in CBT being her intervention of choice. This author explored with Camila the possibility of adding an additional framework to the standard CBT approach. After providing psychoeducation on the various approaches, including AOP, trauma focused and mindfulness based, Camila believed that AOP would be the most beneficial to her treatment. At several points throughout treatment, this author explored if Camila felt that AOP-CBT was working effectively. This stood as an ongoing assessment of the modality and as a reminder that Camila was in control of the direction of her treatment.

Critical Reflection on Self in Practice

In order to provide an adequate AOP approach, the clinician must critically reflect on their personal bias and role in practice. In preparation for Camila's treatment, this author reflected on their views on poverty, parents with child protective services involvement, and systemic oppression. Using journaling as a tool, this author engaged in reflection throughout the course of treatment. For instance, asking self-reflective questions such as "What are my preconceived beliefs about people suffering from poverty? How many of those views are rooted in classism?" Additionally, this author explored the unequal power dynamic that exists in treatment between clinician and Camila as the client. This led to the exploration of both her negative and positive experiences with social services. Camila expressed always entering treatment defensively, due to past experiences where she felt shamed for "being a bad mother." Using this and other feelings of being judged, this author moved into the next principle of an AOP approach, exploring Camila's experiences with oppression.

Critical Assessment of Service Users' Experiences of Oppression

At the onset of treatment, Camila would often express feeling as though she is a failure and hopeless. A traditional CBT approach would work with Camila to restructure her thoughts using cognitive restructuring. This CBT technique assumes that individuals are engaging in irrational thinking and therapy can be used to change these automatic thoughts into more rational thoughts. However, clinicians working with marginalized populations should be mindful of how cognitive restructuring could cause further harm. As a result of the oppression marginalized communities have faced, the "negative" thought patterns are not irrational but based on their lived experiences. For instance, Camila expressed that her symptoms are rooted in her beliefs that she is a bad mom and wife who cannot not properly take care of her children and her husband. In this instance, the author could ask Camila about incidents where she has felt as though she has been a good mom and wife and overall beneficial to her family. While it might be helpful to develop strategies to combat these negative thought patterns, the source of the problem is unchallenged. This traditional approach neglects the larger structural issues that are impacting Camila and creating the conditions for her bipolar disorder.

During the course of treatment with Camila, this author explored the source of her negative thoughts. Camila expressed that when she first got married and had children, she was determined to break the cycle of poverty. She worked long hours, sometimes multiple jobs to support her family, but they remained under or at the poverty level. Camila discussed how her bond with her children was fractured due to frequent and extended work hours. When she sought various social services and resources for help, Camila often left feeling embarrassed and berated. Camila noted one incident in which her son's doctor questioned her about taking proper care of her children because she struggled to attend appointments to further assess his autism. She attempted to explain how she could not afford to take off work to bring him but was quickly dismissed and threatened with a child protective service call.

In such cases as these, where the client feels as though they were oppressed, clinicians should explicitly validate these feelings of mistreatment. Taking the traditional CBT framework of questioning the validity of the client's claims could be looked at as a microaggression that can contribute to and exacerbate the client's experiences of shame and mistrust and hinder the therapeutic bond. Adding the AOP approach, this author validated the painful emotions that Camila experienced during these interactions and acknowledged that we live in a society where these types of hurtful incidents occur.

Empowering Service Users

Additionally, while validating Camila's experience, the primary goal of an AOP approach is to empower the client. This was achieved by reframing what the experience meant to Camila. Cognitive restructuring can address the biases of living in an oppressive society, without challenging the client on perceived discrimination. For example, in the incident with the doctor, this author began by validating those emotions that came up when she felt judged or discriminated against. Her automatic thoughts were "I am a bad mother and wife because I can't provide for my family" and "everyone just looks at me as poor." In treatment, this author focused on the internalization of her financial means by asking her questions that focused on her self-worth. For example, "What evidence do you have that supports that you do not provide for your family?" Camila was able to find solace in recently finding employment and cooking for her family and also acknowledging that her husband often praised Camila for how hard she worked for the family, despite her struggles with bipolar II disorder.

The goal of this questioning was to help Camila start to build a defense against the internalization of the classism that she had experienced. This defense could help her understand that the negative thoughts she has when she is discriminated against are not a reflection of her but rather of systemic oppression. Most importantly, these thoughts were untrue. The response she developed to these negative thought patterns was, "Even though others try to make me feel worthless, I have always provided for my family and my effort is valued." By validating her feelings and exploring the systemic oppression undertones, Camila was able to see that despite her lower socioeconomic position, she was a valuable member of her family and society.

Working in Partnership

In order for most therapeutic interventions to be beneficial, the therapeutic alliance must be strong. In the AOP approach, the therapeutic bond is considered a partnership. The client is expected to be involved in all processes that require decision-making.

This aligns with the values of the community-based mental health clinic where Camila was seeking treatment; the clinic encourages its clinicians to complete a treatment plan which outlines treatment goals and objectives to focus on with the client. Camila expressed wanting to focus on reducing her symptoms of depression first, before further exploring her hypomania symptoms. Additionally, her psychiatrist at the clinic strongly suggested that she combine medication with her psychotherapy treatment. Camila was against using medication due to past experiences of adverse side effects. This author validated and supported her decision. Camila was seen as the primary change agent in her treatment. The role of the author was to help facilitate healing, so Camila could develop skills to problem-solve without the author's assistance.

Minimal Intervention

In order to reduce codependency, the principles of AOP are based on minimal intervention in social services. Psychotherapy is meant to be a tool to offer temporary assistance in reducing emotional distress. The client is not learning to adjust to oppression but to challenge it. For instance, Camila inquired about the possibility of the author advocating to her child protective service worker to receive assistance with childcare. Upon further exploration, Camila admitted that she did not feel confident that if she asked on her own, she would receive the necessary childcare assistance. If someone in a higher position thought she needed it, Camila believed it would validate her. This author validated Camila's anxiety due to her past experiences but also addressed the importance of minimal intervention to help her identify her own strengths. Though it took multiple attempts, Camila was able to successfully advocate for herself to receive childcare assistance. She expressed being extremely proud of herself for being assertive, even when her case worker did not originally want to grant the request. Throughout the remainder of the treatment, Camila was able to develop and work through a list of steps that would assist her in addressing her mental health concerns and empowering herself against oppression.

Reflections and Clinical Implications

Considering the reviewed evidence indicating the link between poverty and increased vulnerability for emotional distress, adapting an AOP approach in psychotherapy is vital. The impact of systemic oppression is felt by every member of our society. While every client comes into treatment with biases, flaws, and preconceived notions, so too does every clinician. Through this author's work with Camila and other clients from similar backgrounds, it has deepened their understanding of the emotional health impact of poverty. While the trauma of being oppressed is a wound that is familiar to the author, the devastation that poverty can cause has led to further reflection on how we can hold both privileges and disadvantages simultaneously.

The following implications for clinical practice are drawn from the review of relevant empirical and clinical literature as well as the author's work in community-based mental health:

1. **Just as race, gender identity, and sexuality should be addressed in a meaningful way in psychotherapy, so too should the socioeconomic position of your clients.** Talking about finances in therapy can be difficult because it reflects larger societal norms of shaming those who have less. However, avoiding this topic can display an indifference to the clients you work with, especially impoverished clients. For instance, a Black male suffering from depression

who has a stable sufficient income will likely have more access to resources and solutions to lower his depression than a Black male who lives under the poverty line. Poverty can seep into every facet of an individual's life, and leaving this topic out is a failure to fully understand the lived reality of the people we work with.

2. **Impoverished individuals could benefit from individually tailored strategies to reduce internalized stigma.** While empowering individuals is a fundamental aspect of AOP, it takes time to reduce the subjective experience of internalized oppression. The clinician should help clients work through specific experiences, emotions, and beliefs but appreciate that internalized stigma can still linger. For instance, while a client could understand and verbalize that living in a shelter does not make them any less of a person, they can still display symptoms of inferiority. The clinician should target the specific emotions (in this example, shame) that may impact an individual's mental health, such as maladaptive coping (e.g., detachment and internalization) and emotional suppression. Collaborate with your client to develop healthier coping skills based on their individual needs, replacing the internalized stigma.
3. **Empowering clients to engage in their communities and build supportive relationships could help in reducing symptoms of emotional distress.** Poverty does not exist in a bubble but is experienced in communities. However, people often feel alone in dealing with the trauma of poverty and could benefit from others' support, especially those that share this burden. While individualized treatment can be extremely beneficial to impoverished clients, community participation is also important. This could mean encouraging clients to join local support groups, becoming peer mentors, and attending informational meetings at organizations that offer supportive services. For instance, in the case of Camila, she saw a significant decline in her symptoms when she joined a local support group for women suffering from bipolar disorder. Building a support system outside of therapy allowed her to see that her insight was valuable to others.
4. **When working with disenfranchised populations, critical self-reflection is not a one step process but an ongoing one.** Psychotherapy with impoverished individuals could possibly be laborious for the clinician, because of being a witness to the injustices their clients are facing. Critical self-reflection can lead to the discovery of unconscious classist biases, unchallenged assumptions, and blind spots. Additionally, feelings of helplessness and hopelessness can emerge when exploring the multifaceted barriers that make it difficult to escape poverty. This author was aware of the pitfalls of projecting these feelings in treatment through countertransference. Therefore, the author engaged in daily acts of self-reflection to process their own areas of discomfort. Through self-reflection the author's feelings of helplessness were tied to a great sense of care that their clients leave treatment feeling empowered. The author used this as a motivator to gain a deeper understanding of their client's lives and how they define empowerment.

Conclusion

Based on the review of literature and the author's clinical implications, it is the author's hope that this will add to the growing body of literature that speaks to the effectiveness of AOP in psychotherapy. Acknowledging and challenging oppression when working with impoverished clients have the potential of improving treatment outcomes in community-based mental health clinics. While this author discussed how AOP can strengthen CBT, other therapeutic interventions should be explored. Additionally, this author encourages clinicians, both established and emerging, to explore the connection between class and emotional distress with their clients who live under or at the poverty line. As social work practitioners, we have a duty to empower our clients to challenge and overcome systemic oppression. Using an anti-oppressive approach can provide further insight into how we reduce oppression in our society.

Reflection Questions for Beginner Clinicians

1. How have you benefited from the classist system in our society? In what ways have you been disadvantaged?
2. How do you believe we can bring social justice into the therapeutic setting? How can this benefit the clients you work with?
3. Camila entered into treatment guarded, due to prior incidents of feeling oppressed by social service agencies. What would be your approach to building a therapeutic bond with clients who are hesitant to trust you as a clinician? What is your positionality and its relation to Camila's case and how does this impact the treatment?
4. Are there any additional approaches or interventions that you believe Camila could have benefited from?
5. When working with underprivileged clients, how can you provide support to your clients while empowering them to fight against oppression? What does empowerment look like in the setting you work in or plan to work in?

References

Areán, P. A., Mackin, S., Vargas-Dwyer, E., Raue, P., Sirey, J. A., Kanellopolos, D., & Alexopoulos, G. S. (2010). Treating depression in disabled, low-income elderly: A conceptual model and recommendations for care. *International Journal of Geriatric Psychiatry, 25*(8), 765–769. https://doi.org/10.1002/gps.2556

Baines, D. (2017). *Doing anti-oppressive practice: Social justice social work.* Fernwood Publishing.

Ballo, E., & Tribe, R. (2023). Therapeutic work with clients living in poverty. *International Journal of Social Psychiatry, 69*, 1043–1050. https://doi.org/10.1177/00207640221139798

Beeber, L. S., Schwartz, T. A., Martinez, M. I., Holditch-Davis, D., Bledsoe, S. E., Canuso, R., & Lewis, V. S. (2014). Depressive symptoms and compromised parenting in low-income mothers of infants and toddlers: Distal and proximal risks. *Research in Nursing & Health, 37*(4), 276–291. https://doi.org/10.1002/nur.21604

Beech, B. M., Ford, C., Thorpe, R. J., Jr., Bruce, M. A., & Norris, K. C. (2021). Poverty, racism, and the public health crisis in America. *Frontiers in Public Health, 9*, 699049. https://doi.org/10.3389/fpubh.2021.699049

Benfer, E., Robinson, D., Bulter, S., Edmonds, L., Gilman, S., McKay, K., Owens, L., et al. (2020). *The COVID-19 eviction crisis: An estimated 30–40 million people in America are at risk*. Aspen Institute. Retrieved April 22, 2023, from https://www.aspeninstitute.org/blog-posts/the-covid-19-eviction-crisis-an-estimated-30-40-million-people-in-america-are-at-risk/

Bureau of Labor Statistics. (2020). A profile of the working poor, 2018. https://www.bls.gov/opub/reports/working-poor/2018/home.htm

Burnette, C. E., & Figley, C. R. (2017). Historical oppression, resilience, and transcendence: Can a holistic framework help explain violence experienced by indigenous people. *Social Work, 62*(1), 37–44. https://doi.org/10.1093/sw/sww065

Centers for Disease Control and Prevention. (2008). Prevalence of self-reported postpartum depressive symptoms—17 states, 2004–2005. *Morbidity and Mortality Weekly Report, 57*(14), 361–366.

Centre for Innovation in Campus Mental Health. (n.d.). *Anti-oppressive practice: A guide for moving from theory to action*. Retrieved from https://campusmentalhealth.ca/wp-content/uploads/2022/03/CICMH-Anti-Oppressive-Practice-Toolkit.pdf

Choi, J. W., Kim, T. H., Shin, J., & Han, E. (2019). Poverty and suicide risk in older adults: A retrospective longitudinal cohort study. *International Journal of Geriatric Psychiatry, 34*(11), 1565–1571. https://doi.org/10.1002/gps.5166

Chu, B., Marwaha, K., Sanvictores, T., & Ayers, D. (2023). Physiology, stress reaction. [Updated 2022 Sep 12]. In *StatPearls [Internet]*. StatPearls Publishing. https://www.ncbi.nlm.nih.gov/books/NBK541120/

Creamer, J. (2020, September 15). Inequalities persist despite decline in poverty for all major race and hispanic origin groups. United States Census Bureau. Retrieved April 22, 2023, from https://www.census.gov/library/stories/2020/09/poverty-rates-for-blacks-and-hispanics-reached-historic-lows-in-2019.html

Creamer, J., Shrider, E., Burns, K., & Chen, F. (2022, September 23). Poverty in the United States: 2021. United States Census Bureau. Retrieved April 22, 2023, from https://www.census.gov/data/tables/2022/demo/income-poverty/p60-277.html

Cummings, J. R., Allen, L., Clennon, J., Ji, X., & Druss, B. G. (2017). Geographic access to specialty mental health care across high- and low-income US communities. *JAMA Psychiatry, 74*(5), 476–484. https://doi.org/10.1001/jamapsychiatry.2017.0303

Daniel-Robinson, L., & Moore, J. E. (2019). Innovation and opportunities to address social determinants of health in Medicaid managed care. *Institute for Medicaid Innovation, 1*, 1–24.

Dashiff, C., DiMicco, W., Myers, B., & Sheppard, K. (2009). Poverty and adolescent mental health. *Journal of Child and Adolescent Psychiatric Nursing: Official Publication of the Association of Child and Adolescent Psychiatric Nurses, Inc, 22*(1), 23–32. https://doi.org/10.1111/j.1744-6171.2008.00166

David, D., Cristea, I., & Hofmann, S. G. (2018). Why Cognitive Behavioral Therapy is the current gold standard of psychotherapy. *Frontiers in Psychiatry, 9*, 4. https://doi.org/10.3389/fpsyt.2018.00004

Doser, S. (2022, September 26). Pregnancy and poverty: Forging a path forward for families. APHSA influence build connect. Retrieved April 19, 2023, from https://aphsa.org/APHSABlog/mhhspp/pregnancy-and-poverty-forging-a-path-forward-for-families.aspx

Ekono, M., Jiang, Y., & Smith, S. (2016). *Young children in deep poverty*. National Center for Children in Poverty. Retrieved from http://www.nccp.org/publications/pub_1133.html

(2021, September 17). *Expanding community-based mental health services and support*. Mayor's Management Report. Retrieved April 22, 2023, from https://www.nyc.gov/assets/operations/downloads/pdf/mmr2021/community_mental_health.pdf

Francis, L., DePriest, K., Wilson, M., & Gross, D. (2018). Child poverty, toxic stress, and social determinants of health: Screening and care coordination. *Online Journal of Issues in Nursing, 23*(3), 2. https://doi.org/10.3912/OJIN.Vol23No03Man02

Garfield, L., Holditch-Davis, D., Carter, C. S., McFarlin, B. L., Schwertz, D., Seng, J. S., Giurgescu, C., & White-Traut, R. (2015). Risk factors for postpartum depressive symptoms in low-income women with very low-birth-weight infants. *Advances in Neonatal Care: Official Journal of the National Association of Neonatal Nurses, 15*(1), E3–E8. https://doi.org/10.1097/ANC.0000000000000131

Garland, A. F., Haine-Schlagel, R., Brookman-Frazee, L., et al. (2013). Improving community-based mental health care for children: Translating knowledge into action. *Administration and Policy in Mental Health, 40*, 6–22. https://doi.org/10.1007/s10488-012-0450-8

Gaynes, B. N., Gavin, N., Meltzer-Brody, S., Lohr, K. N., Swinson, T., & Miller, W. C. (2005). Perinatal depression: Prevalence, screening accuracy, and screening outcomes. *Evidence Report/Technology Assessment, 119*, 1–8.

Gresl, B., Fox, R., & Fleischmann, A. (2016). Home-based parent-child therapy in low-income African American, Caucasian, and Latino families: A comparative examination of treatment outcomes. *Child & Family Behavior Therapy, 6*(1), 33–50. https://doi.org/10.1080/07317107.2014.878193

Healy, K. (2014). *Social work theories in context: Creating frameworks for practice* (2nd ed.). Palgrave Macmillan.

Hodgkinson, S., Godoy, L., Beers, L. S., & Lewin, A. (2017). Improving mental health access for low-income children and families in the primary care setting. *Pediatrics, 139*(1), e20151175. https://doi.org/10.1542/peds.2015-1175

Hoffmann, J., Farrell, C., Monuteaux, M., Fleegler, E., & Lee, L. (2020). Association of pediatric suicide with county-level poverty in the United States, 2007–2016. *JAMA Pediatrics, 174*(3), 287–294. https://doi.org/10.1001/jamapediatrics.2019.5678

Jiang, Y., Ekono, M., & Skinner, C. (2015). *Basic facts about low-income children: Children under 18 years, 2013*. National Center for Children in Poverty.

Keefe, R., Rouland, R., & Brownstein-Evans, C. (2018). Postpartum depression among low-income mothers of color: A womanist perspective. *Journal of sociology and social welfare, XLV*, 3–16.

Kim, H., & Burgard, S. (2022). Housing instability and mental health among renters in the Michigan recession and recovery study. *Public Health, 209*, 30–35., ISSN 0033-3506. https://doi.org/10.1016/j.puhe.2022.05.015

King, M. L., Jr. (1994). *Letter from the Birmingham jail*. Harper San Francisco.

Knifton, L., & Inglis, G. (2020). Poverty and mental health: Policy, practice and research implications. *BJPsych Bulletin, 44*(5), 193–196. https://doi.org/10.1192/bjb.2020.78

Llosa, J. A., Agulló-Tomás, E., Menéndez-Espina, S., Rivero-Díaz, M., & Iglesias-Martínez, E. (2022). Self-criticism in in-work poverty: The mediating role of social support in the era of flexibility. *International Journal of Environmental Research and Public Health, 19*(1), 609. https://doi.org/10.3390/ijerph19010609

Ludwig, J., Duncan, G. J., Gennetian, L. A., Katz, L. F., Kessler, R. C., Kling, J. R., & Sanbonmatsu, L. (2012). Neighborhood effects on the long-term Well-being of low-income adults. *Science (New York, NY), 337*(6101), 1505–1510. https://doi.org/10.1126/science.1224648

Manhica, H., Straatmann, V. S., Lundin, A., Agardh, E., & Danielsson, A. K. (2021). Association between poverty exposure during childhood and adolescence, and drug use disorders and drug-related crimes later in life. *Addiction, 116*(7), 1747–1756. https://doi.org/10.1111/add.15336

Mani, A., Mullainathan, S., Shafir, E., & Zhao, J. (2013). Poverty impedes cognitive function. *Science (New York, NY), 341*(6149), 976–980. https://doi.org/10.1126/science.1238041

Mary C., Acri Lindsay A., Bornheimer Lauren, Jessell Aminda, Heckman Chomancuzuk Joshua G., Adler Geetha, Gopalan Mary M., McKay (2016) (2017) The intersection of extreme poverty and familial mental health in the United States Social Work in Mental Health 15(6) 677–689. https://doi.org/10.1080/15332985.2017.1319893

Merriam-Webster. (n.d.). Citation. In Merriam-Webster.com dictionary. Retrieved April 15, 2023, from https://www.merriam-webster.com/dictionary/oppression

Mohamoud, Y. A., Kirby, R. S., & Ehrenthal, D. B. (2019). Poverty, urban-rural classification and term infant mortality: A population-based multilevel analysis. *BMC Pregnancy and Childbirth, 19*(1), 40. https://doi.org/10.1186/s12884-019-2190-1

Norcross, J. C., & Wampold, B. (2018). A new therapy for each patient: Evidence-based relationships and responsiveness. *Journal of Clinical Psychology., 74*(2), 1–18. https://doi.org/10.1002/jclp.22678

Older Women and Poverty. (2018, December). Justice in aging. Retrieved from https://justiceinaging.org/wp-content/uploads/2020/08/Older-Women-and-Poverty.pdf'

Payne, B. K., Brown-Iannuzzi, J. L., & Loersch, C. (2016). Replicable effects of primes on human behavior. *Journal of Experimental Psychology: General, 145*(10), 1269–1279. https://doi.org/10.1037/xge0000201

Reddy, U., Bettegowda, V., Dias, T., Yamada-Kushnir, T., & Willinger, M. (2011). Term pregnancy: A period of heterogeneous risk for infant mortality. *Obstetrics and Gynecology, 117*(6), 1279–1287. https://doi.org/10.1097/AOG.0b013e3182179e28

Ridley, M., Rao, G., Schilbach, F., & Patel, V. (2020). Poverty, depression, and anxiety: Causal evidence and mechanisms. *Science (New York, NY), 370*(6522), eaay0214. https://doi.org/10.1126/science.aay0214

Rubin, A. (2020). Can anti-oppressive clinical practice be compatible with evidence-informed clinical practice? *Journal of Social Work Education, 56*(4), 626–629. https://doi.org/10.1080/10437797.2020.1764807

Spruha, Joshi Stephen J., Mooney Andrew G., Rundle James W., Quinn John R., Beard Magdalena, Cerdá (2017) Pathways from neighborhood poverty to depression among older adults Health & Place 43138–143. https://doi.org/10.1016/j.healthplace.2016.12.003

Spiegel, J., Graziano, P., Arcia, E., Cox, S., Ayala, M., Carnero, N., O'Mara, N., & Sundari Foundation. (2022). Addressing mental health and trauma-related needs of sheltered children and families with trauma-focused Cognitive-Behavioral Therapy (TF-CBT). *Administration and Policy in Mental Health, 49*(5), 881–898. https://doi.org/10.1007/s10488-022-01207-0

The National Center for Children in Poverty. (2016). Quick Facts. Retrieved from nccp.org/about.html

The National Institute on Aging. (n.d.). Understanding the dynamics of the aging process. Retrieved from https://www.nia.nih.gov/about/aging-strategic-directions-research/understanding-dynamics-aging

The State of the Nations Housing. (2022). Joint center for housing studies. Harvard University. Retrieved from https://www.jchs.harvard.edu/sites/default/files/reports/files/Harvard_JCHS_State_Nations_Housing_2022.pdf

van Os, J., Guloksuz, S., Vijn, T. W., Hafkenscheid, A., & Delespaul, P. (2019). The evidence-based group-level symptom-reduction model as the organizing principle for mental health care: Time for change? *World Psychiatry, 18*(1), 88–96.

White, A. M., Philogene, G. S., Fine, L., & Sinha, S. (2009). Social support and self-reported health status of older adults in the United States. *American Journal of Public Health, 99*(10), 1872–1878. https://doi.org/10.2105/AJPH.2008.146894

Windsor, L. C., Jemal, A., & Alessi, E. J. (2015). Cognitive behavioral therapy: A meta-analysis of race and substance use outcomes. *Cultural Diversity & Ethnic Minority Psychology, 21*(2), 300–313. https://doi.org/10.1037/a0037929

Witters, D., & Agrawal, S. (2022, November 3). The economic cost of poor employee mental health. Gallup. Retrieved April 22, 2023, from https://www.gallup.com/workplace/404174/economic-cost-poor-employee-mental-health.aspx

Chapter 12
Unconscious Bias in Social Work: Identifying Culturally Responsive Interventions with BIPOC Clients

Phara Gladden

Introduction

It has been 50 years since the passing of Dr. Martin Luther King Jr., and yet his mission toward social justice, equality, and inclusion remains even more relevant in today's modern world. The landmark legislation of the Civil Rights Act of 1964 was the beginning of a new era and the end to discrimination based on race, class, gender, and religion. A quote by Dr. Martin Luther King Jr. states, "Oppressed people cannot remain oppressed forever. The yearning for freedom eventually manifests itself" (King, 2017, p. 6.). As Bankston (2002) notes, "The civil rights activities during the 1950s were a long struggle to achieve equal rights for all groups of people in the United States. These activities were met with opposition from many White Americans, but many Americans began to recognize the injustice of racial inequality" (p. 4).

The long-haul fight toward ending discrimination, racial oppression, and segregation has resurfaced and is evident in our institutions, education, housing, legal system, and healthcare. Bankston (2002) argues that throughout the nineteenth century, state and local governments limited African Americans and members of other minority groups from freedom and forced segregation of minority groups from major institutions. Empirical research indicates that disparities and inequities in our healthcare system are prevalent in historically racial and ethnic marginalized communities. "The mental health disparities African Americans experience are due to a host of inequities associated with their race and manifest in the form of racism, discrimination, provider bias and stereotyping, poor quality care, culture, and stigma among others" (Armstrong-Mensah et al., 2020, p. 26).

P. Gladden (✉)
Silver School of Social Wor, New York University, New York, NY, USA
e-mail: pgladden77@gmail.com

C. Tosone et al. (eds.), *Reframing Social Work with an Anti-Oppressive Lens*, Essential Clinical Social Work Series,
https://doi.org/10.1007/978-3-031-91391-4_12

According to a 2001 report by the US Surgeon General, Department of Health and Human Services, this was the first mental health report that provided information to the public on the debilitating effects of mental illness, effective treatment, and acknowledged the disparities in mental healthcare for racial and ethnic minorities and future directions for eliminating disparities. Satcher (2001) posits that the science base on minority mental health is inadequate and has resulted in unmet mental health needs and poor-quality mental health services. The lack of research and the knowledge gap in minority mental health continue to perpetuate systematic racism and oppressive practices. Polanco-Ramoan et al. (2016) postulate that "very little is known about how racial and ethnic groups cope with discrimination and how it may impact the risk of mental health" (p. 3). Furthermore, racial and ethnic minorities have less access to mental health services than their counterparts and are less likely to receive equitable care. Implicit bias is the driving force that has led to unequal treatment and disparities in care for racial and ethnic groups. The term "bias" is typically used to refer to both implicit stereotypes and prejudices and raises serious concerns in healthcare. As Kabir and Zaidi (2022) observe: "Bias is a prejudice against an individual or a group of people which stems from either negative or positive beliefs and ideologies" (p. 23). FitzGerald and Hurst (2017) state that implicit bias refers to unconscious attitudes and internalized discrimination based on common stereotypes that influence an individual's actions, judgments, and overall interaction. As we move toward a more progressive era, we must acknowledge one's race, culture, and identity and how we intersect with one another. As a "progressive society," it is important to continue the work of Dr. King and his mission toward equality and inclusivity of vulnerable and underserved groups. It is our responsibility to redefine what is meant as "different" or "other." These two words have led to implicit associations and biases that society has constructed for its gain. At the same time, vulnerable and stigmatized groups continue to be muted and voiceless in a society that claims to promote diversity and inclusion.

This chapter will introduce and define the concept of unconscious and implicit bias, the historical role of the social work profession and its involvement in discriminatory practices, an overview of empirical studies and evidence-based practice approaches to mitigating unconscious biases, and a discussion of the prevalence of racial attitudes and interpretation that perpetuate disparities in healthcare services for Black Indigenous People of Color (BIPOC) communities.

Positionality Statement

As an Afro-Caribbean therapist working in the social work area for the past 23 years, I have chosen to contribute to existing knowledge and give attention to BIPOC communities and individuals that have historically been unrecognized and overlooked due to their racial and ethnic identity, internalized racism, and implicit bias of others. The knowledge put forth in this chapter will encompass both my personal and clinical experiences working with marginalized racial and ethnic groups, as well as assisting clients in being conscious of their self-identity and its intersection with and influence on their lived experiences of racial bias and trauma. My positionality allows me the space to share my wisdom and for you as the reader to be aware of unconscious biases that interfere with providing equitable treatment to BIPOC and marginalized groups. Furthermore, this chapter includes the interventions and strategies I have used to promote self-efficacy, resiliency, empowerment, and collective growth. In reading this chapter, I hope that you are open-minded and willing to explore potential biases, preconceived notions, and misinformation. This chapter will also provide you with clinical tools that are grounded in dismantling oppressive practices in clinical settings. The information suggested in this chapter will be useful to beginning social workers, clinicians, educators, and instructors to develop an awareness of their personal biases and unconscious thoughts, feelings, and behaviors working with BIPOC individuals and groups. Challenging these personal biases will help promote culturally responsive practices and reduce unilateral approaches and negative perceptions of BIPOC and marginalized groups/communities.

The Evolution of Social Work Practice

It is crucial to understand the emergence of social work as a discipline and as a profession and trace its development to the present time. The social work profession began during the late nineteenth century at a time when societal problems were caused by industrial changes. The purpose and the mission of social work were to enhance human well-being and participate in community action programs that assisted in alleviating environmental and personal stressors that impact one's psychological, emotional, and physical health. Dan and Amra (2013) observe that the "social work profession promotes social change, problem-solving in human relationships and the empowerment and liberation of people to enhance well-being" (p. 413). Hare (2004) argues that promoting empowerment and liberation of people are important social work processes: "Since the beginning, social work has been concerned with people who are vulnerable, and oppressed, as well as those who are coping with problems of living" (p. 413). Social work utilizes theories of human behavior and social systems to assist disadvantaged individuals and groups in successfully interacting with their environments.

The Settlement House Movement was founded by Jane Addams in the late 1800s. Addams was recognized as the first social worker who worked toward social change by implementing community programs that served the poor, vulnerable, and disenfranchised. At the time of the nineteenth century, there was a strong emphasis on social justice, human rights, and the formation of welfare programs created to assist individuals struggling with economic and social conditions. Addams established the first American settlement house, Hull-House in Chicago. "A settlement house was both a residence and a community center that aimed to assist migrants that are poor to adjust to the industrial, urban life" (Hounmenou, 2012, p. 43). Lundbland (1995) indicates that the American Settlement House Movement and the Charitable

Organization Society (COS) movement came together to form the profession of social work. Addams's work as a social reformer and organizer helped create the social reforms that developed during the Progressive Era of 1890–1915. Her role in social movements forced the issues of poverty and injustice into society's consciousness. Addams also was aware of the unique problems Black Americans encountered as a result of racial discrimination and put forth the concept of respecting differences among races and nationalities (Lundbland, 1995).

While the social work profession promotes social justice, equality, and economic opportunities for all, this was not the case for marginalized groups, in particular, African Americans who migrated from the South to the North. During the progressive era, social workers participated in and promoted social injustices toward disadvantaged, marginalized groups due to racial biases and preferential treatment of the dominant groups. Hounmenou (2012) argues that the failure of mainstream settlement houses to assist Blacks led to the creation of segregated housing and Black settlement houses. Social workers also participated in discriminatory practices and excluded African Americans, women, and children of color due to their race and racial identity. The general belief among White settlement house leaders was that Blacks "could best progress" on their own through separate self-help or racially oriented organizations but not through the settlement house movement (Lasch-Quin, 2017, p. 5). In response to the refusal of the mainstream house to assist needy Black migrants, African-American female activists and reformers became involved in the establishment of the separate settlement house movement. Thus it can be argued that Black settlement houses provided a safe haven for the poor, opportunities for education, and free space for activism.

According to a news release by the National Association of Social Work (2021), the NASW acknowledges that the social work profession has not always lived up to the mission of social justice and apologized for supporting and participating in discriminatory practices, policies, and activities that have harmed people of color. These unjust practices included social work involvement in the following: segregated settlement houses, support of eugenic theories, and the recruitment of Black men in the Tuskegee experiment. As we move toward a more inclusive and anti-oppressive practice, social work as a profession needs to demonstrate awareness and responsibility and be attuned to the historical trauma experienced by BIPOC groups and communities. It is also essential that social workers acknowledge their positionality and how it may influence cultural biases and disparities in providing culturally responsive treatment interventions to racial and ethnic groups.

An Overview of Current Research on Unconscious and Implicit Bias

The presence of implicit biases among healthcare professionals and clinical care is a cause for concern. It is widely documented that the impact of racial disparities in healthcare is a result of implicit racial bias. Fridell and Brown (2015) argue that implicit biases are similar to explicit biases in that the biased person links individuals to stereotypes or generalizations associated with their group or groups. But, unlike explicit biases, implicit biases are not based on animus or hostility, and these "implicit associations" can impact perceptions and behavior outside of conscious awareness. This is true even for individuals who, at the conscious level, reject prejudice and stereotyping. Hall et al. (2015) define implicit bias as an "unconscious bias, that refers to the unconsciously held thoughts, feelings or behaviors towards a person or group of people that are present but unconsciously held or recognized, affecting our actions and decisions without us realizing" (p. 3). The cause of disparities in health outcomes for stigmatized groups is the implicit biases held by healthcare providers. Several stigmatized racial and ethnic groups experience persistent health disparities; for example, African Americans and American Indians have shorter life spans than their White peers (Williams & Mohammed, 2009). The cause of such disparities is connected to three factors which include genetics/biological antecedents, socioeconomic predictors, and psychological processes that contribute to biased healthcare (Adler & Rehkopf, 2008; Schnittker & McLeod, 2005). Research studies conducted by the National Institutes of Health (NIH) on health disparities suggest that implicit prejudice and stereotyping can impact the judgment and behavior of healthcare providers when interacting with stigmatized patients. This, in turn, has led to negative health outcomes and inadequate healthcare services and treatments for racial and ethnic groups. To begin, persistent concerns about provider bias in healthcare delivery continue to perpetuate health disparities. Finucane and Carrese (1990) examine providers' perceptions of patients: "African American patients were perceived in more negative terms than their white patients" (p. 122). Controlled experiments have found that providers' perceptions and treatment recommendations were strikingly different for White patients with the exact same symptoms (Paradies et al., 2013).

How Does Unconscious Bias Impact Our Healthcare System?

Implicit biases can influence preconceived judgment and behavior. According to FitzGerald and Hurst (2017), the evidence indicates that healthcare professionals exhibit the same levels of implicit bias as the wider population. A report by the Institute of Medicine (IOM) concluded that implicit bias among healthcare providers may contribute to health disparities (Smedley et al., 2003). Based on the evidence and inferences from observational studies and survey data in the IOM report, the findings indicate that "intergroup bias is implicated in interpersonal interactions and biased behavior. In comparison to other populations healthcare providers exhibit more negative attitudes toward African Americans than Whites" (Blair et al., 2011, p. 49). Several studies report that African-American patients report fewer clinical interactions with providers who have prominent levels of implicit bias and favor Whites over Blacks (Blair et al., 2011; Cooper et al., 2012; Oliver et al., 2014).

Moreover, providers' implicit bias has a negative impact on clinic visits with both African-American and White patients. Williams et al. (2019) contend that research indicates that across virtually every type of diagnostic and treatment intervention, Blacks and other minorities receive fewer procedures and poorer-quality medical care than Whites (p. 110). Blair et al. (2011) argue that despite discussion about the potential role of bias in health disparities, little research has directly examined the bias among healthcare professionals (p. 72). The existing evidence does suggest that implicit bias may affect clinical judgment and decision-making. Future research is needed to determine the association between implicit bias and clients' perceptions and behavior in clinical settings.

Evidence-Based Practice Interventions

Empirical evidence indicates that there is very little research on understanding implicit biases and identifying practice approaches to mitigate and reduce biases. However, there have been various approaches and interventions that have been suggested to assess unconscious biases, one of which is the Implicit Association Test (IAT), which was developed in 1988 by two social psychologists, Dr. Mahzarin Banaji and Dr. Anthony Greenwald. Ocejo defines IAT as "a psychological test whose objective is to reveal unconscious attitudes, automatic preferences, and hidden biases by measuring the time that takes an individual to classify concepts into two categories" (p. 1). IAT measures a respondent's implicit attitudes and unconscious bias. IAT is an online test that healthcare and educational organizations have used in addition to training to help healthcare providers develop an awareness of their mental processes, biases, and stereotypes, which can influence negative health outcomes in stigmatized groups. Banaji and Greenwald (2016) argue that while we may not have much power to eradicate our prejudices, we are often capable of counteracting them. The first step is to turn a hidden bias into a visible one. Pritlove and colleagues (2019) note that "Implicit bias training can make individuals aware of their unintentional involvement in the perpetuation of discrimination and inequity as well as the unrecognized advantages they enjoy based on group membership" (p. 502). However, the validity and reliability of IAT vary across studies. Based on a systematic review conducted by FitzGerald and Hurst (2017), they indicated that the most convincing studies from the review are those that combine IAT and a method measuring the quality of treatment in the actual world. These studies provide evidence for a relationship between bias that is measured and behaviors by clinicians that contribute to health disparities. In addition to IAT as a measurement tool, other evidence-based practice approaches have also been supported which include cognitive behavioral therapy (CBT) and mindfulness. Both approaches have been used to reduce unconscious bias and implicit associations.

Cognitive Behavioral Therapy (CBT)

In the 1960s, Aaron Beck developed cognitive behavioral therapy (CBT). CBT has been widely recognized as valuable in the treatment of clinical depression, stress, anxiety, and other mental health disorders; it focuses on the interconnectedness of emotions and actions and the potential to negatively impact each other in a vicious cycle (National Mental Health Service, 2019). CBT is effective in alleviating the influence of unconscious prejudices and stereotypes in the healthcare profession (Prieto 2021). According to Sokol and Fox (2019), CBT shows that initial situations may influence and trigger reactions and feelings and physiological responses. The main components of CBT that are involved are (1) identifying troubling situations, conditions, and problems that are disruptive; (2) identifying negative thoughts, emotions, and behaviors; and (3) reshaping and challenging negative, inaccurate, and irrational thinking patterns.

While CBT has been used extensively by mental health providers, researchers (Dobson and Dobson, 2018) have observed that CBT only focuses on current problems and issues and fails to address underlying causes of mental health conditions. Furthermore, CBT focuses on clients' thoughts, feelings, and behaviors and does not take into consideration problems with systems or family which may directly impact an individual's health and well-being.

Mindfulness

Another alternative approach that can be used with BIPOC and stigmatized groups is mindfulness. Current research has established that mindfulness could reduce discriminatory behaviors and cause people to rely on their instincts (Lueke & Gibson, 2015). Mindfulness is described by Kabat-Zinn (1994) as paying attention to the present in a purposeful and nonjudgmental way. In psychotherapy, it allows clinicians to remain in the present and focus on the intrapsychic connection while practicing empathy and attunement with the client. The use of mentalization enables clinicians to not only examine their own thinking but become more acute in the ability to see their clients' minds. Applegate and Bonovitz (1995) state "Clinician empathy is necessary to establish the 'holding environment'" (p. 84).

Therapeutic empathy is fostered by the qualities of attention, affect regulation, and attunement of mindfulness. Mindfulness is introduced to clients as nonjudgmental awareness. Furthermore, mindfulness can be used to reduce unconscious bias and is beneficial to social work practice, particularly when working with vulnerable and stigmatized groups and being able to empathize and understand their lived experiences and trauma.

A systematic review conducted by FitzGerald and Hurst (2017) indicates a paucity of research in identifying evidence-based practices to reduce unconscious bias; unconscious bias is a ubiquitous phenomenon that is difficult to measure and eliminate. However, I do feel that in-person training and collaborative intergroup interaction between ethnic and nonethnic groups would help to increase familiarity and sensitize individuals to stereotypes and negative attitudes about race and ethnicity. I also think that each individual views the world through their own lens which is based on experiences and culture and what they have learned from their family of origin. Our perception of ourselves and how we see others is based on early childhood experiences and implicit associations. As social workers working with BIPOC and stigmatized groups, it is important that we understand our clients' sociocultural history and undo racial biases and practices that will further perpetuate health disparities and non-egalitarian treatment.

The practice approaches that I have outlined are a few evidence-based practices that research has supported working with BIPOC and stigmatized groups to mitigate and reduce biases. In addition to evidence-based practices, there are theoretical and anti-oppressive frameworks that I have found useful as a clinician working with BIPOC and stigmatized groups.

Social Work Contributions to Anti-oppressive Approaches

Anti-oppressive social work practice includes a variety of approaches and interventions that can be used to address social injustice in BIPOC communities. Integrating cultural competency and anti-oppressive approaches for marginalized communities is essential to social work practice. As agents of change, social workers need to work on conceptualizing and redefining culturally relevant skills and interventions that may be used to treat BIPOC communities. The impact of the COVID-19 pandemic and the racial and social justice during 2020 called for a systemic change that would incorporate cultural awareness and social diversity. In 2021, the National Association of Social Workers (NASW) amended the professional code of ethics to address the importance of professional self-care and cultural competence standards for social workers.

Anti-oppressive practice refers to diverse practice approaches that social workers and other mental health practitioners can use when working with racial and ethnic groups.

Over the past few years, there has been an increase in social work practice literature and empirical research that has contributed to our theoretical understanding of oppression. The role of the social worker as a "change agent" is salient to the practice of social justice and community activism. Social workers use multifaceted approaches to eliminate oppressive practices and eradicate institutional racism. Social workers have not developed any theories of oppression but have "relied on theoretical and conceptual frameworks, related to feminist, anti-racist, critical, conflict, empowerment, or social justice theory" (Robbins, 2011, p. 377).

A theoretical framework is vital in introducing a research problem or phenomenon and provides support in validating and challenging theoretical assumptions using the scientific method. As indicated, there are several different theoretical frameworks that can be applied to implicit and racial biases and the negative outcomes of health disparities.

The following is a list of theoretical frameworks and approaches that I have used to address social injustice and oppressive practices when working with BIPOC clients. These include historical and intergenerational trauma, critical race theory (CRT), intersectionality, radical healing, healing methodologies, and the intersubjective relationship between the clinician and the BIPOC client.

Historical and Intergenerational Trauma

The theory of historical trauma was first developed by Maria Yellow Horse Brave Heart in 1980 while working with tribal communities. In her work, Brave Heart explained the historical and current problems that Native Americans encountered. Native Americans and other racial-ethnic groups have all experienced colonialism, loss of identity, and displacement from their native land. Suicide rates for Native American adults and youth are higher than the national average, with suicide being the second leading cause of death for Native Americans. Native American individuals are reported as having the lowest income, least education, and the highest poverty level of any group—minority or majority—and the lowest life expectancy of any population in the United States.

As a theoretical framework, historical trauma can be applied to different ethnic groups who have also experienced similar trauma of racial violence and colonialism. "Over the last several decades, American Indian, African American, and other indigenous scholars have posited that adverse health outcomes may be rooted in historically situated traumatic events in combination with persistent systemic oppression" (Evans-Campbell, 2008, p. 11). The primary focus of historical trauma is transferred to subsequent generations through biological, psychological, environmental, and social means, resulting in a cross-generational cycle of trauma (Sotero, 2006). Although the validity of historical trauma remains ambiguous due to a lack of evidence, empirical research (Evans-Campbell, 2008; Gone, 2009) suggests that there is uncertainty about the validity of this theory due to the ambiguity of some of the concepts with little empirical evidence. The comprehensiveness of trauma prevention and intervention strategies is limited due to the primary focus on the individual, without integrating political, economic, social, or historical group traumas (Comas-Diaz et al., 1998).

The historical trauma framework applies not just to Native Americans but to other ethnic groups who have experienced cross-generational trauma, thereby contributing to emotional, physical, and psychological trauma that is passed down through generations. Ortega-Williams et al. (2021) argue that historical trauma exists in nonindigenous racial and ethnic groups that have experienced pervasive, historical, political, economic, and social oppression such as racial subjugation and colonization.

Critical Race Theory

Critical race theory (CRT) was influenced and founded by the philosophical writing of Derrick Bell, an African-American civil rights lawyer and the first black professor to teach at Harvard Law School. In addition to Derick Bell, several legal scholars including Kimberle Crenshaw have been involved in the intellectual movement and core idea that race is a social construct and racism is not based on individual bias or prejudice but is embedded in our legal systems and policies. Bell and other scholars created the CRT framework for legal analysis to examine race and racism and its effect on racial and ethnic stigmatized communities. "CRT focuses on the experiential knowledge of ethnic minoritized communities of origin concerning race and race relations" (Delgado & Stefancic, 2023, p. 113). CRT allows for examining structural power that has sustained racial inequities and programs that promote social injustice, inequality, and disharmony (Kolivoski et al., 2014). CRT can also be used to scrutinize race and racism and its effects on ethnic minorities. Hitchcock (2002) argues that "Internalized dominance is a belief system grounded in miseducation and the politics of social inequality. The belief system is a result of an advantaged relationship to privilege, power, and cultural affirmation" (p. 5).

Intersectionality

Intersectionality is a theoretical framework that was originally coined by Kimberlé Crenshaw, an African-American women's civil rights advocate and law professor at Columbia Law School. Crenshaw introduced the concept of intersectionality to describe the oppression, bias, and violence against African-American women but became widely used as an analytic tool to examine the social categorizations of race, class, gender, and sexuality and the interconnection to diverse populations that experience different forms of discrimination and racism. According to Crenshaw (2017), "intersectionality is a lens through which you can see where power comes and collides, where it interlocks and intersects" (p. 1). Collins and Blige (2016) suggest that "These intersecting power relations influence social relations across diverse societies as well as individual experiences in everyday life" (p. 2). Researchers have used intersectionality to understand the complexities of social problems in the world, people, and human experience.

Radical Healing and Healing Methodologies

The concept of healing in oppressed communities can be unconvincing to the larger community. Healing, as a construct, reflects more than just the individual but collective approaches to improving self and society (Heilbron & Guttman, 2000). Healing is described differently in certain cultural/ethnic groups. For the purposes of this paper, healing refers to being able to cope, survive, and thrive within an oppressive society. Lewis et al. (2019) have clearly defined the concept of racial healing, stating that social and racial justice is necessary; racial healing is interpreted as "the policies, actions, and practices which aid individuals and their groups to live out their full potential in societies with a history of racial oppression" (p. 6). The concepts of radical healing frameworks and methodologies include collectivism, critical consciousness, strength and resistance, cultural authenticity, and self-knowledge. Radical healing allows the individual or group to develop "the agency to challenge and change oppressive conditions by striving for wellness through social, community, and individual mechanisms" (Toporek & Williams, 2006, p. 24).

The Intersubjective Relationship Between the Social Worker and BIPOC Clients

The role of a social worker is tantamount to working with BIPOC and stigmatized clients. The interactive intersubjective relationship between the social worker and the client is the foundation that allows the client to feel safe and begin to develop trust in the social worker. Winnicott (1960) argues one of the primary purposes of the therapist is to provide a "holding environment" for the client so that the client may begin to recognize and meet previously neglected ego needs and facilitate the emergence of the true self.

Dr. Janice Edwards, a professor at Howard University School of Social Work, provides her observation on engagement and interactional treatment dyad of clinical social work with clients from diverse and ethnic backgrounds. Her work has lent support to "the paradigm of cultural intelligence (CQ) as a lens for understanding diversity and cultural differences in clinical social work" (Edwards, 2016, p. 220). Edwards (2016) indicates that social workers are involved in a reciprocal relational matrix, which includes us, the client, and the client systems that we engage. The intersubjective experience is a combination of the client's and the social worker's subjectivities, consisting of knowledge, experiences, and feelings on conscious and unconscious levels. "It's the relational exchange that is reciprocal and can both affect and mutually influence the clinical relationship and treatment process" (Edwards, 2016, p. 214).

There has been an emergence of research studies on race, culture, and ethnicity in clinical settings. However, empirical studies remain ill-equipped in identifying culturally responsive treatment interventions to reduce implicit biases, internalized oppression, and discriminatory practices that are experienced by racial and ethnic groups. Social workers need to demonstrate cultural humility and allow themselves to be informed by clients' diversity, cross-cultural practices, and intersecting identities when working with BIPOC and diverse groups. The cross-cultural framework has been used to examine and understand communities with cultural, racial, or ethnic differences (Cohen & Ahmed, 2007). Laird and others who write from this perspective encourage us to engage in an ongoing process of learning about others and to operate as much as possible from a "not-knowing" position (Anderson & Goolishian, 1992). Laird states that we must be "informed not-knowers". As social workers, we need to be adaptive in our practices and utilize current perspectives that will help us to develop awareness and learn about others as well as ourselves.

Based on empirical research and existing theoretical frameworks and postmodern perspective, the social work roles and principles that I have incorporated in my practice working with BIPOC and stigmatized groups in clinical settings are as follows:

- The social worker values and respects clients' dignity and worth.
- The social worker creates a safe "holding environment" free of judgment and biases.
- The social worker recognizes clients' shared values, intersecting identities, and collectivism.
- The social worker conducts a culturally responsive and tailored assessment based on the client's needs, culture, ethnicity, and strengths.
- The social worker identifies the clients' personal and environmental stressors.
- The social worker practices from a person-centered perspective.
- The social worker examines sociocultural histories and cross-cultural differences to inform practice.
- The social worker needs to be attentive to the client's and therapist's dyadic experiences (i.e., transference-countertransference matrices, co-constructed beliefs).
- The social worker advocates and empowers clients to challenge social constructs and beliefs and navigate through oppressive societal systems and institutional racism.
- The social worker promotes resiliency.
- The social worker restores wellness, strength, and hope by practicing healing approaches to enhance individual and group well-being.

These aforementioned principles are incorporated into the case example that follows.

Clinical Case Example

Mr. R is a 35-year-old, single Guatemalan male who has been working at a construction site for the past 15 years. He has no previous psychiatric history and was referred by the employee assistance program (EAP) for continued counseling and recommendation to return to work. As per his employer, Mr. R was observed coming to work intoxicated, had difficult relationships with his coworkers, and recently confided in his supervisor that he had passive suicidal thoughts, stating "I wish it would all just come to an end, and I can just live my life freely." Mr. R's supervisor referred him to the EAP, suggesting that he take time off from work and explore counseling. The client was reluctant to meet with the EAP worker and minimized his anxiety, describing himself as "overworked and just going through life." After several missed sessions with the EAP clinician, it was noted that Mr. R was difficult, hostile, and uncooperative at his employer's request. His supervisor labeled him as being disruptive and unfit to continue working. Despite repeated attempts from his employer to provide him with counseling, Mr. R was put on administrative leave and asked to leave his work site.

Mr. R is a first-generation immigrant who migrated to the United States 5 years ago with his family due to unlivable conditions and the need for healthcare treatment for his 5-year-old daughter, who was diagnosed with sickle cell disease. Mr. R is currently employed and unable to afford health insurance.

During his intake, Mr. R reported that he came to the United States for a "better life and to seek employment to care for my family and daughter." Mr. R reports initially that he had difficulty finding work and is grateful to his employer for allowing him to be able to work and pay for his daughter's treatment and medical expenses. Mr. R often minimized his substance use: "It's just a drink, I'm just trying to get through life." Mr. R was very prideful and seldom talked about himself and his family, and when he did, it was mostly about his work and how he missed being at the job site. Mr. R also questioned the therapist's expertise and cultural background and how women of color can help him with his problems.

During his weekly sessions, Mr. R became more comfortable and began to develop a therapeutic rapport with the therapist. He was also apologetic for the abruptness and condescending statements that he made about being in therapy. As we began our work together, it was important for me to create a safe space where the client felt valued. I was also mindful of the client's intersecting identity as a Hispanic male and how his gender, culture, and immigration status influenced implicit biases by his employer and being labeled as being "difficult and hostile."

It was important that I refrained from pathologizing and "blaming the victim" but rather understand the client's wants and needs and help him to navigate through macro-systems that are oppressive and promote racial biases. In addition, I had to be cognizant of my own preconceived biases and beliefs and acknowledge socially constructed labels that may influence the assessment and treatment process. As we worked through our relational experiences, it was vital to explore the transference-countertransference matrix present in the client-therapist dyad. The client became more engageable and forthcoming and able to identify his feelings and process his emotions.

The client shared his early experience working with his father in construction, masonry, and building wells for his community. After several sessions, the client acknowledged that he never talked about his home life because he describes it as being "too painful." The client admitted it was hard leaving his country but needed to get medical care for his daughter. The client also shared that his drinking had increased due to his inability to process his daughter's illness, for which he blamed himself. Mr. R reported feeling isolated not being in his community and feeling inadequate in asking for help. The client denied suicidal ideation but reported increased anxiety and worry about making ends meet to pay for his daughter's medical treatment. The client reported feeling shame and unable to share his experience with his family and friends and often drinks to numb his feelings.

As the client's treatment came to an end, Mr. R reduced his drinking to once a week. Mr. R was able to process his emotions and develop insight and awareness into his anxiety and behavior. Based on my clinical assessment, the client's symptoms improved. He was able to use counseling to identify maladaptive behaviors and patterns used to cope with his personal and environmental stressors.

My recommendation was for the client to return to work and continue therapy. I also referred the client to Alcoholics Anonymous (AA) meetings near his home and the local Department of Social Services (DSS) where he can apply for medical insurance for his daughter. In retrospect, I realized that the client had not had the opportunity to work on himself and identify personal stressors in his life (being an immigrant, acculturating to a dominant culture, ill daughter, financial issues, lack of health insurance, and community support). Mr. R realized that he was using alcohol to cope with unwanted feelings that he had repressed. Mr. R's culture and ethnicity were also explored during his treatment, as well as how his intersecting identities influenced his past and current experiences. Mr. R reported that therapy helped him to discover his "true self" and learn adaptive coping skills that will help him to work through negative beliefs and continue to work on his recovery.

Discussion of Treatment Interventions Employed

During my work with Mr. R, I incorporated different treatment interventions to help him in his recovery, by understanding his past trauma and the reason for his drinking. In this section, I will describe three different treatment approaches that were clinically chosen to assist Mr. R.

Cognitive Behavioral Therapy

Using CBT, Mr. R was able to identify that his feelings of inadequacy triggered him to drink. Mr. R recognized that he was using alcohol to cope with unwanted feelings that he had repressed. As the client worked on processing his feelings about his daughter's illness, he began to develop insight into his maladaptive behaviors. Mr. R learned the importance of labeling his emotions and applying cognitive reframing skills to identify negative thinking patterns and replace them with healthier thought patterns.

Mindfulness

Mr. R was also able to explore the painful experiences of his childhood, his daughter's illness, and his migration to the United States. As he talked about his traumatic experiences, the client mentioned the difficulty of accepting his daughter's illness. I introduced mindfulness techniques to Mr. R to help him notice that his past experiences influenced his thoughts and interfered with how he related to his daughter and family. Mr. R used deep breathing exercises to help him decrease his anxiety and stress. As I evaluated Mr. R's progress in his sessions, I noticed a change in his behavior and his willingness to accept the reality of his daughter's illness. Mr. R was able to acknowledge his loss of culture, fear of being accepted, and self-deprecation. He began to focus on his strengths, which helped him to feel empowered and reconnect with his daughter.

Radical Healing

The radical healing framework was selected to help Mr. R heal from the personal and cultural trauma he and his family experienced. The author helped Mr. R process his experience living in a dominant culture and navigating through institutional racism and oppressive systems, which serve as a barrier to maintaining the status quo. Mr. R learned to adapt to his new environment and accept things that were not in his control. However, Mr. R worked on healing himself through therapy by finding his purpose by practicing resiliency, self-care, and being involved in his community.

Practice and Supervisory Wisdom

When working with BIPOC and vulnerable populations, I have found that a strength-based approach can be adapted to any client population. "A strengths-based approach to social work involves building a collaborative, person-centered relationship with your client that treats them as a unique individual by focusing on their personal, relational, and community strengths" (Pulla, 2017, p. 39). Tracing its roots in social work, the strength-based approach uses a different lens to view individuals, families, and communities. Developed as a response to models that focus on the deficit (Seligman, 2005), the strength-based approach seeks to view the individual holistically and explore his abilities and circumstances, rather than focusing on his weaknesses and deficits. It is also concerned with identifying a client's inner and outer resources to promote resilience (Pulla, 2017).

Despite our race, culture, and ethnicity, we all desire three fundamental values: safety, belonging, and mattering. In addition to using the existing theoretical framework and evidenced-based practice, I have also found that strength-based approach and four pillars are the building blocks to remain grounded and committed to helping BIPOC and vulnerable clients to heal, empower, and restore wellness in communities of color:

Pillar I: Self-efficacy
Pillar II: Resiliency
Pillar III: Empowerment
Pillar IV: Collective growth

Author's Reflection

As I ponder on this body of work in this chapter, it is important to note that all theoretical frameworks and perspectives suggested are based on empirical research and evidence. Furthermore, there is a paucity of research on the lack of culturally responsive treatment to mitigate and reduce implicit/unconscious biases, internalized oppression, and discriminatory practices. However, as social workers, we need to continue to undo racism and implement anti-oppressive practices, to assist our clients in navigating through macro-, mezzo-, and microsystems that are influenced by institutional and systemic racism. Practicing from a trauma-informed paradigm allows social workers to be informed of clients' sociocultural history, intergenerational trauma, and cross-cultural practices. Clinicians should consider the use of healing methodologies and interventions that will help empower and restore wellness in BIPOC and stigmatized groups. In addition, social work as a profession needs to contribute to future research and scholarship on adapting existing evidence-based practices and integrating culturally responsive interventions to eliminate negative health outcomes and developing practices that promote social justice and anti-oppressive approaches to social work counseling.

Reflection Questions

1. Am I aware of my own unconscious/implicit biases and how they impact and influence my work with BIPOC and other marginalized clients?
2. How can I use my own positionality to challenge and help clients negotiate and navigate through oppressive systems?
3. How can social workers integrate culturally responsive approaches and evidenced-based practices in our work with BIPOC clients?
4. How can trauma-informed care be adapted to meet the needs of BIPOC and culturally diverse groups?
5. What role do social workers play in undoing racism and implementing anti-oppressive practices in their work and community?
6. How do you engage and validate BIPOC clients' sociocultural history, cultural identity, and experience to inform treatment?

References

Adler, N. E., & Rehkopf, D. H. (2008). US disparities in health: Descriptions, causes, and mechanisms. *Annual Review of Public Health, 29*(1), 235–252.

Anderson, H., & Goolishian, H. (1992). The client is the expert: A not-knowing approach to therapy. In S. McNamee & K. Gergen (Eds.), *Therapy as social construction* (pp. 25–39). Sage.

Applegate, J. S., & Bonovitz, J. M. (1995). *The facilitating partnership: A Winnicottian approach for social workers and other helping professionals*. Rowman & Littlefield.

Armstrong-Mensah, E., Patel, H., Parekh, P., & Lee, C. (2020). Mental health inequities and disparities among African American adults in the United States: The role of race. *Research in Health Science, 5*(3), 23–37. https://doi.org/10.22158/rhs.v5n3p23

Banaji, M. R., & Greenwald, A. G. (2016). *Blindspot: Hidden biases of good people*. Bantam.

Bankston, C. L. I. I. I. (2002). *Civil rights movement in the 1950s*. Salem Press Encyclopedia.

Blair, I. V., Steiner, J. F., & Havranek, E. P. (2011). Unconscious (implicit) bias and health disparities: Where do we go from here? *The Permanente Journal, 15*(2), 71.

Crenshaw, K. W. (2017). Race, reform, and retrenchment: Transformation and legitimation in anti-discrimination law. In *Law and social movements* (pp. 475–531). Routledge.

Cohen, C. I., & Ahmed, I. (2007). Working with elderly persons across cultures. In *Textbook of cultural psychiatry* (pp. 512–525). Cambridge University Press.

Collins, P. H., & Blige, S. (2016). *Intersectionality*. Polity Press.

Comas-Diaz, L., Lykes, M. B., & Alarcon, R. D. (1998). Ethnic conflict and the psychology of liberation in Guatemala, Peru, and Puerto Rico. *American Psychologist, 53*(7), 778.

Cooper, L. A., Roter, D. L., Carson, K. A., Beach, M. C., Sabin, J. A., Greenwald, A. G., & Inui, T. S. (2012). The associations of clinicians' implicit attitudes about race with medical visit communication and patient ratings of interpersonal care. *American Journal of Public Health, 102*(5), 979–987.

Dan, M. Z., & Amra, K. (2013). The historical development of social work practice with individuals. *Middle East Journal of Scientific Research, 14*(5), 703–711.

Delgado, R., & Stefancic, J. (2023). *Critical race theory: An introduction* (Vol. 87). NYU Press.

Dobson, D., & Dobson, K. S. (2018). *Evidence-based practice of cognitive-behavioral therapy*. Guilford Publications.

Edwards, J. B. (2016). Cultural intelligence for clinical social work practice. *Clinical Social Work Journal, 44*(3), 211–220.

Evans-Campbell, T. (2008). Historical trauma in American Indian/Native Alaska communities: A multilevel framework for exploring impacts on individuals, families, and communities. *Journal of Interpersonal Violence, 23*(3), 316–338.

Finucane, T. E., & Carrese, J. A. (1990). Racial bias in presentation of cases. *Journal of General Internal Medicine, 5*, 120–121.

FitzGerald, C., & Hurst, S. (2017). Implicit bias in healthcare professionals: A systematic review. *BMC Medical Ethics, 18*(1), 1–18.

Fridell, L., & Brown, S. (2015). Fair and impartial policing: A science-based approach. *The Police Chief, 82*(6), 20–25.

Gone, J. P. (2009). A community-based treatment for Native American historical trauma: Prospects for evidence-based practice. *Journal of Consulting and Clinical Psychology, 77*(4), 751.

Hall, W. J., Chapman, M. V., Lee, K. M., Merino, Y. M., Thomas, T. W., Payne, B. K., Eng, E., Day, S. H., & Coyne-Beasley, T. (2015). Implicit racial/ethnic bias among health care professionals and its influence on health care outcomes: A systematic review. *American Journal of Public Health, 105*(12), e60–e76.

Hare, I. (2004). Defining social work for the 21st century: The International Federation of Social Workers' revised definition of social work. *International Social Work, 47*(3), 407–424.

Heilbron, C. L., & Guttman, M. A. J. (2000). Traditional healing methods with First Nations women in group counselling. *Canadian Journal of Counselling and Psychotherapy, 34*(1).

Hitchcock, J. (2002). *Lifting the white veil: An exploration of white American culture in a multiracial context*. Crandall Dostie & Douglass Books.

Hounmenou, C. (2012). Black settlement houses and oppositional consciousness. *Journal of Black Studies, 43*(6), 646–666.

Kabat-Zinn, J. (1994). *Mindfulness meditation for everyday life*. Piatkus.

Kabir, R., & Zaidi, S. T. (2022). Implicit bias against BIPOC patients in clinical settings: A qualitative review. *Spectra Undergraduate Research Journal, 2*(1), 3.

King, M. L. (2017). Letter from the Birmingham city jail. In *Applied ethics* (pp. 233–243). Routledge.

Kolivoski, K. M., Weaver, A., & Constance-Huggins, M. (2014). Critical race theory: Opportunities for application in social work practice and policy. *Families in Society, 95*(4), 269–262.

Lasch-Quinn, E. (2017). *Black neighbors: Race and the limits of reform in the American settlement house movement, 1890-1945*. UNC Press Books.

Lewis, J. A., Williams, M. G., Moody, A. T., Peppers, E. J., & Gadson, C. A. (2019). Intersectionality theory and microaggressions: Implications for research, teaching, and practice. *Microaggression Theory*, 48–64.

Lueke, A., & Gibson, B. (2015). Mindfulness meditation reduces implicit age and race bias: The role of reduced automaticity of responding. *Social Psychological and Personality Science, 6*(3), 284–291.

Lundblad, K. S. (1995). Jane Addams and social reform: A role model for the 1990s. *Social Work, 40*(5), 661–669.

National Association of Social Workers. (2021). NASW apologizes for racist practices in American social work.

Oliver, M. N., Wells, K. M., Joy-Gaba, J. A., Hawkins, C. B., & Nosek, B. A. (2014). Do physicians' implicit views of African Americans affect clinical decision making? *The Journal of the American Board of Family Medicine, 27*(2), 177–188.

Ortega-Williams, A., Crutchfield, J., & Hall, J. C. (2021). The colorist-historical trauma framework: Implications for culturally responsive practice with African Americans. *Journal of Social Work, 21*(3), 294–309.

Paradies, Y., Priest, N., Ben, J., Truong, M., Gupta, A., Pieterse, A., Kelaher, M., & Gee, G. (2013). Racism as a determinant of health: A protocol for conducting a systematic review and meta-analysis. *Systematic Reviews, 2*, 1–7.

People, H. (2013). Conclusion and future directions: CDC health disparities and inequalities report—United States, 2013. CDC Health Disparities and Inequalities Report—United States, 2013, 62(3), 184.

Polanco-Roman, L., Danies, A., & Anglin, D. M. (2016). Racial discrimination as race-based trauma, coping strategies, and dissociative symptoms among emerging adults. *Psychological Trauma: Theory, Research, Practice, and Policy, 8*(5), 609.

Prieto, E. C. (2021). Cognitive-behavioral therapy (CBT) for reducing implicit biases among healthcare professionals.

Pritlove, C., Juando-Prats, C., Ala-Leppilampi, K., & Parsons, J. A. (2019). The good, the bad, and the ugly of implicit bias. *The Lancet, 393*(10171), 502–504.

Pulla, V. (2017). Strengths-based approach in social work: A distinct ethical advantage. *International Journal of Innovation, Creativity and Change, 3*(2), 97–114.

Robbins, S. P. (2011). Oppression theory and social work treatment. In *Social work treatment: Interlocking theoretical approaches* (pp. 343–353).

Satcher, D. (2001). *Mental health: Culture, race, and ethnicity—A supplement to mental health: A report of the surgeon general*. US Department of Health and Human Services.

Seligman, M. E. P., Steen, T. A., Park, N., & Peterson, C. (2005). Positive psychology.

Schnittker, J., & McLeod, J. D. (2005). The social psychology of health disparities. *Annual Review of Sociology, 31*(1), 75–103.

Smedley, B. D., Stith, A. Y., & Nelson, A. R. (2003). Racial and ethnic disparities in diagnosis and treatment: A review of the evidence and a consideration of causes. Unequal treatment: Confronting racial and ethnic disparities in health care.

Sokol, L., & Fox, M. (2019). *The Comprehensive Clinician's Guide to Cognitive Behavioral Therapy*. Eau Claire. https://www.readpbn.com/pdf/The-ComprehensiveClinician's-Guide-to-Cognitive-Behavioral-TherapySample-Pages.pdf

Sotero, M. (2006). A conceptual model of historical trauma: Implications for public health practice and research. *Journal of Health Disparities Research and Practice, 1*(1), 93–108.

Toporek, R. L., & Williams, R. A. (2006). Ethics and professional issues related to the practice of social justice in counseling psychology. In *Handbook for social justice in counseling psychology: Leadership, vision, and action* (pp. 17–34).

Williams, D. R., & Mohammed, S. A. (2009). Discrimination and racial disparities in health: Evidence and needed research. *Journal of Behavioral Medicine, 32*, 20–47.

Williams, D. R., Lawrence, J. A., Davis, B. A., & Vu, C. (2019). Understanding how discrimination can affect health. *Health Services Research, 54*, 1374–1388.

Winnicott, D. W. (1960). The theory of the parent-infant relationship. In *The maturational processes and the facilitating environment*. International Universities Press, 1965.

Part III
Anti-oppressive Practice in the Criminal Justice System

Chapter 13
The Sankofa of American Prisons: The Case for Abolitionist Social Work

Kirk "Jae" James and Erin George

Introduction

In Fyodor Dostoevsky's novel *The House of the Dead*, he asserts, "The degree of civilization in a society can be judged by entering its prisons" (p. 216). In the United States and much of the colonized world, jails and prisons are emblematic of the extreme manifestations of oppression, white supremacy, and racialized capitalism found in the larger society. The COVID-19 pandemic and its aftermath have further exposed these institutions as places of neglect and suffering, marked by inadequate healthcare, unsanitary conditions, trauma, violence, and widespread inhumanity (Franco-Paredes et al., 2020). The pandemic also brought to light tensions within the social work profession, which is theoretically grounded in social justice but often aligns with the carceral system—inclusive of jails, prisons, policing, the child welfare system, and the school-to-prison pipeline (Jacobs et al., 2021).

As social workers and people who believe in abolition—a world without police, jails, and prisons (and varied oppressive ideas and practices)—and the reimagining of our social response to harm, we write to illuminate the historical amnesia of prisons within the United States and to challenge social workers and other helping professions who feel things have just "gone astray" and who continue to call for *reformist reforms* that ultimately maintain the status quo and perpetuate the existence of the carceral state.

K. J. James
Silver School of Social Work, New York University, New York, NY, USA
e-mail: kirkajames@nyu.edu

E. George (✉)
The Bail Project, Los Angeles, CA, USA
e-mail: ering@bailproject.org

C. Tosone et al. (eds.), *Reframing Social Work with an Anti-Oppressive Lens*, Essential Clinical Social Work Series,
https://doi.org/10.1007/978-3-031-91391-4_13

We honor the history of prisons, particularly the men of Attica, and the legacy of the 1971 riots, which directly called out to helping professions like social work and gave their lives to bring attention to the inherent degradation of prisons. The Attica riots are also significant in that they ushered in decades of hyper-criminalization, reformist reform, and the steroid-fueled growth of mass incarceration—a period that would set in motion a prison boom like none other in history. In the two decades post-Attica, the US prison system would go from averaging about 200,000 prisoners to over 2 million. With less than 5% of the world's population, the United States can claim 25% of the world's prisoners—of whom most are Black and poor and can trace their ancestors back to chattel slavery (James & Smyth, 2014a, 2014b).

We write this chapter to illuminate the history of atrocities associated with prisons and to invite present and future social work practitioners to abolition through the utilization of "Sankofa"—a word and practice from the Akan tribe in Ghana that teaches that to understand our present and ensure our future, we must know our past. And to move forward, we must look back. Sankofa, often represented by a bird looking back over its shoulder, symbolizes the pursuit of knowledge based upon thoughtful investigation and critical examination of historical events—learning from the past to build the future.

Utilizing the principle of Sankofa, this chapter explores the genesis of prisons in Colonial America and its varied iterations. The article concludes by calling social work—as a profession and as people to embrace abolition as a theory of change.

Lastly, in writing this chapter, we utilize the era's language, which can be dehumanizing. We ask that while reading, you remember that the millions of people who have experienced the brutality of the carceral system are sons, mothers, fathers, brothers, sisters, and human beings first and foremost—no matter their actions.

Punishment in Prerevolutionary America

In early American colonies, crime and sin were viewed synonymously, and sanguinary punishment such as public whippings, pillory, mutilations, and even castrations were utilized to address acts of civil disobedience. This lack of distinction between crime and sin informed and perpetuated a belief that crime was "the devil's work" and not worthy of further exploration (Blomberg & Lucken, 2010). Specific emphasis was placed on public displays of punishment to deter crime. It was said that colonial authorities and their brand of punishment often mirrored that of a stern father seeking to change the behavior of their wayward children (Hirsch, 1992). For instance, before being executed in 1789 for robbery, Rachel Wall's public confession mirrored that of a disobedient child as she not only pled guilty to her crimes but also confessed to lying and stealing from her family and breaking the Sabbath (Williams, 1993).

Social control was loosely regulated by a few colony members who acted in a quasi-law enforcement capacity. The formation of systematized "policing" did not exist except for slave patrols. However, in colonies considered "backcountry," it was not unusual to have breakdowns in systems of social control—where retribution was exponentially more brutal if the "perpetrators" happened to be from outside the community. Efforts to rehabilitate people held in makeshift jails (or otherwise confined) were inconceivable as colonists had no real expectations of eradicating crime and focused their efforts solely on retribution.

The Genesis of Prisons

Until the eighteenth century, prisons as we know them today did not exist. What existed were holding facilities for those accused of committing crimes or public offenses contrary to the religious zeitgeist. Individuals were usually held for a short term until a verdict (Rotman, 1990). But by the late 1700s, the "Age of Enlightenment" would drastically alter the response to crime in the colonies. Fathers of the soon-to-be republic were drawn to the work of French thinkers such as Montesquieu, Voltaire, and Diderot. They were also impressed by Italian thinker Cesare Beccaria—whose anonymous essay on *Crimes and Punishment* is considered a catalyst in birthing the new paradigm (Allen et al., 1975). Seeking to find a middle path, retributive practices were allegedly cast aside—with its critics condemning them as barbaric and antiquated. "The rhetoric of the Enlightenment suggested that misguided individuals could be persuaded to exercise moral restraint, good judgment, and self-control" (Blomberg & Lucken, 2010, p. 29). Rule breakers were no longer to be punished based on religious virtue or offenses deemed by the Bible to be against God. Instead, they would be judged by the commission of acts contrary to the welfare of their community—an ideological shift that would ultimately birth the settlement house movement and the social work profession.

As cities formed, there would be a substantial increase in "crime"—Benjamin Rush, a founding father of the United States, initiated discourse with interested reformers to discuss ways to address it. This resulted in the recommendation that "criminals"[1] serve sentences as their punishment, versus capital or corporal punishment, the established custom (Williams, 2006). This recommendation would drastically change the utilization of prisons in the United States.

The Industrial Revolution, the influx of new immigrants, and the *emancipation* of slaves were all seen as an affront to the idealized nation that early colonizers had sought to create. And as the US population became less homogeneous, the utilization of Black codes, convict leasing, and prisons as a means of social control and racialized capitalistic exploitation became more normalized.

[1] To honor the integrity of the research, we use dehumanizing language such as "offenders," "convict," "prisoners" etc., but we ask, as a first practice toward abolition, that social work and other practitioners humanize the men, women, and children who have caged by referring to them as people—formerly incarcerated, incarcerated, or adjacent to the carceral system. See: https://ir.lawnet.fordham.edu/pp/5/.

The "panopticon" was designed by Jeremy Bentham (2020) in the United Kingdom and would become the model for prisons in the United States and worldwide. The panopticon design featured a square wheel with cell blocks arranged like spokes around the hub—which enabled prisoners to be kept separate while allowing a guard to be placed at the central observation point in the middle. The separation, isolation, and design of early prisons were considered integral for rehabilitation. It was said that "The features of separation and surveillance were intended to divide time, space, and bodies in such a way as to purify the pathological, prevent the spread of 'disease', and render each man arbiter of his own monitoring and control" (Blomberg & Lucken, 2010, p. 50). Panopticon design principles, particularly observation that obscures a detainee's ability to know whether or not they are being watched, would ultimately be exported to sanatoriums and other "locked" treatment facilities—a line of continuity across varied forms of imprisonment and mental health services that remains to this day.

The Auburn and Pennsylvania Systems

To better understand the ethos of modern-day prisons, we present a brief analysis of two of its oldest. First, the Auburn system, developed during the post-revolutionary war period, became known as the "congregate" system. In contrast, the Pennsylvania system became known as the "separate" system as it always espoused prisoners' silence and separateness. While the two approaches differed primarily regarding the time spent in solitary confinement, they maintained numerous similarities as they both strove to maintain discipline by enforcing stringent rules (Barnes, 1921).

In 1821, prison administrators at Auburn designed an experiment to test the efficacy of the Pennsylvania system. They took 80 of the men they felt were most resistant to reform and placed them in solitary confinement, enforcing idleness for a period ranging from Christmas 1821 to 1823. While the design was criticized as certain facets did not accurately match that of the Pennsylvania system, the results demonstrated that most men became mentally or physically sick, leading to the experiment's early termination. Proponents of the Auburn system would also cite its ability to produce income via prison labor as a factor to favor that system. "Bigger and cheaper" was the motto, selling points that would incentivize states, from the North to the South, to build 35 new prisons, with Auburn as the prototype, from 1825 to 1869 (Allen et al., 1975).

Southern Prison Economy

The racial and financial dependence on slavery and a nefarious loophole in the 13th Amendment of the US Constitution—which proclaimed, "Neither slavery nor involuntary servitude, except as a punishment for crime whereof the party shall have been duly convicted, shall exist within the United States, or any place subject to their jurisdiction"—allowed Southern states to adopt laws that essentially criminalized every facet of Black life post-emancipation (U.S. Const. amend. XIV, n.d.).

"Black Codes" and slave catchers rebranded as "police" targeted former slaves for being poor, homeless, jobless, or stealing food. Vagrancy laws and a myriad of racially coded regulations were enforced primarily against poor Black people (Brucato, 2020; Oshinsky, 1997). Once "duly convicted," which they often were, they could then be *legally* held in servitude and subsequently leased out to the same plantations that once enslaved them (James & Smyth, 2014a, 2014b). Once convicted, they were sent anywhere in the United States that demanded labor. Treatment and living conditions were deplorable. David Rothman, a researcher of US prison history, captures the rationale for maintaining a broken system in this statement: "If nothing else, penal institutions were convenient because they housed the 'strange alien hordes' such as 'negroes', immigrants, and other challenges to the status quo" (Rothman, 1971, p. 59).

The Reform Era

The American Prison Congress of 1870, organized by Enoch Wines, came together to design the perfect penal system. It featured wardens, "penal experts," and over 130 representatives from various countries and most states within the nation (McKelvey, 1977). The meetings were acrimonious as presenters jockeyed for their ideas to be the prototype all others would follow. However, one proposal stood out—Zebulon Brockway, who represented the New York delegation, gave a speech titled "Ideal for a True Prison System for a State." Brockway had a long and respected career in prisons and proposed that a nonpolitical commission be created and given total authority to build and control juvenile reform schools for youth. He suggested that discipline be administered by grades and marks—which would then be used to determine release dates for individuals with indeterminate sentences. Brockway's paper became the center of a stormy discussion, but most of his recommendations were approved (McKelvey, 1977).

At its core, the Declaration of Principles argued that instead of focusing on the nature of the offense, attention should be given to the nature of the "offender," a paradigm shift that would birth the foundational logics of early social work practice: the "Reform Movement" and its first reformatory, Elmira, in upstate New York (Allen et al., 1975). Zebulon Brockway served as Elmira's first superintendent and experimented with privileges for good conduct to maintain compliance and discipline.

Halfway-type housing was utilized as a prelude to release in an attempt to reorient the individual to society after their incarceration. Brockway reasoned that the old way relied on a "mystic morality" that was not quantifiable and thus unmeasurable in assessing the institution's efficacy (Petersilia & Reitz, 2012).

This new "scientific application" was primarily intended for first-time male "offenders" incarcerated between the ages of 16 and 30. This age range was thought to be less hardened in criminal behavior and more susceptible to reform. This new medical model approach assumed that "offenders" were sick and attempted to "cure" them (Rotman, 1990). Similar to psychiatric hospitals, "prisoners" were now referred to as "inmates"—with the belief that the new designation would instill greater character and accountability. The vernacular and work of the staff also mirror that of the medical profession. Daily activities were quantified and thus measured, allowing staff to track and reward each satisfactory stage completed. Once satisfactory progress had been demonstrated, the "offender" would be released into a period of community supervision known as parole (Blomberg & Lucken, 2010). Parole, coupled with the indeterminate sentence, was the carrot that penologists envisioned would lead "inmates" to the well of reform.

The application of this system, however, failed to replicate theoretical expectations. Guidelines for intermediate sentencing were mostly nonexistent; when they did exist, they were often not followed. What was intended to create uniformity and thus eliminate disparities in sentencing did precisely the opposite. "Indeterminate sentencing without guidelines fueled sentencing disparities, with 'offenders' of identical legal status serving sentences of different lengths" (Blomberg & Lucken, 2010, p. 80).

Calculating prison wardens, who were always searching for new ways to control their increasing populations, began to utilize the threat of denying parole to maintain control of their prisons. It is also within the development of parole and probation that we see the further integration and co-optation of social work, forensic psychology, and criminology in the ideological ethos and practice of prisons and the carceral apparatus.

The original conception of parole release involved a team of behavioral experts serving as the "parole board"—whose duties were to appropriately review facets of the "offender's" institutional record, as well as the "offender's" insight into the crime and their plans for the future. However, the parole boards were composed mainly of politicians and their friends. The parole board interview often lasted no more than 5 min (Rotman, 1990). With no formal guidelines to follow, the meetings focused on arbitrary factors like appearance, likeability, or their ability to convince the parole board that they were indeed *reformed* (Blomberg & Lucken, 2010).

Individuals, once released to parole, were mandated to stay away from communities held in "criminal repute"—an almost insurmountable task considering many had no choice but to go back to the same poor, over-policed, crime-ridden neighborhoods from which they came (Blomberg & Lucken, 2010). The fallacy inherent within this stipulation would result in high revocation and violations. Mays and Winfree classified these early years of parole as essentially a "merry-go-round" that always returned criminalized people back to prison (Mays & Winfree, 2013).

"Probation" was intended as an alternative to prison for crimes not considered too egregious. The theory was that some "offenders" would be best served with community rehabilitation versus prison (Blomberg & Lucken, 2010). Yet, like its sister agency parole, probation officers were under-skilled, underpaid, and overworked—sometimes responsible for caseloads totaling almost 300 individuals (Rothman, 1971). "The ability of probation officers to provide informed decisions to judges, and supervision to 'offenders' was predictably impeded" (Blomberg & Lucken, 2010, p. 82). Contact between probation officers and "offenders" was mandated and ranged from once weekly to monthly. However, in many cases, the contact was rare and, in some jurisdictions, amounted to no more than 10 min a year. Consequently, presentence investigations, often conducted by social workers, consisted of few facts and much speculation and were given little consideration.

Enoch Wines, a prominent reformer of the time, condemned the reform movement for its "over-incarceration" and unfair sentencing of Blacks in proportion to whites. Reform movement leaders were also criticized for lacking the ability to discern between punishment and abuse (Wines, 1879). Reports would show Zebulon Brockway, the man many considered the face of the reformatory movement, vigorously administered paternal discipline in his reformatory. As Blomberg and Lucken (2010) note, "Euphemisms, such as spanking of the patients, positive extraneous assistance, or harmless parental discipline, essentially gave scientific credibility to beatings and cruelty" (p. 79).

The reform era spawned an ideological ethos leading to varying clinical approaches toward understanding and addressing "crime." By 1926, most prisons had a psychiatrist or psychologist. The emerging field of social psychiatry influenced a more "inclusive" view of the "offender" (McKelvey, 1977). The lens of causation (a determinant of treatment) shifted from myopic—perceiving the accused as sick and needing healing—to a more holistic approach, which considered various social and economic factors in assessment and subsequent treatment (Rotman, 1990). In theory, this new approach appeared to be "right" as it addressed many of the incongruities that had long plagued theoretical explanations of crime; however, with time, it too would exist more in theory than practice. Reform era influence is still present in the forms of parole and probation, alternative courts, and mandated treatment—with many of these positions held by social workers (Allen et al., 1975).

Capitalism and the Rise of Super Prisons

The decades during and preceding the Great Depression witnessed a substantial boom in prisons and prisoners to fill them. During this period, the number of people in US prisons increased by almost 200%—more than ten prisons were built, most utilizing Auburn as the model (Allen et al., 1975). This period was also known as the "Industrial Era" of prisons. Utilizing various facets of the industry, prisons essentially became self-sufficient entities. With no labor or commercial laws to restrict them, prisons had carte blanche authority to produce and sell products generated from the exploited labor of incarcerated people. However, opposition was mounting, and the push for greater labor regulation witnessed under President Franklin D. Roosevelt brought it all to a head.

The *Hawes-Cooper Act* of 1929 and the *Ashurst-Summers Act* of 1935 economically affected prison industries by regulating prison products in relation to sale and distribution. As the economy worsened during the Depression, 33 states passed laws effectively prohibiting the sale of prison products on the open market, dealing a severe blow to the prison industry (Allen et al., 1975). As money once generated by the industry began to wane, so did euphoria and attempts at prison reform.

Alcatraz, the super maximum-security prison in San Francisco Bay, epitomized more than any prison of its era the fear of "criminals." The prison exemplified isolation and did not permit visitors, which added to its allure. Alcatraz was also allegedly impossible to escape—whether true or not, it was a proclamation intended to assuage a society suffering from "convict bogey" (Wellman, 2008).

The lack of income generated by former industries and the rising prison population reduced the meager attempts at prison reform even further, resulting in unprecedented prison riots starting in 1929 and continuing through to World War II. Yet the riots would continue shortly after the war as prisoners became increasingly less tolerant of the inhumane conditions they experienced throughout the country. Alcatraz would have its first riot in 1946, setting the tone for almost 200 more nationwide prison riots between 1950 and 1966 (Wellman, 2008).

The endemic violence in US prisons in the 1950s and the 1960s was arguably exacerbated by the Civil Rights era—where millions of oppressed and marginalized people stood up and demanded equality. McKelvey (1977), a researcher of this period, stated:

> As in the larger society, these uprisings not only protested deficiencies in housing, sanitation...but also challenged basic aspects of the system. Confronted, by demands that they could not satisfy...officials hastened to suppress the protesters with force. The crescendo of violence however brought a series of investigations and prompted citizens and legal scholars alike to look again at the basic philosophy of the system. (p. 350)

The American Prison Association proclaimed the reform era a failure and thus began to reshape its charter and purpose. In 1954, it changed its name to the "American Correctional Association" and encouraged states to rename their prisons "Correctional Institutions." A revised manual of correctional standards was issued. However, these surface changes would do little to quell the riots and resistance by prisoners tired of being brutalized under the guise of rehabilitation.

The Politicization of Prisoners

The racial hostility inherent in the 1960s and 1970s added to the mounting tension between the primarily Black prisoners and their white prison guards. Many incarcerated Black people began to consider themselves "political prisoners"—victims of capitalism, racism, and a legalized system of subjugation, a belief that was further exacerbated as numerous civil rights and anti-war activists were incarcerated.

The "political prisoner" narrative was further fueled by nationalistic organizations such as the "Black Panthers" and the "Black Muslims," whose membership rose exponentially under the mounting racial tensions (McKelvey, 1977). Both elegant and defiant, George Jackson, a member of the Black Panther Party, came to embody the mantle of *the* political prisoner. Sentenced to a minor charge at 18, Jackson spent over a decade in prison due to numerous parole board denials and trumped-up prison charges.

On January 16, 1970, Jackson was thrust into the national spotlight when he was charged along with two other prisoners—collectively known as the "Soledad Brothers"—for the killing of a white guard at Soledad Prison in California (Liberatore, 1996). The case made national headlines and, in many ways, cemented Jackson's legacy among fellow prisoners. However, his notoriety and legend were further boosted by a series of deadly events—beginning with the trial of the "Soledad Brothers."

Jonathan Jackson, the 17-year-old younger brother of George Jackson, disillusioned with the justice system and its treatment of George, took matters into his own hands when he staged an armed takeover of Marin County Courthouse, demanding the freedom of his brother George (who was not in court) and the "Soledad Brothers" (Liberatore, 1996). But Jonathan's attempt was thwarted, and he was killed along with the judge during a shoot-out with the police as he attempted to escape.

The courthouse takeover made national headlines and spawned one of the most famous manhunts in United States history in search of Angela Davis—a college professor, activist, and known member of the Black Panther Party—whose registered guns were allegedly used by Jonathan in the failed attempt. George Jackson never left prison alive. His final protest came on August 21, 1971, as he "was shot down, allegedly in a frantic dash across the yard for freedom" (Liberatore, 1996, p. 354). The circumstances of his death remain questionable to this day. Still, his murder would make him a martyr and trigger a string of prison riots across the country—including the infamous Attica riots (Liberatore, 1996).

Attica and the Demand for Human Rights

Attica State Prison, while located thousands of miles away from San Quentin, mirrored its racially abusive conditions and was thus fertile soil for the Black Muslims, the Black Panthers, and its Puerto Rican equivalent, the Young Lords. These organizations formed an allegiance after participating in a sociology class led by incarcerated individuals in the summer of 1971 (McKelvey, 1977). Their goal, as articulated by their manifesto, was "to change forever the ruthless brutalization and disregard for the lives of prisoners here and throughout the United States" (Levinson, 2008, p. 1232).

The Attica Brotherhood echoed the political sentiments of George Jackson and thus saw his death as the catalyst for action—they started by organizing an all-day fast and silence in his honor, which served to create solidarity among prisoners usually divided and controlled along racial lines. Emboldened by this mass cohesion, the leaders among the prisoners began to write grievances challenging the "barbaric conditions" that existed at Attica; however, when the administration considered none of their recommended reforms, the prisoners took matters into their own hands—for 5 days, beginning September 9th to the 13th, 1971, more than 1200 prisoners rebelled and seized control of the prison, burning many of its buildings and taking 39 hostages, consisting of both guards and civilian prison staff.

"We are men. We are not beasts, and we do not intend to be beaten or driven as such" (Kaba, 2021, p. 11) was the call to arms by one of the rebellion leaders, L. D. Barkley, who, along with other leaders, would craft a "manifesto" protesting, in a historical manner, the inhumanity of Attica and every other prison in the world.

The *men* of Attica, without scholarly access to the historical genesis of prisons, or maybe even knowledge of the 13th Amendment, nonetheless articulated sentiments echoing a clear understanding that prisons, and their role in them, were nothing more than a perverse continuation of the legalized control, subjugation, and commodification of Black people (and other undesirables) within America. The event garnered national headlines. Twenty-seven high-profile celebrities came to Attica as "neutral observers" to end the hostage situation; however, things did not end well:

> Just before ten in the morning, on September 13th, a National Guard helicopter dropped tear gas into the prison yard. Then some five hundred and fifty New York State Police troopers, augmented by more than two hundred sheriff's deputies—and with the Attica correction officers unconscionably mixed in—entered the prison and mounted the catwalks. Armed with shotguns deliberately loaded with wide-arc buckshot and .270 rifles loaded with unjacketed bullets, of a kind banned by the Geneva Conventions, they started shooting, firing at everything they saw. "The bullets were coming like rain," one hostage recalled. (Gopnik, 2016, para. 21)

The subsequent massacre at Attica by the State Police and the numerous illuminative reports that preceded it served to further jolt the consciousness of the American people and Congress to the problem of prisons in the nation (Zimbardo, 2011). Numerous commissions and hearings took place due to the confluence of violence at San Quentin and Attica; the hearings further illuminated inhumane practices and conditions that festered and grew in prisons (Rotman, 1990). The subsequent reports produced by the various commissioned inquiries led to a renewed attempt at prison rights, improved prison conditions, and programming that could be substantiated through evaluative methods; however, what happened in the subsequent decades not only mirrored the violence and inhumanity emblematic of prisons in the United States since their genesis but expanded to unprecedented heights.

History of Prisons in the United States Post-Attica Uprising (1971–Present)

1970s: Aftermath of Attica and Policy Changes

The prison population in the 1970s post-Attica stood at about 200,000. However, well-coordinated events would create a prison boom never seen on planet Earth in any nation, much less one that considers itself the paragon of democracy. The first event was the "war on drugs" initiated by the Comprehensive Drug Abuse Prevention and Control Act of 1970, which classified *drugs* in varied levels of seriousness and punishment. Then, in 1971, President Richard Nixon declared drug abuse as "public enemy number one," leading to the creation of the Drug Enforcement Administration (DEA) in 1973 to consolidate federal efforts against drug use (Stuart, 2011).

Nelson Rockefeller—who served as Governor of New York from 1959 to 1973, had high political aspirations, and later served as Vice President of the United States under President Gerald Ford—did not want to appear soft on crime on a national level, which many argue led to his decision to send in the national guards and instigate the massacre at Attica (Thompson, 2014). However, Rockefeller's enduring legacy would be a drug law, which would be praised and emulated by many states and countries throughout the world and would have an enduring legacy on the history of policing, jails, prisons, and millions of black and brown people.

Rockefeller's drug law bore his name and set the stage for what we would call "mass incarceration." However, before the passage of the laws, he was a proponent of treatment and rehabilitation but shifted course to align with the "tough-on-crime" movement and the political zeitgeist. The *Rockefeller Drug laws* were dubbed draconian and inhumane as they took discretion away from judges and instead created mandatory minimums of 15 and 25 years with a max of life imprisonment for people convicted of possessing as little as two ounces of cocaine. The laws were *supposed* to be a deterrent and targeted at drug kingpins, but most of the people locked up were poor Black and Brown people seeking to escape the perpetual traumas of White supremacy through substance use (Drucker, 2002).

1980s: War on Drugs and the Prison Boom

Reminiscent of the Black Codes of 1865, the "war on drugs" fueled by draconian laws, over-policing, anti-blackness, and racial profiling would see the prison population almost double from the previous decade to almost 400,000 people and climbing with no end in sight. "In 1985, President Reagan hired media staff to paint the portrait of the war on drugs as a Black problem. Images of Black drug dealers, 'crack whores,' 'crack babies,' and the decay of inner-city neighborhoods' permeated the public consciousness" and numbed any empathy or curiosity about the unparalleled rise in incarceration rates (James & Smyth, 2014a, 2014b, p. 109).

Nancy Reagan's infamous "Just Say No" catchphrase and campaign further oversimplified, dehumanized, and negated the myriad of socioeconomic factors substance users faced, allowing for trust and overreliance on the federal government, which responded by using The *Rockefeller Drug laws* as a model for the Anti-Drug Abuse Act of 1986, which introduced harsher penalties for drug offenses, mandatory minimums, and similarly took away discretion from judges. The 1986 Act established a 100:1 sentencing disparity between crack and powder cocaine, meaning possession of just 5 g of crack cocaine triggered the same mandatory minimum sentence as 500 g of powder cocaine (Tonry, 1995). The drug laws of the 1980s were not passed in a vacuum. What made them so dangerous was the prevalence of widespread trauma, poverty, suffering, and the introduction of crack cocaine to inner city neighborhoods—which much evidence suggests was intentionally done (Blum, 1996).

The Iran-Contra affair was a political scandal that was exposed in 1986 involving high-level government officials within the Reagan Administration who were *illegally* selling guns to Iran to aid in their flight with Iraq who the United States considered an enemy. The proceeds from the guns were then smuggled to Contras—a rebel group supported by the United States fighting the Sandinista government in Nicaragua. Journalist Gary Webb's "Dark Alliance" series in 1996 alleged that the CIA was involved or turned a blind eye to drug smuggling by the Contras and other groups, allowing for the proliferation of crack cocaine in the inner city (Blum, 1996).

1990s: Mass Incarceration

By the 1990s, tough-on-crime policy, the drug war, and the omnipresent policing of Black and Brown bodies created a period of incarceration that by the end of the decade, there were "More African Americans …in prison or jail, on probation or parole—than were enslaved in 1850 before the Civil War began" (Alexander, p. 175). The decade, like the previous, also introduced policies like the 1994 Crime Bill—drafted by then-senator Joe Biden and signed into law by President Bill Clinton—which furthered mandatory minimum sentences, three-strikes laws, increased policing and prevalence of inner-city communities, and incentivized states to create more punitive laws and build more than 200 new prisons by providing almost 10 billion dollars in federal funds (Alexander, 2011). It was reported that a new prison was opened every 15 days. Most were built in remote and economically distressed communities to replace lost income.

Similarly to previous decades, politicians furthered anti-blackness and rallied support for punitive bills by negating socioeconomics and other factors that precipitate what we call crime, furthering the narrative of them vs us and prioritizing punishment over rehabilitation. In advocating for the 1994 crime bill, Joe Biden stated during a senate debate that "We must take back the streets," while Hillary Clinton, in support of the bill, labeled Black children involved with the carceral system as "super predators" with "no conscience, no empathy" and who could only be controlled through strict punishment (Cooper, 2023).

Research throughout the decade showed that drug usage was about equal between Blacks and Whites; however, when "a survey asked people to close their eyes and envision a drug user. The results were published in the Journal of Alcohol and Drug Education found that 95% of participants pictured a Black drug user, while only 5% envisioned other races" (James & Smyth, 2014a, 2014b, p. 110). By the decade's end, the prison population had surged from less than 200,000 in the 1970s to almost 2 million.

African Americans comprised about 40% of the prison population despite being only about 13% of the US population (Mauer, 1999). Research further indicated that one in three Black men could be expected to be incarcerated during their lifetime. The never-before-seen levels of incarceration had a devastating impact not only on incarcerated individuals but also on their communities, families, and friends.

A content analysis of hip-hop music during the era from artists like Wu-Tang Clan, Tupac, Biggie, and Nas all spoke to the varied impact of incarceration on their communities—it was a cry for help, but no one was listening! The criminalization of Blacks, which began with the 13th Amendment and Black Codes of 1865 and continued through various racialized ideologies and practices, finally solidified the narrative of Black criminality in the United States and much of the world (Shabazz, 2021).

When discussing "mass incarceration" during the 1990s, a factor often overlooked is the passage of the Illegal Immigration Reform and Immigrant Responsibility Act (IIRAIRA), which, like the 1994 crime bill, took away judicial discretion and made many minor crimes more serious. The law also had a provision for mandatory detention and deportation. It was made retroactive, leading to millions of people being targeted by the carceral state for minor offenses, often decades old. Like the crime bill, implementing the IIRAIRA through federal funding and grants such as the State Criminal Alien Assistance Program (SCAAP) incentivizes states to detain immigrants and expand detention facilities (Fragomen, 1997).

Many immigration prisons were run by capitalistic-oriented private prison companies with little regard for the humanity of their prisoners. Still, they had contracts from the federal government assuring them guaranteed bed minimums and thus a steady income stream. Law enforcement was similarly incentivized to detain immigrants through federal dollars, leading to the daily detention population average rising from about 7500 in 1995 to close to 20,000 by the end of the decade (Detention Watch Network, 2016).

While the racial aspect of incarceration is often highlighted, it should be noted that the hyper-incarceration of Black and Brown people is a very intentional form of racial capitalism similar to slavery. The American Legislative Exchange Council, better known as "ALEC," is a nonprofit organization of conservative state legislators and private sector representatives that has played a crucial role in the growth of prisons and incarceration. It promotes and drafts tough-on-crime laws, including three-strikes laws, mandatory minimum sentencing, and truth in sentencing. ALEC has strong ties and support from the private prison industry, including companies like Corrections Corporation of America and GEO Group (Cohen, 2013).

ALEC bills like the "Prison Industries Act" support establishing and expanding prison industries where incarcerated individuals work for private companies like Victoria's Secret, which benefit economically from the cheap labor provided by incarcerated individuals, who are often paid significantly less than the minimum wage allowing businesses to reduce their labor costs and increase profits (Cao, 2018). Policies promoted by ALEC increase incarceration rates and contribute to a larger pool of available prison labor. This creates a cyclical relationship where tough-on-crime laws benefit private companies that rely on cheap prison labor and perpetuate a form of modern-day slavery (Sawyer, 2017).

2000s: Continued Growth and Beginning of Reform

The early 2000s saw incarceration rates continue to rise, peaking at around 2008 with 1.6 million incarcerated individuals (BJS, 2009). However, the number was significantly greater when you factored in people detained or under other forms of carceral control, including probation, parole, or immigrant detention (Glaze & Bonczar, 2009). The drastic increase in prisoners and prisons exponentially exacerbated the historical inhumane conditions emblematic of jails and prisons.

In states like California, which had the largest prison population then, the Supreme Court case Brown v. Plata (2011) mandated that they address inadequate healthcare issues and prison overcrowding by reducing the population. However, immigrant detention facilities continued to increase, leading to the creation of the Department of Homeland Security (DHS) in 2003 to manage them. DHS contracted private prisons like "Corrections Corporation of America," which was plagued by overcrowding, inhumane conditions, and violence (Detention Watch, 2016).

By the 2000s, the United States, with less than 5% of the world population, had nonetheless managed to incarcerate over 25% of the world's prisoners and was far and away the world's leader in all facets of incarceration (James & Smyth, 2014a, 2014b). "Mass incarceration" was now mainstream, with many advocates and politicians highlighting its racial, societal, and economic impact, leading to attempts at *reform*. A primary policy was the Second Chance Act of 2007, which aimed to lower the likelihood that people returned to jail post-release (recidivism) by providing funding for education, job training, and varied substance use treatment. Alternative to incarceration (ATI) models were also utilized throughout the country to provide drug courts, probation, treatment, and varied alternatives to incarceration for mostly nonviolent offenders (Petersilia, 2004). Even with attempts at *reform*, research would still conclude that Black and Brown people remained overrepresented in every facet of the prison population. Black women would also become the fastest-growing prison population statistically, with little research to extrapolate the impact on their families and communities, which were already compromised.

2010s: Reform and Decline

For the first time in decades, the prison population declined slightly—reaching about 1.5 million by 2019 (BJS, 2009). Books like Michelle Alexander's *New Jim Crow* would further highlight the issues of jails and prisons by providing empirical and historical research on how the United States managed to create a new form of slavery and social control through the carceral system. The book brought widespread attention to what Alexander argues is a racial caste system disproportionality impacting Blacks and other minorities.

Varied advocacy led to legislative changes, such as the Fair Sentencing Act of 2010 (U.S. Congress, 2010) and the First Step Act of 2018 (U.S. Congress, 2018), which aimed to reduce sentences for nonviolent offenses and improve prison conditions. Many states, no longer seeing prisons and jails as profitable, have invested in sentencing laws, parole policies, and mental health treatment and ended cash bail, leading to a further decline in the prison population.

2020s: Ongoing Reforms and COVID-19 Impact

March 2020 and the global lockdown put in place to mitigate the impact of COVID-19 are moments that the people who survived will never forget. It was also a moment, furthered by the killings of George Floyd, Breonna Taylor, and others, along with movements like Black Lives Matter, which again highlighted the historical racial disparities in the carceral system (James, 2021).

The widespread outbreaks in correctional facilities throughout the United States, including San Quintin State Prison in California, saw more than half of its population (1600 people) test positive for COVID-19 (Cloud et al., 2020). The mortality rates among prisoners were also significantly higher than the general population. By the end of 2020, more than 2700 deaths had been reported in state and federal prisons (Franco-Paredes et al., 2020), and a research study found that the mortality rate of the virus was almost three times higher for prisoners than the general population (Saloner et al., 2020).

In June 2021, with admittedly poor testing and the inability to socially isolate, there were almost 400,000 reported cases of COVID-19, with an infection rate over 5 times higher than the general population (Saloner et al., 2020). The pandemic, again, challenged the larger society to see people in jails and prisons as human, empathize with their plight, and demand change in a broken system—leading many states to implement decarceration strategies, restorative justice, and varied practices to reduce prison populations including of releasing nonviolent offenders, elderly, and people with preexisting health conditions. However, as of 2023, there are approximately 3.9 million people in the United States still under some form of community supervision, and more than 1.5 million people are incarcerated (Davis, 2023).

Conclusion

It has been almost five decades since Attica. Yet the call for justice and humanity by people affected by prisons—witnessed since their genesis in early colonial America—still echoes loudly to this day (Selke, 1993). It is said that "Attica is every prison, and every prison is Attica" (New York State Special Commission on Attica, 1972). Despite decades of reform efforts, US jails and prisons remain inhumane sites of violence, harm, and unprecedented trauma—just as they were designed to be. Between 1972 and 2009, the US prison population increased by almost 700%—fueled by racist policies and practices versus actual increases in "crime." Most people incarcerated are poor, of color, and historically marginalized within the rhetoric of "democracy."

In 1971, the Attica manifesto called for social workers—and, today, the social work profession—is embedded in numerous spaces aimed at addressing the harms of the carceral system, not limited to reentry services, alternatives to incarceration, specialized courts, mandated mental health and substance use treatment, community supervision, training of and collaboration with law enforcement, and policy reform advocacy. And while the positive impact of these interventions may reduce immediate harm to people impacted by the carceral system—which is needed—on the whole, they achieve only incremental change to a system rooted in the ethos of slavery and White supremacy.

Ending mass incarceration requires the uprooting of ideologies that allow for its continued existence. The punishment paradigm upon which prisons are built extends far beyond the walls of any of the physical structures designed to lock people away from their families, communities, and support networks. Punishment and marginalization remain at the core of many "criminal justice reform" efforts—hence why they have consistently replicated carceral outcomes.

The Sankofa of prisons demonstrates that jails, prisons, and "alternatives" are doing precisely what they were designed to do and thus cannot be "tweaked" or reformed. Eddie Ellis, a former Black Panther and prisoner during the Attica riots, often shared the story of McDonald's and its billboards boasting of "millions served"—before asking his audience to imagine: what would happen if half those people returned their food? He would let the question sit for a while, then say: "McDonald's would go out of business!" So imagine now that the likelihood of a person being sent back to prison within 5 years of being released is nearly 50% (Benecchi, 2021) and that many of the challenges associated with jails and prisons today, such as racial targeting, access to bail, capitalistic labor exploitation, lack of mental health services, educational programming, pre- and post-release planning inclusive of parole and probation, and solitary confinement, are not things that have simply gone wrong and need to be fixed but are emblematic of an inhumane system (Saloner et al., 2020).

Social workers must resist fearmongering by the media and "tough-on-crime" politicians' depiction of "crime waves" driven by decarceration. The carceral system is complex and constantly evolving—an organism seeking homeostasis. When one aspect of the system is reformed, it self-corrects in another area to maintain the status quo. Audre Lorde says, "The master's tools will never dismantle the master's house" (2007, p. 112). "Reform" is the master's tool and negates the insidious history of prisons.

As Mariame Kaba states, "One thing that remains constant for me is that the system—the prison industrial complex—isn't broken. The system of mass criminalization we have isn't the result of failure" (2021, para. 2). We must therefore acknowledge the inherent limitations of *reforming* a system that is achieving its true purpose and move forward under radically divergent, abolitionist models.

Abolition, a theory of change, has always been intersectional and much more than eradicating slavery, police, jails, and prisons. Abolition is imagining new systems of living, working, education, healthcare, and community investments. The social work profession, rooted in understanding the many histories, systems, and factors that impact people and communities, is uniquely positioned to reject criminalization, envision possibilities, and create anew. If we, as social workers, are to be true to the core values of our profession, i.e., social justice, the dignity and worth of all people, and the dismantling of all systems, structures, and practices that uphold dehumanization and the punishment paradigm, then abolition is the only option.

The work of abolition can and must occur in the myriad professional settings where social workers find themselves. Social work within carceral spaces is inherently challenging. Yet liberatory practice does not exist in conflict with nor negate the value of harm reduction. Balancing the objective of advancing abolition while simultaneously meeting the needs of human beings captured by jails and prisons in this "now" is our responsibility. It requires diligently envisioning and creating new possibilities while also bringing light into the darkness of current systems. Holding the tension of work in carceral spaces while actively building a liberatory society is a critical part of our charge.

We must reject interventions that criminalize and punish and speak out against the expansion of carceral institutions and practices into schools, mental health treatment, social services, and all other settings. We must follow the wisdom of the late Eddie Ellis and abandon dehumanizing language in favor of terminology that puts *people* first (Ellis, 2007). When serving marginalized, pathologized, and criminalized populations, we must move away from domination and othering toward partnership; we must be trauma informed and embrace what bell hooks terms a "love ethos" (2000).

Finally, for social work to honor its values as a profession, we must reject the carceral state, embrace abolition, and imagine a world in which police, jails, prisons, and the underlying ideologies that spawned them are all obsolete—except as written testimonies and a warning to future generations of the darkness that existed within them.

Reflection Questions

1. How does the concept of good and evil and racism impede or assist us in a critical analysis of what we call "crime"?
2. In what ways do you think the legacy of slavery informs our carceral system and social work practice?
3. How can social workers who believe in abolition practice harm reduction within the carceral system?

References

Alexander, M. (2011). The New Jim Crow. *New York, NY*: New Press.

Allen, H. E., Simonsen, C. E., & Latessa, E. J. (1975). *Corrections in America: An introduction* (p. 120). Glencoe Press.

Barnes, H. E. (1921). Historical origin of the prison system in America. *Journal of the American Institute of Criminal Law and Criminology, 12*, 35.

Benecchi, L. (2021). Recidivism imprisons American progress. *Harvard Political Review, 8*.

Bentham, J. (2020). *The panopticon writings*. Verso Books.

Blomberg, T. G., & Lucken, K. (2010). *American penology: A history of control*. Routledge.

Blum, W. (1996). The CIA, contras, gangs, and crack. *Foreign Policy in Focus, 1*.

Brucato, B. (2020). Policing race and racing police. *Social Justice, 47*(3/4, 161/162), 115–136.

Cao, L. (2018). Made in America: Race, trade, and prison labor. SSRN Electronic *Journal*. https://doi.org/10.2139/ssrn.3136654

Cloud, D. H., Ahalt, C., Augustine, D., Sears, D., & Williams, B. (2020). Medical isolation and solitary confinement: Balancing health and humanity in US jails and prisons during COVID-19. *Journal of General Internal Medicine, 35*(9), 2738–2742.

Cohen, M. (2013). ALEC's influence over criminal justice legislation in the United States. The Nation. Retrieved from https://www.thenation.com/article/archive/alecs-influence-over-criminal-justice-legislation-united-states/

Cooper, H. (2023). *Put y'all back in chains: How Joe Biden's policies hurt black Americans*. Simon and Schuster.

Davis, A. (2023). *The state of mass incarceration in America*. Random House.

Detention Watch Network. (2016). *Banking on detention: Local lockup quotas & the immigrant dragnet*. Retrieved from https://www.detentionwatchnetwork.org/pressroom/releases/2016/banking-detention-local-lockup-quotas-immigrant-dragnet

Dostoevsky, F. (1967). *The house of the dead* (A. M. D. P., Trans.). New American Library. (Original work published 1862).

Drucker, E. (2002). Population impact of mass incarceration under New York's Rockefeller drug laws: An analysis of years of life lost. *Journal of Urban Health Bulletin of the New York Academy of Medicine, 79*(3), 434–435.

Ellis, E. (2007). An open letter to our friends on the question of language. New York, NY. Center for NuLeadership [online]. Available at: https://prisoneducation.nyu.edu/wp-content/uploads/2015/05/CNUSlang-ltr_regular.pdf.

Fragomen, A. T., Jr. (1997). The illegal immigration reform and immigrant responsibility act of 1996: An overview. *International Migration Review, 31*(2), 438–460.

Franco-Paredes, C., Jankousky, K., Schultz, J., Bernfeld, J., Cullen, K., Quan, N. G., et al. (2020). COVID-19 in jails and prisons: A neglected infection in a marginalized population. *PLoS Neglected Tropical Diseases, 14*(6), e0008409.

Glaze, L. E., & Bonczar, T. P. (2009). *Probation and parole in the United States, 2008 (NCJ 228230)*. Bureau of Justice Statistics, U.S. Department of Justice. Retrieved from https://www.bjs.gov/content/pub/pdf/ppus08.pdf

Gopnik, A. (2016). Learning from the slaughter in Attica: What the 1971 uprising and massacre reveal about our prison system and the liberal democratic state. The New Yorker, August 22, 2016. Retrieved from https://www.newyorker.com/magazine/2016/08/29/learning-from-the-slaughter-in-attica

Hirsch, A. J. (1992). *The rise of the penitentiary: Prisons and punishment in early America* (Vol. 84). Yale University Press.

hooks, b. (2000). *All about love: New visions*. William Morrow.

Jacobs, L. A., Kim, M. E., Whitfield, D. L., Gartner, R. E., Panichelli, M., Kattari, S. K., et al. (2021). Defund the police: Moving towards an anti-carceral social work. *Journal of Progressive Human Services, 32*(1), 37–62.

James, K. J. (2021). Black lives, mass incarceration, and the perpetuity of trauma in the era of COVID-19: The road to abolition social work. In *Shared trauma, shared resilience during a pandemic: Social work in the time of COVID-19* (pp. 281–290).

James, K., & Smyth, J. (2014a). Deconstructing mass incarceration in the United States through a human rights lens: Implications for social work education and practice. In *Advancing human rights in social work education*. CSWE Press.

James, K., & Smyth, J. (2014b). If George Zimmerman were found guilty, would the criminal justice system be considered just?: A racial analysis of American criminal justice in the aftermath of Trayvon Martin. In *Trayvon Martin, race, and American justice* (pp. 107–111). Brill.

Kaba, M. (2021). Towards the horizon of abolition. Retrived from https://thenextsystem.org/learn/stories/towards-horizon-abolition-conversation-mariame-kaba

Levinson, D. (Ed.). (2008). *Encyclopedia of crime and punishment* (Vol. 1). Sage.

Liberatore, P. (1996). *The road to hell: The true story of George Jackson, Stephen Bingham, and the San Quentin Massacre*. Atlantic Monthly Press.

Lorde, A. (2007). The master's tools will never dismantle the master's house. In *Sister outsider: Essays and speeches* (pp. 110–114). Crossing Press.

Mauer, M. (1999). Why are tough on crime policies so popular. *Stanford Law & Policy Review, 11*, 9.

Mays, G. L., & Winfree, L. T., Jr. (2013). *Essentials of corrections*. John Wiley & Sons.

McKelvey, B. (1977). *American prisons: A history of good intentions* (p. 383). Patterson Smith.

New York State Special Commission on Attica. (1972). Attica: The official report of the New York State Special Commission on Attica. Bantam Books.

Oshinsky, D. M. (1997). *Worse than slavery*. Simon and Schuster.

Petersilia, J. (2004). What works in prisoner Reentry? Reviewing and questioning the evidence. *Federal Probation, 68*(2), 4–8. Retrieved from https://www.uscourts.gov/federal-probation-journal/2004/12/what-works-prisoner-reentry-reviewing-and-questioning-evidence

Petersilia, J., & Reitz, K. R. (Eds.). (2012). *The Oxford handbook of sentencing and corrections*. OUP.

Rothman, D. J. (1971). *The discovery of the asylum: Social order and disorder in the new republic*. Routledge.

Rotman, E. (1990). *Beyond punishment: A new view on the rehabilitation of criminal offenders* (p. 115). Greenwood Press.

Saloner, B., Parish, K., Ward, J. A., DiLaura, G., & Dolovich, S. (2020). COVID-19 cases and deaths in federal and state prisons. *JAMA, 324*(6), 602–603.

Sawyer, W. (2017). How much do incarcerated people earn in each state? *Prison Policy Initiative*. Retrieved from https://www.prisonpolicy.org/reports/wages.html

Selke, W. L. (1993). *Prisons in crisis* (Vol. 814). Indiana University Press.

Shabazz, R. (2021). "We gon be alright:" containment, creativity, and the birth of hip-hop. *Cultural Geographies, 28*(3), 447–453.

Stuart, S. (2011). War as metaphor and the rule of law in crisis: The lessons we should have learned from the war on drugs. *The Southern Illinois University Law Journal, 36*, 1.

Thompson, H. A. (2014). Lessons from Attica: From prisoner rebellion to mass incarceration and Back. *Socialism and Democracy, 28*(3), 153–171.
Tonry, M. (1995). *Malign neglect: Race, crime, and punishment in America*. Oxford University Press.
U.S. Congress. (2010). Fair sentencing act of 2010. Public Law, 111–220. Retrieved from https://www.congress.gov/bill/111th-congress/senate-bill/1789
U.S. Congress. (2018). First step act of 2018. Public Law 115–391. Retrieved from https://www.congress.gov/bill/115th-congress/house-bill/5682.
U.S. Const. amend. XIV. (n.d.).
U.S. Department of Justice, Office of Justice Programs, Bureau of Justice Statistics. (2009). Prisoners in 2008 (NCJ 228417).
Wellman, G. L. (2008). *A history of Alcatraz Island: 1853–2008*. Arcadia Publishing.
Williams, D. E. (Ed.). (1993). *Pillars of salt: An anthology of early American criminal narratives*. Rowman & Littlefield Publishers.
Williams, M. (2006). *Virtually criminal: Crime, deviance and regulation online*. Routledge.
Wines, E. C. (1879). *The state of prisons and of child-saving institutions in the civilized world*. J. Wilson & son.
Zimbardo, P. (2011). *The Lucifer effect: How good people turn evil*. Random House.

Chapter 14
Invisible Casualties: Youth Justice Work

Peleya Patterson

Background

The history of youth justice and social work intersects at many different points throughout history. Youth justice can be traced back to the child-saving movement in the late 1800s (Platt, 1969). Viewed as an alternate way of combatting the challenges of urban "wayward" youth caused by an unregulated capitalist society, this work started as a rehabilitative way to address and reform troubled youth (Young et al., 2017). Parenthetically, this notion sounds familiar, like "corrective' in our current corrections system. Successful lobbying for a new rehabilitative approach led to the creation of the juvenile court model in Cook County, Illinois, on July 3, 1899—led by Jane Addams and fellow reformers. Jane Addams was an American settlement activist, feminist, advocate for women's rights, Nobel Peace Prize winner, and social worker. Her work had an overarching theme of giving a voice to the voiceless, which most often included women and children.

The goal of the work within this new juvenile court was the protection of the public, now known as public safety, and rehabilitating youth. This differed from the punitive approach often used in the adult criminal legal system. The new juvenile court would also address the needs of abused and neglected children. The model was adopted across the United States and Canada by 1925 and in other countries in Europe and South America. During the 1950s and 1960s, the juvenile court's philosophy of rehabilitation through individualized justice was questioned by professionals as it led to an increased number of youths being institutionalized indefinitely in the name of treatment. In a series of decisions made by the US Supreme Court in

P. Patterson (✉)
Silver School of Social Work, New York University, New York, NY, USA
e-mail: peleyap@gmail.com

C. Tosone et al. (eds.), *Reframing Social Work with an Anti-Oppressive Lens*, Essential Clinical Social Work Series,
https://doi.org/10.1007/978-3-031-91391-4_14

the 1960s, the juvenile courts were required to become more formal, akin to the criminal courts (McNamara & Burns, 2017).

Almost 50 years after the national adoption of the juvenile court system, the Juvenile Justice and Delinquency Prevention Act of 1974 was established by the Office of Juvenile Justice and Delinquency Prevention (OJJDP) to support local and state efforts to prevent delinquency and improve juvenile justice systems. As a part of the Office of Justice Programs within the US Department of Justice, OJJDP works to prevent and respond to youth delinquency and protect children. Through its divisions, OJJDP sponsors research, program, and training initiatives. OJJDP also develops priorities and goals, sets policies to guide federal juvenile justice issues, disseminates information about juvenile justice issues, and awards funds to states to support local programming (OJJDP, 2023).

Most recently, beginning April 10, 2017, the age of criminal responsibility was raised in New York State from 16 to 18 because of the Raise the Age (RTA) legislation (New York State Unified Court System, Office for Justice Initiatives, n.d.). The goal was to ensure that young people in New York who commit nonviolent crimes receive the intervention and evidence-based treatment they need. The legislation was enacted over 2 years, with 16-year-olds removed from the adult system in 2018 and 17-year-olds removed in 2019. Although the legislation increased the age of criminal responsibility, it does not consider the developmental stages of the adolescent brain. The adolescent brain is prewired for sensation-seeking and risk-taking, which aligns with the heightened motivation for reward, as it often leads to careless behaviors (Jadhav & Boutrel, 2019). More specifically, research indicates that the brain's cerebral cortex/frontal lobe, responsible for advanced cognitive and rational functioning, undergoes significant changes during puberty and throughout adolescence. This part of the brain is not fully developed until 25–30 years of age (Campellone & Turley, 2023; Williams, 2020; Mercurio et al., 2020). In addition, many of our youth may also be experiencing interpersonal traumatic events during a host of co-occurring biological changes attributed to brain development and puberty. The concept of epigenetics is often absent from the dialogue on youth brain development. Epigenetics suggests that our genes can carry memories of trauma experienced by our ancestors, which influence the ways that we respond to trauma and stress (Pember, 2016). Recent research on epigenetics suggests that the genes of children can be altered based on their prenatal exposure to trauma. From a biological perspective (in the life of a child), the impact can take place as early as conception. The father's sperm may carry specific markers on their DNA (pre-fertilization) and be transferred to the child. It can take place while the child is in utero as the mother is enduring various environmental stressors, including emotional stress, community violence, poor nutrition, drug exposure, and daily encounters with racism. Finally, the child may be impacted after birth by maternal caregiving and infant physiology (Curley et al., 2023). If we couple these biological factors with the complex trauma and environmental factors that many of our marginalized youth are exposed to daily, we increase the likelihood of youth encountering the child welfare and youth legal system (Teska, 2023).

Today, our youth courts continue to strive for those same goals of public safety and rehabilitation but look more like a combination of rehabilitative and punitive. There is also now a youth part within Supreme court because of the Raise the Age Legislation (n.d.). Before Raise the Age, the age of criminal responsibility in New York City was 16. New York was one of two states in the United States that held minors accountable in criminal court at age 16. Following the passing of Raise the Age, youth are now seen in family court or the youth part in Supreme court until age 18. For our youth, ages 18–24, we can still provide services as directed by the court and probation. On the rehabilitative side, we have diversion, alternative to detention, alternative to placement, and alternative to incarceration programs. On the punitive side, there are nonsecure detention, secure detention, nonsecure placement, limited-secure placement, and jail and prison facilities.

Populations Served

As an African American cisgender woman who is also a mother to three Black children, I often identify with the youth and families I serve. As a mother of a young Black man, I have many of the same fears, concerns, and hopes as the caregivers. Unfortunately, the trauma of being Black and raising children in systems that often do not see, hear, or value them bonds us. As a clinician, I use the resources I have gained through life experience, education, and professional networks to assist youth, staff, families, and the community in any capacity needed.

As professionals seeking more impactful programming, we must step back to see where we are and want to be in the work. Ultimately, the goal is to work ourselves out of a job. The current work resembles a harm reduction model where we aim to become more preventive/proactive and less punitive/reactive. Through time and maturity, children can learn, grow, and change, but the systems involved often hinder capacity through harsh sentencing, legal scars (criminal records), and unrealistic expectations from community supervision.

Youth courts have become the catchall for youth who fall through the cracks of other systems, particularly Black youth, and families from underserved communities. In 2016, African Americans represented 61% of arrests in youth justice cases for children under 16 and 52% of arrests in youth justice cases for ages 16 and 17 (Citizens Committee for Children of New York, 2016; Rovner, 2021). It should be noted that the division of the two age groups was before the passing of Raise the Age in 2017. As clinicians working with arrested youth, we collaborate with several other city and/or state agencies and programs. Table 14.1 presents a list of some of our most frequent collaborators.

Most often, youth justice staff are working in partnership with child welfare agencies, mental health agencies, the Department of Probation (DOP), and the New York City Department of Education (DOE) on issues that have gone unaddressed and/or ignored and have resulted in court involvement. Passages Academy, part of District 79 under the DOE, currently serves youth held in secure and

Table 14.1 Potential collaborators for youth in the carceral system

Governing agency	Program name	Purpose and partnership
Administration for Children's Services (ACS)	Alternative to Detention (ATD)	Community-based programs monitor youth as they attend court. Youths are given the program in lieu of being held in Non-Secure Detention (NSD) or Secure Detention (SD).
Juvenile Operations Department of Probation (Family Court DOP)	Alternative to Placement (ATP)	Community-based programs provide services to adjudicated youth in lieu of placement in Non-Secure Placement (NSP) or Limited Secure Placement (LSP). The goal is to prevent further involvement in the legal system while successfully navigating community supervision (probation).
Administration for Children's Services (ACS)	Limited Secure Placement (LSP)	Locked placement for youth, usually located on campuses, similar to city jails but designated for youth.
Administration for Children's Services (ACS)	Non-secure Detention (NSD)	Community-based organizations provide group home settings that house family court youth as they fight their delinquency case, and communicate with facilities about youth and court date outcomes.
Department of Education (DOE)	Passages Academy, District 79 (D79)	Services youth under 18 who are detained in secure or non-secure facilities by providing alternate academic settings. We obtain all school records to ensure a smooth transition back into the community. Most youth are reconnected to their home school (if they had one) after a period of detention.
Community-Based Organization (CBO)	Functional Family Therapy (FFT)	Provides in-home, family-based therapy free of charge.
Administration for Children's Services (ACS)	Non-Secure Placement (NSP)	Group homes ran by community-based organizations located within communities; part of the Close to Home (CTH) initiative to keep youth and families as close as possible throughout placement.
Administration for Children's Services (ACS)	Children's Center	Foster-care housing for youth.
Criminal court and supreme courts	Sentencing mitigation	Advocacy from social workers, who usually gather information to help decrease sentences and tell the story of the youth to the court.
Community-based organizations	Multi-systemic therapy	Provide multi-systemic-based therapy as needed.
Department of Education (DOE)	Court liaisons	Court liaisons provide DOE information but are housed in family courts.
Administration for Children's Services (ACS)	Secure Detention (SD)	Locked facilities, a similar setting to city jails, but designated for youth.
Department of Education (DOE)	East River Academy	Services youth ages 18–21 (22 if they receive special education services) who are incarcerated on Rikers Island for 10 or more days. As youth are released from Rikers Island, social workers attempt to obtain all school records (including high school equivalency preparation documents) to assist in facilitating a smooth transition back into community.

(continued)

Table 14.1 (continued)

Governing agency	Program name	Purpose and partnership
Human Resources Administration (HRA)	Benefits	Connect youth and families to benefits.
Department of Homeless Services (DHS)	Shelter system	Communicate with case managers to advocate for vouchers and/or movement within the shelter system for youth and families.
Department of Education (DOE)	Lyfe Centers	Provides free childcare for youth enrolled in high school, designated sites at schools throughout New York City.
Community-Based Organization (CBO)	Community partnership programs	The goal is to decrease the number of ACS reports within neighborhoods with high report rates and provide concrete resources to assist families in avoiding SCR reports.
Department of Corrections (DOC)	Discharge planning	Should provide community connections for returning citizens as well vital documents and benefits (Medicaid).
Community supervision	Parole	Youth returning home often come home with a length of time on parole. Provide emotional support as well as community resources to youth and families as youth re-enter society.
Community-Based Organization (CBO)	Re-entry planning and resources	Community-based agencies provide resources for returning citizens; connect youth and families to services such as employment, housing, etc.

nonsecure detention and placement facilities throughout New York City. In 2023, 60% of their population had an active Individualized Education Plan (IEP). Are we looking at the correlation between disabilities and court involvement? What proactive measures have we taken to address this? This is not a new phenomenon, as it was reported in July 2000 that large numbers of youth involved in the juvenile justice system across America had education-related disabilities (Buurrell & Warboys, 2000). Often, court-involved youth are not successful in school for various reasons, and thus they are not engaged or simply stop going. Research has shown that probation youth with special education needs are significantly associated with greater mental health problems, lower self-regulation skills, and more school exclusion experiences (Bo-Kyung et al., 2021). The current education system does not address youth with various types of intelligence and/or different learning styles. We typically meet the basic education needs of visual and/or auditory learners, but what about kinesthetic learners or aural (musical) learners? They often fall through the cracks and disconnect from education, and the time spent outside of school (truancy) can contribute to the need for police contact. By the time youth with learning disabilities are out of school for 3–5 years, 31% have been arrested, and by the time youth with emotional disturbances have been out of school for 3–5 years, 58% have been arrested (Buurrell & Warboys, 2000).

Approximately 20% of students with emotional disturbances are arrested at least once before they leave school (Buurrell & Warboys, 2000). For those who remain in school and begin to cause disruptions or display disruptive behaviors, interactions may result in suspension or police contact through school safety. This practice is known as the *school-to-prison pipeline*, referring to education and public safety policies that push students into the criminal legal system. Schools send students into the pipeline through zero-tolerance disciplinary policies, which involve the police in minor misbehavior and often lead to arrests and youth detention referrals (New York Civil Liberties Union, 2023). These spaces and/or incidents are opportunities for restorative practice and/or justice. *Restorative practices* are tools and techniques used to build relationships and strengthen community bonds. The main three principles are repairing harm, stakeholder involvement, and transforming the role of government and community through open communication and a shared sense of community (Kimbrell et al., 2023). *Restorative justice* (RJ) is a philosophy or process inspired by Indigenous practices, used to respond to conflict. The process elevates the needs of the person or community harmed while holding the harmer accountable for their impact on the person and/or community.

During my time as a forensic social worker, I had a youth who stole our program van and crashed it. After finding out, program leadership faced deciding whether to press charges on the participant. As a team, we decided not to press charges but instead have a restorative justice (RJ) circle. We first asked the youth if he was willing to participate since the conference was necessary for him to return to the center. He agreed, and we scheduled the conference with all impacted parties (Buurrell & Warboys, 2000). The facilitator asked the standard six questions of everyone in the circle, and consequences were agreed on. The participant had to complete 2 months of community service and participate in substance abuse groups for at least 2 months. However, he would be allowed to return to the center after three substance abuse groups. The RJ process allowed us to resolve the issue in the community without putting a permanent mark on this young man's record. It also allowed us to get to the root of the problem which was substance use and poor coping strategies for complex trauma. Lastly, by welcoming the youth back into the community after the incident, staff displayed unconditional positive regard which helped the youth with a sense of belonging and acceptance. Restorative justice aims for the parties to reach a mutual agreement on how to repair harm based on an understanding of the conflict and its impact (New York Peace Institute, 2022). By building a stronger sense of community while using less punitive approaches and discipline, we observed a decrease in conflict and discharges and increased communication between staff and participants. It is a culture and tool that teachers and school staff can use to decrease the number of school suspensions (Gwathney, 2021; Alvarez, 2022). Restorative practices are viewed as prevention, while restorative justice is responsive. Both seek to see all parties as humans while creating space for all parties to see humility and commonality in each other and the community.

Focusing on New York City, African Americans represented 40% of ACS investigation cases for child abuse and neglect in 2020 (Citizens Committee for Children, 2020). Our youth and families make up 40% of the reports, although we account for just 25% of the population. Many of those youths and families are involved in family court proceedings (on the delinquency side) as well. Often, poverty is the root cause of many cases of neglect. Research has shown that families living in urban poverty face any number of family stressors, such as family conflict, violence and dissolution, victimization/incarceration or death of a family member, and more neglect and maltreatment than families living in more affluent communities. They are also prone to experiencing financial hardship, residential instability, homelessness, and racial discrimination (Collins et al., 2010).

Families are unable to provide the city's standard for basic needs and are often reported to and monitored by our child welfare system. Instead of penalizing families for not having adequate resources, we must examine why they do not have them and then in partnership with families create opportunities to help families sustain themselves. For example, in East New York, Brooklyn, we have partnered with a Community Partnership Program whose goal is to decrease the number of reports made to the State Central Registry (SCR) out of the East NY community. Instead of reporting a family that may not have groceries, they will provide groceries and a referral to a benefits assistance program and food distribution resources throughout the community. The program also builds relationships with schools, churches, senior centers, and community centers to get the word out about the services available to families. While community programs like these address the concrete needs of youth and families, restorative practices can also be used to enhance communication between case managers/workers and families and between caregivers and children.

Roles of a Forensic Social Worker in Nonprofit Settings

As a youth justice service provider, I work with youth ages 13–24 who are involved with the legal system, including family, criminal, supreme, and sometimes federal courts (Maschi & Leibowitz, 2017). You may be the lone social worker in the room if working in such settings. As such, we are often charged with wearing various hats determined by the setting. Within the court or extensions of the court (law enforcement), your primary roles are to educate and advocate. You are educating officers, lawyers, and others on your youth and families and the many ways to view their successes and opportunities for growth. You may also find yourself educating them on the many ways to recognize their privilege and positionality within the context of power dynamics and judgment and the importance of cultural humility.

Youth justice workers are educating, elevating, and advocating for our families. Forensic social workers educate families on their rights as parents/caregivers, generational trauma and its impact, resources within the community, and the inherent strengths of their children and themselves. We also educate families on court system practices, the roles of the people involved in the various systems, and how to navigate those relationships for their best interests. In many legal and law enforcement spaces, youth and families are not regarded as the experts on their own lives, and we are charged with creating spaces where the voices of youth and families are heard. Lastly, I believe that our education and empowerment efforts inform our policy and/or advocacy work. Our advocacy work occurs on the micro, mezzo, and macro levels.

Social work has long used a two-pronged approach to facilitate change: (a) assisting individuals and families with functioning to their best potential and (b) combating unjust and unfair community and societal conditions through strategies of social reform (Bartlett, 1958).

Interventions

Cognitive behavioral therapy (CBT) and sometimes trauma-focused cognitive behavioral therapy (TF-CBT) are often used with youth justice populations. CBT is the most frequently endorsed empirically supported treatment (EST) as per the American Psychological Association (APA) Task Force on evidence-based practice (Dobson et al., 2019). In reducing engagement in violence and crime, CBT offers individuals a practical way to address the emotional causes of these behaviors and helps people develop more effective and prosocial strategies (Baldwin et al., 2018). Other trauma-informed practices are used as well. We find that few interventions and/or evidence-based practices began with court-involved youth and/or black males as the research subject. As such, interventions such as CBT need to be adapted to better meet the needs of our population (Steele, 2020; Steele & Newton, 2022). For example, at the beginning of my career, we used TF-CBT, in which the client was required to write a narrative. When working with my youth, the process would always stall at this part of the intervention. Without stating it, I considered what the apprehension might be for a young person. Could it be a literacy issue, lack of engagement, or maybe concern about how participating may look to peers? I brought it up in a group check-in, which involves stating one's name, current feeling (on a scale of 1–10), goal, and question of the day. When I asked the participants about the narrative exercise, I realized that the narrative was being compared to writing a negative statement in some youth circles. Instead, I substituted the written narrative for a musical narrative (Kallio, 2022). Each youth had to discuss their traumatic event(s) through a series of sounds or songs, like a soundtrack. The youth willingly participated, and I learned so much about them, their traumatic experience(s), their community of support, their viewpoints, and their taste in music. As there are limited culture-specific interventions made for our target audience, it is important to know when to pivot and try something new. The opportunity to cocreate alternative approaches with your youth only strengthens the therapeutic relationship: the foundation of the work. While there are numerous city youth organizations, some of which are incentive based, my observation is that the relationships with staff keep them engaged.

We also must be able to acknowledge incremental success. Yes, we would love for our youth to go to school every day, but if they go 2 days more than they went last week or last year, celebrate them! If they have conflicts or outbursts at school, and there was one less conflict or outburst this week, celebrate them! If they have a curfew mandate and made it multiple times this week (but not all 7 days), celebrate them! The youth are more likely to respond to someone who celebrates them and their incremental successes than someone who operates from a deficit model. To this point, many will say what about compliance? As social workers, we need to consider compliance. Still, it should include the youth's participation in the process as to what they are realistically able to do rather than unattainable mandates.

Families and communities do have the power to heal themselves if given space, resources, and opportunity (Quintero, 2020); this two-generation approach is often absent in programs. These interventions are all client centered but do not always acknowledge the daily stressors of institutional and structural racism and the daily racist encounters at school, work, or in the community. Social workers are operating from a harm reduction model as we do not have the power to completely remove our youth (and families) from the systems that are harming them and are reminders of White supremacy. Programming alone does not change the way the world views our Black youth. Bell hooks (2015) describes the racist picture of Black masculinity as one of failure: psychologically damaged, dangerous, violent sex maniacs whose insanity is informed by their inability to fulfill their phallocentric masculine destiny in a racist context. Thus, in many spaces, our Black males are feared unjustly. As a Black woman and social worker, I am constantly in a space of deconstructing the picture of Black masculinity and protecting our youth as much as possible from the harsh realities of the systems and society at large. DeGruy (2017) discusses this notion of women protecting their children from the larger White society for fear of harm; she traces this need in the African American community to the origins of slavery, labeling the collective experience as *post-traumatic slave syndrome*. DeGruy discusses the generational trauma that plagues African American communities and families, as well as how the continuous structural and institutional exposure to racism (Wilkins, et al., 2013) and lack of access to opportunities over generations are contributing factors to many of the challenges within the African American community.

Representation Matters

As a Black female social worker and mother to a Black male and two Black females, I often struggle with my countertransference reactions while serving my youth and families as they often remind me of my own family. They truly become extended relatives as many of our youth can be with us for over 2 years; termination is often difficult.

I believe that our current legal system is steeped in anti-Blackness and built on a platform of racism and oppression, which is evident based on courtroom staffing, procedures, processes, practices, sentencing, and related matters. There is an unspoken level of understanding from a historical perspective. There is also an understanding of what youth and families face within their communities and our current legal system. As we navigate the legal system together, I often see myself and my family in the people I serve.

Credible Messengers and the Credible Messenger (CM) Model

Credible messengers are neighborhood leaders, experienced youth advocates, and individuals with relevant life experiences whose role is to help youth transform attitudes and behaviors around violence. They serve young people whose needs go far beyond the traditional mentoring approach of companionship, confidence building, and typical academic, social, or career guidance. They can connect with the most challenging young people because they (1) come from the same communities, (2) are formerly incarcerated or were involved in the justice system, (3) have turned their lives around, (4) demonstrate integrity and transformation, and (5) are skilled and trained in mentoring young people (DC.gov, 2023).

Throughout my youth justice career, credible messengers have been the backbone of our work. The impact of the youth's relationship with an adult who has navigated the same communities and systems as them and yet came out on the other side is paramount; a huge part of mentoring is modeling behavior for our youth. It is a real-life, tangible example of possibility. Their existence says there is life beyond the gang, the block, and the jail or prison and simply beyond today. The credible messengers look like them, talk like them, dress like them, and even know some of the same people. The difference is the direction their lives are going in and their choice to invest in preventing the next generation of the community from getting further involved in the legal system (Austria & Peterson, 2017).

As these returning citizens work to redeem themselves and become first responders for their youth and/or communities, cities and governing agencies place little value on their lived experiences and areas of expertise. Although they are often first to respond to potentially life-threatening events, they are not paid accordingly. The average salary for a credible messenger is 38 K–40 K per year. This challenge also speaks to our values as a society. We will invest 556 K to keep someone housed on Rikers Island. Still, we will not invest that same money in rebuilding communities, creating safe spaces for youth and families, providing affordable housing, or supporting the successful transition of returning citizens (New York City Comptroller, 2021).

I am often faced with the reality that although I have the best intentions, I am still part of the larger machine that often oppresses staff and communities, whether it be intentional or unintentional. For instance, as we empower the community by hiring from within the community, we cannot pay them a living wage. Although I successfully advocate for salary increases, I am still unable to give them what they need and deserve to sustain their own families as they come to work daily to support the families of others. Although credible messengers are effective and efficient, their wages are usually linked to levels of education, which is also an oppressive practice, especially considering the lack of financial resources and/or access to college education.

To date, implementing the credible messenger model has been the most successful within youth justice programming; arrests and recidivism are down compared to those not enrolled in CM programs. Although the credible messenger model started in Chicago, it has spread to other cities nationwide (U.S. Attorney's Office, Northern

District of Georgia, 2025). The New York City leadership has taken notice as our mayor has a credible messenger on his advisory team as the gang czar (Rubenstein & Mays, 2022). In 2023, the mayor asked that all youth arrested on weapons charges be connected to a credible messenger program (Probation Staff, 2021).

Even in Failure There Is Success

The truth is we cannot help everyone. The goal is to plant a seed that blossoms as the youth and family grow. At times, it is hard to keep this in mind, but the work has a way of reminding you. During my second year as a professional social worker, I met a participant who was referred to the program for an assault while attending middle school. As with all new participants, we completed his intake at home with his family to establish a relationship with everyone. This intake includes all preliminary paperwork, releases, applications, and our strengths assessment. Following our initial meeting, I often visited the youth as the assigned clinician, but he usually ran from me, sometimes hiding in the stairways during school visits. I took these opportunities to talk with school staff about how he presented at school. The reports were negative and often ended with questions about why I continued to come to see him. After several suspensions, the school was out of ideas. During one of these suspensions, I offered him to come out and eat with me. He agreed, even choosing the restaurant; we ate, and the rest is, as they say, "history." We began to talk daily, peeling back another "layer" of his hard exterior every day.

After conversing for some time, we began cocreating his genogram, documenting the members of the family and their ages, as well as the ones he was closest to geographically and in terms of relationship. It was our project, and we would make updates every so often. He began participating in group activities and secured a summer youth job through the vulnerable youth selection process. As we worked together, the history of family incarceration and family mental health challenges were revealed. He also acknowledged that the family had previous ACS involvement. As he continues to engage, I remind him that our conversations are safe with me, and I explain confidentiality again. Parenthetically, I typically explain my role as a mandated reporter at the intake and inform them of what I must report versus what can remain confidential. It is essential to be as transparent as possible, as families have often been through multiple systems and find it hard to trust people/programs based on their experiences. Unfortunately, many court-involved youth and families have had several negative experiences with various systems that lead them to err on the side of caution when encountering new people, programs, and systems. Stating my intentions and obligations as the clinician from the beginning decreases the distrust on the part of the family.

After some time, he was pushed out of middle school due to his behavior. This process is called *social promotion*. During this time, the school elects to move the child to the next school setting regardless of academic progress (Chen, 2022). Just like that, we are now in high school. Unfortunately, this program ended after

9 months, and we had to close the case. It was deemed a successful closure because he avoided additional arrests and further engagement with the legal system. However, I felt unsettled with terminating at this point. It could have been because of the time we spent together or the strained familial relationships. It could have also been because I lost my mother at 13 and had feelings of abandonment following her death; I felt like I was abandoning this youth by closing the case. I talked with my supervisor, who assured me that he would be welcome to attend any group or trip that we had to offer and that he and his family were still welcome in the center at any time. After a couple of months, he completed probation. We held a graduation and celebrated his program accomplishments and completion of probation. I even wrote them a personal letter and bought flowers for his mother because this was a celebration for the family as well. After this, I started to see less of him, but he continued to call sporadically. After a couple of months, he informed me that he was going to become a father.

At this point, I was super concerned but wanted to be as supportive as possible. Being a parent is hard as an adult but even more challenging for a 15-year-old with limited family support. I asked him how he felt about becoming a parent, and he seemed genuinely happy. Thus, I supported his choice and used our agency resources to secure things for the baby. Things were hard for the new parent, and we continued to help him in any way possible. The family had limited financial resources, and the parent (our client) was not old enough to get a job. A few months after the child was born, our youth was involved in a very high-profile gang assault. My immediate reaction was denial, but then I was confronted with the video. Immediately, I thought, this is not the young person I spent the last 2 years getting to know. As the news reports came in, I was defensive. The reports called them animal names, and the social media commentary was worse. As I am sitting at work 1 day trying to figure out what I could have done differently, he calls. He reflected on our time together and thanked me for "being there." Over the next year, I supported him by attending court dates, visiting him at different facilities, and even keeping in touch with the family. He was later sentenced to several years in prison and continued to communicate via letters and email over that time. Because this happened years before Raise the Age (RTA), he went to adult prison at 16 years of age.

This experience taught me so many lessons. This was when I learned to separate the deed from the doer. Although he made a decision I disagreed with, I could still support the person with whom I had built a relationship for over 2 years. I also learned that it is naïve and borderline arrogant to believe that your presence alone can change someone's life, no matter how committed you are to the person and the work. Yes, your work contributes to change, but your presence alone is not enough. It is your job to plant the seed, and doing the work consistently is the fertilizer to ensure the seed can grow. In retrospect, I thought about the ways to include parents more in our programming. Parents will be with their children far longer than any program. How can we better support parents and caregivers? I was grateful for a supervisor who was skilled, humane, and realistic. She guided me through the process as a new professional in the field and helped me reflect on my strengths and areas for development. The most important thing I learned from this experience is the power of relationships (Bailey et al., 1992). Today, the participant is home and adjusting to life as an adult and parent. He is working full-time and volunteers to speak with youth about his life experiences to deter them from following in his footsteps to prison. We still talk often. A relationship that was built over 10 years ago is still standing. Even in failure, there was success.

For those of you thinking about a career in forensic social work, ask yourselves: Why do I want to do this work? Can I be committed to the work when commitment is not popular or does not feel good? How will I use my power and positionality to uplift youth, families, and communities? Is my end goal the dismantling of carceral systems for youth?

Practice and Supervisory Wisdom: Ten Things I Wish I Knew Then But Know Now

1. Do not take it personally. It was never about you, and it will never be about you. Often, when youth respond in a "disrespectful" way, it is not about you. It can be a learned trauma response, and in many settings, that response has been successful in getting people to leave.
2. Learn to separate the deed from the doer. You must separate the person from the decision and the action from the intention. Get to know the young person aside from his or her offense.
3. Youth and families are experts in their lives. Regardless of how many degrees you have or how many theories you know, you will never know more about youth and their families than they do. Be an active listener and a forever student for youth, families, and community.
4. Leave your judgments at the door. Even if it is different from what you would do, it does not make it wrong. Families know what they need to sustain themselves. This is also part of cultural humility as you practice respecting the cultural practices of various ethnic groups.
5. Learn everybody's name; it is the little things that matter. Make it a point to learn the name of each young person. Greeting them by name lets them know that they are important to you. Even if they are not directly reporting to you, greet them and ask their name.
6. School is a great foundation, but experience is the best teacher. Master of Social Work (MSW) school is a great foundation, but it does not fully prepare you for the work. Most of your learning will come from hands-on practice. You will learn the most from your youth, families, community, and colleagues. Most social work programs do not require classes specific to forensic social work. As such, you will do most of what you learn on the job.
7. Learn your community. You are not in the community to just deliver services; you are there to be of service. For example, learn who runs the neighborhood tournaments, tenant/block association, and when is "Old Timers Day." It is important to learn about your community and have staff from it. Community

reinvestment is important to any youth justice initiative. It is good to see someone they know when they enter the space.

8. Culture is not just about race. Often when people hear culture, they automatically think of skin color and ethnic groups. However, there is culture within a community, within age groups, and even within workspaces. Be aware of the cultures in your space and how you impact the culture in those spaces. Also, be aware of your power and positionality in those spaces.
9. It is not what is wrong with you; it is what happened to you. Often youth are faced with daily consequences of the decisions of the adults in and around their lives. The question "what's wrong with you?" implies that the blame is on the youth and that they are solely responsible for the situation. "What happened?" is from a space of wanting to hear the youth's voice and story. Unfortunately, our youth are not usually heard or seen as often as needed.
10. Finally, the goal is to work yourself out of a job. The long-term goal is always to work yourself out of the job. As we realize that detention, placement, jails, and prisons are not spaces for humans, especially youth, we must elevate our voices to deconstruct and dismantle oppressive practices, legislation, and spaces. The goal is abolition, the ultimate anti-oppressive practice.

Reflection Questions

1. Have you explored your implicit biases and how they may impact your youth, families, and/or community?
2. Are you conscious of the messages being sent to the youth by the legal, education, and community supervision systems? Do you reinforce or negate the negative messages?
3. Are you able to see the youth aside from his or her poor decision?
4. Are you cocreating interventions, taking into account the inherent strengths of the youth and family as the starting point? How are those strengths translated into interventions?
5. Are you operating from a strength-based perspective? This is crucial in reframing and replacing negative cognitions.
6. How do you define success? Does this conflict with youth and families' definition of success?
7. Are you content with working yourself out of a job? What are you doing to work toward this goal daily?

References

Alvarez, B. (2022). *What educators can do to help dismantle the school-to-prison pipeline*. neaToday.

Austria, R., & Peterson, J. (2017). *Credible messenger mentoring for justice-involved youth*. The Pinkerton Papers.
Bailey, D. B., Buysse, V., Edmondson, R., & Smith, T. M. (1992). Creating family-centered services in early intervention: Perceptions of professionals in four states. *Exceptional Children, 58*(3), 298–309.
Baldwin, M., Chablani-Medley, A., Marques, L., Schiraldi, V., Valentine, S. E., & Zeira, Y. (2018). *Cognitive behavioral theory, young adults, and community corrections: Pathways for innovation*. Program in Criminal Justice Policy and Management, Harvard Kennedy School.
Bartlett, H. M. (1958). Working definition of social work practice. *Social Work, 3*(2), 5–8.
Buurwell, S., & Warboys, L. (2000). Special education and the juvenile justice system. *OJJDP Juvenile Justice Bulletin*.
Campellone, J., & Turley, R. K. (2023). Understanding the teen brain. University of Rochester Medical Center Health Encyclopedia. Retrieved May 1, 2023, from https://www.urmc.rochester.edu/encyclopedia/content.aspx?
Chen, G. (2022). *Is social promotion crippling our children's future? The debate*. Public School Review.
Citizens' Committee for Children of New York. (2016). Juvenile arrests. In Keeping Track Online database. Retrieved from https://data.cccnewyork.org/data
Citizens' Committee for Children of New York. (2020). Keeping Track of New York City's Children: Child welfare and community safety [Data set]. Retrieved May 1, 2023, from https://data.cccnewyork.org/data/map/3/child-abuseand-neglect-investigations
Collins, K., Connors, K., Davis, S., Donohue, A., Gardner, S., Goldblatt, E., Hayward, A., Kiser, L., Strieder, F., & Thompson, E. (2010). *Understanding the impact of trauma and urban poverty on family systems: Risks, resilience, and interventions*. Family Informed Trauma Treatment Center.
Curley, J. P., Mashoodh, R., & Champagne, F. A. (2023). Chapter 24 - transgenerational epigenetics. Elsevier Inc.
DeGruy, J. (2017). *Post traumatic slave syndrome: America's legacy of enduring injury & healing*. Uptone Press.
District of Columbia Department of Youth Rehabilitation Services. (n.d.). Credible Messenger Initiative. DC.gov. https://dyrs.dc.gov/page/credib
Dobson, K. S., & Dozois, D. J. A. (Eds.). (2019). *Handbook of cognitive-behavioral therapies* (4th ed.). Guilford Press.
Gwathney, A. N. (2021). Offsetting racial divides: Adolescent african american males & restorative justice practices. *Clinical Social Work Journal, 49*(3), 346–355.
Hooks, B. (2015). *Black looks race and representation*. Routledge Taylor & Francis Group.
Jadhav, K. S., & Boutrel, B. (2019). Prefrontal cortex development and emergence of self-regulatory competence: The two cardinal features of adolescence disrupted in context of alcohol abuse. *The European Journal of Neuroscience, 50*(3), 2274–2281.
Kallio, A. A. (2022). The transformative potentials and politics of music in juvenile justice settings. *Music Education Research, 24*(4), 405–416.
Kimbrell, C. S., Wilson, D. B., & Olaghere, A. (2023). Restorative justice programs and practices in juvenile justice: An updated systematic review and meta-analysis for effectiveness. *Criminology & Public Policy, 22*(1), 161–195.
Maschi, T., & Leibowitz, G. S. (Eds.). (2017). *Forensic social work: Psychosocial and legal issues across diverse populations and settings*. Springer Publishing Company, Incorporated.
McNamara, R., & Burns, R. (2017). *Multiculturalism, crime, and criminal justice*. Oxford University Press.
Mercurio, E., García-López, E., Morales-Quintero, L., Llamas, N. E., Marinaro, J. Á., & Muñoz, J. M. (2020). Adolescent brain development and progressive legal responsibility in the latin american context. *Frontiers in Psychology, 11*, 1–13.
New York City Comptroller. (2021, December 6). *Comptroller stringer: Cost of incarceration per person in New York City Skyrockets to all-time high* [Press release]. https://comptroller.

nyc.gov/newsroom/comptroller-stringer-cost-of-incarceration-per-person-in-new-york-city-skyrockets-to-all-time-high-2/

New York State Unified Court System, Office for Justice Initiatives. (n.d.). Raise the age. https://ww2.nycourts.gov/ip/oji/raisetheage.shtml

New York Civil Liberties Union. (2023). School-to-prison pipeline. *NYCLU*. https://www.nyclu.org/en/school-prisonpipeline

Office of Juvenile Justice and Delinquency Prevention (OJJDP). (2023). About OJJDP | Office of Juvenile Justice and Delinquency Prevention (ojp.gov). https://ojjdp.ojp.gov/about

Pember, M. A. (2016). Intergenerational trauma: Understanding natives' inherited pain. Retrieved from http://amberic.org/

Platt, A. (1969). The rise of the child-saving movement: A study in social policy and correctional reform. *The Annals of the American Academy of Political and Social Science, 381*(1), 21–38.

Quintero, A. (2020). The multigenerational transmission process of healing social cultural wounds within the Black community: A comprehensive analysis. *Counseling and Family Therapy Scholarship Review, 3*(1), 1–14.

Rovner, J. (2021). Black disparities in youth incarceration. *Montana, 113*(1485), 13–14.

Rubinstein, D., & Mays, J. C. (2022, June 2). Mayor Adams names longtime ally as gun violence czar despite past scrutiny. The New York Times. https://www.nytimes.com/2022/06/02/nyregion/andre-mitchell-gun-violenceczar.html

Steele, J. M. (2020). A CBT approach to internalized racism among african americans. *International Journal for the Advancement of Counselling, 42*(3), 217–233.

Steele, J. M., & Newton, C. S. (2022). Culturally adapted cognitive behavioral therapy as a model to address internalized racism among african american clients. *Journal of Mental Health Counseling, 44*(2), 98–116.

Teska, J. (2023). *Complex trauma in children and adolescents: An overview*. Social Work Reference Guide.

Tsui, J. C. (2014). Breaking free of the prison paradigm: Integrating restorative justice techniques into Chicago's juvenile justice system. *Journal of Criminal Law & Criminology, 104*(3), 634–666.

U.S. Attorney's Office, Northern District of Georgia. (2024, August 26). Project Safe Neighborhoods (PSN). U.S. Department of Justice. Retrieved June 27, 2025, from U.S. Department of Justice, Northern District of Georgia archives.

Young, S., Greer, B., & Church, R. (2017). Juvenile delinquency, welfare, justice and therapeutic interventions: A global perspective. *BJPsych Bulletin, 41*(1), 21–29.

Wilkins, E., Whiting, J., Watson, M., Russon, J., & Moncrief, A. (2013). Residual effects of slavery: What clinicians need to know. *Contemporary Family Therapy: An International Journal, 35*(1), 14–28.

Williams, A. (2020). Early childhood trauma impact on adolescent brain development, decision making abilities, and delinquent behaviors: Policy implications for juveniles tried in adult court systems. *Juvenile and Family Court Journal, 71*(1), 5–18.

Chapter 15
Anti-oppressive Practice Within Youth Diversion Programs

Laura A. Smith

Introduction

"Congratulations, you have completed the program, and your case has been dismissed." A sigh of relief escapes and a smile of joy appears on the client's face. These are the moments that make it all worth it. Working as a social worker in a youth diversion program has challenges and rewards. Youth diversion programs (YDP) work with adolescents ages 19–24 who have committed a first-time nonviolent offense. These programs intend to prevent further involvement in the criminal legal system. The programs allow for an alternative method to incarceration through court-mandated monitoring and supervision (NeMoyer et al., 2020). Social workers are key agents in a system that can be difficult to navigate. Unjust practices often manifest within legal systems, impacting a participant's likelihood of success in these programs. As social workers, the NASW Code of Ethics (NASW, 2017) and initiatives like the Grand Challenges of Social Work (2023) guide our ethical responsibility to embrace and implement anti-oppressive practices.

Overview of Alternative to Incarceration Programs

Alternative to incarceration (ATI) programs continue to be created to aid the youth who have been charged with crimes. Depending on the severity of the crime, ATI programs provide services to youth involved in felony crimes to be able to reduce their charges to misdemeanors or dismiss the charges in their entirety. The purpose

---

L. A. Smith (✉)
Silver School of Social Work, New York University, New York, NY, USA
e-mail: las9987@nyu.edu

C. Tosone et al. (eds.), *Reframing Social Work with an Anti-Oppressive Lens*, Essential Clinical Social Work Series,
https://doi.org/10.1007/978-3-031-91391-4_15

of these programs is to decrease the court's dependence on incarceration, reducing the jail population by enabling individuals to stay within their communities while enhancing their stability and well-being. Today, multiple forms of ATI programs were created for the specific needs of the participants. The developed programs focus on community service, mental health, drug treatment, juvenile delinquency, and more. These programs emphasize structured treatment interventions as the primary source of change designed to alleviate the problem of mass incarceration and overcrowding within the prison system.

The programs require participants to adhere to strict rules to have their cases reduced or ultimately dismissed. Compliance is a fundamental requirement, entailing a rigorous commitment to various conditions such as following a curfew, wearing electronic monitoring devices, undergoing drug tests, and regularly checking in with assigned supervisors. Noncompliance can result in violations, potentially leading to incarceration.

Introduction to Youth Diversion Programs (YDPs)

The push toward diversion of youth from the criminal legal system started over 30 years ago, coinciding with the increased evidence for the effectiveness of youth treatment programs (Wilson & Hoge, 2013). Youth diversion courts were designed as diversion programs based on the problem-solving court model. These programs are offered to participants with nonviolent offenses ages 18–26. This was established as an alternative in the criminal legal system as policymakers were concerned about placing low-status offenders with serious offenders (Pope & Jones, 2020).

Historically, the juvenile court system has wavered between the extremes of punishment and rehabilitation, contingent on societal perceptions of juvenile offenders. Sometimes, harsh punitive measures were considered paramount, but there has always been a powerful draw toward restoration, mainly when young individuals showed a potential for reform (Cochran & Mears, 2015). Terms such as "superpredator" in the mid-1990s exacerbated misperceptions about juvenile crime rates, insinuating an increase when, in fact, there was a notable decline (Allen & Whitt, 2020). Amid these shifting paradigms, the primary aim of YDPs stands out: to decrease the chances of participants facing rearrest by equipping them with constructive resources and fundamental tools to fulfill their essential needs.

Studies have shown that diversion programs can lower recidivism. Recidivism, as defined by the National Institute of Justice (NIJ), refers to the occurrence of criminal acts that lead to rearrest, reconviction, or a return to prison, with or without a new sentence, within 3 years after a person's release. In 2017, Human Impact Partners conducted a study that followed 73 juvenile diversion programs within the United States. On average, there was a 10% lower recidivism rate than traditional juvenile system processes, 31.5% for diversion programs compared to 41.3% for traditional juvenile justice processing (Human Impact Partners, 2017). Although there are statistics surrounding recidivism, it is still a complex variable to measure. According to NIJ, determining the occurrence of recidivism is more complicated for criminologists. A challenge in assessing recidivism is the presumption that everyone studied faces the same risk of rearrest. Recognizing variations in risk environments is crucial for those looking at the impact of interventions. Suppose an individual from one program is placed in a "riskier" setting than another from a different program or a control group. In that case, the observed recidivism disparities stem from this differing risk, not the program itself.

Challenges of Youth Diversion Programs

While youth diversion programs (YDPs) offer numerous benefits, they also present several challenges. Common obstacles include participant resistance, the persistence of punitive outcomes, and difficulties participants face in securing employment after program involvement. These issues can undermine program effectiveness and hinder long-term success for youth particularly those from marginalized communities.

Understanding Participant Resistance

Many individuals who initially participate in youth diversion programs tend to hesitate, often due to a deep distrust of authority figures. Most have experienced unfair treatment or harassment by law enforcement and mistrust toward police and legal authorities. Disproportionate interactions with law enforcement have contributed to a cycle of distrust, especially among Black and Latinx boys, who often feel betrayed and mistrusted by adults. Black youth tend to have more negative and hostile feelings toward police, seeing them as a force of oppression rather than community protection (Human Impact Partner, June 2017). A national survey of young people ages 18–29 found that 55% of Black youth reported harassment by the police, nearly double the rate of other groups. Only 44% of Black youth said they trusted the police, compared to 76% of Asian American, 72% of White, and 60% of Latinx youth (Human Impact Partner, June 2017). The mistrust can make it difficult for participants to comply with diversion program requirements. When social workers adopt roles that resemble law enforcement, it can further intensify these feelings, complicating engagement and rapport.

The Return of Punitive Approaches

The criminal legal system has a history of cycling between "rehabilitative" and punitive punishment when working with youth. The establishment of juvenile courts started in the late 1800s with the guiding optimistic principle that the young person could be reformed. Juvenile courts handle most matters as civil cases, viewing the youth as an individual who needs rehabilitation and supervision and treating delinquency as a social problem instead of as a crime (Mallett & Tedor, 2019).

In the 1960s, a juvenile delinquency committee was appointed during the Kennedy Administration. The committee focused on preventative measures for at-risk children and adolescents, such as establishing diversion alternatives away from delinquency adjudication (Mallett & Tedor, 2019). This created the first federal grant-making law: the Juvenile Justice and Delinquency Prevention Act of 1974.

During the 1990s, the Tough on Crime movement marked a return to punitive approaches in both juvenile and adult court systems. The law and order philosophy emphasized public safety and accountability, leading to harsher penalties, increased detainment, and the transfer of youth into the adult criminal legal system. These shifts were often justified by rising crime rates and the perception that juvenile courts were too lenient. Critics argued that prevention and intervention programs were ineffective, especially for serious or repeat offenders. However, more recent frameworks including systemic racism theory and critical race theory have challenged these assumptions, pointing to the structural biases that may have driven such policies. Punitive legal reforms increased juvenile detainment and incarceration and the wholesale transfer of many youthful offenders into the adult criminal legal system (Mallett & Tedor, 2019). The prevailing belief was that juvenile courts were soft on crime and ineffectual and that preventative or intervention programs do not work with delinquent adolescents, particularly those considered serious and chronic offenders (Mallett & Tedor, 2019). However, contemporary theories such as "The New Jim Crow," systemic racism theory, and critical race theory have challenged these assertions, highlighting the potential systemic and structural biases that could be influencing these beliefs and policy changes.

Since the early 2000s, diversion programs serving youth and young adults have expanded significantly. Although these services are designed to prioritize rehabilitation, a shift toward more punitive measures has become increasingly evident. In 2019, state and local police departments in the United States made over 153,000 arrests for unlawful use of weapon offenses, an increase of 9% compared to 2014 (Motivans, 2022).

Youth diversion programs serving primarily Black and Latinx adolescents often impose harsher sanctions for noncompliance. For instance, missing curfew may result in placement of an electronic monitoring system. Similarly, if a participant is pulled over while driving with a suspended license, the program may request that the individual be remanded for a period of weeks. Cochran and Mears (2015) found that minority youth particularly Black adolescents, are more likely to be perceived as threatening and criminal, which lead courts to impose more punitive, control-oriented punishments. Even within diversion contexts, juvenile courts demonstrate less willingness to assign more resource-intensive and rehabilitative programming to youth of color.

Difficulty Obtaining Employment

Although job development and employment assistance are available in diversion programs, participants often face significant challenges in securing employment. All participants are required to take a conditional plea, which means they plead guilty to the offense, under the condition that the case will be dismissed upon successful program completion. In many cases, participants are arrested for possession of a weapon that is found on them, rather than for its use However, once the conditional plea is entered, the charge appears as a conviction on the participant's paperwork until the program is completed. Although the individual has not been formally convicted of a felony, the pending charge frequently shows up on background checks and may result in lost job opportunities. As a result, some participants lose existing employment or struggle to find work, which can hinder their ability to maintain financial stability during the program. Courts are becoming increasingly aware of this issue, and in some instances, judges have provided letters for participants to submit to employers. Despite these challenges, youth diversion programs remain an essential tool for keeping young people on track and continue to play a vital role in communities across the country.

The Social Work Role in Youth Diversion Programs

In criminal legal system agency settings, it is common for administrators who have no training or education in social work or psychology to maintain that criminally involved individuals are unable to change, and innocent people are not falsely convicted. By contrast, social workers believe that highly motivated individuals can change into productive and law-abiding citizens if they are provided with the correct services (Brownell & Roberts, 2002).

When accepted, the participant has a list of program mandates that they must comply with to complete. The list is as follows:

- Weekly check-in sessions with an assigned social worker
- Maintaining enrollment in school and/or being gainfully employed
- Remaining substance-free (client is subject to random drug testing)
- Completion of community service hours
- Complying with curfew (client is subject to having an ankle monitor tracking device placed on them; if they do not comply, the client is also subject to random home visits by law enforcement to ensure the client is following curfew)

- Avoiding rearrests
- Avoiding travel without permission from the program and court
- Attending all court dates

The social worker has multiple roles in youth diversion, including case management, counseling, and court advocacy.

Case Management

Social workers assess the needs of participants and collaborate with clients to create a comprehensive plan that caters to their unique needs and objectives. This may involve providing referrals for education, employment, or vocational opportunities. Additionally, social workers are responsible for monitoring compliance to ensure that clients are following program mandates. Overall, social work case management aims to empower clients, enabling them to attain self-sufficiency and enhance their quality of life throughout participation and after completion.

Counseling

Counseling is a critical component of youth diversion programs. The experience of major life stressors, such as exposure to violence, death of loved ones, or serious illness, is prevalent among court-involved youths and has an adverse impact on developmental outcomes. These outcomes can include delinquency and emotional/psychological dysfunction, such as post-traumatic stress disorder (PTSD) (Dembo et al., 2012). There are numerous approaches to counseling in youth diversion programs, including cognitive behavioral therapy (CBT), which can help the participant recognize and change negative thought patterns that contribute to behaviors. Additionally, counseling can focus on building positive relationships and developing social skills.

Court Advocacy

Social workers need to attend court hearings to report on the progress of program participants. In these reports, social workers provide updates on the client's educational or employment status, progress with community service, and any legal updates, such as rearrests or additional court dates. Attending court hearings and providing updates are a crucial aspect of a social worker's role, ensuring that the court is fully informed about the progress of program participants and any updates that may impact their compliance with the program.

Systemic Oppression in the Criminal Legal System

The criminal legal system is deeply rooted in oppression. Racial disparities have historically been the target of deliberate discrimination and oppression in the criminal legal system, which has led to an inaccurate perception of crime that falsely associates individuals with criminality (Hinton et al., 2018). Manifest oppression, defined as an observable occurrence of cruel and unjust treatment, is closely associated with this (Boyd, 2010). To understand manifest oppression, we must examine the US penal system and its treatment of Blacks. The prison system is a "comprehensive and well-disguised system of social control" (Alexander, 2012, p. 4). For those who are unable to receive an opportunity for diversion, there is the possibility of incarceration.

In 2020, the Bureau of Justice Statistics (BJS) reported that there were a total of 1,430,800 individuals incarcerated in state and federal prisons, 10% of which were young adults. Including local jails, the total amounts to 146,300 young adults in the carceral system. A large percentage of those incarcerated identified as Black. BJS notes that 39% of these young adults were Black. This affects the individual as well as their families, and if a person is released from serving time, they still face challenges. The individual's felony status can cause discrimination in obtaining employment, housing, education, and public benefits. If the basic needs are not met, there is a higher chance of recidivism (Kelly & Varghese, 2018).

Theoretical Frameworks Associated with Oppression in Youth Justice

Youth living in lower-income and over policed communities frequently report experiences of surveillance, profiling, and unjust treatment by law enforcement. These patterns reflect broader systemic inequalities and are often explained through criminological frameworks such as strain theory and labeling theory. These theories help illuminate how structural disadvantage, discriminatory practices and social construction of deviance contribute to the overrepresentation of marginalized youth in the criminal legal system. Together, they provide a lens through which to understand the intersection of poverty, racial bias, and punitive responses to youth behavior.

Strain Theory

Strain theories explore how systemic barriers impact individuals, particularly those from marginalized communities. Robert Merton (1968) first conceptualized strain theory, arguing that societal structures create pressures that can lead individuals to engage in crime when legitimate pathways to success are blocked. According to

Merton, the "American Dream" is defined by financial success, but individuals in lower socioeconomic positions often lack the means to achieve this goal through socially approved channels. As a result, some may turn to alternative means, including crime, to access resources. Early strain theorists largely framed these issues through a capitalist and class-biased lens, reinforcing the idea that middle-class norms were superior while dismissing the struggles of lower-income populations.

Over time, strain theory evolved to incorporate a broader understanding of how stressors impact behavior. By the 1980s and 1990s, scholars moved beyond purely structural explanations, emphasizing psychological and emotional responses to strain. Robert Agnew (2001) developed general strain theory (GST), which proposed that crime can be a response not only to blocked opportunities but also to negative life experiences. Agnew highlighted three primary sources of strain:

- Failure to achieve positively valued goals (e.g., financial success, education)
- Removal of positive stimuli (e.g., loss of a loved one, end of a significant relationship)
- Presence of negative stimuli (e.g., abuse, neglect, discrimination)

According to Agnew, individuals experiencing these strains—especially when they perceive their treatment as unjust—are more likely to develop negative emotions such as anger and frustration. When coping resources are limited, crime may serve as a means of alleviating strain or regaining control over their circumstances.

This perspective is particularly relevant to youth in marginalized communities, who often face economic hardship, social stigmatization, and aggressive policing. Many report that encounters with law enforcement create additional stressors that reinforce feelings of oppression. The assumption that they are criminals based on their neighborhood or appearance reflects a systemic pattern of labeling that can perpetuate cycles of criminalization and marginalization.

By applying strain theory to real-world scenarios, it becomes evident that systemic inequalities exacerbate the challenges faced by vulnerable populations, influencing their interactions with the criminal justice system. Rather than viewing crime solely as an individual failing, strain theory highlights how institutional barriers and societal pressures shape behavioral responses.

In 1994, Steven F. Messner and Richard Rosenfield developed institutional anomie theory (IAT). IAT was drawn from Merton's classical strain theory. However, IAT incorporated a macrostructural perspective. "The distinguishing feature of IAT is its principal focus on culture and social structure as manifested in social institutions". Messner and Fieldman examined the following: (1) the system of institutions, such as the economy, education, and the family; (2) the institutional norms that regulate behaviors; and (3) the interplay and functions of institutional norms and their influence on the functioning of individuals. Social institutions like schools, families, and government play a key role in maintaining established social systems. IAT reinforces the idea that these institutions are essential for a stable society. IAT utilizes functionalist orientation and highlights the importance of these institutions in shaping the social structure (Poulter, 2005). Nguyen and Ngo (2021) believes that IAT falls short by holding individuals responsible when they are seen as unable to meet the expectations associated with these social institutions. Consequently, engaging in criminal activities is linked to personal shortcomings in upholding the shared moral standards of society.

The stress and strain from law enforcement contribute to the behavior of youth within diversion programs. Police misconduct can affect behavioral outcomes among criminally involved youth. It has been found through studies that in disadvantaged communities, incidents of police misconduct can lead to an increase in violent crimes among community members (Zapolski et al., 2018). This emphasizes the importance of fair and just policing practices to ensure the safety and well-being of all members of a community.

Labeling Theory

Labeling theorists contend that youths who have been labeled as juvenile delinquents or criminals continue to engage in unlawful activities in response to prejudicial attitudes and discriminatory treatment from members of the public (Nguyen & Ngo, 2021). In the twentieth century, sociologists noticed how youth were perceived within their community based on delinquent behaviors. The foundation of labeling theory was developed by Frank Tannenbaum and later expanded on by Edwin Lemert. Both scholars explain how the process of labeling occurs for youth through the concept of social tagging and suggest the mechanism that leads them to recommit crime (Nguyen & Ngo, 2021). Tannenbaum (1938) made observations of the interactions between the community and youth who have engaged in delinquent acts. He indicates that when youth committed delinquent activities, the community would tag them as delinquent, and they would consequently receive adverse treatment.

Lemert (1951) provided additional insight into the reasons behind deviant behavior, and he proposed two types of deviance: primary and secondary. Committing the initial offense would be considered primary deviance. Youth do not self-identify as offenders; instead, they try to rationalize criminal activities. During this stage, the labeling process affects the individual self-identity and self-concept. However, if the youth's perception of self is weak, Lemert believes that this will lead to the response of secondary deviance. The more negatively intensified societal reactions the youth offender is exposed to, the more they reengage in the first offenses, which fit the delinquent labels given by the community and society (Lemert, 1951). Tannenbaum and Lemert's primary focus was exploring the potential outcomes of social labeling rather than examining the underlying reasons why young individuals engage in deviant activities.

A contemporary view of labeling theory can be seen through sociologist Howard Becker. In 1963, Becker wrote *Outsider: Studies in the Sociology of Deviance*. Becker described the process of labeling, through the image of outsiders who were considered deviants for breaking the rules enacted by the dominant groups and used the term *deviant careers* to predict how individuals engage in crimes (Nguyen & Ngo, 2021). Becker identified several steps in the process, which included (1) committing nonconforming acts, (2) experiencing being caught and labeled a deviant, and (3) subscribing to a different organized group. When youth commit nonconforming acts that lead to violating regulations, the violations are either unintended or intended (Becker, 1963). Becker believed that lack of awareness did not lead to further criminal acts; instead, it intended nonconformity-concerned individuals to achieve their aspirations, motivating them to commit more deviant acts (Becker, 1963). When young people engage in intentional deviant behavior, they often face harsh judgment from society. This judgment gives the public the power to label and treat the individual involved in negative ways. Becker (1963) believed that organized deviant groups, such as gangs, implied that the labeled individuals seek to be among other like-minded people with similar values and experiences to deal with the discrimination. Becker's analysis does not successfully address the complexities of oppression that are formed by the dominant groups.

Diversion programs often reflect patterns consistent with strain and labeling theory. Participants are frequently labeled as defendants and may continue to carry this label even after successful program completion, reinforcing stigma and potentially impacting their long term reintegration into the community. It is concerning that these clients are usually subject to a one-size-fits-all approach by the administration and are still being monitored by law enforcement post-program. This perpetuates a cycle of oppression within a population that is already vulnerable. It is important for these diversion programs to be mindful of the impact that labeling can have on participants and to take steps to avoid perpetuating harmful stereotypes. Instead, the focus should be on providing support and resources to individuals to help them make positive changes in their lives.

Now that the background and participant experiences in youth diversion programs (YDP) have been explored the focus shifts to anti-oppressive practices (AOPs) and the ethical challenges they present. To deepen this understanding, two case scenarios commonly encountered in YDP settings will be examined.

Pathways Through Diversion: Two Case Studies

The following two case scenarios of Jeremy and Mara present two different trajectories with the Transforming Steps Beyond (TSB) Program, a youth diversion initiative designed for individuals charged with nonviolent offenses. These examples offer insight into how systemic barriers, institutional responses, and individual circumstances intersect to shape youth outcomes within diversion settings.

Jeremy

Jeremy identifies as a 19-year-old African American cisgender male who was arrested for possession of a firearm. At the time of the arrest, he was in a vehicle with three other passengers all over the age of 21 and with prior criminal records. According to the case file, Jeremy took responsibility for the weapon and subsequently booked and detained at a local jail. The bail for Jeremy's release was $25,000 with a bond of $5000. Jeremy's immediate family consists of his mother who works for a neighborhood daycare and two 8-year-old twin brothers. Jeremy's mother was unable to afford the set bond for Jeremy who remained incarcerated for over 3 months; within that time, Jeremy's public defender was reassigned four times. Since this was Jeremy's first offense, his attorney referred him to the TSB program. Jeremy's attorney was confident that Jeremy would get accepted to the 18-month program. If Jeremy completed the TSB program the criminal possession of a weapon in the second degree (CPW2) he was charged with would be dismissed and expunged from his legal record. However, if Jeremy failed to complete the youth diversion program, he would be considered to be in violation of the program, resulting in being charged with a felony and mandated to serve 5 years in a maximum prison facility and 5 years post release supervision (PRS).

Jeremy was transported to the TSBprogram from the local jail to meet with the program staff, which consisted of the assigned social worker, an additional social worker, and the program director. Jeremy was brought into a room where he was handcuffed to a seat with limited mobility. The program staff explained the program requirements to Jeremy, who was eager to start work and take his General Education Development (GED) exam.

An assessment for the TSB program typically takes 4–6 weeks. The assessment includes an interview with a family member and potential participant, followed by an extensive interview process with the individual. During this time, the potential participant will participate in the program on a trial basis. Specifically, this consists of attending meetings and checking in for curfew; some candidates would even begin community service hours that count toward program participation. For Jeremy to be able to participate, he would have to take the plea immediately after he was released from jail. The assessment interview with Jeremy and the assigned social worker was completed within two hours. Jeremy was scheduled to be accepted and take the program plea.

After Jeremy took his conditional plea of guilty, he headed over to the TSB program to meet with the social worker and program director. The program director stated that an ankle monitor would be placed on Jeremy, to ensure he is monitored after his release and complies with curfew. TSB does not typically place electronic monitoring devices on incoming participants, but this was a requirement for Jeremy to be released to the program. Because Jeremy's phone was taken as evidence during the arrest three months prior, he was required to check in using a landline. During the first three weeks, he consistently checked in, met with his assigned social worker, and complied with all curfew and monitoring requirements. The social worker located a local GED prep course for Jeremy to enroll in. He was registered and was expected to start in the coming weeks. However, before he could start the social worker was informed that Jeremy was rearrested for being outside of his building after midnight with a group of people. Because Jeremy had an open case, he was taken to central booking. Jeremy was later released and given a summons with a deadline to pay a fine. After the arrest, Jeremy's participation declined: he stopped coming in consistently, did not charge his device or check-in for curfew, and did not attend the GED prep class. The assigned social worker had multiple case conferences with Jeremy to discuss progress and the importance of remaining in compliance. Jeremy said he would begin checking in with the social worker; he was consistent for a day or two, but then would stop. The program director stated that he would request that Jeremy be remanded to jail for 2 weeks due to noncompliance.

The court granted the request, and after returning from custody, Jeremy initially resumed compliance with the program requirements. However, he was rearrested again, for loitering outside a neighborhood store, where an alleged shooting had occurred earlier that day, though there was no indication that Jeremy was involved in the incident. Following this arrest, Jeremy shared with the social worker that the same officers in his neighborhood were constantly harassing him. His participation declined once again. After four months in the program, Jeremy failed to meet expectations and was deemed non compliant due to multiple missed curfew check-ins. and Jeremy was terminated from the TSB program due to noncomplaince, leading to the reinstatement of the CPW2 felony charge. Per the terms of his conditional plea he was required to serve the agreed-upon sentence of incarceration and PRS.

Reflection Questions

1. What oppressive factors contributed to Jeremy's violation of the TSB program?
2. When reading about Jeremy's case, do any personal judgments or feelings of countertransference arise for you? If they do, what specific thoughts or emotions emerge?
3. What do you believe Jeremy would have needed to complete the TSB program?

Mara

Mara identifies as a 21-year-old Hispanic, cisgender woman. At 19 years old, Mara was arrested for possession of a weapon as a gun was found in her purse. At the time, Mara was with her boyfriend who had prior arrests and an open court case. Mara had multiple court dates before receiving the TSB program and was hesitant when initially being assessed. Mara was frustrated with the process but also hesitant to talk with the assigned social worker because she stated that she does not trust anyone.

As Mara continued the assessment, she started to build rapport with the social worker, allowing her to become more open. Mara was already employed prior to the program and had a high school diploma. While she worked for a local diner, Mara stated that she is always looking for better work opportunities. Her goal was to work within the school system, but she is currently unable to because of the open case. Mara shared her frustration with finding different jobs because the case appears on her background checks.

Mara was unable to have any family members participate in the assessment interview. She shared that she has a difficult relationship with her mother and had to move out of the home when she was 20 years old. Mara has a close relationship with her father, but he is currently incarcerated and expected to be released in 3 years. Mara was raised by her maternal grandmother, who recently moved to another state, and she now lives with her aunt and cousins, all of whom have busy work schedules.

Mara acclimated quickly during the trial of TSB and 6 weeks later took her plea to the court. Mara attended all scheduled sessions with social workers, started volunteering for her community service requirement, and checked in consistently for curfew. As Mara started to build a therapeutic relationship with her social worker, she found counseling very helpful. In her neighborhood, she was losing many people she grew up with to gun violence or incarceration. These traumatic experiences have caused her stress and anxiety but motivated Mara to complete the program so she can reset her life. Mara had instances when she would attend sessions frustrated after arguing with her mother. Mara and her social worker collaborated to develop a plan that involved utilizing her support network, including her grandmother and close friends. The social worker also suggested incorporating stress-relief strategies like taking walks and practicing breathing exercises.

Mara lost her job at the local diner. Subsequently, she met with the social worker and discussed job possibilities. Mara had an interest in working in culinary arts, so the social worker referred her to a community-based culinary arts internship. In the 12-week program, Mara would receive paid training and job experience, as well as job placement at a restaurant within the community.

After a year and a half, of consistent engagement, Mara successfully completed the TSB program. Her case was dismissed and expunged. Three months later, she reconnected with her social worker to share that she had secured employment within the school system. In addition to relocating to a new neighborhood, Mara also began therapy to continue supporting her mental health and personal development, demonstrating the long term impact of a supportive, anti-oppressive intervention.

Reflection Questions

1. What factors do you believe contributed to Mara's success within the program?
2. How would you handle a client's resistance when meeting with you?

3. How has your awareness of countertransference influenced your understanding of Mara's case study? What steps would you take to manage any countertransference that may surface?

Ethical Clinical Practice in Youth Diversion Programs

Social work is grounded in ethical practice. The National Association of Social Workers (NASW) Code of Ethics is used as a guide for social workers' professional behavior and is especially relevant for those working in youth diversion programs. NASW states that the code of ethics sets forth values, principles, and standards to guide social workers' conduct. The Code is relevant to all social workers and social work students, regardless of their professional functions, the settings in which they work, or the populations they serve (National Association of Social Workers, 2017). The core values of the Code of Ethics are service, social justice, dignity and worth of the person, importance of human relationships, integrity, and competence. Despite their commitment to ethical clinical practice, social workers in youth diversion programs may face challenges when working within the criminal legal system, as it may create a conflict between legal and social work ethics.

Implementing Anti-oppressive Practices in Social Work

Anti-oppressive practice in social work is essential within criminal legal settings. The population has experienced oppression and marginalization. As a social worker in these settings, I incorporate five anti-oppressive practices that are essential to working with the population:

1. Removing the label associated with the individual who was involved with the crime

   It is common in court involved settings to refer to individuals as defendants. Your first step within this setting is to remove the oppressive labels. It is imperative that we are mindful of the language we use. For instance, the term "rehabilitative approaches" inadvertently suggest that the participant is "broken" or lacking in some way and requires fixing. Moving beyond such terminology allows us to see the client as more than just a case. It is essential to ensure our documentation and interactions with legal personnel consistently use language that upholds the dignity and humanity of the individuals involved.
2. Seek supervision

   If you are new to this setting, and need more experience working with a population in youth diversion, it is important to have supervision with a licensed social work clinician. In this space, you will be able to discuss feelings of countertransference and questions or concerns you may have while working with the population. This allows you to have open discussions while building your competence.

3. Empower your participants

   As you get to know your participants, you will learn more about their personalities, interests, and, most importantly, their strengths. Invest in your clients. Take an interest in what they enjoy and encourage them to follow their ambitions, as Mara did. Reassure your clients often that the reason why they are in this situation does not define them. This will build confidence for the client during and after program completion.

4. Do not use a "one size-fits-all approach"

   No client is the same; each has its own needs that must be met. Your job is to assess each client's needs separately and create the best course of action for that individual. Grouping and labeling the population do a disservice to the client and may do more harm than good.

5. When in doubt, refer out

   As discussed, you will face challenges maintaining ethical practice within your agency or setting. Your responsibility is to advocate for your clients; if you find yourself in a challenging situation where you are stuck between the responsibilities of your job and your ethical practice, it is essential to reach out to the best advocate for the client. For example, if the prosecution asks the client to provide information that may further incriminate them or is unrelated to their current case, using it as leverage to keep them in the program, the social worker needs to advise the client to consult their attorney.

Conclusion: Advancing Anti-Oppressive Youth Work

While anti-oppressive practices in youth diversion have advanced, significant work remains. As social workers, your ongoing commitment to equity, dignity and justice will continue to shape the evolution of these practices. Diversion programs remain a vital alternative to incarceration, offering young people a chance at meaningful change. Entering these spaces with critical awareness and a drive for systemic transformation is essential to building more just and effective interventions.

Reflective Practice Questions

1. What motivated you to pursue a career in court-related and criminal justice environments?
2. What difficulties do you anticipate while working with young people in diversion programs? How would you address these challenges?
3. In your work with participants, how do you think the theories of strain and labeling will impact your approach?

4. When working with youth in the criminal legal system, do you think taking a punitive or rehabilitative approach is more effective? What are your thoughts on this?
5. Considering legal limitations, how do you believe your personal values and ethical principles will affect your approach to anti-oppressive practices?

References

Agnew, R. (2001). Building on the foundation of general strain theory: Specifying the types of strain most likely to lead to crime and delinquency. *Journal of Research in Crime and Delinquency, 38*(4), 319–361.

Alexander, M. (2012). *The new Jim crow: Mass incarceration in the age of colorblindness*. The New Press.

Allen, T. T., & Whitt, A. (2020). An examination of the relationship between media exposure and fear of victimization: Implications of the Superpredator narrative on juvenile justice policies. *Juvenile & Family Court Journal, 71*(4), 23–34. https://doi-org.proxy.library.nyu.edu/10.1111/jfcj.12185

Becker, H. S. (1963). *Outsiders: Studies in the sociology of deviance*. Free Press.

Boyd, N. M. (2010). Forum: Oppression in the mundane of management. *Administrative Theory & Praxis (M.E. Sharpe), 32*(3), 445–449. https://doi.org/10.2753/ATP1084-1806320311

Brownell, P., & Roberts, A. R. (2002). A century of social work in criminal justice and correctional settings. *Journal of Offender Rehabilitation, 35*(2), 1–18.

Cochran, J. C., & Mears, D. P. (2015). Race, ethnic, and gender divides in juvenile court sanctioning and rehabilitative intervention. *Journal of Research in Crime and Delinquency, 52*(2), 181–212.

Dembo, R., Briones, R., Gulledge, L., Karas, L., Winters, K., Belenko, S., & Greenbaum, P. (2012). Stress, mental health, and substance abuse problems in a sample of diversion program youths: An exploratory latent class analysis. *Journal of Child & Adolescent Substance Abuse, 21*(2), 130–155. https://doi-org.proxy.library.nyu.edu/10.1080/1067828X.2012.662115

Grand Challenges for Social Work. (2023, June 9). https://grandchallengesforsocialwork.org/

Hinton, E. K., Henderson, L., & Reed, C. (2018, May 1). An unjust burden. Vera Institute. https://www.vera.org/publications/for-the-record-unjust-burden

Human Impact Partners. (2017). *Reducing youth arrests keeps kids healthy and successful: A health analysis of youth arrest in Michigan*. Human Impact Partners.

Kelly, D. C., & Varghese, R. (2018). Four contexts of institutional oppression: Examining the experiences of blacks in education, criminal justice and child welfare. *Journal of Human Behavior in the Social Environment, 28*(7), 874–888. https://doi-org.proxy.library.nyu.edu/10.1080/10911359.2018.1466751

Lemert, E. M.. (Edwin M. 1912–1996) (1951). *Social pathology: A systematic approach to the theory of sociopathic behavior*. McGraw-Hill.

Mallett, C. A., & Tedor, M. F. (2019). *Juvenile delinquency pathways and prevention: Chapter 2 the history of juvenile justice and today's*. Juvenile Courts Sage Publications 27–42 Sage Publications.

Merton, R. K. (1968). *Social theory and social structure*. Free Press. 1910–2003.

Motivans, M. (2022, December 1). *Federal Justice Statistics, 2021 – bjs.ojp.gov*. Federal Justice Statistics 2021. Retrieved May 4, 2023, from https://bjs.ojp.gov/sites/g/files/xyckuh236/files/media/document/fjs21.pdf

National Association of Social Workers. (2017). Code of ethics of the National Association of Social Workers. Retrieved from https://www.socialworkers.org/About/Ethics/Code-of-Ethics/Code-of-Ethics-English

NeMoyer, A., Gale-Bentz, E., Goldstein, N. E. S., & Pema Harvey, L. (2020). Factors associated with successful completion of a community-based, Postarrest juvenile diversion program and subsequent rearrest. *Crime & Delinquency, 66*(5), 603–626. https://doi.org/10.1177/0011128719842377

Nguyen, Q. H., & Ngo, H. V. (2021). Strain theories and labelling theories: A critical examination through an anti-oppressive lens. *Critical Social Work, 22*(1), 76–95. https://doi.org/10.22329/csw.v22i1.6900

Pope, R. J., & Jones, J. N. (2020). Exploring organizational strategies and participant experience in the young adult diversion court. *Victims & Offenders, 15*(2), 267–290.

Poulter, J. (2005). Integrating theory and practice: A new heuristic paradigm for social work practice. *Australian Social Work, 58*(2), 199–212. https://doi-org.proxy.library.nyu.edu/10.1111/j.1447-0748.2005.00204.x

Tannenbaum, F. (1938). *Crime and the community* (pp. 1893–1969). Ginn.

Wilson, H. A., & Hoge, R. D. (2013). Diverting our attention to what works: Evaluating the effectiveness of a youth diversion program. *Youth Violence and Juvenile Justice, 11*(4), 313–331.

Zapolski, T. C. B., Banks, D. E., Lau, K. S. L., & Aalsma, M. C. (2018). Perceived police injustice, moral disengagement, and aggression among juvenile offenders: Utilizing the general strain theory model. *Child Psychiatry & Human Development, 49*(2), 290–297. https://doi.org/10.1007/s10578-017-0750-z

Chapter 16
Anti-oppressive Practice with Women in Carceral Spaces

Allison McCullough

The number of women incarcerated in the United States has exploded in the past 30 years. Women are the most rapidly growing population of incarcerated people in the country, growing at double the rate of men (Kajstura & Sawyer, 2024). Since 1980, there has been an over 700% increase in the number of women experiencing incarceration, rising from a total of 26,378 women in 1980 to 224,845 women in 2019 (The Sentencing Project, 2020). The explosion in the population of incarcerated women has been largely attributed to the pursuit of the war on drugs and mandatory sentencing minimums, changes that have disproportionately led to an increase in the number of incarcerated Black women (Alexander, 2010) who are incarcerated at nearly twice the rate of White women (Carson, 2020).

Even though racialized and poor people are incarcerated at disproportionate rates, social work practice within the criminal legal system[1] does not typically utilize an anti-oppressive framework (Leotti, 2021; O'Brien & Willison, 2022; Pollack, 2004). Anti-oppressive practice's foundations lay on a staunch commitment to social justice and a dedication to examining systemic issues that maintain social hierarchy and oppression; anti-oppressive practice works to dismantle those systems in pursuit of liberation for all (Larson, 2008).

[1] A note on language. This paper will use the term "criminal legal system," not "criminal justice system," because there is nothing just about a system that dehumanizes, racializes, and entraps human beings. This author also recognizes individuals who identify as female or nonbinary are sometimes placed in male facilities because the carceral system does not always honor gender identity.

A. McCullough (✉)
Silver School of Social Work, New York University, New York, NY, USA
e-mail: Acm257@nyu.edu

C. Tosone et al. (eds.), *Reframing Social Work with an Anti-Oppressive Lens*, Essential Clinical Social Work Series,
https://doi.org/10.1007/978-3-031-91391-4_16

For social work to be anti-oppressive, the social context in which people come to be incarcerated must be incorporated into practice (Pollack, 2004). Social workers must examine inevitable power dynamics in their work and commit to powering sharing to the fullest extent possible (Larson, 2008). Many of the interventions utilized in jails and prisons fail to use an anti-oppressive framework because they ignore structural inequities and reinforce the notion of "criminal thinking" stemming from individual deficits, not forms of systemic oppression.

This chapter discusses the White supremacist, patriarchal, and classist lenses through which women's behavior has been criminalized and controlled and examines social work's complicity in this process. It reviews work currently being done with women in carceral spaces and asks the reader to think about ways that social workers can practice anti-oppressive work in inherently oppressive spaces. How can we seek to understand the lives of people experiencing incarceration within the oppressive contexts that led to their incarceration? How can we ensure that our work does not further oppress marginalized populations? This chapter seeks to answer those questions and to provide best practices informed by a social worker with years of experience working within carceral spaces.

White Femininity and Social Control: The Foundation of Women's Imprisonment

The ideals associated with dominant systems of heteropatriarchy and white supremacy are embedded in the foundations of social work and in the creation of women's carceral institutions in the United States. Social work's foundation is built upon the professionalism of white femininity (Baldwell, 2014) and early women's imprisonment aimed to reform "fallen" whose behavior was criminalized for deviating from hegemonic norms (Hahn Rafter, 1983; Leotti, 2022; O'Brien & Willison, 2022).

As public punishment began to fall out of favor with the rise of enlightenment ideals, the legal system transitioned to the custodial model of punishment that included prisons that housed people convicted of crimes. Crime was viewed as a result of idleness, and the focus of prisons was to instill values of obedience and hard work through physical labor (O'Brien & Willison, 2022). Women did not make up a large percentage of the incarcerated population and were held in the same prisons as men, in separate areas that often had much worse conditions (Dodge, 1999; Rafter; 1983).

In 1870, the emergence of the Progressive Era ushered in the creation of the reformatory model of incarceration for women. At the foundation of this model was the gendered notion of a "true womanhood" that required women to be submissive and both morally and sexually pure (Harrell, 2022; Leotti, 2022). This construction of femininity was rooted in White, heteronormative ideals that led to the criminalization of racialized and poor women. Women were expected to remain in the home and working outside of the home for pay was viewed as improper. White middle- and upper-class women were able to meet these behavioral expectations while poor women, who were disproportionately Black, had to work outside of the home due to economic necessity or forced exploitation (Leotti, 2022).

Women were convicted mostly of crimes against chastity, including adultery, fornication, lewd cohabitation, and lewdness, and crimes against public order, including drunkenness, idle and disorderly behavior, and stubbornness. Women who were found to have engaged in sex work, alcohol consumption, and other criminalized behaviors were the antithesis of feminine ideals and served as a warning of the consequences of deviance (Leotti, 2022; Rafter, 1983). The goal of reformatories was to reform women—a form of social control that shaped women to comply with hegemonic norms and behavioral expectations. Women sent to reformatories were believed capable of a salvation that would occur once they conformed to fit feminine norms (Harrell, 2022). Most Black women were not considered capable of reform and true womanhood and continued to be sentenced to custodial institutions in which they performed hard physical labor (Leotti, 2022; Rafter, 1983).

The women, mostly poor and White, were housed in reformatories that were run by middle- and upper-class women, often social workers, who were compliant with dominant female norms, with the assumption that such women would act as role models. Reformatories provided training in domestic duties to prepare women for life as an acceptable woman upon release. The reformers and social workers who had pushed for reformatories did not situate their work in the context of larger social or economic factors. Their reform efforts emphasized individual "deficits" and maintained the ideal of a true womanhood based on White, upper-class values. The reformers of the time believed they were improving life for female prisoners by moving them from custodial institutions and focusing on care rather than punishment. However, reformatories perpetuated social control over women (Rafter, 1983). Rather than challenging the social and economic oppression of women, social workers perpetuated gender norms and the criminalization of deviance.

Many of these social work reformers gathered at the annual National Conference of Charities and Corrections. The conference was originally named the Conference of Boards of Charities; Corrections was added to the title in 1879 to reflect the organization's increasing focus on corrections (in the case of reformatories, "correcting" women's behavior) and delinquency. In 1917, the conference was renamed The National Conference of Social Work and became a hallmark conference for the profession (Harrell, 2022). As demonstrated by its role in the reformatory model, social work has been complicit in the control of criminalized women since its beginnings. Social work evolved, in part, to legitimize White femininity (Bussey et al., 2021) and, as a profession that continues to be comprised predominantly of White women, must recognize this and incorporate that knowledge into current practice.

Current Practices

The hegemonic norms at the foundation of women's imprisonment in the United States continue to inform how we incarcerate women. The carceral system continues to be a system of control and punishment for poor and marginalized communities and for others who deviate from dominant ideals of gender; it continues to criminalize those who fail to conform. Crime and notions of criminal behavior have always been social constructions framed by the sociopolitical values of the time (Pollack, 2004). The guiding carceral programming and interventions are reflective of the ideological climate and create a social construct of what is considered "criminalized behavior." Neoliberal values of individual responsibility and accountability maintain a focus on problems as a result of individual behaviors, not systemic failures or policies and structures that create and maintain oppressed and marginalized communities (Leotti, 2022). The relationship between socioeconomic exclusion and criminalization is ignored (Pollack, 2009). Resistance to oppression, including protecting oneself against an abusive partner, resisting poverty, and substance use to cope with manifestations of oppression, is criminalized (Pollack, 2004). Statistical correlations between race, gender, and class are reflective of the values and practices of the carceral system, not individual behavior (O'Brien & Willison, 2022). The social construction of crime is further evident in the inconsistencies between the ways in which the federal government and individual states define and respond to criminalized behaviors (Pollack, 2004, O'Brien & Willison, 2022).

The social construction of criminality is also evident in the explosion of the US prison population because of policies related to the pursuit of the war on drugs and mandatory sentencing minimums (Alexander, 2010). The increase in drug-related criminalization had a more dramatic increase on the incarceration rates of women than men (Harmon & Boppre, 2016) because substance use conflicts with the hegemonic narrative of women as mothers and caretakers (Harmon & O'Brien, 2011).

Dominant ideals of motherhood, again based on White supremacist, middle-class, heteronormative values, frame how the carceral system engages with poor mothers of color. In the nine states in which prison nurseries exist, mothers may be denied entrance based on the nature of their charges or a history of involvement with the child welfare system (Goshin & Byrne, 2009), another system that punishes families who do not conform to dominant familial norms (Cénat et al., 2021). The carceral system determines who is fit to be a mother and separates the rest from their newborn children.

As in the reformatory model where behavioral correction was the goal and larger systemic issues were ignored, today's services are largely focused on individual "deficits" that continue to fail to acknowledge social and environmental issues that contribute to incarceration (Leotti, 2022). As has been the case since colonial times, behaviors and thought processes in need of correction continue to be identified through a lens that idealizes White, heteronormative, patriarchal values of womanhood. Carceral interventions aiming to correct these behaviors reinforce and perpetuate these hegemonic ideals and continue to punish those who do not conform (O'Brien & Willison, 2022; Pollack, 2004).

Despite the racial and economic disparities in the US prison population, social work within the carceral system has not typically been approached with an anti-oppressive framework (Leotti, 2021; O'Brien & Willison, 2022; Pollack, 2004). Anti-oppressive practice emphasizes and examines dynamics of power and oppression in the lives of clients who have been marginalized and oppressed. Anti-oppressive social work must also acknowledge the power present in services provided by social workers (Donohue-Dioh et al., 2021; Pollack, 2004, 2009). This work is especially necessary for social workers practicing in carceral spaces that, by design, function to deny autonomy and to punish and control. The frameworks guiding programming are reflective of the ideological climate of the time and create a social construct of what is considered "criminalized behavior." Neoliberal values of individual responsibility accountability maintain a focus on problems because of individual behaviors, not systemic failures or policies and structures that create and maintain oppressed and marginalized communities (Leotti, 2022).

Cognitive behavioral programming is widely viewed as the most effective programming in prisons (Allen et al., 2001; O'Brien & Willison, 2022; Pollack, 2004). The National Institute for Corrections published an article on its website titled "Preventing Future Crime with Cognitive Behavioral Therapy: One Form of Psychotherapy Stands Out in The Criminal Justice System" (Clark, 2010). The article highlighted the ability of cognitive behavioral interventions to improve social skills, critical reasoning, moral reasoning, and self-efficacy and made no mention of poverty, racism, or other systemic oppressions. The cognitive behavioral approach suggests that criminalized individuals think differently than non-criminalized individuals because of faulty thinking indicative of lower levels of moral development or poor ability to think rationally (Allen et al., 2001; O'Brien & Willison; 2022; Pollack, 2004).

Central to cognitive behavioral interventions is the idea that "criminal thinking" leads to incarceration. The social context in which people come to experience incarceration is ignored. The theoretical underpinnings of cognitive behavioral approaches perpetuate an us versus them dichotomy between service providers and criminalized individuals that discourages the realization that systems of oppression are inextricably linked to who ends up in prison and who does not (Leotti, 2021). The frameworks guiding programming are reflective of the ideological climate of the time and create a social construct of what is considered "criminalized behavior." Neoliberal values of individual responsibility and accountability maintain a focus on problems because of individual behaviors, not systemic failures or policies and structures that create and maintain oppressed and marginalized communities (Leotti, 2021, 2022).

The cognitive behavioral interventions used in prisons decontextualize behavior. The focus is not on capabilities and strengths but on individual "deficits." Incarcerated women are commonly viewed to lack rationality, reason, self-esteem, and adequate coping skills. When the larger systems of power and oppression are ignored, they remain unchallenged (O'Brien & Willison, 2022). The cognitive behavioral models used in prisons are heavily manualized and do not address issues of cultural identifiers including gender, class, or race. Such prescriptive, evidence-based models also fail to allow space for criminalized women to define needs and success on their own terms (Leotti, 2021).

Participant discussions about the impact of systems of oppression are viewed as denials and rationalizations of incarceration (Pollack, 2004), not as meaningful ways to explore and understand their lives. Cognitive behavioral interventions encourage individuals to adopt the "criminal personality" storyline while ignoring the constructs of identity and lived experience. Women are conditioned to adopt a "victimhood" narrative that ignores strengths and resiliencies. In adopting this narrative, the carceral system becomes the hero who redeemed women in need of correction (Pollack, 2020).

Much of the gender-specific programming in women's prisons assumes that criminalized behavior is related to low self-esteem. Interventions aim to raise self-esteem to reduce future interaction with the criminal legal system (Leotti, 2021). Incarceration is the result of low self-worth, not limited social and economic opportunity. Rather than examining structural factors such as racism, sexism, interpersonal violence, or poverty, the issue in need of intervention becomes an individual deficit. The intentions of such carceral programs may be empowerment, but they are ultimately disempowering when they fail to incorporate a holistic view of the systems that limit a woman's power to make decisions. The choices women make are often not indicative of low self-esteem but of the opportunities available to them (Pollack, 2020).

The high rates of trauma among women experiencing incarceration have been well documented (DeHart, 2008; Dholakia, 2021). Anti-oppressive work must recognize past trauma and acknowledge the additional trauma caused by incarceration. The psychological effects of trauma, including depression, hypervigilance, and mistrust, are often exacerbated in a prison setting. In the cognitive behavioral frameworks that dominate programming in carceral spaces, behavior is decontextualized from the social structures and inequities that perpetuate trauma. Women are often labeled as "resistant, manipulative, hostile, or uncooperative"—descriptors that decontextualize individual behavior and do not examine the intersection of oppression and trauma. The controlled environment of incarceration and the authority of prison guards can recreate abusive dynamics and trigger trauma responses that should be viewed as coping responses to trauma, not pathologized (Pollack, 2004 p. 698).

A qualitative study conducted by Pollack (2009) interviewed incarcerated women about their experiences with programming and found that, despite programmatic goals of empowerment, most women did not find the programming in prison to be empowering. Participants shared that the emphasis on individual traits ignored the realities of their lives, and the majority wanted the carceral system to be held accountable for false claims of rehabilitation.

The most recent document on social work in carceral spaces written by the National Association of Social Workers (NASW), the largest membership association of professional social workers in the world entitled *Criminal Justice Social*

Work in the United States: Adapting to New Challenges (Kelly et al., 2010), makes no mention of power, oppression, or racism. Such systems are inextricably linked to incarceration and are crucial to an understanding of how individuals become trapped in the carceral system. In the absence of a critical approach to examining mass incarceration, it is concerning that later in the same publication, the NASW calls for social workers to be leaders in the creation of criminal legal policy (NASW refers to it as criminal justice policy). The NASW does state that "leadership requires a re-examination of how Criminal Justice Social Work (CJSW) functions within the American criminal justice system, and how the profession's leadership voice can be heard as the criminal justice system goes through its own self-examination" (Kelly et al., 2010, p. 4). There is no urgent call for social work to examine its own history of compliance within the creation and maintenance of the punitive carceral system and no mention of the need for anti-oppressive or anti-racist practices.

Despite social work being a profession that emphasizes a person-in-environment framework, that value does not seem to carry over to carceral settings. Social work has been criticized for moving away from challenging systemic issues of oppression toward individualized services that pathologize behavior and fail to incorporate environmental and systemic issues. The perceived divide between social justice-oriented macro practice and individualized practice has been perceived as a shift that occurred when social work moved to professionalize itself and gain legitimacy within positivist realms of science (Abramovitz, 1998; Bussey et al., 2021).

In its quest to be viewed as a legitimate profession, social work came to rely on evidence-based practices (including the cognitive behavioral interventions discussed earlier in this chapter) which have been criticized for failing to center the voices and honor the lived experience of participants (Abramovitz, 1998). Social work has been complicit in the creation and maintenance of oppressive systems when it fails to value the lived experience of clients and to examine the effects of structural and institutional oppression (O'Brien & Willison, 2022). The application of an anti-oppressive framework to social work practice would ensure that both the symptoms of marginalization and oppression, such as homelessness or depressed mood, were addressed while seeking ways to work with the individual to combat the oppressive systems. Anti-oppressive work does not abide by a false binary of macro versus micro practice and engages both individuals and communities in the struggle for liberation.

Anti-oppressive practice requires social workers to challenge existing systems of oppression. Carceral spaces are designed to control and punish, and incarcerated individuals are constantly reminded of their lack of autonomy. Empowerment and self-determination, two hallmark values of social work (NASW, 2008), are in stark contrast to the intentionally oppressive design of carceral spaces. Social workers must resist practices that further oppress or control criminalized individuals. While it is imperative that social workers engage in practices that do not further oppress criminalized individuals, the profession must also continue to fight for alternative responses to harm that dismantle the legal system's overreliance on incarceration.

Best Practices

How can social workers work within the carceral system but not be a part of it? How do we resist bending to the pervasive values of the carceral system when we are immersed in those values in our places of work? Scholars have challenged the idea that individuals can receive empowering services that promote healing while in an environment designed to be oppressive (Kendall, 1994). The cognitive behavioral interventions that are the predominant form of treatment in prisons do not challenge this assertion, but social work can find ways to honor the humanity and highlight the strengths of women who are incarcerated. Social work can resist the dominant constructs of criminalized women and partner with clients in anti-oppressive practices that view incarceration as the result of choices made from lives lived within intersecting oppressive systems. This section will offer suggestions for social workers, and I will provide examples from my experience working with women incarcerated in a New York City jail.

Anti-oppressive social work requires the development of critical consciousness to examine the oppressive structures in the lives of our clients, in addition to the power inequities that exist within the social worker's relationship with clients. The development of critical awareness is necessary before one can actively engage in critical action (Bussey et al., 2021). Critical consciousness is especially necessary when working in carceral spaces at the intersection of multiple oppressive systems.

Critical consciousness was originally described by Paolo Freire (1973) who found that social injustices flourished when communities were not aware of the systemic oppressions that impacted their lives (Jemal, 2017). In addition to fostering an understanding of the systems and structures that create and sustain inequity, critical consciousness empowers oppressed people to develop a sense of agency and to resist oppressive conditions (El Amin, 2022).

Working with clients to develop critical consciousness about the systems that continue their criminalization enables them to resist the carceral rhetoric that their behavior is a result of individual faulty thinking. It allows clients to think about their lives in the context of the sociopolitical systems in which they live and invites them to develop a more complex understanding of their criminalization and ways to resist the "criminal" narrative.

Anti-oppressive social work cannot be done by a practitioner who has not examined their own positionality in relation to systems of oppression. This requires more than knowing one's racial and gender identities and socioeconomic identities; it requires continuous critical reflection on intersecting identities and impact on the services they provide (Kishimoto, 2016).

There are inevitable power imbalances in a social worker's relationship with clients, and critical consciousness challenges social workers to recognize them. The power imbalances have nurtured social work's role as social controllers (Sakamoto & Pitner, 2005). Within an anti-oppressive framework, critical consciousness calls on social workers to critically examine ways in which their own identities have been shaped by dominant ideologies and ways in which their identity influences work with clients. Social workers must further interrogate how their identities have contributed to, or upheld, systems of oppression (Mullaly, 2002). Social control/helping tensions that have plagued social work since its inception are especially visible in carceral settings that are designed to control, punish, and surveil (Leotti, 2022). Social work's role in women's reformatories is a prime example of the profession's complicity in upholding social constructs of gender.

Suggested Practices

- *Examine your power and be humble.* There are inevitable power dynamics within the social worker/client relationship but strive to dismantle them to the extent possible by emphasizing client's knowledge, strengths, and abilities (O'Brien & Willison, 2022). Approach social work practice with humility. You are not the expert; the client is the expert. They have been living their lives for many years, and you are just meeting them. It is arrogant to think you know what is best for someone and that behavior mirrors social work's legacy as agents of social control. The lived experiences of incarcerated women must guide the work you do; be humble and willing to admit that you do not know what is best. Clients in carceral spaces have very little power and autonomy. Do what you can to give them choice in what happens in the work you do together.
- *Resist the dominant narrative.* On an individual client level, resist the labels that have been given to clients. Challenge the popular notion of women as deceitful and manipulative (Pollack, 2004). Be curious about behavior. Think about ways in which the carceral environment might be motivating current behavior and ways in which past trauma may be reexperienced and exacerbated by incarceration. Look for the strengths, humor, and love within the clients with whom you work.
- *Resist the artificial separation of micro- and macro-level work.* There are certainly tensions that occur when using an anti-oppressive framework in a carceral setting because anti-oppressive work requires practice on both the individual and larger societal levels. Social workers are challenged to balance the need to maintain access to the carceral space and to resist the carceral system. On a macro-scale, look for ways to become engaged in advocacy work including rallies and social protests. If your workplace is not active in advocacy work, educate them on the importance of macro-level change and the need to bring attention to the oppressive policies that lead to the incarceration of your clients.
- *Examine your motivations.* Engage in constant reflection as to why you do this work and as to how you relate to the clients with whom you work and how they relate to you. Think about your social identity and how it impacts client relationships. Do people want or need your help? What puts you in a position to offer help? The false us versus them dichotomy present in carceral programming interventions must be resisted by social workers (O'Brien & Willison, 2022). Anti-oppressive work is not possible if a social worker views criminalized people as

anything other than capable members of their community whose choices have been limited by the systems in which they live.

- *Be critical of social work.* "Any profession that does not examine its oppressive and racist tendencies is indeed creating harm to society" (Donohue-Dioh et al., 2021, p. 1047). Social workers must be aware of the tension between care and control that has been endemic to the profession since its inception. Examine the foundations and dominant epistemologies of the schools where you were educated. There is no neutral education (Freire, 1973). Identify the assumptions about criminalized individuals that were made and examine the extent to which your school encouraged you to explore social work's complicity in maintaining systems of oppression.

Case Example and Author Positionality

Samantha[2] had been arrested on allegations of assault after a fight with her former partner, Chris. She could not afford the $7500 bail set on her case and was detained on Rikers Island while her case moved through the courts. Samantha, 32, identified as a cisgender Black woman. She had a history of steady employment as a retail cashier where she earned minimum wage, a salary on which she struggled to support herself and her 2-year-old son. At the time of her arrest, she had been residing in a homeless shelter with her son.

The charges alleged that Samantha and Chris got into a verbal and physical altercation outside of the shelter. When Samantha was arrested, her son was placed into the custody of the Administration for Children's Services (ACS). As a social worker, my job was to work with Samantha to create a plan to present to the court as part of release advocacy so that she could return to the community while awaiting sentencing.

It was crucial to gather Samantha's understanding of her current circumstances rather than rely on court documents and correctional records. I did not read her Record of Arrests and Prosecutions (RAP) sheet or other court documents prior to meeting with her, and I wanted my first impression of her to be within her control.

Samantha's life was highly controlled in jail, and I tried to allow her as much autonomy as possible so as not to be another person simply taking away her capacity to make decisions for herself. During our first meeting, this included asking what she liked to be called, asking her permission to take notes while we spoke, asking if I could take a minute to explain my role, and then stressing that I was not the expert in our dyad. To minimize the power imbalance between us, I emphasized that I had a lot to learn from the experiences she would come to share and that it was she who had the deep understanding of her abilities and needs, not me. Together, she and I would work on a plan to present to the court, and I would read that plan with her so that she was aware of everything being said on her behalf.

[2] All identifiable information has been changed to protect confidentiality.

It was critical to explore the larger systems of oppression that were linked to Samantha's current incarceration so that her behavior was not mistakenly viewed as a result of faulty thinking or personal deficits. We discussed the persistent poverty and structural racism in her life and explored the ways in which they had constrained her choices. We also examined her relationship with Chris through a patriarchal lens of power and control. Her love for her son and her ability to be a working parent to a young child in the face of interpersonal, economic, and housing insecurity were incredible strengths.

At times, I had difficulty engaging with Samantha. She could be quick to anger if she felt I was not fully understanding her, and, at times, she (reasonably) questioned my ability to write an effective release advocacy report detailing her life. Rather than view Samantha as difficult or resistant, a label attached to many incarcerated women, I put the onus on myself to explore her reactions and use different skills to engage her. While I did not assume that there was definite trauma or abuse in her past, I left open the possibility that her ways of interacting with me were manifestations of behaviors developed because of past trauma. In time, Samantha shared the traumas that she had experienced.

Samantha and I examined the ways in which her past trauma was triggered in the highly controlled carceral environment. She had been emotionally and physically abused by her father and had experienced intimate partner violence (IPV), including physical, sexual, and emotional abuse, in most of her romantic relationships. When correctional officers acted disrespectfully or made threats, the internalized negative cognitions she developed during her traumatic experiences flooded her. The return to these cognitions triggered a return to behaviors she had used to cope with the trauma of the abuse, mainly outward aggressions, self-harm, and substance misuse.

Samantha and I acknowledged the blatant disregard for her humanity that she experienced while incarcerated and identified strengths and resources she could call upon to try to cope with the trauma of incarceration. At the end of every meeting, I offered to do a grounding exercise (and eventually, Samantha came to lead them), acknowledging the trauma and vulnerabilities of being incarcerated and the risk she took in discussing past trauma in a carceral environment where safety was not guaranteed. We ended with a reiteration of her strengths.

As much as I tried to dismantle some of the power differentials, every single action I took was infused with power. Regardless of the outcome of our meeting, I would go home at the end of the day; Samantha would not. Even though I tried to assure Samantha that I valued her experiences and her knowledge of what she needed, at the end of the day, I was the one who would speak at her court appearance, not her. We both lived in a world where my existence was validated more than hers; my knowledge as a White woman pursuing a doctoral degree was more privileged than hers. As social workers, we must continue our efforts to dismantle this privilege; much of it is unearned, and it is harmful to the populations with whom we work.

An important part of my work with Samantha included my own vigilance in regularly reflecting upon my identity, including my own biases and positionality. I am a White cisgender woman who has never experienced incarceration. The social work profession was founded on the dominant values of people who share many of my privileged identities and has criminalized the survival behaviors of people who do not. There is no doubt that White women, women like me, have contributed to the criminalization of oppressed women. There is also no doubt that I have been complicit in the maintenance of these structures, as much as I try to dismantle them. I am a feminist, and White feminism has been dismissive, at best, but more realistically harmful, to women of color. White feminism has a history of failing to fight for the liberation of all women—including poor and women of color—and therefore allows racism and social exclusion to continue (Beck, 2021; Evans & Bussey-Chamberlain, 2021).

I work in a carceral system that privileges my identities and that does not seek to control my behavior or punish me in the ways in which it does the women with whom I work. I go home at the end of the day; I see my family at the end of the day. A lifetime of work remains in the examination of my own biases and privileges; a failure to do this puts me in jeopardy of reproducing and maintaining the harms caused to individuals ensnared in the carceral system.

Conclusion

An anti-oppressive framework calls upon social workers to be critical of the role of social work in the creation and maintenance of the carceral system. Past efforts that have contributed to the social control of marginalized groups of women must be acknowledged and examined if we are to avoid engaging in the same harmful practices that uphold those systems of oppression and control. Social workers in carceral spaces must honor the lived experience and wisdom of the people with whom they work. The systems of white supremacy, patriarchy, heteronormativity, and poverty that contribute to incarceration must be incorporated into practice and used as lenses through which services are provided. When working in carceral spaces, social workers must also challenge the idea that incarceration is necessary to address community harms and continue to fight for solutions that focus on decarceration and dismantling the reliance on prisons and jails.

Reflection Questions

1. How have you benefited from the dominant notions of femininity that social work has upheld?
2. How will you resist reproducing harm and oppression in carceral spaces?
3. Where do your ideas of gender, criminality, race, and other social constructions come from and how do they benefit you? How do they harm others?

4. How would you work with Samantha in a carceral setting? What would you do the same or differently? How would your positionality impact your work together?

References

Abramovitz, M. (1998). Social work and social reform: An arena of struggle. *Social Work, 43*(6), 512–626. https://doi.org/10.1093/sw/43.6.512

Alexander, M. (2010). *The new Jim Crow: Mass incarceration in the age of colorblindness*. The New Press.

Allen, C. L., MacKenzie, D. L., & Hickman, L. J. (2001). The effectiveness of cognitive behavioral treatment for adult offenders: A methodological, quality-based review. *International Journal of Offender Therapy and Comparative Criminology, 45*(4), 498–514. https://doi.org/10.1177/0306624X01454009

Baldwell, H. (2014). Colonial encounters: Racialized social workers negotiating professional scripts of whiteness. *Intersectionalites: A Global Journal of Social Work Analysis, Research, Policy, and Practice, 3*, 1–23. https://journals.library.mun.ca/index.php/IJ/article/view/996

Beck, K. (2021). *White feminism: From the suffragettes to influencers and who they leave behind*. Simon & Schuster.

Bussey, R. B., Jemal, A., & Caliste, S. (2021). Transforming social work's potential in the field: A radical framework. *Social Work Education., 40*(1), 140–154. https://doi.org/10.1080/02615479.2020.1723536

Carson, A. E. (2020). *Prisoners in 2019*. Office of Justice Programs, Bureau of Statistics. http://csat.bjs.ojp.gov/

Cénat, J. M., McIntee, S., Mukunzi, J. N., & Noorishad, P. (2021). Overrepresentation of Black children in the child welfare system: A systematic review to understand and better act. *Children and Youth Services Review, 120*, 105714. https://doi.org/10.1016/j.childyouth.2020.105714

Clark, P. (2010). *Preventing future crime with Cognitive Behavioral Therapy: One form of psychotherapy stands out in the criminal justice system*. National Journal of Justice Journal.

DeHart, D. D. (2008). Pathways to prison: Impact of victimization in the lives of incarcerated women. *Violence Against Women, 14*(12), 1362–1381. https://doi.org/10.1177/1077801208327018

Dholakia, N. (2021, May 17). *Women's incarceration rates are skyrocketing. These advocates are trying to change that*. Vera Institute of Justice. https://www.vera.org/news/womens-incarceration-rates-areskyrocketing#:~:text=Women%20are%20more%20likely%20to,little%20to%20address%20their%20needs

Dodge, L. M. (1999). "One female prisoner is of more trouble than twenty males": Women convicts in Illinois prisons, 1835–1896. *Journal of Social History, 32*(4), 907–930. https://www.jstor.org/stable/i292610

Donohue-Dioh, J., Wilson, J., & Leota, S. (2021). The woke disrupter: A call to action. *Advances in Social Work., 21*(2/3), 1045–1063. https://doi.org/10.18060/24164

El Amin, E. (2022). Critical consciousness. https://kappanonline.org/critical-consciousness-key-student-achievement/

Evans, E., & Bussey-Chamberlain, P. (2021). The problems with feminist nostalgia: Intersectionality and white popular feminism. *European Journal of Women's Studies, 28*(3), 353–368. https://doi.org/10.1177/13505068211032058

Freire, P. (1973). *Education for critical consciousness*. Continuum.

Goshin, L. S., & Byrne, M. W. (2009). Converging streams of opportunity for prison nursery programs in the United States. *Journal of Offender Rehabilitation, 48*(4), 271–295. https://doi.org/10.1080/10509670902848972

Harmon, M. G., & Boppre, B. (2016). Women of color and the war on crime: An explanation for the rise in black female imprisonment. *Journal of Ethnicity In Criminal Justice, 16*, 1–24. https://doi.org/10.1080/15377938.2015.1052173

Harmon, M. G., & O'Brien, R. M. (2011). Gendered arrests or gendered sentencing: Explaining the narrowing of the gender gap in imprisonment over time: 1970–2008. *Sociological Perspectives, 54*, 641–664. https://doi.org/10.1525/sop.2011.54.4.641

Harrell, S. (2022). Social work & corrections in the progressive era: What we remember, what we obscure. *Journal of Progressive Human Services, 34*(1), 55–74. https://doi-org.proxy.library.nyu.edu/10.1080/10428232.2022.2109359

Jemal, A. (2017). Critical consciousness: A critique and critical analysis of the literature. *The Urban Review, 49*(4), 602–626. https://doi.org/10.1007/s11256-017-0411-3

Kajstura, A. & Sawyer, W. (2024, March 5) *Women's mass incarceration: The whole pie 2024*. Prison Policy Initiative. https://www.prisonpolicy.org/reports/pie2024women.html

Kelly, J., Clark, E.J., Whitaker, T., Wilson, M. (2010). *Criminal justice social work in the United States: Adapting to new challenges*. National Association of Social Workers.

Kendall, K. (1994). Therapy behind prison walls. A contradiction in terms? *Prison Services Journal, 96*, 2–11.

Kishimoto, K. (2016). Anti-racist pedagogy: From faculty's self-reflection to organizing within and beyond the classroom. *Race Ethnicity and Education, 21*(4), 540–554. https://doi.org/10.1080/13613324.2016.1248824

Larson, G. (2008). Anti-oppressive practice in mental health. *Journal of Progressive Human Services, 19*(1), 39–54. https://doi.org/10.1080/10428230802070223

Leotti, S. M. (2021). Social work with criminalized women: Governance or resistance in the carceral state? *Affilia, 36*(3), 302–318. https://doi.org/10.1177/08861099211014773

Leotti, S. M. (2022). The keepers and the kept: Social work and criminalized women, an historical review. *Journal of Progressive Human Services, 33*(2), 151–175. https://doi.org/10.1080/10428232.2022.2049184

Mullaly, B. (2002). *Challenging oppression: A critical social work approach*. Oxford University Press.

National Association of Social Workers (NASW). (2008). Preamble to the code of ethics. https://www.socialworkers.org/About/Ethics/Code-of-Ethics/Code-of-Ethics-English

O'Brien, P. & Willison, J.S. (2022). *Anti-Oppressive Social Work Practice and the Carceral State*. Oxford University Press.

Pollack, S. (2004). Anti-oppressive social work practice with women in prison: Discursive reconstructions and alternative practices. *British Journal of Social Work, 34*, 693–707. https://doi.org/10.1093/bjsw/bch085

Pollack, S. (2009). "You can't have it both ways": Punishment and treatment of imprisoned women. *Journal of Progressive Human Services, 20*, 112–128. https://doi.org/10.1080/10428230903306344

Pollack, S. (2020). Transformative praxis with incarcerated women: Collaboration, leadership, and voice. *Affilia: Journal of Women and Social Work, 35*(3), 344–357. https://doi.org/10.1177/0886109919886133

Rafter, N. H. (1983). Prisons for Women, 1790–1980. *Crime and Justice, 5*, 129–181. The University of Chicago Press.

Sakamoto, I., & Pitner, R. O. (2005). Use of critical consciousness in anti-oppressive social work practice: Disentangling power dynamics at personal and structural levels. *British Journal of Social Work, 35*(4), 435–452.

Chapter 17
Using Trauma as a Form of Oppression: How Intersectional Trauma Keeps Women Incarcerated

Renee Rosiecki

Introduction

Incarcerated women are an especially vulnerable population experiencing victimization through sexual violence, domestic violence, and state violence. Survivors of violence have already had their power and control taken away, and imprisonment simply magnifies this phenomenon. Trauma-informed interventions provide social workers with the ability to practice in an anti-oppressive manner acknowledging the victimization their clients have endured. This chapter presents a framework for forensic social workers to work with incarcerated female survivors including feminist theory, trauma-informed practice, and intersectionality. This author strongly recommends that forensic social workers are competent in trauma-informed therapies and have an understanding of intersectionality.

Note: It is important to note the use of terminology based on sources, date of publication, and field of publication. The terms survivor and victim have been reclaimed by many victim-centered movements and are used interchangeably (RAINN, 2024). Restorative justice language discourages the use of terms such as inmate, felon, offender, perpetrator, abuser, batterer, etc., and gives preference to person who caused harm (Center for Court Innovation, 2019; Furio, 2002). This author has made effort to avoid the use of stigmatizing language; however, many sources regarding the criminal legal system incorporate those terms. Criminal legal system is given preference over criminal justice system. Therapists, clinicians, and mental health professionals include clinical social workers, counselors, and psychologists. Gender-based violence is a broad term describing violence influenced by gender; however, this article focuses on women and those who identify as women

R. Rosiecki (✉)
Silver School of Social Work, New York University, New York, NY, USA
e-mail: rnw4675@nyu.edu

C. Tosone et al. (eds.), *Reframing Social Work with an Anti-Oppressive Lens*, Essential Clinical Social Work Series,
https://doi.org/10.1007/978-3-031-91391-4_17

(The United Nations, 1994). Domestic violence is primarily used as that is the term many clients identify the most with but is interchangeably used with intimate partner violence (National Coalition Against Domestic Violence, 2020; Pennell, 2018).

How Have We Come to Understand Trauma?

To work with incarcerated survivors of domestic and sexual violence, a social worker must understand trauma and oppression. Throughout the years, trauma has been understood through hysteria, shell shock, combat neuroses, domestic and sexual violence, and most recently post-traumatic stress disorder (PTSD). During the women's liberation movement in the 1970s, psychiatric nurse Ann Burgess and sociologist Lynda Holmstrom studied the psychological effects of rape in which they labeled as a rape trauma syndrome including insomnia, nausea, startle responses, nightmares, dissociation, and numbness (Herman, 1997). In the 1980s, psychologist Lenore E. Walker described survivors of domestic violence with psychological reactions to their abuse as having battered woman syndrome (Walker, 2016). It is important to note, that the original concept of battered woman syndrome has been challenged by black feminism as stereotypes of societal constructs of appropriate behavior for white women (Allard, 1991). Currently, the American Psychological Association (2023) defines trauma as an emotional response to a terrible event including rape, natural disasters, or an accident.

Consequently, our understanding of trauma has changed, and PTSD as a formal clinical diagnosis has also evolved. It was not until DSM 5 that sexual violence would be added as a form of trauma (APA, 2013). Currently, PTSD is described by the following criteria for more than 1 month: exposure to actual/threated death, serious injury, or sexual violence; intrusive symptoms associated with the trauma; avoidance of stimuli associated with the trauma; negative cognitive alterations; hyperarousal and reactivity; and significant impairment in daily areas of functioning and may include dissociation (APA, 2022).

Violence and Trauma as a Means of Power and Control

Violence is a very powerful, intentional, and effective method of control. This chapter will focus on domestic and sexual violence against women. Sexual violence is defined as any sexual act, attempt to obtain a sexual act, unwanted sexual comments or advances, or acts to traffic against a person's will using coercion regardless of their relationship, in any setting (World Health Organization, 2002). Sexual assault includes a variety of sexual activities including unwanted touching, grabbing, oral sex, anal sex, sexual penetration with an object, and/or sexual intercourse (National Center for PTSD, 2022).

The National Coalition Against Domestic Violence (NCADV) defines domestic violence as the willful intimidation, physical assault, sexual assault, and/or other abusive behavior as part of having power and control perpetrated by one partner against another (National Coalition Against Domestic Violence, 2020). Other common terms used for domestic violence are women abuse or intimate partner violence (IPV) (Pennell, 2018). It is important to note that some organizations use the term intimate partner violence for violence in romantic/intimate relationships and interpersonal violence for violence in family or intimate relationships; both terms are used interchangeably with domestic violence in literature, depending on the time frame and source. Both domestic violence and sexual violence assert power and control over a victim.

The power and control wheel, formally known as the Duluth model, was developed by the Domestic Abuse Intervention Programs (DAIP) in the 1980s to empower victims who had minimal choices, to offer men's programs, and to end violence against women (Domestic Abuse Intervention Programs, 2017a). There are now updated models that include information for same-sex relationships and male victims (Domestic Abuse Intervention Programs, 2017b). As per the wheel, domestic violence is a pattern of behavior including physical violence, sexual violence, economic abuse, coercion, threats, intimidation, emotional abuse, isolation, using children against the victim, minimization, denial, blaming, and male privilege (National Domestic Violence Hotline, 2023). Sexual violence can occur using the same tactics. Violence not only elicits an emotional response of anxiety or fear but also a physical response.

Merriam-Webster (2023) defines oppression as the unjust or cruel exercise of excessive authority or power. When I have worked with incarcerated female survivors, they experience PTSD symptoms which make them vulnerable, decrease their decision-making abilities, and increase emotional dysregulation. When a victim is in a traumatized state, they are more susceptible to manipulation and revictimization. As social workers working within forensic settings, we need to consider the clinical and environmental impact of trauma instead of pathologizing and criminalizing survival responses.

Social Work's Mission to Address Trauma Within Forensic Settings

What Is Anti-oppressive Social Work Practice?

Social work is grounded in a set of core values that give perspective to the profession's positionality on anti-oppressive work. According to Curry-Stevens (2016), anti-oppressive practice (AOP) is rooted in social justice and working within a lens exploring power dynamics and outcomes based on identities or affiliations. The goal of AOP is to minimize power hierarchies by empowering the marginalized and reducing power imbalances for the privileged (Curry-Stevens, 2016). Social workers are in a unique position where we have authority, power, and privilege that we must examine to engage in anti-oppressive work. We must acknowledge that we benefit from the system that oppresses our clients as we are paid employees. So, should social workers work in prisons, jails, and other correctional settings?

According to the National Association of Social Workers (NASW), social workers must follow a set of core values including service, social justice, dignity and worth of the person, importance of human relationships, integrity, and competence (National Association of Social Workers, 2023). From a micro standpoint, we must continue to serve incarcerated people and value them. From a macro lens, we must work to advocate for policy changes and abolish oppressive systems such as the carceral system. To engage in anti-oppressive practice, we must simultaneously provide services for our clients while dismantling the system in which we work.

The History of Forensic Social Work

There are various definitions of forensic social work. Forensic social work is defined as an integrated social work practice approach encompassing generalist, forensic/legal, and collectivist knowledge and skills (Maschi et al., 2017). The National Organization of Forensic Social Work (2020) defines forensic social work as social work relating to the law and legal system. Maschi et al. (2017) discuss multiple perspectives of forensic social work including working in the context of a legal environment, the intersection of mental health and law, and working with victims and/or incarcerated persons. Forensic social work has evolved over time and continues to expand to consider more timely social concerns.

In the late 1800s and early 1900s, there were social workers working toward social reform regarding law and justice but specifically developing juvenile systems so that children were not incarcerated with adults (Center on Juvenile and Criminal Justice, 1999; Maschi et al., 2017). After the creation of juvenile courts, prisons became more focused on repentance and reform aligning with the mission of social work (Blakely & Bumphus, 1999). As a result, social workers became "correctional treatment specialists" focusing on casework in correctional treatment programs (Roberts & Brownell, 1999). In the 1980s, the general American societal perspective shifted from social to individual responsibility, and as a result rehabilitative programs decreased, criminal sentences became harsher, and social work shifted to focus more to victim services than prison reform (Maschi et al., 2017).

Currently, forensic social work has been concerned with issues of police brutality, mass incarceration, and the disproportionate amount of Black people in the criminal justice system (Maschi et al., 2017). Forensic social workers continue to work within the criminal legal system in prisons, jails, detention centers, juvenile facilities, probation, drug/recovery court, domestic violence agencies, and policy advocacy. Social workers in these settings can provide direct services while simultaneously acknowledging trauma is a response to systemic oppression. This chapter will focus on one aspect of forensic social work, specifically working with incarcerated female survivors of domestic and sexual violence. In order to practice within an anti-oppressive framework, we must consider the intersectionality of systemic trauma.

The Intersectional Trauma of Gender-Based Violence and State Violence

Intersectionality and Oppression

Kimberlé Crenshaw (1989) introduced intersectionality, defining it as the study of intersecting social identities and subsequent systems including race, gender, class, ability, sexual orientation, age, religion, nationality, and other identities. Crenshaw, along with Patricia Hill Collins, explored intersectionality within oppressive systems, not just identities (Moradi, 2017). Collins extended intersectionality as a structural matrix of domination among multiple forces of oppression that shape people's experiences, such as sexism and racism (Collins, 2000). Intersectionality challenges single dimensional oppression and highlights what Crenshaw terms as double-discrimination, which is the dynamic of multiple forms of intersecting oppression (Crenshaw, 1989; Moradi, 2017). This chapter will explore intersectional forms of state violence and gender-based violence against women.

State violence is defined broadly by social scientists including direct political violence, genocide, and the use of social services for surveillance (Torres, 2018). For this chapter we will be focusing on mass incarceration as a method of state violence. Mass incarceration is defined as the criminal justice system and the broader laws and policies that control those labeled as criminal in and outside of prison (Alexander, 2010).

It is important to note the complexity of traumas, social identities, and oppressive systems that intertwine with forensic social work. For example, race and racism are major components undeniably interwoven within the carceral system. While there are many important social identities and systems of oppression for forensic social workers to acknowledge and challenge, this chapter will focus on the intersectionality between gender-based violence (specifically domestic and sexual violence) and state violence. While this chapter focuses specifically on the experience of victimized, incarcerated women, it is this author's strong recommendation to new practitioners to familiarize yourself with the types of oppression within carceral system, especially racism, in order to practice within an anti-oppressive framework.

Rates of Domestic Violence, Sexual Violence, and Trauma for Incarcerated Women

Currently, women are the fastest growing population in correctional institutions in America as the rates of incarcerated women have more than quadrupled between 1990 and 2019 (The Sentencing Project, 2020). Physical and sexual abuse of women in custody is so inhumane and prevalent, it has been labeled as a human rights issue (Amnesty International, 1999). According to Green et al. (2005), of the 90% of incarcerated females who reported interpersonal trauma, 50% reported experiencing sexual abuse as children. Another study found that 79% of women in federal and state prisons experienced physical abuse and 60% experienced sexual abuse (Lapidus et al., 2005), whereas in the community, 27.3%–35.6% of women have experienced sexual violence, physical violence, or stalking in their lifetime by an intimate partner (Black et al., 2011; Breiding et al., 2014). A study at Bedford Hills Correctional Facility found that over 80% of incarcerated women have a childhood physical and sexual abuse; more than 90% have experienced physical or sexual assault in their adult lives (Browne et al., 1999). Of incarcerated women with mental illness, 78% reported prior physical or sexual abuse (Ditton, 1999).

Disproportionate amounts of imprisoned persons, especially women, have experienced childhood and adult sexual abuse prior to their incarceration (Tripodi & Pettus-Davis, 2013). Rates of childhood sexual abuse for imprisoned females before the age of 11 are over two thirds (Browne et al., 1999). Another study reported that 70% of female inmates reported child sexual abuse (Johnson & Lynch, 2013). For domestic violence, incarcerated females experience higher rates than in the community. According to the 2011 National Intimate Partner and Sexual Violence Survey, 31.5% of women experience physical violence from an intimate partner (Breiding et al., 2014; Smith et al., 2017).

In regard to trauma, 12.5% of incarcerated people in prisons and 15.9% of incarcerated people in jail have been diagnosed with post-traumatic stress disorder (PTSD) (Bronson, & Berzofsky, 2017). The prevalence of PTSD in prison populations is higher than in community populations (Facer-Irwin, et al., 2019). One study demonstrated that 21% of women in correctional settings had PTSD (Facer-Irwin, et al., 2019). Compared to their community counterparts, imprisoned women report higher rates of lifetime exposure to cumulative trauma, including physical and sexual victimization (Bloom et al., 2003). Additionally, a 2014 study suggests that PTSD increases the risk of criminal recidivism (Sadeh & McNeil, 2015). Forensic social workers need to focus on incarcerated women as they are oppressed through victimization and incarceration.

Traumatization and Re-traumatization

Incarceration and victimization are degrading, dehumanizing experiences. Both events are traumatizing, making incarcerated survivors an especially marginalized group in need of social work intervention. After women experience sexual or intimate partner violence, 23.7% were fearful, 20.7% were concerned for their safety, 20.0% experienced one or more PTSD symptoms, 13.4% were physically injured, 6.9% needed medical care, 3.6% needed housing services, 3.3% needed victim advocate services, 8.8% needed legal services, 9.1% missed at least 1 day of work or school, 1.3% contracted a sexually transmitted infection, and 1.7% became pregnant (Breiding et al., 2014).

Incarceration is traumatizing for any incarcerated person but especially for a survivor of domestic and sexual violence. From my professional experience, carceral institutions are authoritarian environments that have the potential for re-traumatization and mimicking the dynamics of past abuse including the presence of male officers supervising incarcerated women, lack of control, and invasive security protocols such as including cavity/strip searches, pat downs, and shake downs. Prisons and jails are triggering environments with shackles/handcuffs, overcrowding in confined spaces, and loud noises from codes, fights, and cell doors slamming. The threatening environment can lead to an increase in trauma symptoms such as hypervigilance and exaggerated startle responses. Furthermore, there is a lack of therapeutic and coping resources in many facilities such as mental health treatment, exercise equipment and spaces, nutritious food, and privacy for mindfulness or self-regulation. It is important for forensic social workers to understand carceral spaces with knowledge of trauma for proper context.

Beyond the environmental impact of correctional facilities, sexual assault is prevalent, especially for women. Annually, 800,000 inmates are sexually assaulted (Department of Justice, 2013a). One study concluded that 80,600 inmates were sexually assaulted or raped annually in the United States (Department of Justice, 2013b). As per the 2012 prisoner survey, an estimated 200,000 inmates are sexually abused in American detention facilities annually (Santo, 2018). Davis acknowledges the frequency of sexual assault in women's correctional facilities being taken for granted. Inmate-on-inmate sexual victimization is nearly 4x higher for incarcerated women (212 per 1000) than incarcerated men (43 per 1000) (Wolff et al., 2006). According to the Bureau of Justice Statistics, although women only represented 7% of the correctional population, they accounted for 22% of peer-aggravated sexual victimizations and 33% staff-aggravated sexual victimizations from 2009 to 2011 (Beck et al., 2018). The most recent sexual victimization reported by adult correctional facilities from 2012 to 2015 did not include information on gender.

Gendered Punishment

Prisons are gendered structures with gendered punishment that reflect the larger gendered society. Incarcerated women are usually labeled as insane, immoral, and oversexualized opposed to men who are labeled as criminal or deviant. Experiencing physical or sexual abuse increases the risk for women to be incarcerated (Dichter & Osthoff, 2015). One study found that childhood victimization increased incarceration rates (Saxena & Messina, 2021). Victim's survival responses to domestic violence may include being coerced into criminal behavior leading to the incarceration of survivors (Dichter & Osthoff, 2015). Since women have high rates of victimization before incarceration, high rates of revictimization during incarceration, and victimization increases incarceration, incarcerated women are systemically stuck in a cycle of oppression.

Practice Approaches and Contemporary Frameworks: The Role of the Social Worker in Anti-oppressive and Clinical Practice

Anti-oppressive Frameworks Within Forensic Social Work

For forensic social workers to maintain an anti-oppressive framework, this author suggests micro and macro interventions based on feminist theory, trauma-informed practice, and intersectionality.

Feminist Theory Feminist theory focuses on how gender relates to power and oppression in society and posits that all women are oppressed and powerless in ways men are not (Collins, 2000). Paulo Freire's concept of critical consciousness explains the awareness of oppression within society and the implications of oppression (Freire, 1973). Forensic social workers should practice from a position of critical consciousness to promote social justice and empowerment whether working for prison reform or with sexual abuse survivors (Turner, 2017). It is important to note that traditional feminism was not developed for incarcerated survivors as it does not take intersectionality or incarceration status into account.

Trauma-Informed Social Work To treat trauma, we must first understand it. All social workers must practice with competence and within their scope of practice as per the NASW Code of Ethics (2023), and this writer urges all forensic social workers to become knowledgeable about trauma. However, there are so many limitations on how we understand trauma. For example, the trauma- and stressor-related disorders, specifically including PTSD, do not sufficiently envelope the breadth of trauma, especially from an intersectionality and culturally informed lens. Forensic social workers should seek to understand the foundation of trauma theory, clinical understandings of trauma such as PTSD diagnostic criteria, the physiological trauma responses including central nervous system responses, and the specific responses to subtypes of trauma such as sexual violence, domestic violence, and incarceration. Phillips et al. (2015) define trauma-informed approaches for domestic and sexual violence survivors as careful listening to survivors, responding to the effects of trauma, providing trauma education, a commitment to ongoing trauma-informed efforts, and a commitment to staff well-being. Forensic social workers should understand trauma the context of individuals and systems.

Intersectionality Intersectionality encourages social workers to consider individual social identities and large systems that are used to oppress and maintain oppression. In forensic social work practice, the application of intersectionality requires that practitioners engage in critical self-reflection of identity, power, privilege, oppression, biases, assumptions, and beliefs (Moradi, 2017). Within the context of the helping relationship, power is contextual, relational, and unequal between an interventionist and a survivor of gender-based violence (Moradi, 2017). Forensic social workers must acknowledge the power differentials specifically to avoid recreating power and control dynamics from abusive relationships. Forensic social work grounded in anti-oppressive practice should be rooted in the empowerment aspect of intersectionality advocating to integrate experiences of those marginalized into clinical and macro practice (Moradi, 2017). Practice with incarcerated victims can be improved by avoiding generalizations or assumptions about violence which inhibit survivor safety and empowerment (Moradi, 2017). Without intersectionality, forensic social workers may neglect to address the trauma of state violence and gender-based violence that both trauma-informed and feminist practice fail to fully address.

Micro Practice: Clinical Forensic Social Work with Incarcerated Female Survivors

Feminist Therapy Female criminals are viewed as immoral, oversexualized, or insane with little to no chance of rehabilitation. In order to help survivors heal, we must believe them. I have found when working with survivors of domestic and sexual violence that a therapist believing them is one of the most therapeutic actions a therapist can do. Beyond belief, forensic social workers can work to integrate empowerment and cognitive restructuring in line with feminist theory. Empowerment is the primary goal of feminist therapy which frames psychological and social distress as the result of living in a patriarchal society, regardless of gender (Mintz & Tager, 2012). Within the field of social work, strengths-based practice is common, aligned with empowerment practice, focusing on strengths and resilience (Saleeby, 1997). An example of this is in forensic practice reframing in feminist therapy with sexual abuse survivors to externalize blame (Turner, 1993). This is crucial while working with female incarcerated survivors to challenge the self-blaming cognitions to process any misplaced guilt, shame, or other negative emotions and to internalize their resilience.

In my clinical experience, trauma treatments must be victim centered. The term victim centered is commonly used in domestic violence, Intimate partner violence (IPV), and sexual violence and has similar principles to person-centered therapy. Person-centered therapy was developed by Carl Rogers in the 1940s and is grounded in the premise that the therapist works in a nondirective manner to enhance the independence of the individual, rather than focusing on the therapist solving the problem, and the client is seen as the expert on their own life (Yao & Kabir, 2023). Rogers emphasized reflective listening, empathy, and acceptance in therapy over that traditional Freudian interpretation of behaviors or unconscious drives (Hill & Nakayama, 2000). This is the foundation of victim-centered work. For instance, a social worker may think a victim should press charges against a person who sexually abused them; however, from a victim-centered approach, the social worker will provide the client with options and elicit the client's opinion on how they want to proceed. This is directly aligned with the social work principle of self-determination (NASW 2023). The goal of a forensic social worker when working with incarcerated victims is to restore their sense of power and control as they have already had that compromised through incarceration and victimization.

Trauma-Informed Therapy In addition to being victim centered, forensic social workers should practice holistic, trauma-informed treatment to address the complex influence of trauma on a person's life. A holistic approach includes addressing emotional, psychological, physical, and interpersonal symptoms of trauma. Pierre Janet developed his triphasic model for post-traumatic stress treatment with the goals of symptom-oriented treatment and stabilization, exploration of traumatic memories, and personality reintegration and rehabilitation (Hart et al., 1989). According to Janet, the stages are sequential as processing cannot occur until the client feel stable and safe and can achieve a level of functioning to perform tasks of daily living (Rothschild, 2010). Judith Herman developed a model about trauma recovery based off the work of Janet called the stages of recovery including safety, remembrance and mourning, and reconnection (Herman, 1997).

Herman's model of conceptualizing and treating trauma explains that trauma recovery requires relational context as trauma is relational, incorporating the relationship with the therapist (Herman, 1997). The therapist is neutral, focused on the recovery of the patient, attuned to the power differential, collaborative, aware of one's countertransference, and conscious of vicarious traumatization (Herman, 1997). Therapists focus on validation of experience versus behavior modification as the client is in control of their life (Herman, 1997). Effective trauma treatment is when the therapist helps the patient regain control after a trauma, rather than focusing too heavily on the client's feelings of helplessness, which is more likely to unintentionally disempower the patient and perpetuate trauma symptoms (Herman, 1997). It is important for clients to have a sense of autonomy which is aligned with the social work ethical principle of respecting the dignity and worth of a person.

The primary goal of trauma treatment is restoring a sense of safety and control which was lost after the trauma including meeting basic needs including a safe living environment, physical safety, medical/physical needs, and a safe support system (Herman, 1997). In stage two, the client tells their story of the trauma, so through the reconstruction, it can eventually be integrated (Herman, 1997). Reconstruction includes the therapist witnessing the client's story, the therapist maintaining safety, and the client mourning the losses of the trauma to reclaim their emotions (Herman, 1997). The final stage of reconnection involves the survivor developing a new sense of self, new beliefs, and new relationships as part of their new future as well as understanding their prior victimization within context (Herman, 1997). The trauma is not necessarily ever fully resolved as different life events and/or milestones can cause traumatic memories to resurface or take on different meaning (Herman, 1997).

It is important to consider what the goal of therapy is from the beginning as trauma survivors will have different goals; however, all clients need to be able to attain a daily functionality. Not all clients may desire to recall, reexperience, and process their traumatic memories, so this may not be the therapeutic goals for all clients (Rothschild, 2010). This is the brilliance within Janet's model and sequentially Herman's model. It addresses the commonalities of trauma such as dysregulation and negative impact on functioning as the foundation of clinical work but also incorporates a person-centered approach where the client's input is valued.

Herman's framework can be applied through various clinical modalities and specifically for incarcerated female survivors. The safety aspect of treatment incorporates the client's ability to build rapport during a vulnerable state as the carceral environment is threatening and there is a staunch power dynamic with authority figures. The second stage aligns with the client's need to make sense of their extraordinary experience of incarceration, another potentially traumatizing event, and a safe space to process this and former victimization. The final stage of reintegration aligns with reentry planning for incarcerated persons to prevent recidivism. Incarcerated persons need support and interventions to explore and plan to avoid further criminal activity as survivors need plans to cope with triggers for their traumas.

Trauma-informed care is rooted in understanding the person-in-environment perspective (PIE) (Kondrat, 2008) and the impact of adversity on maladaptive coping, including criminal behavior (Grady et al., 2017). Trauma-informed care seeks to develop a safe environment using collaboration, emphasizing empowerment, and avoiding recreating abusive dynamics in the helping relationship (Elliott et al., 2005). Trauma-informed care recognizes the impact that violence and victimization have on psychosocial development and relational skills (Elliott et al., 2005). Evidence-based trauma treatments to consider include eye movement desensitization and reprocessing (EMDR) therapy, cognitive processing therapy (CPT), prolonged exposure (PE) therapy, internal family systems (IFS), sensorimotor therapy, somatic experiencing, and trauma-informed yoga (National Center on PTSD, 2025; Shapiro, 2017; van der Kolk, 2014). All trauma treatments aim to decrease trauma symptoms, but forensic social workers should practice within a victim-centered, feminist, and intersectional framework.

Intersectionality in Clinical Practice Forensic social workers must embrace intersectionality as part of clinical interventions with clients. In therapy honoring intersectionality, the clinician reflects on how the client constructs themselves in interpersonal and structural power dynamics; how do these dynamics shape my client, and how do these dynamics co-construct my client's presenting problem (Moradi, 2017)? A pertinent example of this in correctional settings is considering the intersectionality of racial trauma and post-traumatic slave syndrome (PTSS). DeGruy lists the symptoms of PTSS as vacant esteem, ever-present anger, and racist socialization in which she explains incorporating collective blame and humiliation (DeGruy, 2005). PTSS is very apparent in correctional settings with incarcerated Black people, and a prevalent example of intersectional trauma as incarceration mimics the power and control dynamics from slavery. An intersectional therapy application may include liberation psychology to address racial trauma concurrently with the trauma of incarceration.

Intersectionality and forensic social work cannot be discussed without discussing the influence of race and cross-racial therapy. Bryant-Davis strongly suggests decolonizing therapy to incorporate intersectionality through having more diverse therapists and creating space for the voice of the oppressed (2019). One study suggests there are different ways to broach the subject of race in the therapeutic alliance, and the most effective is when the therapist is aware and accepts it is their responsibility to broach the subject (Day-Vines et al., 2007). In a study regarding cross-racial therapy, clients reported satisfaction when the therapist had an active style, had culture-specific knowledge, was self-disclosed, was attentive, and was nonjudgmental (Chang & Berk, 2009). Research has proven positive impact on building rapport between White therapists and clients of color when the therapist acknowledges racism, is open to discussing race, validates the client's race-related experiences, and is willing to self-disclose their own bias (Burkard et al., 2006).

Intersectionality is effective at exploring the clinical implications of multiple traumas. Bryant-Davis (2019) discusses how people who experience multiple forms of oppression are at a higher risk for PTSD. Individual trauma models overlook community and collective trauma and the cultural experience of mass suffering (Bryant-Davis, 2019), which applies to incarcerated, victimized women. Warrier (2022) believes that an understanding of the patriarchy alongside intersectionality is crucial when conducting any individual work with survivors.

The concept of post-traumatic growth acknowledges the impact of trauma and is strengths based. It aligns with an intersectional application of feminist theories emphasizing empowerment and trauma therapies. Intersectional trauma work also incorporates cultural adaptions of trauma treatments such as EMDR, CPT, PE, and dialectical behavioral therapy (DBT) (Bryant-Davis, 2019). Traditional Western-based modalities focus on symptom reduction and coping, whereas cultural-based trauma models explore the oppression of the trauma socially, spiritually, internally, or systemically (Bryant-Davis, 2019).

Macro Practice: Abolitionist Social Work

I would be remiss to solely focus on clinical applications after pleading forensic social workers to consider individuals and systems. When practicing in any carceral space, social workers must understand mass incarceration and abolitionist social work. Abolitionist practice aims to eradicate and reduce harm, as well as the path to prison (Purnell, 2021). Abolition is not the divestment of the police and prisons but the creation and redistribution of resources and priorities (McLemore, 2020). Abolitionist social work is defined as a theoretical framework with the aim of abolishing punishment, prisons, police, and other carceral systems that cause physiological, cognitive, economic, and political harms to incarcerated people, their families, and their communities (Toraif & Mueller, 2023).

Although this chapter delves into clinical practice, clinicians can also serve as advocates within carceral systems. Individual casework and advocacy are not enough to promote social change; public policy change is required to address the intersectionality of gender-based violence (Warrier, 2022). Social workers are tasked with advocating for the oppressed, including access to services at correctional facilities and larger policy reform. Social workers must work toward expanding mental health services for incarcerated survivors during and after their sentences. Social workers can advocate for legislative changes including sentencing reform, parole reform, bail (wealth-based incarceration) reform, prosecutorial reform, and elimination of mandatory minimums. Rehabilitative approaches such as diversion programs can replace traditional punitive incarceration. Alternatives to incarceration should be considered for survivors of violence, especially as they are predisposed to mental health issues and would benefit from treatment. The goal for forensic social workers is to eradicate the current trauma of incarceration and prevent further traumatization.

Case Example

For this chapter, the client will be referred to as Grace, and all case information is an amalgamation of similar cases to protect the identity of clients. Grace is a middle-aged, Black, Christian, lesbian female serving a lengthy sentence for aggravated manslaughter that was reduced from first-degree murder. Grace was a self-referred client attending voluntary, individual sexual assault and domestic violence counseling at a women's state prison.

This client presented with anxiety, ruminations, inappropriate guilt, nightmares, flashbacks, hypervigilance, poor body image, codependency, repeated victimization, and negative cognitions about herself, others, and the world. Grace has an extensive history of childhood physical and sexual abuse, as well as child neglect, adult sexual violence, and domestic violence. The client had a job at the prison, attended college courses, legal services, and other programs offered. Grace was not engaged in mental health services at the institution beyond her voluntary 16 weeks of domestic and sexual violence therapy. She initially engaged in behaviors resulting in institutional infractions her first few years but was charge free for many years prior to treatment and was then housed in the minimum compound.

The client and therapist discussed the goals of therapy and the therapeutic relationship, including race dynamics. This client received psychoeducation on trauma and resourcing (coping skills) including guided imagery, diaphragmatic breathing techniques, and progressive muscle relaxation. Initially, strength-based counseling and motivational interviewing were utilized to engage the client and build rapport. Grace also participated in cognitive behavioral therapy (CBT); however, her trauma-based cognitions remained rigid. EMDR was introduced as a trauma-informed intervention, and the client met criteria for clinical appropriateness for this intervention.

Within those clinical modalities, Grace and I discussed how she felt her sentence was unfair. Grace and I processed Grace's inability to afford a private lawyer and feeling failed by the system and her public defender based not only on her socioeconomic status but mainly her gender, sexuality, and race. She was an astute woman who observed the lesser sentencing of her white peers with the same charges. Within our cross-racial therapeutic alliance, we explored the impact of race in her sentencing, and Grace expressed feeling comfortable to be candid in sessions. Grace processed her original charges and her anger toward her severe sentencing with a focus on post-traumatic growth and faith. Grace continued to pursue her commitment to receiving her bachelor's degree in prison studying criminal justice with a research interest in domestic violence.

Grace and I explored the variety of trauma she had experienced including domestic violence, sexual violence, and state violence. We discussed systemic oppressions, especially as she had deep shame and self-blame for engaging in a same-sex relationship against her family's Christian values. Grace engaged with religious services and social services simultaneously stating that the prison pastor and social worker helped her heal this component of her trauma. Grace engaged in EMDR and processed the specific domestic and sexual victimization she had experienced prior to her incarceration.

Grace reported feeling a more positive generalized mood, decreased anxiety, improved ability to set boundaries in interpersonal relationships, decreased guilt, and continued motivation for therapy addressing her sexual and domestic victimization. Grace completed her 16 weeks of domestic and sexual violence counseling and was referred to mental health as needed. One consideration for future treatment would be to have a therapist of color and/or a therapist specifically trained in racial trauma for clients like Grace, which are common in carceral settings.

Practice Wisdom

Neophyte social workers may be eager to dive into trauma-informed interventions to address the trauma, but do not do this. This may sound strange after reading this chapter, but this knowledge is gained after years of experience working with traumatized persons in correctional settings. The goal for trauma-informed care is to provide safety, stabilization, and eventually, if clinically advised and victim centered, trauma processing. Concurrently, forensic social workers are advised to use an intersectional framework to address all types of traumas and oppression.

It is also important to acknowledge that being trauma informed means that clinicians are aware and practicing in a manner to honor their clients' experiences. Honoring a client's history of victimization may mean validating their triggers and working to reduce symptomatic responses through coping skills. Other clients may desire to process their domestic or sexual abuse through traditional psychotherapies or more body-based interventions requiring fewer verbal accounts of their trauma, while other clients may present with specific culturally based traumas that require specific culturally informed interventions. There is no one right way to do trauma work.

However, there is a wrong way. Forensic social workers who fail to acknowledge their positionality fail their clients. As social workers, we have degrees, licenses, titles, education, and authority that automatically creates a power differential with our clients. If we introduce our individual identities, this can become very complicated. I am a White woman working within carceral systems. My clients have ignored, commented, or been annoyed by my race. In some cases, my race represents those who have abused my clients or those who created the systems that oppress my clients. As stated earlier, it is the therapist's responsibility to broach the subject of race in the therapeutic alliance and also in terms of the client's treatment needs. One study suggests that clients who are ethnic minorities are less satisfied with mental health treatment when race and ethnicity are not included in their care and that clients felt it was important that their therapist understood their experienced discrimination (Meyer & Zane, 2013). If the therapist is avoidant or pathologizes cultural values, it can be seen as minimizing and reinforce unequal power dynamics (Day-Vines et al., 2007; Sue et al., 2007). This is a continual area of growth within my practice that I urge all forensic social workers to further explore to practice from an anti-oppressive lens.

Reflection Questions

1. What ways can social workers, especially white social workers, take accountability and further understand their positionality?

2. How has the social work profession taken part in the social control of incarcerated, victimized women?
3. What other treatments may be clinically appropriate for Grace's case?

References

Alexander, M. (2010). *The New jim crow: Mass incarceration in the age of colorblindness*. The New Press.

Allard, S. A. (1991). Rethinking battered woman syndrome: A black feminist perspective. *UCLA Journal of Gender and Law, 1*. https://doi.org/10.5070/L311017550

American Psychiatric Association. (2013). *Diagnostic and statistical manual of mental disorders* (5th ed.)

American Psychiatric Association. (2022). *Diagnostic and statistical manual of mental disorders* (5th ed., Text Revision).

American Psychological Association. (2023). *Trauma*. American Psychological Association. https://www.apa.org/topics/trauma

Amnesty International. (1999). *"Not part of my sentence": Violations of the human rights of women in custody*. http://web.amnesty.org/library/Index/ENGAMR510191999?open&of=ENG-360#top

Beck, A. J., Rantala, R. R., & Rexroat, J. (2018). *Sexual victimization reported by adult correctional authorizer, 2009–2011*. U.S. Department of Justice: Office of Justice Programs: Bureau of Justice Statistics. https://www.prearesourcecenter.org/sites/default/files/library/sexualvictimizationreportedbycorrectionalauthorities2009-2011.pdf

Black, M. C., Basile, K. C., Breiding, M. J., Smith, S. G., Walters, M. L., Merrick, M. T., Chen, J., & Stevens, M. R. (2011). *The National Intimate Partner and Sexual Violence Survey (NISVS): 2010 Summary Report*. National Center for Injury Prevention and Control, Centers for Disease Control and Prevention. https://www.cdc.gov/violenceprevention/pdf/nisvs_report2010-a.pdf

Blakely, C. R., & Bumphus, V. W. (1999). American criminal justice philosophy: What's old—What's new? *Federal Probation: A Journal of Correctional Philosophy and Practice, 63*(1), 62–66.

Bloom, B., Owen, B., & Covington, S. (2003). *Gender-responsive strategies: Research, practice, and guiding principles for women offenders*. National Institute of Corrections.

Breiding, M. J., Smith, S. G., Basile, K. C., Walters, M. L., Chen, J., & Merrick, M. T. (2014). Prevalence and characteristics of sexual violence, stalking, and intimate partner violence Victimization: National intimate partner and sexual violence survey, United States, 2011. *Centers for Disease Control and Prevention: Morbidity and Mortality Weekly Report, 63*(8) https://www.cdc.gov/mmwr/pdf/ss/ss6308.pdf

Bronson, J., & Berzofsky, M. (2017). *Indicators of mental health problems reported by prisoners and jail inmates, 2011–12*. Bureau of Justice Statistics. https://bjs.ojp.gov/content/pub/pdf/imhprpji1112.pdf

Browne, A., Miller, B., & Maguin, E. (1999). Prevalence and severity of lifetime physical and sexual victimization among incarcerated women. *International Journal of Law and Psychiatry, 22*, 301–322.

Bryant-Davis, T. (2019). The cultural context of trauma recovery: Considering the posttraumatic stress disorder practice guideline and intersectionality. *Psychotherapy, 56*(3), 400–408. https://doi.org/10.1037/pst0000241

Burkard, A. W., Knox, S., Groen, M., Perez, M., & Hess, S. A. (2006). European American therapist self-disclosure in cross-cultural counseling. *Journal of Counseling Psychology, 53*(1), 15–25.

Center for Court Innovation. (2019). *A national portrait of restorative approaches to intimate partner violence: Pathways to safety, accountability, healing, and well-being*. https://www.

innovatingjustice.org/sites/default/files/media/document/2019/Report_IPV_11262019.pdf?fbclid=IwAR2Y88DTTzKXVU9Ll1Il3XeAuQNQAz5tIXBJRVA5FBfC8V2fP5uWGarH1v0

Center on Juvenile and Criminal Justice. (1999). *Second chances: Giving kids a chance to make a better choice.* Retrieved from https://www.ncjrs.gov/pdffiles1/ojjdp/181680.pdf

Chang, D. F., & Berk, A. (2009). Making cross-racial therapy work: A phenomenological study of clients' experiences of cross-racial therapy. *Journal of Counseling Psychology, 56*(4), 521–536. https://doi.org/10.1037/a0016905

Collins, P. H. (2000). *Black feminist thought: Knowledge, consciousness, and the politics of empowerment.* Routledge.

Crenshaw, K. W. (1989). Demarginalizing the intersection of race and sex: A black feminist critique of antidiscrimination doctrine, feminist theory and antiracist politics. *University of Chicago Legal Forum, 1989*(1), 139–167.

Curry-Stevens, A. (2016). *Anti-oppressive practice.* Oxford University Press. https://doi.org/10.1093/OBO/9780195389678-0203

Day-Vines, N. L., Wood, S. M., Grothaus, T., Craigen, L., Holman, A., Dotson-Blake, K., & Douglass, M. J. (2007). Broaching the subjects of race, ethnicity, and culture during the counseling process. *Journal of Counseling & Development, 85*(4), 401–409.

DeGruy, J. (2005). *Post traumatic slave syndrome: America's legacy of enduring injury and healing.* Uptone Press.

Department of Justice, Office of Justice Programs, Bureau of Justice Statistics. (2013a). *Female victims of sexual violence: 1994–2010.*

Department of Justice, Office of Justice Programs, Bureau of Justice Statistics. (2013b). *Sexual victimization in prisons and jails reported by inmates: 2011–2012.*

Dichter, M. E., & Osthoff, S. (2015). *Women's experiences of abuse as a risk factor for incarceration: A research update.* National Online Resource Center on Violence Against Women. https://vawnet.org/sites/default/files/materials/files/2016-09/AR_IncarcerationUpdate.pdf

Ditton, P. M. (1999). *Mental health and treatment of inmates and probationers.* U.S. Department of Justice, Office of Justice Programs: Bureau of Justice Statistics. https://bjs.ojp.gov/content/pub/pdf/mhtip.pdf

Domestic Abuse Intervention Programs (DAIP). (2017a). *About us.* https://www.theduluthmodel.org/about-us/

Domestic Abuse Intervention Programs (DAIP). (2017b). *Wheels.* https://www.theduluthmodel.org/wheels/

Elliott, D. E., Bjelajac, P., Fallot, R. D., Markoff, L. S., & Reed, B. G. (2005). Trauma-informed or trauma-denied: Principles and implementation of trauma-informed services for women. *Journal of Community Psychology, 33*(4), 461–477.

Facer-Irwin, E., Blackwood, N. J., Bird, A., Dickson, H., McGlade, D., Alves-Costa, F., & MacManus, D. (2019). PTSD in prison settings: A systematic review and meta-analysis of comorbid mental disorders and problematic behaviours. *PLoS One, 14*(9). https://doi.org/10.1371/journal.pone.0222407

Freire, P. (1973). *Education for critical consciousness.* Seabury.

Furio, J. (2002). *Restorative justice: Prison as hell or a chance for redemption.* Algora Publishing.

Grady, M.D., Levenson, J., & Prescott, D. S. (2017). In Maschi, T., & Leibowitz, G. S. (Eds.). *Forensic social work: Psychosocial and legal issues across diverse populations and settings.* Springer Publishing Company, Incorporated.

Green, B. L., Miranda, J., Daroowalla, A., & Siddique, J. (2005). Trauma exposure, mental health functioning, and program needs of women in jail. *Crime & Delinquency, 51*, 133–151.

Hart, O., Brown, P., & van der Kolk, B. (1989). Pierre Janet's treatment of post-traumatic stress. *Journal of Traumatic Stress, 2*(4), 1–11. https://doi.org/10.1007/978-1-4899-1034-9_12

Herman, J. (1997). *Trauma and recovery: The aftermath of violence from domestic abuse to political terror.* Basic Books.

Hill, C. E., & Nakayama, E. Y. (2000). Client-centered therapy: Where has it been and where is it going? A comment on Hathaway (1948). *Journal of Clinical Psychology, 56*(7), 861–875.

Johnson, K. A., & Lynch, S. M. (2013). Predictors of maladaptive coping in incarcerated women who are survivors of childhood sexual abuse. *Journal of Family Violence, 28*, 43–52.
Kondrat, M. E. (2008). Person-in-Environment. In T. M. L. E. Davis (Ed.), *Encyclopedia of social work* (20th ed.). National Association of Social Workers Press and Oxford University Press.
Lapidus, L., Luthra, N., Verma, A., Small, D., Allard, P., & Levingston. (2005). *Caught in the net: The impact of drug policies on women and families*. ACLU, Brennan Center & Break the Chains. https://www.aclu.org/sites/default/files/field_document/asset_upload_file431_23513.pdf
Maschi, T., Leibowitz, G. S., & Killian, M. L. (2017). Conceptual and historical overview of forensic social work. In Maschi, T., & Leibowitz, G. S. (Eds.). *Forensic social work: Psychosocial and legal issues across diverse populations and settings*. Springer, Incorporated.
McLemore, B. (2020). *Defunding the police is not the end goal. It's the first step.* Truthouttruthout. https://truthout.org/articles/defunding-the-police-is-not-the-end-goal-its-the-first-step/
Meyer, O. L., & Zane, N. (2013). The influence of race and ethnicity in client's experiences of mental health treatment. *Journal of Community Psychology, 41*(7), 884–901. https://doi.org/10.1002/jcop.21580
Mintz, L. B., & Tager, D. (2012). Feminist therapy with male clients: Empowering meant to be their whole selves. In C. Z. Enns & E. N. Williams (Eds.), *The Oxford handbook of feminist multicultural counseling psychology*. Oxford University Press. https://doi.org/10.1093/oxfordhb/9780199744220.013.0017
Moradi, B. (2017). (Re)focusing intersectionality: From social identities back to systems of oppression and privilege. In K. A. DeBord, A. R. Fischer, K. J. Bieschke, & R. M. Perez (Eds.), *Handbook of sexual orientation and gender diversity in counseling and psychotherapy* (pp. 105–127). American Psychological Association. https://doi.org/10.1037/15959-005
National Association of Social Workers. (2023). *Code of ethics.* NASW. https://www.socialworkers.org/About/Ethics/Code-of-Ethics/Code-of-Ethics-English
National Center for PTSD. (2022). *Sexual assault against females.* PTSD: National center for PTSD. https://www.ptsd.va.gov/professional/treat/type/sexual_assault_female.asp
National Center for PTSD. (2025). *Understand PTSD treatment.* PTSD: National center for PTSD. https://www.ptsd.va.gov/understand_tx/talk_therapy.asp
National Coalition Against Domestic Violence. (2020). *Domestic violence and the Black community.* https://assets.speakcdn.com/assets/2497/dv_in_the_black_community.pdf.
National Domestic Violence Hotline. (2023). *Power and control.* https://www.thehotline.org/identify-abuse/power-and-control/
Pennell, J. (2018). Domestic violence. In T. Maschi & G. S. Leibowitz (Eds.), *Forensic social work: Psychosocial and legal issues across diverse populations and settings* (2nd ed.). Springer, Incorporated.
Phillips, H., Lyon, E., Fabri, M., & Warshaw, C. (2015). *Promising practices and model programs: Trauma-informed approaches to working with survivors of domestic and sexual violence and other trauma.* National Center on Domestic Violence, Trauma, and Mental Health. https://ncdvtmh.org/wp-content/uploads/2022/10/NCDVTMH_PromisingPracticesReport_2015.pdf
Purnell, D. (2021). *Becoming abolitionists: Police, power, and the pursuit of freedom*. Astra House.
Rape Abuse & Incest National Network (RAINN). (2024). *Key terms and phrases.* https://www.rainn.org/articles/key-terms-and-phrases
Roberts, A. R., & Brownell, P. (1999). A century of forensic social work: Bridging the past to the present. *Social Work, 44*, 359–369.
Rothschild, B. (2010). *8 keys to safe trauma recovery: Take-charge strategies to empower your healing*. W. W. Norton & Company.
Sadeh, N., & McNiel, D. E. (2015). Posttraumatic stress disorder increases risk of criminal recidivism among justice-involved persons with mental disorders. *Criminal Justice and Behavior, 42*(6), 573–586. https://doi.org/10.1177/0093854814556880
Saleeby, D. (1997). *The strengths perspective in social work practice*. Longman.
Santo, A. (2018). Prison rape allegations are on the rise. The marshall project. https://www.themarshallproject.org/2018/07/25/prison-rape-allegations-are-on-the-rise

Saxena, P., & Messina, N. (2021). Trajectories of victimization to violence among incarcerated women. *Health Justice, 9*(18). https://doi.org/10.1186/s40352-021-00144-8

Shapiro, F. (2017). *Eye movement desensitization and reprocessing (EMDR) therapy: Basic principles, protocols and procedures* (3rd ed.). Guilford Press.

Smith, S. G., Chen, J., Basile, K. C., Gilbert, L. K., Merrick, M. T., Patel, N., Walling, M., & Jain, A. (2017). *The national intimate partner and sexual violence survey (NISVS): 2010–2012 state report.* National Center for Injury Prevention and Control, Centers for Disease Control and Prevention. https://www.cdc.gov/violenceprevention/pdf/NISVSStateReportBook.pdf.

Sue, D. W., Bucceri, J. M., Lin, A. I., Nadal, K. L., & Torino, G. C. (2007). Racial microaggressions and the Asian American experience. *Cultural Diversity & Ethnic Minority Psychology, 13*(1), 72–81.

The National Organization of Forensic Social Work. (2020). *Forensic social work.* https://www.nofsw.org/what-is-forensic-social-work-1

The Sentencing Project. (2020). *Incarcerated women and girls.* The sentencing project. https://www.sentencingproject.org/publications/incarcerated-women-and-girls/

The United Nations' Office of the High Commissioner for Human Rights' Committee on the Elimination of Discrimination against Women. (1994). *Declaration on the elimination of violence against women proclaimed by general assembly resolution 48/104.* https://www.ohchr.org/EN/Issues/Women/WRGS/Pages/VAW.aspx

Toraif, N. & Mueller, J. C. (2023, March 22). *Abolitionist social work. Encyclopedia of social work.* National Association of Social Workers Press and Oxford University Press. https://doi.org/10.1093/acrefore/9780199975839.013.1553

Torres, M. G. (2018). State violence. In A. J. Trevino (Ed.), *The Cambridge handbook of social problems* (Vol. 2, pp. 381–398). Cambridge University Press. https://doi.org/10.1017/9781108550710.023

Tripodi, S. J., & Pettus-Davis, C. (2013). Histories of childhood victimization and subsequent mental health problems, substance use, and sexual victimization for a sample of incarcerated women in the US. *International Journal of Law and Psychiatry, 36*(1), 30–40. https://doi.org/10.1016/j.ijlp.2012.11.005

Turner, S. (1993). Talking about sexual abuse: The value of short-term therapy groups for women survivors. *Journal of Group Psychotherapy, Psychodrama, and Sociometry, 46*, 110–121.

Van der Kolk, B. (2014). *The body keeps the score: Brain, mind, and body in the healing of trauma.* Penguin Books.

Walker, L. E. A. (2016). *The battered woman syndrome* (4th ed.). Springer.

Warrier, S. (2022). Inclusion and exclusion: Intersectionality and gender-based violence. In R. Geffner, J. W. White, L. K. Hamberger, A. Rosenbaum, V. Vaughan-Eden, & V. I. Vieth (Eds.), *Handbook of interpersonal violence and abuse across the lifespan* (pp. 2539–2552). Springer. https://doi.org/10.1007/978-3-319-89999-2_49

Wolff, N., Blitz, C. L., Shi, J., Bachman, R., & Siegel, J. A. (2006). Sexual violence inside prisons: Rates of victimization. *Journal of Urban Health: Bulletin of the New York Academy of Medicine, 83*(5), 835–848.

World Health Organization (WHO). (2002). *World report on violence and health.* https://www.who.int/violence_injury_prevention/violence/global_campaign/en/chap6.pdf

Yao, L., & Kabir, R. Person-centered therapy (Rogerian therapy). (2023, February 9). *National library of medicine: National center for biotechnology information.* https://www.ncbi.nlm.nih.gov/books/NBK589708/#article-147772.r1

Part IV
Additional Anti-oppressive Practice Settings

Chapter 18
The Palliative Social Work Role in Surrogate Decision-Making for Sexual- and Gender-Diverse Older Adults: Opportunities for Anti-oppressive Practice

Heather Menzer

Introduction

Palliative social workers are an integral part of interdisciplinary palliative teams and bring a combination of skills and competencies to their work with patients and families. This is exemplified in the standards set out by leading organizations in the field of palliative and end-of-life care. The National Coalition for Hospice and Palliative Care (NCP) endorses clinical practice guidelines for any clinician who is caring for patients with serious illness, those at the end of life, or those in hospice (National Consensus Project for Quality Palliative Care, 2018). They identify eight domains that incorporate the concepts and practices necessary for high-quality palliative care: (1) structure and processes of care, (2) physical aspects of care, (3) psychological and psychiatric aspects, (4) social aspects of care, (5) spiritual, religious, and existential aspects of care, (6) cultural aspects of care, (7) care of the patient nearing the end of life, and (8) ethical and legal aspects of care (National Coalition for Hospice and Palliative Care, 2018).

While the NCP Guidelines include all clinicians, other standards are more specific to social work. The National Association of Social Workers' (NASW) 11 standards for the practice of PSWs consist of (1) ethics and values, (2) knowledge of the relevant concepts, (3) assessment, (4) expertise with end-of-life intervention and treatment planning, (5) attitude and self-awareness, (6) empowerment and advocacy, (7) documentation, (8) interdisciplinary teamwork, (9) cultural competence (which today might be better referred to as cultural humility or cultural responsiveness), (10) continuing education, and (11) supervision, leadership, and training (NASW, 2004). More recently, the Center to Advance Palliative Care (CAPC) has

H. Menzer (✉)
NYU Langone Health, New York, NY, USA
e-mail: Heather.menzer@nyulangone.org

C. Tosone et al. (eds.), *Reframing Social Work with an Anti-Oppressive Lens*, Essential Clinical Social Work Series,
https://doi.org/10.1007/978-3-031-91391-4_18

recognized the unique contributions of the PSW by adding curriculum specific to the discipline to their online offerings (CAPC, n.d.; Higgins, 2022). Like the NASW, CAPC believes that social workers working with patients with serious illness must be able to assess the needs and concerns of their patients, strengthen the clinician-patient relationship, understand patients' goals for care, manage pain and symptoms, prevent crises and plan ahead (CAPC, n.d.). These organizations emphasize that special attention be paid to the concept of empowerment and advocacy in the palliative social work role as, over time, PSWs will undoubtedly come to see gaps in service to certain groups or populations. This must be done with incorporation of an anti-oppressive lens to ensure that PSWs consider the ways in which their patients have been systematically discriminated against and oppressed (Hulko et al., 2019). PSWs should therefore be advocating for groups that are disadvantaged or marginalized within an anti-oppressive framework. As such, the growing group of sexual and gender-diverse older adults (SGDOAs) should be of particular concern to PSWs.

Situations where surrogate decision-makers (SDMs) are appointed for SGDOAs are specifically deserving of attention. This occurs when a worsening illness or injury renders a patient unable to make their own medical decisions and requires the appointment of an SDM due to the lack of existing advance directives. These situations can be distressing for patients, families and loved ones, SDMs, PSWs, and the larger medical team (Majesko et al., 2012; Wocial et al., 2020). There is also growing concern about the inequities in these laws across the country as SGDOAs are more likely to be supported by friends and partners, yet surrogate decision-making laws often default to biological family members (DeMartino et al., 2017; de Vries et al., 2022). The frequency of these situations is likely only to increase as the US population is aging at such a rate that for the first time in the nation's history, adults 65 and older are expected to outnumber children under the age of 18 by 2035 (Vespa, 2018).

This paper reviews the history of the PSW role and the importance of using an anti-oppressive lens. It examines dilemmas that palliative teams encounter when providing care to SGDOAs who require the appointment of SDMs. It details a composite case narrative to illustrate the role of the PSW in these difficult situations. The author's reflections will be noted, as well as opportunities for future study.

History of Palliative Care Social Work

Palliative social work as a specialty evolved from the history of medical social work or social work in healthcare (Harper, 2011). Massachusetts General Hospital was instrumental in the foundation of medical social work, hiring Garnet Pelton in 1905 and later Ida Cannon as their first two medical social workers (Gehlert, 2019). Simultaneously, medical social work was beginning at Johns Hopkins Hospital in Baltimore, Maryland, and what would eventually become City of Hope National Medical Center in Duarte, California. Across all these institutions social workers were acknowledging connections between patients' illnesses and their emotional states, and their colleagues were beginning to recognize the importance of having a clinician with this skill set as part of the interdisciplinary team (Harper, 2011; Ruth & Marshall, 2017). In 1918, the American Association of Hospital Social Workers was established, and there was a push toward professionalization of the role (Gehlert, 2019).

The beginnings of palliative social work specifically are linked to Dame Cicely Saunders, the pioneer of the hospice movement (Harper, 2011). Saunders was trained first as a nurse and later as a medical social worker and a physician (Saunders, 2001). In the early 1950s, Saunders, along with social workers like Ruth Abrams and Alison Player, wrote about their experiences working with terminally ill patients and what they perceived to be their vital role and contributions (Saunders, 2001). The concept of hospice itself became commonly recognized after Saunders founded St. Christopher's Hospice in London, England, in 1967 (Harper, 2011). She continued to write and lecture on the importance of the care of seriously and terminally ill patients throughout her career, and her work eventually inspired the establishment of the US hospice movement (Harper, 2011).

Medical social services were eventually incorporated into US federal legislation, including in the establishment of Medicare in 1965 (Harper, 2011). Later, the Institute of Medicine (IOM), founded in 1970 as an advising agency to the federal government on issues around health (National Academy of Medicine, 2022), published a series of reports over several decades about the care of the seriously ill and dying. These included *Approaching Death: Improving Care at the End of Life* in 1997 (IOM, 1997), *When Children Die: Improving Palliative and End-of-Life Care for Children and their Families* in 2003 (IOM, 2003), and *Dying in America: Improving Quality and Honoring Individual Preferences near the End of Life* in 2014 (IOM, 2014). These publications served as comprehensive reviews of the state of end-of-life care in the United States, respective to the years in which they were published.

In *Approaching Death* (IOM, 1997), the authors observe that social workers are a valuable part of interdisciplinary teams and that general social work training already puts them at an advantage in palliative care due to their knowledge of family systems and supportive counseling (IOM, 1997). Even with this background they suggest that further specialized instruction in caring for the dying is warranted for social workers. They propose that training focus on how to help dying patients continue a meaningful quality of life throughout their illness, advance care planning (ACP), end-of-life decision-making, and the care of the patient's caregivers, families, and friends (IOM, 1997). At the time of publication, the authors found little evidence of specialized palliative courses in social work schools (IOM, 1997).

Important advancements in palliative medicine and social work have developed since the original 1997 IOM report. The Academy of Hospice Physicians, now the American Academy of Hospice and Palliative Medicine (AAHPM), was established in 1998 with a goal of improving the lives of those suffering from serious illness (AAHPM, n.d.). In 2006 hospice and palliative medicine was officially defined as a medical specialty (AAHPM, n.d.). The Social Work Hospice and Palliative Care Network (SWHPN) was established in 2007 (SWHPN, 2022), and previously existing organizations, like the Association of Oncology Social Work (AOSW), continued to evolve and contribute to the advancement of palliative social work over time (AOSW, 2023).

A landmark project on palliative care and end of life, The Open Society Institute's Project on Death in America (PDIA) funded a variety of initiatives from 1993 to 2003 with a goal of improving death in the United States (Open Society Institute, 2004). Within the PDIA, funding opportunities have extended to social work. This included the founding of the Social Work Leadership Development Awards, devoted to enhancing practice, supporting research, training and policy development for social workers, and promoting collaboration between schools of social work and practice sites (Open Society Institute, 2004). The PDIA also set aside funds to support a Social Work Summit on Palliative and End-of-Life Care in 2002 which provided a space for social workers to meet and work toward shared goals (Clark, 2013). PDIA grant recipients have contributed to the field in important ways. For example, grantee Ellen Csikai, founding editor of the *Journal of Social Work in End-of-Life and Palliative Care*, put out its first issue in 2005 (Clark, 2013). This journal remains an important publication for PSWs and others to publish original research and conceptual articles on an array of topics related to end-of-life and palliative care (Taylor & Francis Group, 2023).

Certification opportunities have been established which have given greater weight and validity to the PSW role. Post-Master's certificate programs have been established, first at Smith College Social of Social Work in 2000 (Berzoff et al., 2006) and later at New York University Silver School of Social Work (Gardner et al., 2015). The NASW's Advanced Certified Hospice and Palliative Social Worker (ACHP-SW) certification and the Advanced Palliative Hospice Social Worker Certification (APHSW-C) have allowed PSWs to legitimize their specialty (Higgins, 2022; NASW, 2023).

Today, palliative social work has a more formally understood role (NASW, 2004). In the first nationwide job analysis of hospice and PSWs in the United States, Head et al. (2019) found that 97.9% of respondents to their survey agreed that the role of hospice and PSWs includes conducting psychosocial assessment, facilitating patient-centered goal setting, forming care plans, providing counseling and casework, assisting with decision-making and ACP throughout the trajectory of serious illness, providing psychoeducation, and referring patients to appropriate resources. These tasks however do not comprehensively portray the complicated nature of the job. Higgins (2022) has offered that to appropriately characterize the role of the inpatient hospital PSW, one should consider how PSWs interact with micro, mezzo, and macro system levels. PSWs first must reconcile their personal boundaries around the work and consider their interactions with team members and other hospital social workers, their role within the hospital at large, and how their work is shaped and affected by institutional, state, and federal policies and laws (Higgins, 2022). These often-competing interests can lead to difficulties in the day-to-day work in the hospital. PSWs are frequently caught between the administrative and task-orientated responsibilities of the job and the more rewarding clinical work (Higgins, 2022). The PSW must find a way to balance these obligations and still stay true to their goal of providing support to and working effectively with patients, families, medical teams, and systems when patients are at the end of life.

PSWs must also incorporate an anti-oppressive lens in their social work practice. Anti-oppressive social work is patient focused and seeks to eliminate oppression and oppressive practices through work with clients and systems (Hulko et al., 2019). It considers that oppression takes place between individuals and systems (Morgaine & Capous-Desyllas, 2014). Ultimately, no part of the work is apolitical. Since it occurs within systems, all of it is susceptible to echoing the politics and power embedded in those systems, even when the social worker is operating with the best intentions (Mattsson, 2014). Consider how social workers document, for example. It is up to the practitioner themselves to decide what is kept in and what is omitted in a patient's record (Lee, 2022). Documentation is therefore reflective of the social worker's positionality, experiences, and beliefs.

Anti-oppressive work also acknowledges that being a member of a group that has historically experienced discrimination or mistreatment is known to be associated with trauma (Hulko et al., 2019). Therefore, it is important that clients who have experienced trauma as a result of oppressive practices receive care from a social worker who is practicing with both anti-oppressive and trauma-informed lenses. Anti-oppressive practice requires practitioner self-awareness at all levels, including personal, professional, and institutional. This self-awareness must incorporate an understanding of the power and privilege held by the social worker (Havig & Byers, 2019; Morgaine & Capous-Desyllas, 2014) and how the profession has contributed to the marginalization and oppression of groups (Havig & Byers, 2019). The anti-oppressive practitioner must consider a client's intersecting identities and the complex ways in which they have been subject to oppression and how they interact and reinforce one another (Mattsson, 2014). In the case of SGDOAs, the social worker must consider at least the patient's gender identity, sexual orientation, class, race, and age as well as the historical oppressions this group has suffered.

Palliative Care for Sexual- and Gender-Diverse Older Adults

The specific needs of SGDOAs receiving care from PSWs have not been adequately addressed in the literature or in social work school curriculum (Arthur, 2015). The role of the PSW in caring for SGDOAs must utilize an anti-oppressive framework to understand how stigma and discrimination have affected the provision of care to this group (Arthur, 2015). SGDOAs are known to experience healthcare discrimination and are more likely than their cisgender, heterosexual counterparts to have their healthcare wishes be disregarded (Candrian & Cloyes, 2021; Su et al., 2016). They may be reticent to access care, even when ill, due to a fear that they will face discrimination (Mirza & Rooney, 2018; White Hughto et al., 2015). These factors contribute to the known health disparities for individuals in this group (Fredriksen-Goldsen et al., 2013; Gaither et al., 2017).

Ongoing discrimination of sexual- and gender-diverse (SGD) patients is acknowledged by healthcare teams. In a study of palliative care and hospice professionals, including social workers, Stein et al. (2020) found that a majority of these clinicians believed SGD patients were more likely to experience discrimination than their cisgender and heterosexual peers. They found that 43% of the professionals had personally observed a patient's spouse, partner, or legal surrogate being treated disrespectfully or having their wishes minimized or ignored (Stein et al., 2020). Professionals were more likely to report these incidences if they worked in states without laws protecting SGD individuals from discrimination or if they had more years of work experience (Stein et al., 2020). These findings however are in direct conflict with the *American Medical Association's (AMA) Code of Medical Ethics for Decisions for Adult Patients Who Lack Capacity* which states that providers should treat surrogate decision-makers with the same respect as they would the patient (AMA, 2022).

Considering that many healthcare providers lack knowledge in how to best treat SGD patients (Shetty et al., 2016), this may not be surprising. Providers who care for SGDOAs may not grasp key concepts including sexuality, sexual orientation, sexual behavior, gender identity, gender expression, gender dysphoria, and gender nonconformity (Acquaviva, 2017). Providers may not understand how legal and ethical issues particularly affect SGDOAs. For example, providers may not be aware that even if a patient legally designates a healthcare agent, the healthcare proxy form does not extend power for that person to make decisions over the disposition of the patient's remains, funeral decisions, and obituaries. Without proper designation of decision-making power after death, these decisions will be defaulted to the patient's next of kin (Acquaviva, 2017).

Members of the SGD community are less likely to reach advanced age with a spouse or child and are most likely to rely on families of choice for care, including friends or non-married partners (Candrian & Cloyes, 2021; de Vries et al., 2022). Those who do have adult children are less likely to receive care from them when compared to their non-SGD counterparts (IOM, 2011). Considering this, PSWs should take an active role in the promotion and facilitation of ACP discussions. ACP, the process of helping patients discuss and document their healthcare wishes, endorses the importance of appointing decision-makers *before* incapacity occurs (National Institute on Aging, 2018). ACP is acknowledged to be an important component of the PSW role (Head et al., 2019; NASW, 2004), yet there are disparities in the provision of ACP to the SGD population (Beringer et al., 2021; Valenti et al., 2022). This may put this group at higher risk to end up without legally designated decision-makers as they approach the end of life.

Surrogate Decision-Making for Sexual- and Gender-Diverse Older Adults

When patients present to palliative teams unable to have ACP conversations and without previously documented wishes or legally designated decision-makers, an SDM may be appointed on the patient's behalf. The process of SDM designation itself is one that may disenfranchise SGD patients. Although this population is more likely to rely on families of choice for support and care than on biological family (de Vries et al., 2022), many states give priority to biological family over families of choice in surrogate decision-making. In fact, only six states and the District of Colombia give domestic partners power equal to married spouses in their surrogate decision-maker laws (DeMartino et al., 2017). In a study of hospitalized older adults who required the appointment of SDMs, Comer et al. (2018) looked at surrogates who were considered traditional (immediate family) and compared them to nontraditional surrogates (other family, friends, partners). They found that the relationships these surrogates had to the patient were essentially the same in terms of how often the surrogate was in contact with the patient and how likely they were to have had conversation about the patient's medical wishes prior to incapacity. As a result, they suggested that states consider expanding their SDM laws to be more inclusive of nontraditional surrogates (Comer et al., 2018).

The actual appointment of a surrogate decision-maker often falls on medical staff (AMA, 2022). The AMA is clear on what the physician's ethical responsibility is to their patient and the SDM in these situations. They are called to

> "(a) identify an appropriate surrogate to make decisions on the patient's behalf; (b) recognize that the patient's surrogate is entitled to the same respect as the patient; (c) provide advice, guidance, and support to the surrogate; (d) assist the surrogate to make decisions in keeping with the standard of substituted judgment, basing decisions on: (i) the patient's preferences (if any) as expressed in an advance directive or as documented in the medical record; and (e) assist the surrogate to make decisions in keeping with the best interest standard when the patient's preferences and values are not known and cannot reasonably be inferred, such as when the patient has not previously expressed preferences or has never had decision-making capacity" (AMA, 2022, "Decisions for Adult Patients Who Lack Capacity" section).

When ethical concerns arise, physicians are instructed to consult an ethics committee (AMA, 2022). This includes situations where SDMs attempt to override a patient's known preferences (The National Consensus Project for Quality Palliative Care, 2018).

While the NASW's Standards for Palliative and End-of-Life Care (2004) acknowledge the importance of ethical decision-making, empowerment, and advocacy, they do not speak specifically to SDM appointment scenarios. This leaves PSWs to approach these situations without clear guidelines, unless their institutions have their own policies.

Due to the emotional nature of these cases, these situations can be distressing to care teams, including PSWs. Teams may be concerned that a legal surrogate decision-maker is not who the patient would have chosen for themselves (Comer et al., 2017). Physicians have been known to experience moral distress in SDM cases or the distress felt when one cannot act in accordance with what one deems ethical and right (Jameton, 1984). Moral distress is more likely to occur for physicians in SDM situations when their patients are older or when life-sustaining treatment decisions are being made (Wocial et al., 2020). Teams may worry that surrogates are making decisions outside the bounds of their moral authority, for example, if they make decisions based on the surrogate's own religious beliefs that the patient does not identify with (Berger, 2017). This may be exacerbated in situations where surrogates are biologically related to the patient but do not have an intimate or personal relationship with them (Berger, 2020).

Role of the Palliative Social Worker in Surrogate Decision-Making Cases

The PSW's role in surrogate decision-making scenarios is a complex one. It mirrors the NASW's Standards for Palliative and End-of-Life Care (2004) but should be done through an anti-oppressive lens to fully honor and protect the SGDOA. In addition to the general role of providing support in crisis, grief, and bereavement, the role also requires the PSW to have knowledge of institutional, state and local policies, a grasp of medical ethics, and an ability to mediate (The National Consensus Project for Quality Palliative Care, 2018). In keeping with an anti-oppressive framework, the PSW should strive toward self-awareness, working to understand how their own beliefs, attitudes, and feelings affect the way they interact with their SGDOA patients (Acquaviva, 2017).

Completing a thorough psychosocial assessment for the incapacitated SGDOA is the recommended starting point. The PSW should verify what family, friends, or support system exists. PSWs must be careful to explore terms like *spouse*, *domestic partner*, *and married* and determine whether or not those relationships exist legally as many states require this in order for a person to be officially designated as an SDM (Acquaviva, 2017). Using knowledge of advance directives and other ACP documents, the PSW should explore if documents already exist for the patient that could avoid surrogate decision-making defaults to go into effect. This may include calling institutions or agencies that have records of these documents, other medical systems and clinics, dialysis centers, nursing homes, methadone clinics, assisted living facilities, home care agencies, and insurance companies.

Once it is determined that no advance directives exist, it may be within the scope of the PSW role to determine who is the patient's legal SDM. This requires a thorough understanding of the state SDM law (The National Consensus Project for Quality Palliative Care, 2018) and knowledge of institutional and state discrimination policies (Blotner & Dotolo, 2022). The PSW should understand what these laws and policies omit as even the most robust state surrogate decision-making laws leave certain factors up to interpretation. For example, does the law dictate how many times a team should reach out to a potential surrogate before deciding to move on to another person? What if there are concerns with the ability of the legal surrogate to make informed decisions? What should be done when several people carry equal weight as surrogate decision-makers? PSWs should look to their institutions or ethics committees for guidance in these situations. In circumstances where patients are known to have intellectual or developmental disabilities, requirements may be higher (The National Consensus Project for Quality Palliative Care, 2018). Patients without known supports also require investigation, and ethics committee referral may be appropriate.

Once designated, the PSW can facilitate conversation with the surrogate to elucidate if the patient ever mentioned their treatment preferences. At this time, it may be prudent to speak to the surrogate about the benefits of allowing the team to talk to a patient's friends, partner, or other contacts (Buckey & Abell, 2010). These interviews can provide invaluable information to a decision-maker, especially when the legally appointed surrogate has experienced estrangement from the patient. The PSW may also need to remind or educate the SDM on their role, which is to honor the patient's preferences, not the SDM's preferences (National Consensus Project for Quality Palliative Care, 2018).

Throughout the case the PSW should use inclusive language that appropriately respects how the patient identifies themselves, including their preferred pronouns (Gay and Lesbian Medical Association, 2006; Rossi & Lopez, 2017). The PSW should carefully document in the medical record so that they are accurately reflecting the names and pronouns that patients prefer in writing. PSWs may also need to educate their teams and hold coworkers accountable when they overhear pronoun misuse and appropriately address a mistake if another clinician misgenders a patient (Gay and Lesbian Medical Association, 2006).

Intersectionality must not be overlooked. SGDOAs represent a variety of cultures, races, religions, languages, and other characteristics (Javier, 2021). PSWs should ensure they are honoring the patient's intersectional identities (Javier, 2021) as well as respecting the culture of the SDM. Anderson et al. (2015) found that culture was seen as a barrier to successful communication with decision-makers of incapacitated ICU patients, so the PSW role should bring a cultural humility lens to the work.

PSWs should consider the SDM's need for support during what can be a very difficult and upsetting time. SDMs are known to experience stress, anxiety, and emotional distress when tasked with making decisions on behalf of another (Rogers & Lopez, 2023). Anderson and colleagues (2023) found that one fifth of surrogate decision-makers in intensive care situations felt moderate to strong regret about the life-sustaining treatment decisions they made. They want emotional support from their healthcare teams and benefit from an individualized approach to receiving difficult news and information (Anderson et al., 2015). PSWs can assess how ready a decision-maker is to receive tough news, prepare families for difficult discussions, and provide feedback to physicians with the decision-maker's concerns (Anderson et al., 2015). PSWs should consider when referral to spiritual care could benefit a patient or SDM. The involvement of spiritual care in these situations has been shown to increase SDM psychological and spiritual well-being and to decrease their anxiety (Torke et al., 2023).

Case Illustration and Author's Reflections

The realities of these situations may be best understood by reviewing how these situations actually unfold. As an inpatient hospital PSW in a large metropolitan health system, I met with John, a 71-year-old cisgender Caucasian male who identified as gay and used he/him pronouns. He presented to the hospital for pain associated with end-stage anal cancer. During my assessment John explained that he had once completed an advance directive naming a partner as his primary healthcare agent but had destroyed the form upon the relationship's end 5 years ago. He said that he was well supported by a network of close friends and still maintained a friendship with his ex-partner. He was open to the idea of completing a new advance directive form but asked for time to consider who he would appoint. As we continued our ACP discussion John said he was not feeling up to speaking about his medical wishes today and asked that I return the next day. Unfortunately, soon after John suffered a medical event that left him unable to communicate, and he did not wake up again. Decisions needed to be made about John's treatment course due to the severity of his condition. The palliative team believed John was dying and his heart would likely stop in the coming days, and I was tasked with finding an SDM. At that point the standard of care dictated that all interventions be attempted to prolong his life, including cardiopulmonary resuscitation in the event his heart stopped since he had not expressed any limitations to treatment.

In the absence of advance directives, I reached out to the emergency contact in John's medical chart, a close friend, Steven. Steven shared that John had a brother, Roger, in a neighboring town although the two had not spoken in many years after a falling out. In accordance with the state surrogate decision-making law, I called Roger who said he felt a familial responsibility to take on the role of SGM, something he believed their parents would have wanted him to do. Roger acknowledged that he knew nothing of John's wishes and expressed feelings of guilt and remorse that he had lost the opportunity to reconcile with his brother. Roger was unaware of who made up John's support network and had not known of his ex-partner. The palliative team often noted their unease with the situation as they believed John would not have chosen Roger as his decision-maker if he had another opportunity to complete an advance directive.

Through targeted conversation and the exploration of John's values, I supported Roger as he decided how to move forward. With Roger's permission I arranged and facilitated a discussion between the palliative team, Roger, John's ex-partner, and several close friends. Roger had initially decided that John would continue receiving life-sustaining treatment interventions as he hoped for recovery, but he changed his mind after listening to John's support system. They related past conversations with John who had been clear that he would not accept a life where he was unlikely to live at home independently again or be able to make his own decisions. Considering this, and the palliative team's recommendations, Roger pursued the withdrawal of life-sustaining treatment on his brother's behalf. Together we planned how to honor and support John during his transition. Roger, his children, and John's friends brought in pictures and shared stories about John. His favorite music played on a speaker Roger brought from home. While John did not identify as religious, a hospital chaplain led the group in prayer as requested by Roger, as he and John had done this when their parents had died. John died surrounded by this support system.

Our role as PSWs involves considering how to best support our most vulnerable patients. At end of life our SGDOA patients may be especially vulnerable, particularly when they can no longer speak for themselves and have not nominated anyone to do so for them. Of course, we do not just support our patients but their friends, families, partners, and even our team as they wrestle with their own grief and emotions around these often-complicated situations. As in John's situation, we can experience internal conflict if we believe a patient would have chosen someone other than the legal SDM to make their decisions. I felt this distress as I thought it unlikely that John would have named Roger as his decision-maker based on our conversation prior to his incapacity. I found myself feeling protective of John and had to remind myself that Roger was doing his best to make decisions, even though I worried that at times they were not in line with what John might want. Luckily, Roger was open to communication with John's ex-partner and friends and took their suggestions into consideration, but this is not always the case.

After John's death I organized and facilitated a case meeting where the team came together to discuss the experience of taking care of John and the difficulties we faced. During and after these types of cases, I also rely on my own supervision to process my feelings. While it is helpful to talk about cases with the larger palliative group, as the only PSW on my team it is important to review the situation with a social work supervisor specifically. Advocating for clearer guidelines within my institution and getting involved in professional associations with the power to influence larger change help me deal with my distress around these situations. It also fulfills my duty to promote equity for the disadvantaged and bring a larger awareness to this issue. The PSW truly lives in the micro, mezzo, and macro space simultaneously. While the day-to-day clinical work is our bread and butter, we cannot truly promote anti-oppression in our field without participating in change on a broader level.

Conclusion

A 2019 report from CAPC and the National Palliative Care Research Center concluded that US hospitals and health systems are falling short in providing adequate care to those with serious illness. They call for more resources to focus on the holistic needs of patients and their families (Morrison & Meier, 2019). This includes the most vulnerable groups, SGDOAs among them. PSWs are well placed to be on the forefront of advocacy for this group at all system levels. This must start by ensuring that new social work graduates receive appropriate palliative care education, and luckily there is more available now than ever before. In 2017 Berkman and Stein invited all MSW programs in the United States and Canada to participate in a study about their palliative care courses and curriculum. Of the 105 that responded, 63 MSW programs said that they had at least some content on palliative care within their curriculum, and 10 offered full courses on palliative care. There are MSW programs that now allow a specific palliative care focus, like New York University Silver School of Social Work's Zelda Foster MSW Fellowship in Palliative and End-of-Life Care (NYU Silver School of Social Work, n.d.) and the Fordham University Graduate School of Social Service's Palliative Care Fellowship (Fordham University, n.d.).

In their ongoing commitment to continuing education, PSWs should participate or lead trainings in how to best care for the SGD population (Stein et al., 2020). PSWs can also advocate for institutional or state-wide-level nondiscrimination policies to be created and enforced to better protect this group (Javier, 2021; Stein et al., 2020).

Creating more opportunities for the SGD population to participate in ACP is crucial, and PSWs are well positioned to lead this effort. Even in the most recent IOM report, authors found that most healthcare systems were not providing adequate clinician-patient communication around end-of-life issues or opportunities for patients and families to participate in ACP (IOM, 2014). PSWs must address patient wishes and facilitate communication between a patient and their decision-makers prior to the loss of decision-making capacity considering that SDMs who have little or no knowledge of a patient's wishes are largely unable to appropriately speak for them (Buckey & Abell, 2010).

PSWs should get involved on a larger scale to support federal legislation efforts that would benefit them and therefore patients and families. In 2018 The Palliative Care and Hospice Education and Training Act (PCHETA) passed the US House of Representatives and was introduced to the Senate in 2022 by Senator Tammy Baldwin. PCHETA would create workforce development, fellowship opportunities, and career incentive awards for PSWs (Morrison and Meier, 2019; H.R. 647, 2019). Also introduced in 2022 by Senator Mark Warner is the Improving Access to Advance Care Planning Act which, among other things, would allow social workers to bill for ACP services under Medicare (S.4873, 2022).

It is an exciting time in the domain of PSW. There is ample opportunity for new social work graduates entering palliative care to make a lasting impact on all system levels by utilizing an anti-oppressive lens to support and protect the most vulnerable as they approach the end of life. Emerging leaders in PSW might consider leading future research efforts examining how surrogate decision-making policies affect not just SGDOA individuals as a whole but the unique populations that make up that group. Future research may also look at ways in which PSWs best cope with their own distress from these emotional cases.

Reflection Questions

1. How would you have intervened as a palliative social worker if Roger was unwilling to hear from John's friends?
2. Did the social worker in John's case provide anti-oppressive practice? If so, what did the palliative social worker do?
3. How can you proceed if you determine your institution does not have policies that best protect sexual and gender minority older adults?
4. How can you support the team around you when they experience moral distress in a surrogate decision-making case? How can you care for yourself?
5. How would you define anti-oppressive social work in the context of palliative social work?

References

Acquaviva, K. D. (2017). *LGBTQ-inclusive hospice and palliative care: A practical guide to transforming professional practice*. Columbia University Press.

American Academy of Hospice and Palliative Medicine. (n.d.). *History of AAHPM*. Retrieved April 30, 2023, from https://aahpm.org/about/history

American Medical Association. (2022) *Decisions for adult patients who lack capacity*. https://www.ama-assn.org/delivering-care/ethics/decisions-adult-patients-who-lack-capacity

Andersen, S. K., Butler, R. A., Chang, C. C. H., Arnold, R., Angus, D. C., & White, D. B. (2023). Prevalence of long-term decision regret and associated risk factors in a large cohort of ICU surrogate decision makers. *Critical Care, 27*(1), 1–11.

Anderson, W. G., Cimino, J. W., Ernecoff, N. C., Ungar, A., Shotsberger, K. J., Pollice, L. A., Buddadhumaruk, P., Carson, S. S., Curtis, J. R., & Hough, C. L. (2015). A multicenter study of key stakeholders' perspectives on communicating with surrogates about prognosis in intensive care units. *Annals of the American Thoracic Society, 12*(2), 142–152.

Arthur, D. P. (2015). Social work practice with LGBT elders at end of life: Developing practice evaluation and clinical skills through a cultural perspective. *Journal of Social Work in End-of-Life & Palliative Care, 11*(2), 178–201.

Association of Oncology Social Work. (2023). *About AOSW.*. https://aosw.org/about-aosw/

Berger, J. T. (2017). The limits of surrogates' moral authority and physician professionalism: can the paradigm of palliative sedation be instructive? *The Hastings Center Report, 47*(1), 20–23.

Berger, J. T. (2020). Marginally represented patients and the moral authority of surrogates. *American Journal of Bioethics, 20*(2), 44–48. https://doi.org/10.1080/15265161.2019.1701732

Beringer, R. M., Gutman, G., & de Vries, B. (2021). Exploring and promoting advance care planning among lesbian, gay, bisexual, transgender, and queer (LGBTQ) older adults living in non-metropolitan British Columbia. *Journal of Gay & Lesbian Social Services, 33*(4), 407–426. https://doi.org/10.1080/10538720.2021.1885552

Berzoff, J., Lucas, G., Deluca, D., Gerbino, S., Browning, D., Foster, Z., & Chatchkes, E. (2006). Clinical social work education in palliative and end-of-life care: Relational approaches for advanced practitioners. *Journal of Social Work in End-of-Life & Palliative Care, 2*(2), 45–63. https://doi.org/10.1300/J457v02n02_04

Blotner, C., & Dotolo, D. (2022). LGBTQ patient palliative care: A queery in quality of life. In T. Altilio, S. Otis-Green, & J. G. Cagle (Eds.), *The oxford textbook of palliative social work* (pp. 153–163). Oxford University Press, Incorporated.

Buckey, J. W., & Abell, N. (2010). Life-sustaining treatment decisions: A social work response to meet needs of health care surrogates. Journal of social work in end-of-life & palliative care, 6(1-2), 27–50.

Candrian, C., & Cloyes, K. G. (2021). "She's dying and I can't say we're married?": End-of-life care for LGBT older adults. *Gerontologist, 61*(8), 1197–1201. https://doi.org/10.1093/geront/gnaa186

Center to Advance Palliative Care. (n.d.). *Clinical training recommendations for social workers caring for patients with serious illness.* https://www.capc.org/clinical-training-recommendations-for-all-clinicians-caring-for-patients-with-serious-illness/clinical-training-recommendations-for-social-workers-caring-for-patients-with-serious-illness/

Clark, D. (2013). *Transforming the culture of dying: The work of the project on death in America.* Oxford University Press.

Comer, A. R., Gaffney, M., Stone, C. L., & Torke, A. (2017). Physician understanding and application of surrogate decision-making laws in clinical practice. *AJOB Empirical Bioethics, 8*(3), 198–204. https://doi.org/10.1080/23294515.2016.1234520

Comer, A., Slaven, J., Montz, A., Burke, E., Inger, L., & Torke, A. (2018). Nontraditional surrogate decision makers for hospitalized older adults. *Medical Care, 56*(4), 337–340.

de Vries, B., Gutman, G., Soheilipour, S., Gahagan, J., Humble, Á., Mock, S., & Chamberland, L. (2022). Advance care planning among older LGBT Canadians: heteronormative influences. Sexualities, 25(1-2), 79–98.

DeMartino, E. S., Sperry, B. P., Mueller, P. S., Doyle, C. K., Siegler, M., Gregory, S. E., Sulmasy, D. P., Dudzinski, D. M., & Kramer, D. B. (2017). Who decides when a patient can't? Statutes on alternate decision makers. *New England Journal of Medicine, 376*(15), 1478–1482. https://doi.org/10.1056/NEJMms1611497

Fordham University. (n.d.). *Graduate school of social service: Palliative care fellowship*. https://www.fordham.edu/graduate-school-of-social-service/academics/palliative-care-fellowship/

Fredriksen-Goldsen, K., Kim, H.-J., Barkan, S. E., Muraco, A., & Hoy-Ellis, C. (2013). Health disparities among lesbian, gay, and bisexual older adults: Results from a population-based study. *American Journal of Public Health, 103*(10), 1802–1809. https://doi.org/10.2105/AJPH.2012.301110

Gaither, T. W., Awad, M. A., Osterberg, E. C., Romero, A., Bowers, M. L., & Breyer, B. N. (2017). Impact of sexual orientation identity on medical morbidities in male-to-female transgender patients. *LGBT Health, 4*(1), 11–16. https://doi-org.proxy.library.nyu.edu/10.1089/lgbt.2016.0097

Gardner, D. S., Gerbino, S., Walls, J. W., Chachkes, E., & Doherty, M. J. (2015). Mentoring the next generation of social workers in palliative and end-of-life care: The Zelda Foster studies program. *Journal of Social Work in End-of-Life & Palliative Care, 11*(2), 107–131.

Gay and Lesbian Medical Association. (2006). *Guidelines for care of lesbian, gay, bisexual and transgender patients*. https://www.glma.org/_data/n_0001/resources/live/Welcoming%20Environment.pdf

Gehlert, S. (2019). The conceptual underpinnings of social work in health care. In S. Gehlert & T. Browne (Eds.), Handbook of health social work (3rd ed., pp. 1–19). Wiley.

Harper, B. C. (2011). Palliative social work: An historical perspective. Oxford textbook of palliative social work, 11–20.

Havig, K., & Byers, L. (2019). Truth, reconciliation, and social work: A critical pathway to social justice and anti-oppressive practice. *Journal of Social Work Values & Ethics, 16*(2), 70–80.

Head, B., Peters, B., Middleton, A., Friedman, C., & Guman, N. (2019). Results of a nationwide hospice and palliative care social work job analysis. *Journal of Social Work in End-of-Life & Palliative Care, 15*(1), 16–33.

Higgins, P. C. (2022). Guess who's coming to dinner?: The evolving identity of palliative social workers. In T. Altilio, S. Otis-Green, & J. G. Cagle (Eds.), *The Oxford textbook of palliative social work* (pp. 65–76). Oxford University Press.

Hulko, W., Brotman, S., Stern, L., & Ferrer, I. (2019). *Gerontological social work in action: Anti-oppressive practice with older adults, their families, and communities*. Routledge.
Institute of Medicine. (1997). *Approaching death: Improving care at the end of life*. National Academy Press.
Institute of Medicine. (2003). *When children die: Improving palliative and end-of-life care for children and their families*. The National Academies Press.
Institute of Medicine Committee on Lesbian, Gay, Bisexual, and Transgender Health Issues and Research Gaps and Opportunities. (2011). *The health of lesbian, gay, bisexual, and transgender people: Building a foundation for better understanding*. National Academies Press.
Institute of Medicine. (2014). Dying in America: Improving quality and honoring individual preferences near the end of life. Washington, DC: National Academies Press.
Jameton, A. (1984). *Nursing practice: The ethical issues*.
Javier, N. M. (2021). Palliative care needs, concerns, and affirmative strategies for the LGBTQ population. *Palliative Care and Social Practice*, 15.
Lee, E. (2022). Assessment as a site of anti/oppressive social work practice: Negotiating with power and the de/professionalisation of social work. *British Journal of Social Work, 52*(7), 4378–4400. https://doi-org.proxy.library.nyu.edu/10.1093/bjsw/bcac038
Majesko, A., Hong, S. Y., Weissfeld, L., & White, D. B. (2012). *Identifying family members who may struggle in the role of surrogate decision maker*. Lippincott Williams and Wilkins.
Mattsson, T. (2014). Intersectionality as a useful tool: Anti-oppressive social work and critical reflection. *Affilia, 29*(1), 8–17.
Mirza, S. A., & Rooney, C. (2018, January 18). *Discrimination prevents LGBTQ people from accessing health care*. The Center for American Progress. https://www.americanprogress.org/article/discrimination-prevents-lgbtq-people-accessing-health-care/
Morgaine, K. L., & Capous-Desyllas, M. J. (2014). *Anti-oppressive social work practice: Putting theory into action*. Sage.
Morrison, R. S., & Meier, D. E. (2019). *America's care of serious illness: A state-by-state report card on access to palliative care in our nation's hospitals*. Center to Advance Palliative Care and the National Palliative Care Research Center. https://reportcard.capc.org/wp-content/uploads/2020/05/CAPC_State-by-State-Report-Card_051120.pdf
National Academy of Medicine. (2022). *About the National Academy of Medicine*. https://nam.edu/about-the-nam/
National Association of Social Workers. (2004). *NASW Standards for social work practice in palliative and end of life care*. NASW Press.
National Association of Social Workers. (2023). *Advanced certified hospice & palliative social worker (ACHP-SW)*.. https://www.socialworkers.org/Careers/Credentials/Apply-for-NASW-Social-Work-Credentials/Advanced-Certified-Hospice-and-Palliative-Social-Worker
National Consensus Project for Quality Palliative Care. (2018). *Clinical practice guidelines for quality palliative care* (4th ed.). National Consensus Project for Quality Palliative Care. https://www.nationalcoalitionhpc.org/ncp
National Institute on Aging. (2018, January 15). *Advance care planning: Health care directives*. https://www.nia.nih.gov/health/advance-care-planning-health-care-directives
NYU Silver School of Social Work. (n.d.). *Zelda Foster Studies*. https://socialwork.nyu.edu/faculty-and-research/faculty-initiatives/zelda-foster-studies.html
Open Society Institute. (2004). *Transforming the culture of dying: The project on death in America, October 1994 to December 2003*.. https://www.opensocietyfoundations.org/uploads/de19b013-003f-45cf-9810-a302a4dac741/a_transforming.pdf
Rogers, A. H., & Lopez, R. P. (2023). Systematic review revisited, 2010–2020: The effect on surrogates of making treatment decisions for others. *Journal of Palliative Care, 38*(1), 71–77.
Rossi, A. L., & Lopez, E. J. (2017). Contextualizing competence: Language and LGBT-based competency in health care. *Journal of Homosexuality, 64*(10), 1330–1349. https://doi.org/10.1080/00918369.2017.1321361
Ruth, B. J., & Marshall, J. W. (2017). A history of social work in public health. *American Journal of Public Health, 107*(S3), S236–S242.

Saunders, D. C. (2001). Social work and palliative care—the early history. *The British Journal of Social Work, 31*(5), 791–799.

Shetty, G., Sanchez, J. A., Lancaster, J. M., Wilson, L. E., Quinn, G. P., & Schabath, M. B. (2016). Oncology healthcare providers' knowledge, attitudes, and practice behaviors regarding LGBT health. *Patient Education and Counseling, 99*(10), 1676–1684. https://doi.org/10.1016/j.pec.2016.05.004

Social Work Hospice & Palliative Care Network. (2022). *Welcome to SWHPN.*. https://www.swhpn.org/about-swhpn.

Standards for Palliative and End-of-Life Care refers to reference below: National Association of Social Workers. (2004). NASW Standards for social work practice in palliative and end of life care. NASW Press.

Stein, G. L., Berkman, C., O'Mahony, S., Godfry, D., Javier, N. M., & Maingi, S. (2020). Experiences of lesbian, gay, bisexual, and transgender patients and families in hospice and palliative care: Perspectives of the palliative care team. *Journal of Palliative Medicine, 23*(6), 817–824. https://doi.org/10.1089/jpm.2019.0542

Su, D., Irwin, J. A., Fisher, C., Ramos, A., Kelley, M., Mendoza, D. A. R., & Coleman, J. D. (2016). Mental health disparities within the LGBT population: A comparison between transgender and nontransgender individuals. *Transgender Health, 1*(1), 12–20.

Taylor & Francis Online. (2023). *Journal of social work in end-of-life and palliative care*. https://www.tandfonline.com/toc/wswe20/current

Torke, A. M., Varner-Perez, S. E., Burke, E. S., Taylor, T. A., Slaven, J. E., Kozinski, K. L., Maiko, S. M., Pfeffer, B. J., & Banks, S. K. (2023). Effects of spiritual care on well-being of intensive care family surrogates: A clinical trial. *Journal of Pain and Symptom Management, 65*(4), 296–307. https://doi-org.proxy.library.nyu.edu/10.1016/j.jpainsymman.2022.12.007

Valenti, K. G., Janssen, L. M., Enguidanos, S., & de Medeiros, K. (2022). "By the time she got sick it was just kind of too late": A qualitative study on advanced care planning among bereaved lesbian, gay, and bisexual older women. *Palliative Medicine, 36*(2), 375–385. https://doi.org/10.1177/02692163211065279

Vespa, J. (2018, October 9). *The U.S. joins other countries with large aging populations. The graying of America: More older adults than kids by 2035.* https://www.census.gov/library/stories/2018/03/graying-america.html

White Hughto, J. M., Reisner, S. L., & Pachankis, J. E. (2015). Transgender stigma and health: A critical review of stigma determinants, mechanisms, and interventions. *Social Science & Medicine, 147*, 222–231. https://doi.org/10.1016/j.socscimed.2015.11.010

Wocial, L. D., Slaven, J. E., Montz, K., Monahan, P. O., Hickman, S. E., Callahan, C. M., Helft, P. R., Sachs, G. A., Inger, L., Burke, E. S., & Torke, A. M. (2020). Factors associated with physician moral distress caring for hospitalized elderly patients needing a surrogate decision-maker: A prospective study. *Journal of General Internal Medicine, 35*(5), 1405–1412. https://doi.org/10.1007/s11606-020-05652-1

Chapter 19
More Humanity Needed in Human Service: An Anecdotal Analysis of Current Homeless Service Practices

Caitlin Krenn

Introduction

As Paulo Freire wisely observed, "the pursuit of full humanity… cannot be carried out in isolation or individualism, but only in fellowship and solidarity; therefore, it cannot unfold in the antagonistic relations between oppressors and oppressed. No one can be authentically human while [they] prevent others from being so" (Freire, 2017, p. 83).

After supervising and teaching dozens of students (also having been one myself), I can say confidently that when asked "why" one feels compelled to do this work, almost every person replies with some version of the phrase, "I want to help people." It is indeed an understatement to say that human services work is *hard*. What is more, doing this work during a global pandemic, looming recession, and continually polarizing political climate makes daily life difficult for any person, to say nothing of those working in communities confronting heightened levels of adversity. Despite these challenges, so many helping professionals, myself included, feel drawn, even called to this work, finding it fulfilling in ways that seem unique to human services work. This pursuit can feel noble, genuine, and necessary, yet many of our social service systems in the United States, not unlike the United States itself, were built on principles and tenets that are oppressive, making the system inherently the same (Braveman et al., 2022; Brown & Homan, 2022). So where does that leave social workers and other human service professionals who want to do this work ethically, nobly, and in ways that honor anti-oppressive and trauma-informed principles? This is a question I continually grapple with and do not believe I have found (perhaps because it does not exist) a definitive answer that feels comforting. This

C. Krenn (✉)
Mental Health Services, The Door – A Center of Alternatives, New York, NY, USA
e-mail: c.krenn@nyu.edu

C. Tosone et al. (eds.), *Reframing Social Work with an Anti-Oppressive Lens*, Essential Clinical Social Work Series,
https://doi.org/10.1007/978-3-031-91391-4_19

question has evolved into an ongoing internal dialogue and unending reflective process.

In this chapter, I share some of my experiences doing social work in various social services sectors in New York City. I analyze these experiences, and their isolated and recurring patterns, to answer the following questions:

- What makes the current systems oppressive?
- What is the impact of these systems functioning the way they do?
- What role can and do social workers play in upholding or dismantling these systems?
- Where can practitioners go from here?

These are ambitious questions, and because much of this analysis will be rooted in personal experience and observations, and will likely not result in specific solutions, however, this chapter aims to provide some foundational understanding of these systems and encourage continued reflection and productive dialogue about the system's limitations, the impact of these challenges, and how to begin moving forward in ways that are anti-oppressive. The purpose of this chapter is to unpack oppressive practices, witnessed and experienced, to identify and discuss the potential for anti-oppressive alternatives. This chapter is about identifying icebergs. It will take ongoing and collective work to identify lifeboats.

Please note that all of the stories in this chapter are true, while names and identifying details of individuals and organizations have been changed or omitted to protect confidentiality. Some vignettes are based on individual cases; others are composites of collective experiences. All anecdotes aim to center the conversation around future-oriented improvements in anti-oppressive practice.

Self-Location

I identify as a White cisgender female. I grew up in a suburban community, in a German and Irish-Catholic family, and was raised by generations of educators. Following a calling I heard as a teenager, I went to public university to work toward my bachelor's in social work (BSW), where I first began working in the community with homeless youth. My education goals took me to New York City (NYC) where I obtained my master's degree (MSW) and social work license. In the decade and a half or so that I have been doing social work in and around NYC, I have worked in multiple sectors of the field including outpatient mental health, schools, child welfare, family shelter, and other homeless service systems. I believe my passion for my work stems from the example of my father and older siblings, all of whom work in various human service professional capacities. I am now a licensed clinical social worker, working primarily with people experiencing homelessness and/or housing instability in NYC. While obtaining my doctorate of social welfare at NYU, my work intently focused on researching and understanding the problems that people experience in these systems to potentially inform policy.

As the late writer and activist Audre Lorde declared, "Oppression and the intolerance of difference come[s] in all shapes... Among those of us who share the goals of liberation and a workable future for our children, there can be no hierarchies of oppression" (Lorde, 1983, p. 3). Social service organizations play a role in upholding the mechanisms of power imbalance in which certain groups have privilege and others do not. Commitment to anti-oppressive work is a continuous and conscious state. Every organization and person functioning within them (providing or receiving services) fall somewhere along the power-privilege continuum. This chapter serves as a personal exercise in evaluating my positionality on that continuum, as well as a reflective process concluding with a renewal of my commitment to being an agent for anti-oppressive advocacy and personal practice - and the encouragement of yours.

Anti-oppressive practice encompasses the principle of reflexivity, a demand that social workers continually contemplate the ways their own social identity and values affect the information they gather and how it informs their work (Burke & Harrison, 1998). This includes a worker's understanding of the social context, as experienced by them and those they work with. I believe doing this work effectively means applying this anti-oppressive principle regularly, with unwavering commitment to a constant awareness of one's identity, presentation, and the impact of each factor on the work and community being served. I extend this belief to my work in academia and will be applying the same efforts to my analysis and discussion of my experiences throughout this chapter.

Establishing Common Language

An "anti-oppressive approach" to practicing social work and human service is broadly understood as a dynamic, multi-disciplined theoretical framework that attempts to promote values of social justice and equality by challenging the power of oppression (Rogers, 2012; Dalrymple & Burke, 1995; Dominelli, 2003). This approach encompasses the essence of various critical frameworks including structural, feminist, and critical race theory, which challenge the social work profession to reconceptualize social services for historically excluded populations to center inclusion, social justice, and social change (Campbell, 2003; Abramovitz, 1998). With this understanding in mind, the term "anti-oppressive" will be used to refer to practices that embody these values espoused by these frameworks. In contrast, the term "oppressive" will be used to describe practices, actions, and structures that are antithetical to these values and ultimately subvert the humanity and progress of the client population in question. There is a considerable amount of literature about anti-oppressive approaches and practices which center clinical interventions and pedagogical concerns (Dominelli, 1998; Dalrymple & Burke, 1995), but it often overlooks the organizational domain (Strier & Binyamin, 2009). In their case for the fundamental restoration of the mission of social service organizations, Strier and Binyamin (2009) argue, "This flaw in anti-oppressive literature is of extreme importance for the simple reason that the implementation of anti-oppressive practice demands deep changes in the organizational structure and institutional culture of social services" (p. 5).

Organizational and Structural Factors

The Nonprofit Industrial Complex

Nonprofit and social welfare organizations are not immune to the larger structural issues, including the economy, national priorities, and values and changes in these (Peters, 2017). In the past few decades, there has been decreased public involvement in social welfare programs (INCITE!, 2007). In an effort to respond to this, nonprofit organizations have adapted to continue providing services, causing fundamental and functional problems and resulting in the emergence of what is described as the nonprofit industrial complex (NPIC) (Samimi, 2019). These nonprofit social service organizations struggle to secure funding from donors in a competitive market. Both those providing and receiving services often feel those who have the power to grant resources are out of touch and lack understanding of the work in ways that can adequately inform their highly influential decision-making. I have seen this in every organization I have worked within; clients and direct providers feel their needs are misunderstood by those in high-level leadership positions. A common sentiment often exists that the needs and humanity of those on the ground (clients and staff alike) are prioritized behind "meeting numbers" and "preparing for audits," oftentimes at the expense of someone feeling heard and seen in their struggle (McGann, 2022; Brodkin, 1997; Lewis, 1977).

Compounding this, many social service organizations are beholden to funders from multiple systems, whether foundation funders, managed care companies, private donors, board members, government, and others. There are auditing and documentation redundancies, all within antiquated technological (or physical) record-keeping systems that result in less time for direct service prioritization while increasing burnout and frustration (Poertner, 1985; Stalker & Harvey, 2002; Lloyd et al., 2002; LeCroy & Rank, 1987; Schepman & Zarate, 2008). I have consistently observed social workers who are inundated with documentation and paperwork demands, made more difficult by record-keeping systems that are outdated, lacking in the technological infrastructure to streamline these processes. The NYC shelter system, for example, still keeps paper charts, which can date back decades and are often physically mismanaged and disorganized because everyone involved in upkeeping them may be overworked, overwhelmed, and improperly or inadequately trained (Maguire, 2005; Ames, 1999; Cairns et al., 2018; Lloyd et al., 2002).

Organizational Missions and Values

Throughout my career I have worked at multiple organizations, and my enchantment with each organization always begins and ends the same way. I find myself feeling frustrated with my current and previous experiences, and then I learn of a new opportunity in a different organization and get excited by their mission and the values they espouse. Once working for them, the work gets off to a promising start, and I work there for some time before becoming exposed to the ways the practices contradict their mission and values, while the people in leadership roles do not see the reality of how the work is being done. The main reason I have left jobs is because once I was fully immersed in the work and saw the way it was being conducted, I did not see that the mission and values the organization espoused were consistent with the way services were provided. Earlier in my career, I believed that by becoming a leader internally, I could ensure the work is being performed in ways congruent with organizational values. However, I quickly learned that despite my leadership role, there were still supervisory entities beholden to pressures, budgetary demands, and other capitalistic justifications preventing social workers from being the agents of change we could be, if we could move with strategic intentionality. In addition, when I would actively work to fix this misalignment, I have been dismissed or, worse, discouraged from prioritizing the organizational values in authentic ways and even labeled as some version of a "troublemaker."

Policies and Policy Enforcement

One of the most prominent ways that oppressive professional behavior is enacted and justified within human service systems is through policies and procedures (Dominelli, 1996, 2003). In the helping professions, especially in the nonprofit sector, I have found that policies will often be pointed to as the metaphorical "bogeyman" who is to blame for why things are as they are. Policy is not always oppressive, and it could be argued that often, they are necessary; however, there are times in which a person's needs should supersede policy. These moments are hard to handle for many social workers, especially early career professionals, trying to acclimate to doing extremely difficult work within difficult systems. When policies are oppressive and there is no permission structure for employees to use their judgment when accessing resources outside of explicit policy, the result can be a disenfranchisement of communities of clients and a disempowerment of service providers (INCITE!, 2007; Bow & Buys, 2003).

One example of this is when a client arrives late or after hours, to a day program that provides food, claiming they are hungry. Despite the organization having food available, some of which may even go to waste, many social workers will feel beholden to policy and turn this person away. This can have negative effects on that client's trust in the organization, as well as on their connection and reliance on providers to understand and prioritize their basic human needs. Most importantly, this can leave a hungry person without food.

Oppressive policies are also enforced and justified in the name of safety. The work that social workers do requires a firm commitment to boundaries and limits that ensure structure and safety while concurrently embodying a compassionate approach that can be flexible to account for a person's humanity and presentation in their most challenging moments.

Safety

In this example, I have observed "safety" used to subvert services from someone in desperate need.

> I worked with a client who identified as a transgender woman of color, who left an abusive home as a young person and has been struggling with homelessness and substance use for most of her life. She had been in and out of carceral systems, almost always placed in male prisons due to the sex she was assigned at birth, resulting in extensive physical and sexual assault by other inmates. This is a person with complex trauma who has spent most of her life fighting for her safety. Further, this is a person who has learned through her lived experiences that navigating discriminatory systems and interactions with prejudiced individuals will often leave her without her basic needs met; therefore, she must find alternative ways to meet her basic needs, including food and shelter. This conditioning can result in maladaptive strategies to meet these needs. Furthermore, she may present with behavior indicative of a trauma response that needs to be understood by professionals through the framework of how her current and past experiences inform her presenting state and behavior.
>
> This client was denied food after program hours. Upon becoming frustrated, she became dysregulated, shouting profanity and "threatening staff." The following day, this client was banned from the program citing "safety concerns." This is a person whose involvement in the program was a direct result of their need for support meeting their basic human needs and desire to develop alternative behavioral responses for moments of stress and frustration, like unfortunate food denial. When we, as the trained professionals poised to help, are quick to dismiss and even ban individuals most in need, our actions are not informed by anti-oppressive values and practices.

An irony within the enactment of oppressive policies is how common it is that little infrastructure exists to ensure safety and quality of service provision. For example, organizations I have worked for have lacked adequate space for assessments to be conducted in confidential ways, little or no procedure or guidelines for client risk assessment and subsequent safety planning, including response to sexual assault, gender-based violence, sexual harassment, suicidality, and so on. These necessary investments are often overlooked and deprioritized while trying to accomplish whatever metrics may be needed to protect the flow of funding (INCITE!, 2007; Perlmutter, 2006). In practice, once again, quality and safety can be compromised, even while "keeping the lights on" to continue providing services (INCITE!, 2007).

The Impact on Individuals

Failure of Policy Enactment

This example demonstrates a scenario in which even when the appropriate infrastructure is in place and clients have gotten approval through often slow-moving and archaic systems, a policy can still be oppressive in execution.

> When I was supervising mental health support services in a transitional family shelter, one resident, a single mother of a medically fragile son, had applied and received approval for a special accommodation to have a humidifier in her unit for her son's asthma. She provided medical documentation to her case manager and the Department of Homeless Services (DHS), and it had been approved and documented in our on-site case records and in the electronic records system. One evening, a staff member conducted an inspection of this family's unit and confiscated the humidifier. The client was not present during the inspection and was therefore unable to advocate for themselves. This staff person did not do their duty in checking for approval before assuming the humidifier was contraband. By the time the client had returned to the residence, they were rightfully distraught that their personal property had been removed without their knowledge and their son would not have the medically necessary equipment to sleep safely that night.

The fallout from this circumstance resulted in a breach of trust and client safety. The client filed a police report stating the item was stolen by the facility staff. The client then organized protests of the shelter in the community. Instances like these have been observed to have lasting impact on attachment and relational capacity with service providers and any potential relational endeavor in the future (Bow & Buys, 2003; Deegan, 2000; Freire, 1970). Anti-oppressive practice needs to be reflected not only in how policies are constructed and written but also in how they are implemented and enacted.

Unjust Structural Policy

This example reflects the discouragement that comes when fighting against oppressive policies that no amount of advocacy seems to impact.

> This family of five was living in a transitional family shelter. The family consisted of a grandmother, her adult son, and three young grandchildren. On top of the family residing in the shelter, making their best attempts to find permanent housing, the adult son was agonizingly ill and needed a vital organ transplant. Our team immediately tried to find the quickest way to get our client on an organ donor list, collaborating with medical providers and searching for organizational resources to support them. We learned that organ donations are not provided to people living in shelters because it is not considered a suitable environment for recovery. Logically, I could understand that rationale, for these facilities were high risk even for the healthiest of people. After sitting with the information, however, I became irate; getting selected from a transplant list is harrowing enough, but to know that even if our client was selected, he could be passed over for no other reason than because he lived in our facility. For more context, the grandmother had an undocumented immigration status, making the application process to anything (e.g., jobs, apartments, supportive housing, etc.)

> extremely difficult. Additionally, with her son dangerously ill, the responsibilities of childcare and generating income were simultaneously falling on the grandmother. Our team advocated daily to anyone in the organization we could reach—often to no avail or without a response. Upon further advocacy, things only became more complicated; nowhere in DHS or various medical systems' policies could I find a written declaration that living in a shelter was an immediate disqualifier for a patient; however, different transplant programs had different standards, and different transplant teams could disqualify individual candidates on a situational means, such as shelter residency (United Network for Organ Sharing, 2023). While our team persisted in our research and advocacy, our client's condition worsened until he passed away.

This loss was one of the most excruciating of my career, largely because I felt, and ultimately was, powerless. My voice was unable to reach the oppressive enactment of a policy or a lack of policy, and despite the frequency or decibel at which I shouted, this inability to cut through the bureaucracy in these systems would be the reason this man lost his life, that his children would lose their father, and this resilient family already facing so much would be further plunged into turmoil, likely to have ripple effects for generations.

Impacts Far and Wide

Decisions on how to carry out policies can have an impact that goes far beyond the individual or the short term. The ways in which organizations choose to execute policies can have a broader impact on the societal functioning of clients. I experienced this firsthand during the 2020 census-taking process:

> While working as a supervisor in a transitional family shelter, I volunteered to support the census-taking process in our shelters. I was motivated to do this seeing how fraught our community was with disinformation about the census taking process, exacerbated by the Trump administration's political tactic to discourage people with an insecure immigration status from completing it. Research indicates that although the citizenship question was not included on the 2020 Census, the odds of responding to the census after the citizenship question announcement were 20% lower than the odds of those responding before the announcement (Walejko et al., 2020).
>
> After communicating with multiple people within the organization, including high-level members of executive leadership, I learned that the organization had been awarded a grant, and a number of iPads, for staff to do data collection activities, including manually supporting clients with filling out the US census online. This was a welcome resource; however, my team was already overworked, under-resourced, and at high risk of contracting COVID-19 due to the nature of our work and our daily commutes on public transportation. I became curious if there were other, more efficient, accurate, and effective ways to collect this information. I began communicating with multiple people at the US Census Bureau Office and learned we were able to report our internal daily census data for the purposes of the US census to ensure accuracy and efficiency. Shelter staff are required to report a daily point-in-time (PIT) count, intended to provide a "snapshot" of shelter occupancy in a given single 24-h period (Continuum of Care Homeless Assistance Programs Homeless Populations and Subpopulations, 2022). This seemed like the perfect solution. I was thrilled to share what I had learned with leadership and eager to ensure my staff did not have to put themselves at

further risk. I was devastated when leadership replied that they were aware we could communicate the information directly but were choosing a manual option because doing so helped them procure the grant and we were thus obligated to utilize the iPads in this specific way.

I began asking general questions about who had been consulted about the feasibility of this, what planning had been done to ensure the support of our monolingual Spanish-speaking clients, what training about not only the electronic census platform but also how to ensure client confidentiality when filling out the form, and what would be done to ensure the health and safety of all of the folks interacting closely (and arguably unnecessarily) throughout this process (Lindenthal et al., 1988). I was perhaps the first person who had any involvement with direct services to be a part of this conversation, so none of these factors seemed to have been considered.

This example demonstrates not only an injustice in how clients are supported, or how an already burnt-out staff was further pressed upon to accomplish risky tasks outside their already demanding daily responsibilities, but this shows how policies and their faulty execution contribute to the continued oppression of people living in shelter systems. The information gathered by the census generates demographic profiles of communities, allocates seats in the House of Representatives, redraws districts, and provides crucial programs and services for US citizens (Berry-James et al., 2020). A fair and accurate census is crucial to help states and local officials make important decisions based on the data they receive through census reports. What is more, the 2020 Census was slated to be used to enforce federal civil rights laws and monitor compliance with antidiscrimination laws (Khan et al., 2018). The housing-insecure population is often politically overlooked, their needs and ultimately humanity often dismissed. As a result of census undercounting, districts with more shelters and therefore greater homeless populations are underrepresented and under-resourced, resulting in the needs of the homeless population going unmet. Despite the availability and viability of a process with far less error potential, like the direct reporting of the PIT numbers to the US Census Bureau, the organization opted for a manual option with great cost to their human capital, all in the name of protecting procured funding.

It is reasonable to assume that the data collection was fraught with gaps and many people were unreachable or unwilling to engage with shelter staff to fill out the census, resulting in the perpetuation of the challenges faced by this population above articulated census-taking problem with this population, even while the organization had an opportunity to report more accurate data that could have translated into increased resources. (Snipp, 2003; Sullivan 2020; Elliott et al., 2019). These competing demands to secure operating funds for human service organizations can sometimes undermine the broader mission of meeting community needs.

There may be room to criticize my characterization of the policies and their enactment in these vignettes; however, these are my lived experiences with these policy enactments and how they impacted my clients and my experiences as someone working to help. I submit that it is noteworthy that I have been in various leadership capacities and still had these experiences.

Under-resourcing

The concern of under-resourcing is rampant throughout the human service sector (INCITE!, 2007; Kimes, 2016; Lizano et al., 2014). Examples of this were simplified during the height of the pandemic when it was made clear to the public that the very health professionals risking their lives to care for our global community did not have adequate availability or quality of protective material (Satiani et al., 2020; Azizi et al., 2021). Just as this was true for medical professionals, the scarcity was as present for those working in other human service sectors, coming in close contact with people, in a shelter, for instance (Jeckler et al., 2020; Guasti, 2020; Carver et al., 2022).

Culturally Competent Staffing Practices

The examples presented reflect how a scarcity of resources impacts the service landscape and can uphold oppressive systems and policies that result in negative outcomes. An omnipresent reality in human services is a lack of adequate staffing and, more specifically, a lack of Spanish/English bilingual (SEB) social workers. This has been a constant reality in organizations I have worked with. Bilingual social workers are in high demand, particularly in larger metropolitan areas made up of high Latinx populations (Fitzhugh Mullan Institute for Health Workforce Equity, 2020). There is an undeniable disparity between the demographics of social work professionals and the demographics of many of the communities we serve (NASW, 2015). An estimated 12%–14% of social workers identify as Hispanic or Latinx (Fitzhugh Mullan Institute for Health Workforce Equity, 2020). These data do not specify the linguistic abilities of these professionals. Within the last decade, the Latinx population in the United States has increased by 23% (Jones et al., 2021), a rate that promises to far outpace the rate at which social work schools are producing bilingual social workers (Cordero & Negroni, 2013).

Without access to bilingual service providers, culturally competent social services cannot be fully achieved. Obtaining linguistically appropriate service providers for non-English speaking clients is a vital component of providing quality services in anti-oppressive ways. When a client is unable to benefit from, or even understand, the services being provided to them due to a language barrier, it is arguably impossible for them to fully benefit from those efforts (Olcoń et al., 2018). Emphasis must be placed on attracting and retaining quality social workers at large, particularly those who are bilingual or multilingual. In my experience, organizations often have little or no recruitment efforts specifically targeting bilingual practitioners. Furthermore, there is often very little incentive offered for this specialized skill set (e.g., a stipend or salary modification to account for the skill and potential additional work this person will do).

What is more, bilingual practitioners are often asked and expected to carry more than their share of caseloads, groups, and other responsibilities because they may be the only or one of few persons able to support this subset of the community. This can increase the likelihood of burnout, job dissatisfaction, and turnover, having devastating effects on the community being served and program/service functionality in general (Engstrom & Min, 2004). Note the following anecdote:

> I have had to manage a short-staffed team where the entire limited English language client population was being served by only one social worker. This social worker was a strong advocate and requested the expedited hiring of another bilingual worker to support the community. Eager to move forward on this request, I began searching for specific forums to target my recruitment efforts, activating my network, and doing research on the current job market. I discovered that we were offering a wage that was significantly below the market salary for a bilingual social worker in NYC. I advocated for an increased salary, consistent with the market rates, and was swiftly denied based on budget constraints. Despite my best efforts, it was not long thereafter that our lone bilingual social worker notified me of their resignation, citing burnout and the lack of any prospects for additional support. For the following months, our Spanish-speaking clients were left without the benefit of a social worker who spoke their language, significantly compromising on the quality of service they were able to receive.

A Path Forward

Organizations should invest in a full review of policies and procedures from charters and board bylaws, to ensure practices are anti-oppressive and account for the humanity of all community members, especially clients. The organization should institutionalize anti-oppressive training for all, and if managers do not have human services backgrounds, they should be required to be trained in the foundational values and practices within human services. Direct service providers should be trained and empowered to apply policies flexibly, as needed to accommodate the humanity of clients (e.g., providing food after program hours). Record-keeping systems should be updated to allow providers to easily track and store client information securely and to avoid creating relational ruptures and retraumatization (e.g., special accommodation approvals). Organizations should have clear and accessible policies regarding interdisciplinary system work that expedite provider understanding and advocacy when it comes to meeting client needs (e.g., organ transplant policies). Finally, organizations should respect the expertise and experiences of staff and, in fact, partner with direct service professionals to find solutions to organizational problems. Organizations should respect and appropriately reward specialized skill sets in ways that do not create inequitable workloads as in the case of bilingual social worker shortages that result in larger workloads without additional compensation.

One way to begin making progress on these issues is to intentionally support the advancement of social workers into leadership roles (Adams, 2019; Bliss et al., 2014; Brilliant, 1986; Lawler, 2007; Mosley & Smith, 2018; Rank & Hutchison,

2000; Sullivan, 2016). Research indicates that leaders with social work training are more highly rated in both organizational factors and transformational leadership (Choy-Brown et al., 2020). Social workers make strong leaders not only because of the transferability of social work skills to leadership roles but also because their management and organizational priorities are informed by the experience of having been service providers. Research has shown that physician-run hospitals score 25% higher than manager-run hospitals in the top 100 hospital rankings (Goodall, 2011). We can hypothesize that a similar impact could occur in a study of social workers who manage social service programs and agencies.

Without upward mobility and leadership opportunities, organizations risk losing loyal and talented social workers who have leadership ambitions (Santora & Sarros, 2001). Organizations risk social workers losing their commitment and enthusiasm for the mission while increasing resentment and negative attitudes that have adverse effects on their service outcomes (Santora & Sarros, 2001). This in turn increases the likelihood of turnover, not only eliminating quality candidates for leadership but also creating perpetual turmoil in service provision with a revolving door of dissatisfied providers.

Investing in social workers in leadership positions could potentially influence problematic policies and execution of such. Leadership strategy and priorities informed by a clear understanding and experience with direct service could impact overall regard for leadership decisions, faith in leadership strategy, morale as it regards social work career advancement, and most importantly more anti-oppressive and humane attitudes woven into the fabric of every organizational output, from reforming and creating policy, to budgetary prioritization, to resource allocation, to hiring practices, to training and managerial supports that emphasize anti-oppressive practice, and so much more.

Conclusion

This chapter only encompasses some of the ways in which these systems can do harm to themselves and those they serve. I would like to place final emphasis on a few observable patterns working within systems that uphold oppressive practices. Rigid policies and procedures can cause devastating harm when not co-occurring with opportunity to make allowances for individual circumstances. Although necessary in many cases, metric-driven outcomes can cause a lack of focus on humanity in human service work and refocus on the accomplishment of tasks for the sake of doing them, not necessarily serving the clients' needs (INCITE!, 2007; Rodríguez, 2007; Pérez, 2007). As demonstrated in the discussion and examples throughout this chapter, these concerns have the potential to result in service dissatisfaction, client disengagement, negative health outcomes, retraumatization, the furthering of attachment concerns, and even death. A lack of emphasis on social work values and those who work through them has an impact at every level, from the scarcity of leadership opportunities for people with service backgrounds to an under-appreciation for those doing the work. These concerns have the potential to result in employee dissatisfaction, burnout, turnover, and more, which, in turn, has a cyclical effect on client progress, relationships, well-being, and more, serving once again to preserve their status in their oppressed state.

Burke and Harrison aptly state, "As social work practitioners, we have a moral, ethical and legal responsibility to challenge inequality and disadvantage" (p. 131). Organizational adaptation to incorporate anti-oppressive values and rework decades-old systems that were predicated on discriminatory intent will not be an easy or simple task. It is my belief that a coordinated, multidimensional effort that incorporates people within and outside of organizations would be necessary to see meaningful systemic change. This would require massive amounts of buy-in to the tenets of anti-oppressive practice and a willingness to challenge the status quo and much of the experiential expertise many pride themselves on having attained. This would require bilateral brainstorming and intervention crafting from both the "top-down" and the "bottom-up." If this were to be accomplished, this would also require a continuous systemic maintenance and regularly renewed commitment to the principles of anti-oppressive practice. This change, and the idea of this as a call to action, is ambitious, to put it mildly, but as necessary as anything that ever was.

Reflection Questions

1. Are anti-oppressive practices workable within the nonprofit human services sector as it currently exists?
2. What changes would be necessary to allow for more anti-oppressive practices?
3. Within the system as it exists, what can social workers do to contribute to meaningful change?
4. What agency does the social worker have in holding the client and community's needs as paramount?

References

Abramovitz, M. (1998). Social work and social reform: An arena of struggle. *Social work, 43*(6), 512–526.

Adams, D. R. (2019). Social work's role in collaborative community–academic partnerships: How our past informs our future. *Social Work, 64*(1), 19–28.

Ames, N. (1999). Social work recording: A new look at an old issue. *Journal of Social Work Education, 35*(2), 227–237.

Azizi, M. R., Atlasi, R., Ziapour, A., Abbas, J., & Naemi, R. (2021). Innovative human resource management strategies during the COVID-19 pandemic: A systematic narrative review approach. *Heliyon, 7*(6).

Berry-James, R. M., Gooden, S. T., & Johnson, R. G., III. (2020). Civil rights, social equity, and census 2020. *Public Administration Review, 80*(6), 1100–1108.

Bliss, D. L., Pecukonis, E., & Snyder-Vogel, M. (2014). Principled leadership development model for aspiring social work managers and administrators: Development and application. *Human Service Organizations Management, Leadership & Governance, 38*(1), 5–15. https://doi.org/10.1080/03643107.2013.853008

Bow, V., & Buys, E. (2003). Sense of community and place attachment: The natural environment plays a vital role in developing a sense of community. In *Social Change in the 21st Century 2003 Conference Refereed Proceedings* (pp. 1–18). Centre for Social Change Research, School of Humanities and Human Services QUT.

Braveman, P. A., Arkin, E., Proctor, D., Kauh, T., & Holm, N. (2022). Systemic and structural racism: Definitions, examples, health damages, and approaches to dismantling. *Health Affairs, 41*(2), 171–178. https://doi.org/10.1377/hlthaff.2021.01394

Brilliant, E. L. (1986). Social work leadership: A missing ingredient? *Social Work, 31*(5), 325–331.

Brodkin, E. Z. (1997). Inside the welfare contract: Discretion and accountability in state welfare administration. *Social Service Review, 71*(1), 1–33.

Brown, T., & Homan, P. (2022). Structural racism and health stratification in the US: Connecting theory to measurement.

Burke, B., & Harrison, P. (1998). Anti-oppressive practice. *Social work: Themes, issues and critical debates*, 229–239.

Cairns, I., Jonas, M., & Wallis, K. (2018). The ethics of sharing: How do social workers decide what to record in shared health records? *Ethics and Social Welfare, 12*(4), 348–369.

Campbell, C. (2003). Anti-oppressive theory and practice as the organizing theme for social work education: The case in favour. *Canadian Social Work Review/Revue Canadienne de Service Social, 20*(1), 121–125. http://www.jstor.org/stable/41670001

Carver, H., Price, T., Falzon, D., McCulloch, P., & Parkes, T. (2022). Stress and wellbeing during the COVID-19 pandemic: A mixed-methods exploration of frontline homelessness services staff experiences in Scotland. *International Journal of Environmental Research and Public Health, 19*(6), 3659.

Choy-Brown, M., Stanhope, V., Wackstein, N., & Cole, H. D. (2020). Do social workers lead differently? Examining associations with leadership style and organizational factors. *Human Service Organizations, Management, Leadership & Governance, 44*(4), 332–342. https://doi.org/10.1080/23303131.2020.1767744

Cordero, A. E., & Negroni, L. K. (2013). Leadership development for Latino community emancipation: An integrative approach in social work education. *Advances in Social Work, 14*(1), 102–124.

Council on Social Work Education. (2010). Diversity, critical multiculturalism, and oppression: Interaction and transformation. *Final report on activity connected to the CSWE sponsored diversity conversations.* Retrieved from http://www.cswe.org/File.aspx?id=44654

Council on Social Work Education. (2017). *Profile on the social work workforce*. Retrieved from https://www.socialworkers.org/LinkClick.aspx?fileticket=wCttjrHq0gE%3D&portalid=0

Council on Social Work Education. (2018). *New social workers results of the nationwide survey of 2017 social work graduates. The national social work workforce study*. Retrieved from https://www.socialworkers.org/LinkClick.aspx?fileticket=C0r5P1zkMbQ%3d&portalid=0

Council on Social Work Education. (2020). *The social work profession: Findings from three years of surveys of new social workers*. Retrieved from https://www.cswe.org/CSWE/media/Workforce-Study/The-Social-Work-Profession-Findings-from-Three-Years-of-Surveys-of-New-Social-Workers-Dec-2020.pdf

Council on Social Work Education. (2022). *Educational policy and accreditation standards for baccalaureate and master's social work programs*. Retrieved from https://www.cswe.org/getmedia/94471c42-13b8-493b-9041-b30f48533d64/2022-EPAS.pdf

Dalrymple, J., & Burke, B. (1995). *Anti oppressive practice social care and the law*. Open University Press.

Deegan, P. E. (2000). Spirit breaking: When the helping professions hurt. *The Humanistic Psychologist, 28*(1–3), 194–209.

Dominelli, L. (1996). Deprofessionalizing social work: Anti-oppressive practice, competencies and postmodernism. *The British Journal of Social Work, 26*(2), 153–175.
Dominelli, L. (1998). Anti-oppressive practice in context. Social work: Themes, issues and critical debates, 3–22.
Dominelli, L. (2003). *Anti-oppressive social work theory and practice*. Palgrave.
Elliott, D., Santos, R., Martin, S., & Runes, C. (2019). *Assessing miscounts in the 2020 census*. Urban Institute.
Engstrom, D., & Min, J. W. (2004). Perspectives of bilingual social workers: "You just have to do a lot more for them". *Journal of Ethnic & Cultural Diversity in Social Work, 13*(1), 59–82.
Fitzhugh Mullan Institute for Health Workforce Equity. The George Washington University. (2020). *The social work profession findings from three years of surveys of new social workers*. https://www.cswe.org/CSWE/media/Workforce-Study/The-Social-Work-Profession-Findings-from-Three-Years-of-Surveys-of-New-Social-Workers-Dec-2020.pdf
Freire, P. (1970). *Pedagogy of the oppressed*. Penguin Classics.
Freire, P. (2017). *Pedagogy of the oppressed*. Penguin Classics.
Goodall, A. H. (2011). Physician-leaders and hospital performance: Is there an association? *Social Science & Medicine, 73*(4), 535–539.
Guasti, N. (2020). The plight of essential workers during the COVID-19 pandemic. *Lancet, 395*(10237), 1587.
HUD 2022 Continuum of Care Homeless Assistance Programs Homeless Populations and Subpopulations. (2022). In *HUD exchange*. US Department of Housing and Urban Development. https://files.hudexchange.info/reports/published/CoC_PopSub_NatlTerrDC_2022.pdf
INCITE! (2007). *The revolution will not be funded: Beyond the non-profit industrial complex*. South End Press.
Jecker, N. S., Wightman, A. G., & Diekema, D. S. (2020). Prioritizing frontline workers during the COVID-19 pandemic. *The American Journal of Bioethics, 20*(7), 128–132.
Jones, N., Marks, M., Ramirez, R., & Ríos-Vargas, M. (2021, August 12). *2020 Census illuminates racial and ethnic composition of the country*. https://www.census.gov/library/stories/2021/08/improved-race-ethnicity-measures-reveal-united-states-population-much-more-multiracial.html
Khan, S., Goldvale, C., & Dutta-Gipta, I. (2018). *Why a fair and accurate census matters to thriving private and public sectors*. Washington, DC: The Leadership Conference Education Fund, Center on Poverty and Inequality, Georgetown Law. Retrieved from http://civilrightsdocs.info/pdf/census/2020/Census-Matters-Private-Public-Sectors.pdf
Kimes, A. T. (2016). *Burnout rates among social workers: A systematic review and synthesis*.
Lawler, J. (2007). Leadership in social work: A case of caveat emptor? *British Journal of Social Work, 37*(1), 123–141.
LeCroy, C. W., & Rank, M. R. (1987). Factors associated with burnout in the social services: An exploratory study. *Journal of Social Service Research, 10*(1), 23–39.
Lewis, V. S. (1977). *The challenges of numbers*.
Lindenthal, J. J., Jordan, T. J., Lentz, J. D., & Thomas, C. S. (1988). Social workers' management of confidentiality. *Social Work, 33*(2), 157–158. https://doi.org/10.1093/sw/33.2.157
Lizano, E. L., Hsiao, H. Y., Barak, M. E. M., & Casper, L. M. (2014). Support in the workplace: Buffering the deleterious effects of work-family conflict on child welfare workers' well-being and job burnout. *Journal of Social Service Research, 40*(2), 178–188. https://doi.org/10.1080/01488376.2013.875093
Lloyd, C., King, R., & Chenoweth, L. (2002). Social work, stress and burnout: A review. *Journal of Mental Health, 11*(3), 255–265.
Lorde, A. (1983). There is no hierarchy of oppression. *Interracial Books for Children Bulletin, 14*(3/4), 9.
Maguire, R. (2005). Lessons learned from implementing an electronic records management system. *Records Management Journal, 15*(3), 150–157. https://doi.org/10.1108/09565690510632337

McGann, M. (2022). Meeting the numbers: Performance politics and welfare-to-work at the street-level. *Irish Journal of Sociology, 30*(1), 69–89.
Mosley, J. E., & Smith, S. R. (2018). Human service agencies and the question of impact: Lessons for theory, policy, and practice. *Human Service Organizations: Management, Leadership & Governance, 42*(2), 113–122.
National Association of Social Workers [NASW]. (2015). *NASW standards and indicators for cultural competence in social work practice.* Retrieved from https://www.socialworkers.org/LinkClick.aspx?fileticket=7dVckZAYUmk%3d&portalid=0
Olcoń, K., Pantell, M., & Sund, A. C. (2018). Recruitment and retention of Latinos in social work education: Building on students' community cultural wealth. *Journal of Social Work Education, 54*(2), 349–363.
Pérez, A. H. Sisters in Action for Power. (2007). *Between radical theory and community praxis: Reflections on organizing and the non-profit industrial complex* (pp. 91–99).
Perlmutter, F. D. (2006). Ensuring social work administration. *Administration in Social Work, 30*(2), 3–10.
Peters, S. C. (2017). Social work leadership: An analysis of historical and contemporary challenges. *Human Service Organizations: Management, Leadership & Governance, 41*(4), 336–345.
Poertner, J. (1985). Purchase of service and accountability: Will they ever meet? *Administration in Social Work, 9*(1), 57–66.
Rank, M. G., & Hutchison, W. S. (2000). An analysis of leadership within the social work profession. *Journal of Social Work Education, 36*(3), 487–502.
Rodríguez, D. (2007). *The political logic of the non-profit industrial complex. The revolution will not be funded: Beyond the non-profit industrial complex.* IW o. CA Violence.
Rogers, J. (2012). Anti-oppressive social work research: Reflections on power in the creation of knowledge. *Social Work Education, 31*(7), 866–879. https://doi.org/10.1080/02615479.2011.602965
Samimi, J. C. (2019). Funding America's nonprofits: The nonprofit industrial complex's hold on social justice. *Columbia Social Work Review, 8*(1), 17–25. https://doi.org/10.7916/cswr.v8i1.1967
Santora, J. C., & Sarros, J. C. (2001). CEO succession in nonprofit community-based organizations: Is there room for insiders at the top? *Career Development International, 6*(2), 107–111. https://doi.org/10.1108/13620430110383429
Satiani, B., Zigrang, T. A., & Bailey-Wheaton, J. L. (2020). COVID-19 financial resources for physicians. *Journal of Vascular Surgery, 72*(4), 1161–1165.
Schepman, S. B., & Zarate, M. A. (2008). The relationship between burnout, negative affectivity and organizational citizenship behavior for human services employees. *International Journal of Humanities and Social Sciences, 2*(4), 242–247.
Snipp, C. M. (2003). Racial measurement in the American census: Past practices and implications for the future. *Annual Review of Sociology, 29*(1), 563–588. https://doi.org/10.1146/annurev.soc.29.010202.100006
Stalker, C., & Harvey, C. (2002). *Professional Burnout in social service organizations: A review of theory, research and prevention.*
Strier, R., & Binyamin S. (2009) Developing anti-oppressive services for the poor: A theoretical and organisational rationale. *British Journal of Social Work*, 1–19. https://doi.org/10.1093/bjsw/bcp122
Sullivan, W. P. (2016). Leadership in social work: Where are we? *Journal of Social Work Education, 52*(September), S51–S61.
Sullivan, T. A. (2020). Coming to our census: How social statistics underpin our democracy (and republic). *Harvard Data Science Review, 2*(1).
United Network for Organ Sharing (UNOS). (2023). *Frequently asked questions: Facts about organ donation.* https://unos.org/transplant/frequently-asked-questions/
Walejko, G., Kriz, B., García Trejo, Y. A., Sandoval Girón, A., Evans, S., & Bates, N. (2020). Use of exact matching to examine media's effect on intended behavior the case of the addition of the 2020 census citizenship question. *Public Opinion Quarterly, 84*(4), 1000–1013.

Chapter 20
The Future of Social Work: Responding to Organizational Workplace Needs

Grace Cosachov Protos

Positionality Statement

This author writes from the perspective of a first-generation American, white woman of Latino heritage who has been a leader in the public, private, and higher education sectors and who has worked to address working women's workforce challenges. Her professional experience is informed by many years of grassroots-level work to understand systemic workforce issues that challenge and impact working women, particularly women of color. In an effort to collectively advance solutions for working women, she directed regional coalitions around the United States, with a variety of political and local leaders and voices in the community. These professional experiences inform her perspective on the lack of government and employer support and the interrelated systems that contribute to oppressive structures for working individuals. Much of her work has been informed by data and lived experiences. This knowledge has helped direct her work toward advocating for systemic change to improve work force environments. She now leads an office at a major global university where her goals include addressing individual and organizational workplace well-being and health.

Workforce and Societal Changes

The workforce in the United States has changed significantly within the last 60 years. Some of these changes include an increase in the number of women participating in the paid workforce. In the 1960s women represented 37% of the labor

G. C. Protos (✉)
Work Life, Office of the Provost, New York University, New York, NY, USA
e-mail: gc495@nyu.edu

C. Tosone et al. (eds.), *Reframing Social Work with an Anti-Oppressive Lens*, Essential Clinical Social Work Series,
https://doi.org/10.1007/978-3-031-91391-4_20

force (BLS, 2017) compared with today's labor participation of over 57% (BLS, 2021). Approximately 75% of working women today are parenting children under the age of 18 (USDOLWB, 2022), and 41% are the sole or co-income earners for their families (CAP, 2019). There has been an increase in dual-income families, single-family homes headed by women, adult caregiving responsibilities, and the growing "sandwich generation," caring for young children and elderly parents (Miller, 1981). These significant labor force changes have challenged employers' understanding of employee needs, and despite major efforts by organizations to address workplace and employee issues, there continues to be an insufficient response to current-day worker issues.

Momentous societal changes have also taken place, most notably rapid advances in technology blurring the boundaries between employer work expectations and employee work-life integration (Waller & Ragsdell, 2012), an aging workforce, multi-generations working together for the first time, and continued growth of immigrant populations participating in the paid economy (BLS, 2017; see also BLS, 2021; CAP, 2019).

The effects of these changes without correlated societal systemic improvements have resulted in increased employee mental health issues, increased stress (Gallup, 2022), disengagement with work, and employees being burdened by caregiving responsibilities with little attention to their own well-being. This can be seen in the increased cost of good-quality, affordable childcare and the discrepancy between the school day and workday hours (Christensen et al., 2011). These hardships have resulted in workers demanding greater support to improve work-life integration. At the same time, organizations have been challenged to recruit, engage, and retain workers, having consequential financial impact. Despite the challenges with work and personal environments and the negative impacts to both employers and employees, organizations have not adequately responded to and have been ill-equipped to expediently address evolving needs.

To better understand existing gaps between what workers need and what is currently offered by employers, it is important to look at the historical evolution of social work and how workplace challenges have been addressed. Focusing on social betterment, the early years of social work began in the early twentieth century through volunteer work, which was recognized as a profession by 1930, when it started focusing on poverty and other social issues facing children and families. After the Great Depression and World War II, there was demand for the profession to refocus on mental health and issues related to veteran support (Stuart, 2019). By the mid-1940s, the emergence of employee assistance programs appeared in large companies looking to address alcoholism and mental health of their employees (Trice & Schonbrunn, 1981). By the mid 1950s the National Association of Social Workers (NASW) was established and created its first Code of Ethics for the profession. In the ensuing decades, the profession developed state-specific requirements and clinical exams leading to different levels of licensure for social workers, including advanced exams for master's degrees and requiring 2–3 years of clinical supervision (Dyeson, 2004). During this decade, the Kennedy Presidential Administration started the Action for Mental Health to address the carceral system, anti-delinquency of youth, poverty, the war on drugs, mental health, and other social issues. This expansion of social government services had a direct impact on the profession and led social workers to incorporate advocacy work, including political advocacy, policy planning, and administration of organizations and programs, and to develop the skill of coalition building (Stuart, 2019). Simultaneously, casework with individuals and families was expanded and rooted itself in psychosocial treatment approaches that understood human behavior and social and environmental factors (González & Gelman, 2015).

By 1998 the profession celebrated its first centennial which included the establishment of training programs, standards, licensing laws, and the Council on Social Work Education (CSWE), an accrediting body for social work education at the bachelor's and master's level. Throughout the more than 100 years of professional recognition, social workers have worked in settlement houses, charity organizations, agencies, and companies all while focusing on social welfare and justice.

While the social work profession was attending to social justice and mental health issues in communities, the workplace was trying to find ways to resolve challenges related to the management of employees (Obedgiu, 2017). In the early twentieth century, the nature of the relationship between employee and employer began to change, influenced by the inception of the Industrial Revolution. Initial workplace challenges included unsafe working conditions and unfair labor practices, often resulting in violent outbursts of employee resistance, walkouts, and strikes. As a result, companies started to focus on the betterment of the employer and employee relationship by aligning the management of people to business strategy and creating personnel management departments. This departmental role continued to evolve into the late twentieth century impacted by increased national challenges related to gender and racial discrimination, as well as the passage of the Civil Rights Act of 1964 and the Equal Employment Opportunity Act. Thus, the human resources' professional role became an enforcer of rules to avoid legal ramifications for companies (Pophal, n.d.). Today, the role continues to oversee the management of necessary employment laws while driving the focus of competitive advantage for organizations. Some of the main areas of focus include the employee experience such as recruitment, training and development, performance management, compensation, and benefits.

Insufficient Workforce Support

Exacerbating current workplace and employee issues are the lack of federal policies supporting employee needs. The United States is one of the only developed countries that does not offer a policy supporting paid leave for employees that need time off for the care of others or themselves (Pew Research Center, 2019). There is no federal earned sick day policy or universal childcare support. Without federal support, a small number of states and cities have passed their own paid leave and earned sick day policies for workers; however, these policies are limited, and while they offer job-protected leave, they may not fully compensate an individual's salary for time off. The lack of federally supportive policies essential for the needs of today's labor force places increased responsibility and urgency on employers to address these issues with a variety of supportive interventions by better understanding both the systems within which we live and work and the needs of workers.

Adding to the urgency of addressing workplace stressors, there have been a number of recent social developments that have resulted in increased personal and workplace stress including racial and social justice tension, tumultuous local and global politics, and increases in economic instability. The COVID-19 global pandemic added concerns to our already challenged work environment that are still affecting the workplace. Issues such as long COVID, grief, trauma, depression, and isolation contribute to the increased level of mental health issues and workplace burnout experienced today. According to a Gallup 2022 survey, the level of stress experienced by workers has continued to rise since 2009 (Gallup, 2022).

Post-Pandemic Workplace: Employer and Employee Challenges

The post-pandemic work environment has changed how and where work gets done by allowing employees to either be fully remote or work a hybrid schedule. This most recent change has made necessary a new set of supervisory skills focused on the employee-manager relationship (McKinsey, 2021) and has shifted the organizing of work and management of employees. Managers that are not skilled to address these new ways of working have left employees feeling disconnected and have negatively impacted the culture and climate of the workplace.

According to a Gallup survey comparing levels of engagement from 2020 to 2022, there has been a continued decline in employee engagement with highest declines in engagement among employees working fully remote jobs. The survey looked at workplace engagement elements such as clear communication of work expectations, recognition, autonomy, and connection to the mission and purpose of the organization, all of which are important for employee satisfaction (Gallup, 2022). Attributable to the decline in employee engagement are workplace elements such as trust, collaboration, and a caring environment, which lead to greater engagement and therefore well-being. Without these elements, employee engagement declines.

Limiting employment workplace flexibility arrangements has also resulted in a decrease in employee engagement (Gallup, 2022) and in difficulties recruiting candidates who are seeking more flexible work schedules to improve their work-life integration. Employees who for decades had been struggling with integrating caregiving responsibilities, work schedules, and societal and systemic barriers found that the pandemic demonstrated they could accomplish their work fully remotely, allowing for better work-life integration. However, when organizations began to return to the office fully or with a hybrid schedule, employees voiced concerns about discontinued workplace flexibility offerings compromising their ability to integrate caregiving responsibilities and self-care including mental health needs.

Mental health issues, such as anxiety, stress, isolation, and depression, have also been on the rise and have been the focus of organizations as they learn about ways of supporting evolving employee needs. Politics and current events play leading roles in increasing anxiety and stress according to a 2022 American Psychological Association survey. Significant sources of stress also included racial climate, increased inflation resulting in economic hardship, and concerns over safety including mass shootings, gun violence, and general crime. The parenting community has worried about the long-term effects of the pandemic on their children as seen in the correlated increase in depression, alcohol and drug use, and an increase in self-harm of younger populations (Lopes et al., 2022). Older workers, who were among the most vulnerable during the pandemic, faced the consequences of social isolation including an increase in mental disorders, a decline in cognition, and greater risks that compromised their immune system (Vrach & Tomar, 2020). Complicating factors that increase tension relate to mental healthcare being prohibitively expensive. Individuals with lower household incomes indicate that stress associated with economic instability is high and access to mental health is unattainable for them.

The Missing Systemic Anti-Oppressive Lens in the Workforce

The organization of work, how it gets done, and the division of labor have existed for centuries and progressed more formally through the Industrial Revolution where machine owners began the process of supervision over those tasked with working on machines. This created a clear division of labor, power, and hierarchy (Kranzberg & Hannan, 2023). This division continued to form in the subsequent 150 years resulting in a labor force today that has oppressed the voices of large communities of workers. Many participating in today's workforce are challenged by poor work policies and the lack of supportive practices in direct conflict with their basic work-life needs.

Changes in the labor force and the lack of policy change alignment are in direct conflict with what the workforce needs today and persistently perpetuate the oppression of workforce communities.

Populations, such as individuals with family responsibilities, in particular, working women, have been oppressed and discriminated against and left out of dominant workforce groups. By example, the corresponding organizational policies and workplace practices that affect pregnant workers have been slow to change and were little represented in the 1980s and 1990s due to a traditional work model built primarily on the white, male workforce. Results of the oppression and discrimination against women workers can be seen by looking at the increase in pregnancy discrimination complaints filed with the Equal Employment Opportunity Commission and other agencies. In 1997 there were 3977 cases filed versus 5797 cases in 2011 (Equal Employment Opportunity Commission [EEOC], n.d.).

Another important policy affecting working women is paid leave. Organizations have been slow to offer paid leave policies for caregiving. In 1992 organizations with 100 or more employees offered paid leave to only 3% of their workers versus 15% in 2012 (BLS, 2013). Offering paid leave to women supports them remaining in the work environment (SHRM, 2020), the lack of which forces women in and out of the labor force adding to their financial instability particularly in their older years. The result of this oppression is a "21st century workforce laboring in a 20th century workplace" (Christensen, 2014).

Recognizing the continued oppressive workplace barriers for working families, the Obama White House led national campaigns to educate and expand efforts to have the federal government and the private sector become leaders to address the identified and continued oppression of certain workforce communities. Two high-profile campaigns were Lead on Leave (Lyles, 2014), a paid leave effort, and The National Dialogue on Workplace Flexibility, an effort to get employers to recognize the importance of incorporating flexibility in how, when, and where work gets done (Tchen, 2010).

What the Workplace Needs Today

The US Surgeon General's Report of 2022, *Workplace Mental Health and Well-Being*, created a call-to-action framework for organizations to use in support of mental health and well-being. In this report, the Surgeon General draws attention to ways in which organizations can be engines of mental health and well-being and provides five recommendations including protecting workers from harm, creating a sense of connection, showing workers they matter, opening space for employees to have lives outside of work, and supporting professional growth (U.S. Department of Health and Human Services, 2024). This framework addresses worker well-being by understanding the relationship between employment settings and individuals and centering the essential workplace practices on the worker's voice. The report supports what has been a priority for higher education work-life offices around the country, namely, that having adequate policies, practices, and supportive resources for employees allows them to have greater well-being both at work and in their personal lives.

This author's professional experience includes numerous years studying labor force needs, trending issues, and the intersections of supportive employer policies, practices, and resources. It is the opinion of this author that to improve individual and organizational health, employers need to be intimately informed and knowledgeable of the nuanced needs and experiences of today's workers, alongside understanding the various workplace and societal systems that negatively impact individuals. Complementary to understanding current-day work environment experiences and challenges, there needs to be an ability to advocate collaboratively for important individual, workplace, and community changes and to apply key principles of anti-oppressive practices, among them an opportunity to advocate against levels of oppression within micro-, mezzo-, and macrostructures (Dalrymple & Burke, 2006).

The Existing Framework

Existing organizational frameworks to address work environment needs have been historically attended to by human resources departments as described at the start of this chapter. In the last several years, through the increase of social justice issues and the pandemic, the role of the human resources unit has evolved by responding to the needs of today's workers through increased and expanded benefits and establishing supportive policies. Within the past couple of years these departments have also addressed the decline in mental health and well-being by increasing access to outsourced employee assistance programs, wellness programs, health apps, and discounts to classes and resources related to personal care (Fraone, 2022). These improvements have been well received and help individuals focus on self-care; however, these efforts have placed new responsibility on human resources departments to take on these critically urgent and specialized needs and to come up with solutions (Routt, 2021) with little knowledge or expertise in human behavior, mental health counseling, and an understanding of the continued systemic oppression impacting these issues.

It is the opinion of this author that these workplace improvements are not sufficiently informed by individual lived experiences and that they lack knowledge of the complex systemic organizational and societal issues that have direct and indirect impact on the employee. Additionally, these solutions, while helpful, are not informed by subject matter expertise and are therefore limited in their ability to provide significant and systemic change. These limitations were seen most recently during the COVID-19 pandemic during which the US caregiving social systems stopped working, resulting in increased work-family conflicts. These challenges needed subject matter knowledge of the complex caregiving systems, direct knowledge of lived experiences, and specialized professionals in human behavior and psychology to provide adequate, immediate support, and organizational solutions (Carnevale & Hatak, 2020).

Fundamentally, the existing organizational framework for addressing employee needs has several gaps that should be improved. In-depth, expert knowledge is needed within the organizational model to better address the ever-changing workplace issues. Understanding psychological and human behavior, expertise in systems theory, and an understanding of systemic and social justice issues are critical. Additionally, creating a trusting and confidential environment to provide direct service would contribute to information gathering that can help inform business decisions. However, the role of human resources has traditionally been to protect the interest of management by creating a work environment that has competitive advantage for the organization (Kazlauskaitė & Bučiūnienė, 2008), a role that represents management's interest first and foremost. As such, the role of human resources is often seen by employees as one that lacks the objectivity and neutrality needed to impartially understand and address employee concerns (Giardino, 2018). In this author's opinion, this deficiency is seen by employees as a relationship with incomplete trust and a setting that may not be truly confidential.

Current Available Literature

Current research discusses the idea that organizations need to quickly adapt to changing events that impact the workplace and find solutions that are more integrated. In particular, the COVID-19 pandemic created an environment whereby organizations needed to learn quickly about unknown areas such as remote work, overwork, and blurred boundaries between work and personal life and to understand an individual's needs as they relate to the work environment (Carnevale & Hatak, 2020). Other available research points to the need for further exploration on incorporating positive psychology into human resource management practices as an avenue for advancement that supports human flourishing at work (Gruman & Budworth, 2022).

To the best of our knowledge, the topic of existing gaps and how to best respond to current-day employee and workplace needs at the organizational level has not been considered in the literature. It is therefore this author's opinion that understanding the existing organizational gaps and possible alternative new approaches can help increase individual and organizational health and can help reduce continued oppressive workplace practices.

A Future Organizational Model to Address Today's Workplace Needs

By creating a dedicated and independent social work unit sitting outside of human resources, with access to senior leadership, there is an opportunity to address existing gaps in organizational workplace needs. Using social work concepts and frameworks as well as professional, knowledgeable voices can inform and provide solutions to organizational business decisions. Social work's focus and expertise are in addressing social justice issues, studying and understanding systems that impact individuals, using clinical theories and concepts to inform patterns of human behavior, and providing direction and advocating for systemic change. The social work profession with the required licenses, accreditation, and trained professionals provides a broad perspective that can be applied to organizational work-life and can be complementary to the existing organizational model. Creating an independent unit outside of human resources will generate trust and confidentiality needed to bidirectionally provide direct service to employees and advise the organization on business decisions based on grassroots information. This feedback loop (see Fig. 20.1) can inform improvements to policies, practices, organizational systems, culture, and climate and can highlight trending and important issues.

Figure 20.1 demonstrates how the proposed independent, social work unit would provide interventions of work at the micro-, mezzo-, and macro-levels of the organization.

In Fig. 20.1, the micro-level would provide direct service through individualized consultations, the creation and facilitation of support groups, and the offering of resource referral options and specialized direct service assessment for addressing caregiving options and other work-life challenges. In this micro-level, direct service in social work involves one-on-one contact with people and groups.

The mezzo-level would be informed by the information learned at the micro-level and possible impacts of the macro-level and would focus on institutional interventions such as collaborating with organizational units to educate and raise awareness of issues, working to improve organizational systems such as mental health and well-being supports and caregiving benefits, advocating and championing healthy and supportive policies and practices, and working to improve workplace culture and climate.

Macro-level work would inform existing systemic oppressive social, political, and governmental structures that impact both the micro- and mezzo-levels. It would focus on gaining knowledge from outside experts, developing community partnerships in order to continue supporting the organizational community, and expanding thought leadership to enhance a community of practice.

A unit practicing social work would complement the existing organizational structures that have been addressing workplace needs but would bring with it a set of new skills to better address the identified gaps. Social workers are trained in understanding human behavior and the social environment. The profession studies the individual in the context of the systems we live in and can identify concerns at multiple levels. It requires skills such as empathy, active listening, interpersonal communication, emotional and cultural intelligence, critical thinking, advocacy, and a social justice lens to accomplish the work. Applying a social work framework through such a unit would bring with it an anti-oppressive lens by incorporating existing knowledge into organizational practices through education, advocacy, and organizing systemic change.

The Organizational Social Worker of the Future

Addressing organizational and employee health is critically important and timely. The social changes that have occurred in the last few years have had a significant impact on workers and employers alike. There exists a timely opportunity for the social work profession to fill existing gaps and deepen its presence within

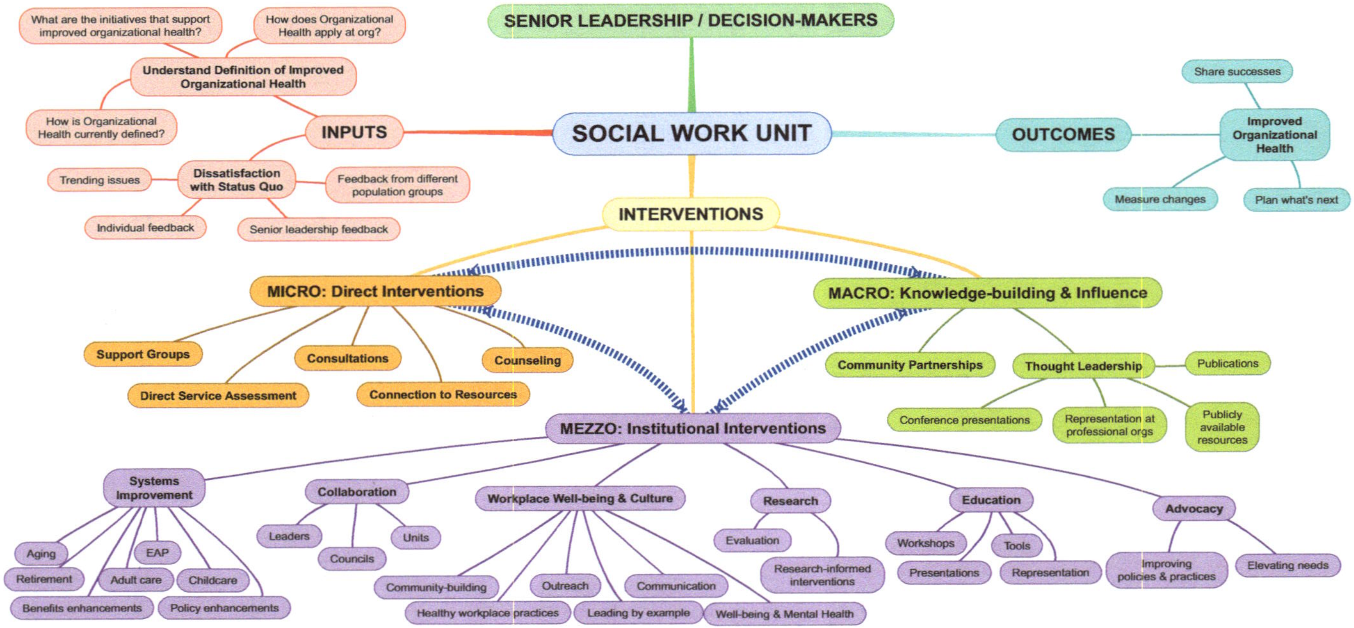

Fig. 20.1 Proposed organizational social work unit

organizational life and be a complementary voice to improving the work-life of individuals while working against anti-oppressive structures. There is also an opportunity for schools of social work to strongly underpin the teaching of occupational social work bringing with it a reengineering of workplace structures to drive supportive solutions for today's workforce.

References

Carnevale, J. B., & Hatak, I. (2020). Employee adjustment and Well-being in the era of COVID-19: Implications for human resource management. *Journal of Business Research, 116*, 183–187.

Center for American Progress. (2019). Breadwinning mothers continue to be the US norm. Retrieved from https://www.americanprogress.org/issues/women/reports/2019/05/10/469739/breadwinning-mothers-continue-u-s-norm/

Christensen, K., Schneider, B., & Butler, D. (2011). Families with school-age children. *The Future of Children, 21*(2), 69–90.

Christensen, K. (2014, January 11). America's families have changed…its workplaces haven't. America's families have changed... its workplaces haven't | Richard Heffner's Open Mind Archive. Richard Heffner's Open Mind Archive.

Dalrymple, J., & Burke, B. (2006). *Anti-oppressive practice: Social care and the law*. McGraw-Hill Education.

Dyeson, T. B. (2004). Social work licensure: A brief history and description. *Home Health Care Management & Practice, 16*(5), 408–411. https://doi.org/10.1177/1084822304264657

Equal Employment Opportunity Commission. (n.d.). Pregnancy Discrimination Charges, EEOC & FEPAs Combined: FY1997 - FY2011. Retrieved from https://www.eeoc.gov/statistics/pregnancy-discrimination-chargeseeoc-fepas-combined-fy-1997-fy-2011

Encyclopedia of Social Work. (n.d.). Retrieved from https://oxfordre.com/socialwork/display/10.1093/acrefore/9780199975839.001.0001/acrefore-9780199975839-e-623

Fraone, J. (2022, November). Mental health. Boston College Center for Work and Family Conference. Boston, MA.

Gallup. (2022). State of the global workplace: 2023 report. Retrieved from https://www.gallup.com/workplace/349484/state-of-the-global-workplace-2022-report.aspx

Gelman, C. R. (2015). Clinical social work practice in the twenty-first century: A changing landscape. *Clinical Social Work Journal, 43*, 257–262.

Giardino, T. (2018, November 9). Three reasons people distrust HR—and what HR can do about it. Forbes.

Gruman, J. A., & Budworth, M. (2022). Positive psychology and human resource management: Building an HR architecture to support human flourishing. *Human Resource Management Review, 32*(3), 100911. https://doi.org/10.1016/j.hrmr.2022.100911

Kazlauskaite, R., & Buciuniene, I. (2008). The role of human resources and their management in the establishment of sustainable competitive advantage. *Engineering Economics, 5*, 78–85.

Kranzberg, M., & Hannan, M. T. (2023, May 11). History of the organization of work. Encyclopedia Britannica. https://www.britannica.com/money/history-of-the-organization-of-work

Lopes, L., Kirzinger, A., Sparks, G., Stokes, M., & Brodie, M. (2022). *KFF/CNN mental health in America survey*. https://www.kff.org/report-section/kff-cnn-mental-health-in-america-survey-findings/

Lyles, L. (2014). In support of paid leave: 25 million stories. Retrieved from https://obamawhitehouse.archives.gov/blog/2014/09/24/support-paid-leave-25-million-stories

McKinsey. (2021, April 28). *Better bosses: Changing the way we lead post-pandemic*. McKinsey & Company. https://www.mckinsey.com/featured-insights/mckinsey-live/webinars/better-bosses-changing-the-way-we-lead-post-pandemic

Miller, D. A. (1981). The "sandwich" generation: Adult children of the aging. *Social Work, 26*(5), 419–423. http://www.jstor.org/stable/23712207

Obedgiu, V. (2017). Human resource management, historical perspectives, evolution and professional development. *Journal of Management Development, 36*(8), 986–990. https://doi.org/10.1108/JMD-12-2016-0267

Pew Research. (2019). Among 41 countries, only the US lacks paid parental leave. Pew Research Center. https://www.pewresearch.org/fact-tank/2019/12/16/u-s-lacks-mandated-paid-parental-leave

Pophal, L. (n.d.). The 100-year history of the human resources department. *Visier*. https://www.visier.com/blog/the-100-year-history-human-resources-department

Routt, D. (2021, June 16). Managing mental health in the workforce: A new role for HR professionals. Forbes.

Stuart, P. (2019, March 26). Social Work profession: History. *Encyclopedia of Social Work*. Retrieved 26 Jun.2025, from https://oxfordre.com/socialwork/view/10.1093/acrefore/9780199975839.001.0001/acrefore-9780199975839-e-623

Tchen, T. (2010). A focus on workplace flexibility. Retrieved from https://obamawhitehouse.archives.gov/blog/2010/12/02/afocus-workplace-flexibility

Trice, H. M., & Schonbrunn, M. (1981). A history of job-based alcoholism programs: 1900–1955. *Journal of Drug Issues, 11*(2), 171–198. https://doi.org/10.1177/002204268101100202

U.S. Bureau of Labor Statistics. (2017). *Women in the workforce, before, during and after the great recession (Spotlight on Statistics)*. Retrieved from https://www.bls.gov/spotlight/2017/women-in-the-workforce-before-during-and-after-the-great-recession/pdf/women-in-the-workforce-before-during-and-after-the-great-recession.pdf

U.S. Bureau of Labor Statistics. (2021). *Women in the labor force: A databook*. Retrieved from BLS Reports. https://www.bls.gov/opub/reports/womens-databook/2020/home.htm#:~:text=In%202019%2C%2057.4%20percent%20of,of%2060.0%20percent%20in%201999

U.S. Department of Health and Human Services, Office of the Surgeon General. (2024). *The U.S. Surgeon General's Framework for Workplace mental health & well-being 2022 — Current priorities of the U.S. surgeon general*. HHS.gov. https://www.hhs.gov/surgeongeneral/priorities/workplace-well-being/index.html

Vrach, I. T., & Tomar, R. (2020). Mental health impacts of social isolation in older people during COVID pandemic. *Progress in Neurology and Psychiatry, 24*(4), 25–29. https://doi.org/10.1002/pnp.684

Waller, A. D., & Ragsdell, G. (2012). The impact of email on work-life balance. *Aslib Proceedings, 64*(2), 154–177.

Glossary of Acronyms and Terms

AAHPM American Academy of Hospice and Palliative Medicine
ABC Activating Event, Beliefs, Consequences
ACA Affordable Care Act
ACE Adverse Childhood Experiences
ACHP-SW Advanced Certified Hospice and Palliative Social Worker
ACP Advance care planning
ACS Administration for Children's Services
ADA Americans with Disabilities Act
ADEI Antiracism, Diversity, Equity, and Inclusion
AMA American Medical Association
AOP Anti-Oppressive Practice
AOSW Association of Oncology Social Work
APHSW-C Advanced Palliative Hospice Social Worker Certification
ATI Alternative to Incarceration
BIPOC Black Indigenous and People of Color
BJS Bureau of Justice Statistics
CAC Child Advocacy Center
CAPC Center to Advance Palliative Care
CBT Cognitive Behavioral Therapy
CDC Centers for Disease Control and Prevention
CFTSI Child and Family Traumatic Stress Intervention
COA Commission of Accreditation
CPT Cognitive Processing Therapy
CPW2 Criminal Possession of a Weapon in the Second Degree
CR-S Culturally Responsive-Sustaining framework
CRT Critical Race Theory
CSWE Council on Social Work Education
DA District Attorney

C. Tosone et al. (eds.), *Reframing Social Work with an Anti-Oppressive Lens*, Essential Clinical Social Work Series,
https://doi.org/10.1007/978-3-031-91391-4

DBT Dialectical Behavior Therapy
DEI Diversity, Equity, and Inclusion
DHS Department of Homeless Services
DJ Disability Justice
DOHMH Department of Health and Mental Hygiene
DREAM Development, Relief, and Education for Alien Minors
DSM Diagnostic and Statistical Manual of Mental Disorders
DWI Driving While Intoxicated
DV Domestic Violence
EMDR Eye Movement Desensitization and Reprocessing Therapy
EMS Emergency Medical Services
EPAS Educational Policy and Accreditation Standards
FDNY Fire Department of New York
FFT Functional Family Therapy
FFT-CW Functional Family Therapy-Child Welfare
FFT-G Functional Family Therapy-Gang
FI Forensic Interview
GSA Gender and Sexuality Alliance
GST General Strain Theory
HBSE Human Behavior and the Social Environment
H&H NYC Health and Hospitals Corporation
IAT Implicit Association Test
IAT Institutional Anomie Theory
IOM Institute of Medicine
IPV Intimate Partner Violence
IRT Instant Response Team
IV Interpersonal Violence
LGBTQ+ Lesbian, Gay Bisexual, Transgender, Queer plus other queer identities
LGBTIA2+ Lesbian, Gay, Bisexual, Transgender, Intersex, Ally, Two-Spirit and/or Plus
LGBTQ2S+ Lesbian, Gay, Bisexual, Transgender, Queer or Questioning, and Two-Spirit
M Mental Illness
MDT Multidisciplinary Team
MST Minority Stress Theory
MST Multisystemic Therapy
MST-CAN Multisystemic Therapy-Child Abuse and Neglect
MTSS Multi-Tiered Systems of Support
NAMI National Alliance on Mental Illness
NASW National Association of Social Workers
NCADV National Coalition Against Domestic Violence
NCCHC National Commission on Correctional Health Care
NCES National Center for Education Statistics
NPIC Nonprofit Industrial Complex

NYC New York City
NYCH&H New York City Health and Hospitals Corporation
NYPD New York Police Department
NYSPCC New York Society for the Prevention of Cruelty to Children
OCA Office of Court Administration
OCD Obsessive-Compulsive Disorder
OCME Office of the City Medical Examiner
PCHETA Palliative Care and Hospice Education and Training Act
PE Prolonged Exposure Therapy
PREA Prison Rape Elimination Act
PRS Post Release Supervision
PTSD Post-traumatic Stress Disorder
PSW Palliative social worker
PWD Person(s) with Disabilities
RAP Record of Arrests and Prosecutions
SCR State Central Registry
SDM Surrogate decision-maker
SEB Spanish/English bilingual
SGD Sexual and gender diverse
SGDOA Sexual- and Gender-Diverse older adult
SMI Seriously Mentally Ill
SST Social Safety Theory
SSW School Social Work
SSWers School Social Workers
SUDS Subjective Unit of Distress Score
SVS Special Victims Squad
SWHPN Social Work Hospice and Palliative Care Network
TF-CBT Trauma-Focused Cognitive Behavioral Therapy
UDL Universal Design for Learning
VA Victim Advocate
VTM Visiting Teacher Movement
WHO World Health Organization
YDP Youth Diversion Programs
YRBS Youth Risk Behavior Survey

Index

C. Tosone et al. (eds.), *Reframing Social Work with an Anti-Oppressive Lens*, Essential Clinical Social Work Series,
https://doi.org/10.1007/978-3-031-91391-4

MIX
Papier aus verantwortungsvollen Quellen
Paper from responsible sources
FSC® C105338

If you have any concerns about our products,
you can contact us on
ProductSafety@springernature.com

In case Publisher is established outside the EU,
the EU authorized representative is:
Springer Nature Customer Service Center GmbH
Europaplatz 3, 69115 Heidelberg, Germany

Printed by Libri Plureos GmbH
in Hamburg, Germany